THE DEATH OF THE FIRST EARTH

THE FACTS BEHIND NOAH'S FLOOD

Book 5 of The Machine or Man Apologetics Series

BY HENRY PATIÑO

The Death of the First Earth
The Facts behind Noah's Flood
Copyright © 2022 by Henry Patiño
Published by Areli Media

Unless otherwise indicated, all Scripture quotations are taken from the New American Standard Bible® (NASB), Copyright © 1960, 1962, 1963, 1968, 1971, 1972, 1973, 1975, 1977, 1995 by The Lockman Foundation. Used by permission. www.Lockman.org.

Scripture quotations marked (NIV) are taken from the Holy Bible, New International Version®, NIV®. Copyright ©1973, 1978, 1984, 2011 by Biblica, Inc.™ Used by permission of Zondervan. All rights reserved worldwide. www.zondervan.com The "NIV" and "New International Version" are trademarks registered in the United States Patent and Trademark Office by Biblica, Inc.™

eISBN: 978-1-7372529-2-4
ISBN: 978-1-7372529-0-0

Special Sales: Most Areli Media titles are available in special quantity discounts. Custom imprinting or excerpting can also be done to fit special needs. Contact Areli Media.

TABLE OF CONTENTS

Chapter 1: The Marvel of the First Earth   1
  Our Judeo-Christian Model   11
  The Two Sources   18
  The Water Vapor Canopy   20
  Diagram 14 - The Water Vapor Canopy   27
  The Underground Saltwater Aquifers   35
  The Hallmarks of the First Earth, Its Death, and the Birth of the Second Earth   45
  The Time of Terror   56
  The Prediluvian Civilization   100
  The Intervention   119
  Diagram 15 – The Continental Drift Theory   120

Chapter 2: The Physical Mechanisms That Caused the Great Flood   121
  Space Rocks and the Continental Drift Theory   122
  The Catastrophic Impacts – The First Horn of Taurus   130
  The Floodgates of the Heavens – The Second Horn of Taurus   132
  The Ancient Chronicles   136

Chapter 3: The Unexpected Space Visitors   141
  The Big Seven   146
    1. The Maniitsoq Crater   147
    2. The Popigai Crater in Siberia   150
    3. The Sudbury Crater in Ontario, Canada   152
    4. The Chicxulub Crater in the Yucatan Peninsula   152

5. The Vredefort Crater in Southwest Johannesburg, Africa	154
6. The Acraman Crater in Australia	155
7. The Wilkes Land Crater in Antarctica	156
The Chicxulub Crater	157
The Wilkes Land, East Antarctic Crater	171
The Land Was Broken Like a Pot	179
The Bulging Crust and Provincial Magma Traps	185
The Seven Shepherds of the Pleiades	191
Chapter 4: The Sumerian Planisphere	**195**
The Star-Planet Sent by An	206
The Path before the Constellations	209
Enduring the Ark	225
Chapter 5: The Fountains of the Deep Were Broken Open (the Hydroplate Theory)	**243**
The First Earth Ripped	245
The Crunching Lateral Forces That Formed Mountains	257
Volcanoes and Supervolcanoes	263
Chapter 6: The Windows of the Heaven Were Opened	**273**
Tsunamis	274
The Storm of All Storms	276
Chapter 7: The End of the First Earth – The First Ice Age	**293**
New Fire Festivals – A Memory of the Second Dawn	295
The Formation of the Mid-Oceanic Ridges and Rifts	303
The Plate Tectonic Theory and Deep Ocean Trenches	307
More Evidence of a Global Hydrological Event	320

Chapter 8: The Scientific Evidence for the Antediluvian World — 327
    The Evidence Regarding a Uniform, Mild Climate — 327
    Evidence in the Ice — 331
    The Genetic Evidence — 345
    Evidence in the Fossils — 350
    Gradual versus Catastrophic Sedimentary Depositions — 360

Chapter 9: The Ark—The Womb of the New Earth — 367
    Argument 6 – No wooden boat could have the measurements described in Scripture. — 368
    1. Ancient Man Could Not Build a Wooden Ship That Large — 370
    2. The Load Capacity of the Ark — 379
    3. Gathering and Caring for the Animals — 383

Chapter 10: The Tower of Babel and the Second Ice Age — 387
    Arrogance and Pride – Nimrod's Folly — 389
    Rapid Deglaciation and the Second Rise of the Ocean Levels — 400
    The New Temperature Regulator – Thermohaline Ocean Conveyor Belt — 402
    The Second Ice Age — 408
    The Second Maximum Glacial Extent — 410

Chapter 11: The Threat of a Future Ice Age — 419
    Global Warming Is Real — 419
    The Intensity of Hurricanes and Tornadoes – A Sign of the End of Our Age — 431
    The Fourth Insurrection — 435

Chapter 12: The Historical Evidence — A Comparison of the Great Flood Accounts, the Creation Stories, and the Division of Languages Worldwide — 443

    Argument 7 – The ancient chronicles regarding a global flood are nothing more than embellished local flood accounts — 444

    A Comparison of the Great Flood Accounts — 445

    1. The Sumerian, Babylonian, and Assyrian Accounts of the Great Flood — 448

    2. The Accounts of the Flood in Europe — 463

    3. The Account of the Flood in the Pacific — 484

    4. The Account of the Flood in Asia — 486

    5. The Account of the Creation and Flood in Africa — 490

    6. The Account of the Flood in South America — 493

    7. The Account of the Flood, the Creation Story, and the Confounding of the Languages According to the North American Indians — 496

    8. The Flood, the Creation Stories, and the Confounding of the Languages According to the Meso-American Indian — 504

Epilogue — 515

Appendix A — 529

References — 549

Index — 559

CHAPTER 1
THE MARVEL OF THE FIRST EARTH

And all earth, and heaven, and sea, were boiling.

—Hesiod

Imagine a world without earthquakes that shatter entire cities and bury people alive, a world without hurricanes and tornadoes that rip through houses and destroy all in their path, a world without tsunamis and floods that wash thousands away into the deep, a world without blizzards and snowstorms that freeze living things and make life difficult in winter months, a world without parched deserts and barren wastelands, a world without lightning and thunderstorms, a world so lush with vegetation that our atmosphere contained 35–37 percent concentration of oxygen, a world protected from cosmic radiation by a thin water vapor canopy and a thick ozone layer, a world whose atmosphere was denser and oxygen saturation to the tissues was twice as efficient, a world whose orbit around the Sun was almost as circular as Venus's and Mercury's orbits, a world whose lunar calendar and solar calendar were in harmony, a world so filled with edible fruits and nuts that humans had but to gather them in order to survive, a world that began filled with peace and security, a world where men and women lived for hundreds of years.

The long life of men gave them the opportunity to grow greatly in knowledge and wisdom. Their understanding of the stars and mathematics would seem miraculous to us. Modern men viewing through evolutionary spectacles consider ancient man inferior and brutish, but he was nothing less than what we are today. Man has always been intelligent. That was the beginning of our First Earth as it was meant to be by God, but greed and lust were kindled by the Religion of the Serpent, and Camelot was lost. The world of spectacular beauty and grandeur became marred by violence and wickedness.

Flavius Josephus writes of Adam's prophetic vision regarding the two forms of destruction that would visit our planet. Our firstfather understood that our world would end once by water and another by fire. The very first man who walked this Earth and breathed our air knew this, for the Lord walked with him in the cool of the Garden at Eden and taught him many things (Genesis 3)—things we may not yet know, things that were buried by the sands of time.

Those who first inhabited our planet used knowledge for good. They discovered the signs of the Zodiac and the message of the Great Deliverer who would come to rescue us from the claws of the Enemy of Man. The Zodiac is the story of the ancient cosmic battle between good and evil. It was the golden age of mankind before it all went wrong. The children of Adam sought to find a way to preserve this knowledge for future posterity. Flavius Josephus, a Jewish rabbi who lived during the time of the destruction of the Second Temple, wrote of this knowledge by those who first inhabited our planet.

> *Now this Seth, when he was brought up, and came to those years in which he could discern what was good, became a virtuous man; and as he was himself of an excellent character, so did he leave children behind him who imitated his virtues. All these proved to be of good disposition. They also inhabited the same country [the Land of Elda] without dissensions,*

and in a happy condition, without any misfortunes falling upon them, till they died. They also were the inventors of that peculiar sort of wisdom which is concerned with the heavenly bodies, and their order. And that their inventions might not be lost before they were sufficiently known, upon Adam's prediction that the world was to be destroyed at one time by the force of fire and at another time by the violence and quantity of water, they made two pillars, the one of brick, the other of stone: They inscribed their discoveries on them both that in case the pillar of bricks should be destroyed by the flood, the pillar of stone might remain, and exhibit those discoveries to mankind (Josephus 1960, 27).

The truth of his prophetic vision is many faceted. Not only will the first destruction be primarily by water and the last destruction by fire, but also the first destruction was first of fire and then of water, as we shall discover. The end came by the baptism of both fire and water.

It was a world of giant conifers 30 stories high. Thick trunks and interwoven roots made them seem to scrape the skies, and yet they remained completely stable, much like the redwoods in California. It was a world rich in fruits of enormous varieties, and only a fraction survived to the Second Earth. There were nuts and berries that grew wild and plentiful, flowers of every color and fragrance, and giant ferns the size of coconut trees that paved the forest floors. Our First Earth was not heaven, the abode of the Creator, but it was the closest our world has ever been to it, and it all went wrong.

It became a place of terror, a world of violence and death, a place of savagery, murder, cannibalism, and the drinking of the blood of human sacrifices. It was here that the blood oath of the Religion of the Serpent introduced human sacrifices and ritual cannibalism. It was here that the Mother Goddesses gave themselves over to the Dark Watchers for the spawning of the Nephilim shamans. It was here that the legend of the Vril was born. The legitimate seed of Eve was threatened with extinction.

So terrible and violent became the First Earth that God had to end it and start all over again. And so our Second Earth was birthed through fire and smoke; through hurling rocks and red molten magma; through steam, water, and howling winds; through ash, ice, and death. But have we learned from our past? Have we understood that the way of peace is right and the way of violence is wrong? Sadly, I think not. The Age of Terror is upon us again with a vengeance. The Religion of the Serpent has morphed into Dar al Harb that hides their crimes against humanity, cloaked as faithfulness to a religion that legitimizes inhuman atrocities in the name of their god Allah in order to centralize power and conquer the world. But that is a story for another book

Once there was a planet, green from top to bottom, filled with luxurious forests and luscious fruit trees of so many varieties that man had to toil little to thrive well. Once there was a planet where the lion ate grass like the ox and predation did not rule nature. Once there was a planet with one single landmass and one single people who spoke one single language. They lived in a world with one single ocean whose water was fresh and pristine for all to drink. But that world vanished because we failed to keep it so. We were entrusted by God to manage our world. Instead, we profaned it.

All of it was washed away in a terrible judgment because the blood of innocents stained the soil crimson red, and the voices of the innocents rising from the Earth cried out for justice to the Almighty. Predation became the way of nature and the way of man. It began in the sixth generation from our firstfather, first with the children of Cain. In time, the time of terror ruled the four corners of the world and eventually seduced even most in the lineage of Seth.

How can man become so cruel as to eat the flesh of other humans? How can man be so cruel as to sacrifice human beings for the selfish notion of gaining greater magical power? And yet, my brothers and sisters, that is our human history. It is the way things became in the First Earth and then again in the Second Earth. The consequence of our rebellion toward God's ways will bring certain judgment on us again if we fail to learn from the past. It behooves us to learn what happened in the First Earth that brought God's wrath upon them.

In the bowels of Mount Baal Hermon, a monstrous plan was hatched in the minds of demons to foil the prophecy of the Dragon Doom uttered by the voice of God in the Garden at Eden. It was through the seed of Eve that the Deliverer was prophesied to come to destroy the Enemy of Man and end the Great Indignation inspired by the Serpent in the First Insurrection. Here, 200 angels began the Second Insurrection against God to thwart the prophecy that God's voice pronounced as a consequence of the First Insurrection at the Garden at Eden (Gen. 3:15).

On the back of the Serpent, selfishness and death entered our planet, and we lost our intended paradise because of the First Insurrection. The angel with the flaming sword kept us from reentering that idyllic paradise since from that fateful day we selfishly chose to be like God. But little did we know then how our peaceful world could so easily be tarnished into a living hell. Hear my words; our choices do have real consequences.

Their demonic, monstrous plan was to profane and destroy the seed of Eve in order to prevent the birthing of the Messiah and foil the fulfillment of the prophecy of the Dragon Doom. For from her seed would come the bane of the Enemy of Man. In that day, the Religion of the Mother Goddesses was spawned in the bowels of Mount Baal Harmon to seduce mankind. Sorcery and the blood oath enticed the selfish, doomed the innocents to oppression, and spurred the wicked to savagery.

It was the wickedness and violence fomented by the Nephilim that forced the hand of God to bring an end to the violence of the First Earth. Will your heart be open to hear the real story of the children of Adam? Will you learn from our past? Have your eyes been dulled by our postmodern scales that dim the truth of our real history? Has the spirit of this world lulled you into thinking that only what you see, touch, and feel can be real? Can you learn to see without eyes? Will you listen to the words and warnings of our ancestors?

There are three events in history that have been universally chronicled by all humanity. The first is the creation of man by God from the clay of the Earth. The second is the Global Deluge, and finally is the dispersion of the nations by the confounding of the languages. No other events in history have been so universally attested in every corner of our planet by every tongue and tribe of our human family. We can ignore the voices of our forefathers and continue in the fog created by the postmodern, self-imposed hallucination, or we can listen to the voices of our ancestors calling to us throughout the millennia to warn us of the impending doom that shall follow us if we again abandon God and choose the selfish way of death.

The ancient chronicles are there for those with eyes to see. To deny the historicity of these events is to claim that we cannot know anything at all about the lives of our ancestors, for there is more historical evidence to support the historicity of these events delineated in the Hebrew Scriptures than there is to support the notion that George Washington led the army of the American Revolution.

But the theological pundits of modern-day "scientism" simply sweep aside such historical evidence on the singular grounds that it simply does not fit within their naturalistic paradigm. To admit that such events really took place would support the notion that a Creator exists, and that simply does not fit in their preferred theological framework. Hence, they nonchalantly sweep aside any such evidence as mythological and historically untrustworthy. Their atheism is nonetheless their theology of scientism. But in the end, no matter how intricate their rationalizations are, every man and woman shall be held accountable to the God of truth.

But if we are to assume that we can know anything at all about our past, then the objective reader must consider that if the historical evidence is universal and yet does not fit with the notions of the naturalistic paradigm, then perhaps it is the naturalistic paradigm that is mythological in nature.

If the biblical narrative is true, then every culture of the world has developed from the funnel of human history that we know as Noah's Flood. That is to say, all cultures have descended from Noah's family and would, therefore, have in their collective memory the knowledge of the same catastrophic event that ended the First Earth. The irony is that all our ancient ancestors have consistently and universally chronicled the death of our First Earth.

Yet in spite of that, evolutionists have completely ignored the impossible odds that would have been necessary for chance to have independently developed almost identical stories of the worldwide Flood in every major culture of the world—accounts that have the same basic elements of the plot in common. Instead, they posit that the Hebrew account was actually borrowed or, less politely, stolen from the earlier Babylonian account. The rewriting of all history with an evolutionary spin has been the most effective tool of Satan to mask the truth that would out his perennial globalist agenda and megalomania.

It is a position evolutionists must take due to the incredible similarity of the two accounts; otherwise, the similarities would be too uncanny for coincidence. There is no denying that the Babylonian account of the Flood very closely parallels the biblical account, but so do most of the other accounts worldwide, a fact that must also be calculated into the equation. If the similarities are universal, then logic dictates that these so-called mythologies must be based on a true historical account. They must point to an event so drastic and catastrophic that it was indelibly inscribed into the memories of all our ancient forefathers. To deny it is tantamount to self-imposed ignorance—a willful leap into the irrational to assuage the typically human desire for moral autonomy.

While it is true that every nation in the world with their own peculiar language has a different name for Noah, we must understand that they speak of the same person and describe the same global disaster that ended our First Earth. When our people were divided into different languages and nations, the names of God, Adam, Eve, and Noah became different, but they spoke of the very same individuals.

Gilgamesh was the fifth king of the Erech Dynasty in early Babylonia. According to this ancient Babylonian account, in one of the king's adventures, he went to visit the Babylonian Noah (Utnapishtim) who told him of the catastrophic Flood that ended the First Earth and how he had escaped it. The account claims that the gods decided to send a deluge as punishment for the wickedness that had swallowed the Earth.

Utnapishtim was ordered to build a ship six stories high and smear it with bitumen (a form of tar) in order to waterproof the wood. He was instructed to take into the ship seed of life of every kind. In the account, like the biblical narrative, the boat runs aground on a mountain. It even speaks of their Noah sending birds out after the rain ceased to see if dry land could be found. Beyond that, like the Noahic account, the epic narrative records Noah offering a sacrifice to the gods after landing on dry ground, after which the gods made a covenant not to flood the earth ever again.

If there were no other Global Flood accounts in the world, then you could effectively argue that the Hebrew account may have been stolen from the Babylonians. But that happens to not be the case. Why is it that almost all other religions and cultures in the world have these exact same parallels?

The Egyptians wrote that their gods at one time purified the Earth by a great worldwide Flood from which only a few shepherds escaped. The Hindu tradition states that Manu, after being warned, built a ship in which he escaped from a great worldwide Flood that destroyed all creatures. The Chinese tradition states that Fa-He, their founder, escaped from a worldwide Flood sent because man had rebelled against heaven. He escaped with his wife, three sons, and three daughters. Eight people survived the First Earth to repopulate the Second Earth. Can such parallels with the Scriptures be accredited to blind, random chance?

There are more than 500 accounts of the worldwide Flood that have been documented throughout all cultures. In the book *The Flood Reconsidered* by Frederick A. Filby, a study by Dr. Richard Andree is cited in which 86 of these accounts were studied (20 Asiatic, three European, seven African, 46 American, 10 Australian and from the Pacific). The conclusion was astounding. Without question, 62 of the 86 accounts of the Flood proved to be entirely independent of any possible influence from the Hebrew or Babylonian accounts (Filby 1970, 58).

Yet their common features cannot be ignored and brushed away as mere coincidence. Such unanimity in their commonalities cannot be objectively ignored. The only possible answer to their concordance must be that there was, in fact, a historical, spacetime event that was witnessed and recorded by the ancients and then remembered by their descendants in widely varying cultures around the world. Any other rationalization must be considered as a purely subjective bias and irrational speculation in every sense of the words.

The universality of the Global Deluge accounts, coupled with the firm common design portrayed by these accounts, must be regarded as absolute proof of the actuality of this historical event as rooted in spacetime history. Such congruity could hardly be expected to arise entirely independently through sheer spontaneous generation without being anchored in a real, actual, spacetime, historical event.

Of course, the objective reader must consider that many of these accounts have been corrupted in time as each culture has eventually mixed into them the normal acculturations and mythological embellishments typical of our human nature, along with the real historical account. The norm in history is always to embellish the deeds of the past. The authenticity of a historical narrative always dims with time. It is our human nature to corrupt and degenerate it.

Like all matter in our universe, we tend to go from a state of order to a state of disorder.

Unfortunately, in so doing, Satan has cleverly managed to discredit in the minds of modern naturalists the veracity of the actual event. But to the objective analyst, the universal commonalities hidden as gems within them attest to the historical reality of the event, separating fact from fiction. Therefore, by cataloging the universal commonalities found within these stories, we can come to know at least the kernel of truth found in each of these historical chronicles.

The following seven facts are universally recorded by diverse and separate cultures worldwide:

1. The Flood was a judgment of God resulting from the wickedness and violence of the antediluvian civilization.
2. God instructed Noah to build an ark.
3. God instructed Noah to save two of every animal, seeds of every kind, and his family.
4. The actual Flood was a worldwide catastrophe, not a local event, that unleashed two sources of water: the fountains of the deep and black rain from the heavens.
5. The ark grounded on a mountain.
6. The world was darkened.
7. The world became cold.

These specific factors cannot be ascribed to mere chance. The evolutionist who insists that these are simply memories of local floods goes against the very narrative recorded, as well as the scientific evidence that substantiates a global catastrophe of unprecedented nature. To hold such a view requires more blind faith than I possess.

In the latter part of this book, I will detail a smattering of these individual accounts chronicled from civilizations around the entire planet so the reader can personally judge whether or not these similarities can be summarily dismissed as coincidence. But presently, I would like to concentrate on the exact nature of the biblical claims and the scientific evidence that corroborates this biblical model.

Our Judeo-Christian Model

The Hebrew Scriptures seem to indicate that the First Earth was a vastly different environment from our Second Earth. The world that was no longer exists. The radical change was caused by the catastrophe of the Great Flood that birthed our Second Earth.

It was a world much closer to the paradise we had lost in the Garden at Eden. From fire, wind, water, and ice our First Earth perished. But few today realize what we lost. Our Second Earth is inferior in so many ways that it is hard for us to even imagine the magnificently designed world that perished so long ago.

Imagine an almost air-conditioned world throughout its entire surface, so fruitful and lush in vegetation that man needed not farm in order to survive. Edible fruits of so many delicate varieties abounded so much that we could not have possibly eaten all the ripe fruit available to us.

Imagine a world with no natural disasters such as tsunamis, hurricanes, tornadoes, earthquakes, floods, and forest fires caused by lightning. It was a world without vast expanses of desert, and there were no blizzards, snow, or harsh freezing winters to survive.

"This is a fairy-tale," you might say. Yes, it sure sounds like a fairy-tale. But it was not. In fact, paradise had already been lost by that time. And although the First Earth was infinitely superior to our present Earth, it had already greatly deteriorated from the magnificent Garden at Eden. Perhaps our fascination with fairy-tales comes from our collective memory of this lost world. We intuitively know this is where we belong. Within the depths of our soul, we sense that this is where we came from. It was our first and intended abode. We inwardly yearn for the world of peace and plenty that we lost so long ago.

Today, like a flickering light too weak to shine brightly, that memory dimly lingers. We long to flee the manmade concrete canyons for the verdure of the unconfined outdoors. Muddling through the work week, we grope for the weekends so we might spend some time even in the dimmest shadow of that garden we long for intuitively, the modern city parks. Or we long for the vacation where we can visit our beautiful national parks.

We decorate our homes with flowers and plant beautiful and elaborate gardens. Yes, that ancient memory still faintly flickers in our souls, even though it continually dims with time. Someday, the souls of many will darken beyond that memory. Someday, night will come, and the shadow shall spread its cloak about our world. The deception of that global ruler who will come crying peace and dragging war shall cloud the minds of most. In that day, the Second Earth shall meet her final fate as did our First Earth when it came to that same crossroad and terrorists ruled our land. Do not be deceived by their shallow promises of global peace. The centralization of power has ever led to tyranny and oppression.

> *They do not know the way of peace, and there is no justice in their tracks; They have made their paths crooked, Whoever treads on them does not know peace.*
> —Isa. 59:8

> *While they are saying, "Peace and safety!" then destruction will come upon them suddenly like labor pains upon a woman with child, and they will not escape.*
> —1 Thess. 5:3

In that day, the intense heat that shall come will diminish our withering world even more. The grass will wither, the trees shall bear no fruit, the rains shall stop, the destroyers shall rage, war shall devastate all in its path, and hunger will grip our planet in a deadly vice followed by pestilence. In that day, judgments from God of diminishing thirds shall announce the beginning of the end of our Second Earth. Violence, war, and pestilence shall profane our Second Earth as the demonic hierarchy once again attempts their New World Order of total global dominance.

In that day, the Four Horsemen of the Apocalypse shall announce the beginning of God's global destruction of our Second Earth throughout the seven years of the Great Tribulation, otherwise known as Jacob's Trouble in the Hebrew Scriptures. That will mark the very last week of years that will end our Second Earth as completely and thoroughly as the Great Flood ended our First Earth. Once again, a global catastrophe will atone for the wickedness of mankind when the promised Deliverer will come to defeat the Antichrist and his destroyers.

Beware of the Four Horsemen who come to conquer mankind and kill one fourth of all humanity in the process. Even the hunger of the wild beasts shall be inflamed as famine strikes all. Pandemics always come riding on the back of famines as our human immune systems begin to fail.

> *I looked, and behold, an ashen horse; and he who sat on it had the name Death; and Hades was following with him. Authority was given to them over a fourth of the earth, to kill with sword and with famine and with pestilence and by the wild beasts of the earth.*
>
> —Rev. 6:8

This shall be a time of testing for all Jews and Christians. Many of the saints shall be hunted like dogs in the street, so deep is hatred for the truth. The Apostle John was given this vision, but he did not fully understand the horror he was seeing, so he asked one of the 24 elders around the throne of God to explain it.

> *Then one of the elders answered, saying to me, "These who are clothed in the white robes, who are they, and where have they come from?" I said to him, "My lord, you know." And*

THE DEATH OF THE FIRST EARTH

> *he said to me, "These are the ones who come out of the great tribulation, and they have washed their robes and made them white in the blood of the Lamb. For this reason, they are before the throne of God; and they serve Him day and night in His temple; and He who sits on the throne will spread His tabernacle over them. They will hunger no longer, nor thirst anymore; nor will the sun beat down on them, nor any heat; for the Lamb in the center of the throne will be their shepherd, and will guide them to springs of the water of life; and God will wipe every tear from their eyes."*
>
> —Rev. 7:13–17

Be patient, my brothers and sisters. The dawning will come, but first will come the Coming Night. The whole world will tremble, literally. Mountains shall crumble. Islands shall fall into the sea. The day of the dark angels shall bring forth the Coming Night, but they shall not stand, for our great God shall once again foil their global conquest. The Blood Moon shall signify the anger of our Holy God that shall atone for the innocent blood that shall be spilt upon our Second Earth by the Dark Stars that have come to rule our planet. When you see these things come to pass, know that the wrath of God shall begin to atone for our Second Earth.

> *I looked when He broke the sixth seal, and there was a great earthquake, and the sun became black as sackcloth made of hair, and the whole moon became like blood; and the stars of the sky fell to the earth, as a fig tree casts its unripe figs when shaken by a great wind. The sky was split apart like a scroll when it is rolled up, and every mountain and island were moved out of their places.*
>
> —Rev. 6:12–14

In the middle of that seven-year period, the demon hordes in full force shall attack the Temple of God in heaven, thinking they can sit upon His Throne. But Michael and his angels shall utterly defeat them. They shall be cast down from heaven and thrust upon the Earth. The demons will rage, knowing that their time is short. God's atonement for their crimes shall not be quenched until the grapes of wrath have been trampled to the last (Rev. 12:1–15).

In the seventh year, the final judgment shall end the seven-year ordeal. A global earthquake of great magnitude shall batter every continent so all of man's work shall crumble to the ground. Every city in the world shall be totally destroyed to dust and ruins, and God shall begin again the Third Earth with a Third Ice Age. I suspect that in that day God shall reunite the seven continents into one supercontinent as it was meant to be during the First Earth. In that day, Jerusalem shall be lifted up, literally. It shall be known from that day forward for eternity as the City of Truth.

> *Then the seventh* angel *poured out his bowl upon the air, and a loud voice came out of the temple from the throne, saying, "It is done." And there were flashes of lightning and sounds and peals of thunder; and there was a great earthquake, such as there had not been since man came to be upon the earth, so great an earthquake* was it, and *so mighty. The great city was split into three parts, and the cities of the nations fell. Babylon the great was remembered before God, to give her the cup of the wine of His fierce wrath. And every island fled away, and the mountains were not found. And huge hailstones, about one hundred pounds each, came down from heaven upon men; and men blasphemed God because of the plague of the hail, because its plague was extremely severe.*
>
> —Rev. 16:17–21

The works of man's hands shall turn to dust and ash and then be pummeled and buried by chunks of ice weighing 100 pounds and raining judgment from the sky. But like before, death shall bring forth a resurrection, and our Third Earth shall rise from the ashes and the crumbled remains of our Second Earth. The blood of the innocents who cried unto heaven for justice shall be avenged, and God shall reward those who, like Noah, remained faithful to the truth in the midst of the Age of Terror called the Great Tribulation.

Do not hearken to the voices of the naysayers who claim that global catastrophes are simply mythological. The Great Flood was no local inundation. Few understand the loss we suffered at the death of the First Earth, which was created with a water vapor canopy that served as a filter that blocked almost all the harmful cosmic radiation and regulated the temperature of the entire planet. It was a world expressly designed for the betterment of mankind. It was an almost perfect world, very superior to the present.

All this was lost in one single cataclysmic event that changed our world forever. This is the story of Noah's Flood. It is the story of the world we lost because of our rebellion toward God. If such a world existed, then the scientific evidence left behind should corroborate it. If such a world ended, then the memory should be etched in the minds of the ancients. If that catastrophe is a real spacetime, historical event, then we should be able to reconstruct the physical mechanisms that brought that world to its fiery and watery death.

With that in mind, I will first give the reader an encapsulated outline of the events believed to have transpired during the deluge that brought the end of the First Earth. Then I will entertain each of these steps in more detail and offer the scientific evidence I believe more accurately explains the empirical facts observed. My purpose is to provide the reader a completely new understanding of the magnificent world we lost in order that the end of the Second Earth does not take us unaware.

It must be noted that I am not claiming with absolute certainty that the Great Flood transpired in every detail exactly in the manner here proposed. What I can say with absolute certainty is that this model is a rational and scientifically adequate model that better explains what we observe today than what the evolutionists offer. What we can say with certainty is that the Great Flood ended the world that was because God judged mankind for the violence and terrorism that had profaned our planet.

The story of the Great Flood is not a myth. It is the story of the death of the First Earth, and it is a spacetime, historical reality. Since we were not there, we must work backward with observable empirical data and construct a physical model that accurately explains the evidence in the rocks and the chronicles of our ancient forefathers that were left behind.

We must not become intimidated and cower in silence by either the terrorism of man's wickedness or the lies of atheistic evolution. We must not turn a blind eye to the horror of this violence or we shall empower wickedness in our own time to thrive. Too often mankind seeks to look away from the consequences of wickedness and in so doing allow their deeds to continue in the dark until they come to call upon us.

Too many of us selfishly worship the idol of personal peace at any price and disengage from our duty to be the salt of the Earth, the light on the hill, and the carriers of the torch of truth. Light must be the antidote to the darkness of the shadow that camouflages wickedness. Those who seek the face of God shall be the light that brings the greatest harvest ever for the Kingdom of God in the midst of the Coming Night.

We must also not be shaken by the horror of the cataclysm. Though the destruction of the First Earth was complete, through His grace He opened up a new way. The same will happen at the end of the Second Earth—not through a great flood but through war, earthquakes, fire, pestilence, and famine.

In this work, I shall address the unique and special characteristics that marked the very nature of our First Earth and provide for the reader the sequence of events that led to its demise. Then I shall proceed with the documentation necessary to back each claim. I will entertain the six major arguments evolutionists use to discredit the historicity of the Great Flood and provide a scientific and rational answer to their specious arguments.

The Two Sources
Argument 1 – Where did the water come from to cover the land?
Naturalists have long attacked the Global Flood as mythological. They insist that all the Flood accounts recorded in the annals of all the ancient civilizations refer to local floods and not a Global Flood. Owing to their evolutionary bias, they have subjectively disregarded much of the scientific data that counters their theology of scientism and have completely disregarded the internal evidence of the ancient chronicles. We can with absolute certainty say that true science is not in contradiction with the biblical narrative. I urge the reader to consider the hard facts with an open mind and a questioning spirit. Only then can men and women of intellectual honesty come to truth.

We begin by providing the sources for the flood water necessary to cover the Earth. The Scriptures are not science books, but they are truth. Hence, when something is declared, it is both intellectually true and scientifically true. That means we can find through the rigors of the scientific methodology the answers that can illuminate the veracity of the historical claims. If it cannot be trusted historically, it cannot be trusted for any spiritual truth.

Consider the following psalm:

> *He established the earth upon its foundations,*
> *So that it will not totter forever and ever.*
> *You covered it with the deep [oceans] as with a garment;*
> *The waters were standing above the mountains,*
> *At Your rebuke they fled [the Great Flood],*
> *At the sound of Your thunder they hurried away.*

The mountains rose; *the valleys sank down*
To the place which You established for them.
You set a boundary that they may not pass over,
So that they will not return to cover the earth (emphasis added).
—Ps. 104:5–9

It is clear that King David understood well that the Genesis record was a historical and not an allegorical account as some modern-day Christians claim as they attempt to merge the atheistic theory of evolution with Christianity. There are four distinct points that David made:

1. The top of the mountains of the First Earth were completely covered by the waters of the Great Flood.
2. After God reduced the waters of the Great Flood, the mountains rose.
3. The earth is presently tottering. This wobble is what causes the precession of the equinoxes.
4. God has promised that He will never allow the Earth to be covered by the same watery cataclysm that was created by the precipitation of the water vapor canopy and the breaking of the fountains of the deep.

Genesis clearly declares that the water that flooded our Earth came from two places: the fountains of the deep and the floodgates of heaven. In other words, there were two water reservoirs alluded to in Scripture that brought forth the Great Flood. The first source of water was a huge network of subterranean chambers filled with salt water below our supercontinent that still exists, as we shall soon document. The second was a water vapor canopy that shrouded our atmosphere.

1. There were and still are vast underground saltwater chambers under the granitic substructure of the Earth's crust. They were under enormous pressure due to the immense weight of the 10 to 16 miles of granitic rock above them that formed our singular supercontinent,

which I call Arza. Because of the enormous pressures in this depth, large volumes of gases and minerals were dissolved into this salt water. As long as the crust of the Earth was intact, this water was stable and stayed contained in the chambers. We propose that this singular supercontinent was struck by seven meteors that cracked the crust of our planet and shattered it into the seven continental plates we have today. The seven impacts were so powerful that they penetrated beyond these reservoirs below the granitic rock of the supercontinent. The impacts uncorked and released the water of the fountains of the deep, which Genesis records.

2. In addition, the First Earth was created with a light water vapor canopy that shrouded the entire Earth prior to the meteor strikes that in one day changed our world forever. This thin vapor canopy created a greenhouse effect that kept the entire surface of the planet at a moderate range of temperature, allowing vast savannahs in areas that today are inhospitable tundra regions. From this limited reservoir came some of the rain that fell on our planet for 40 days and 40 nights. Let us first explore the evidence for these two propositions.

The Water Vapor Canopy

Argument 2 – The naturalist scoffs at the biblical claim that before the Great Flood the Earth had no rain.

The Genesis record informs us that the meteorological system of the First Earth was radically different than ours today. There was no rain in those days. Instead, a mist covered the ground every morning and watered the whole supercontinent of Arza. As our modern farmers have learned, watering through methods of irrigation that are not by sprinklers is much more efficient.

> *For the* Lord *God had not sent rain upon the earth, and there was no man to cultivate the ground. But a mist used to rise from the earth and water the whole surface of the ground.*
> —Gen. 2:5–6

As we shall see, it is quite possible to have an Earth without rain and yet filled with humidity with the ideal temperature for our plant and animal life to thrive. Two enormously important factors were created in the ideal environment of the First Earth:

1. The first was a solid granitic crust cushioned on huge underground saltwater aquifers.
2. The second was a light water vapor canopy that provided marvelous protection against cosmic rays and kept our Earth under a uniform meteorological homeostasis. Consequently, prior to the Great Flood, the meteorological processes on our planet were quite subdued and peaceful. There were no hurricanes or tornadoes. There were no earthquakes or tsunamis since our stable crust provided a habitat free of them. Our planet was much closer to being the idyllic paradise of the Garden at Eden.

Evolutionists dogmatically insist that the continental landmasses that broke into our continents have been crushing together and pulling apart for 4.5 billion years. They deny that our First Earth had a solid and unbroken singular supercontinent. They believe that the continents, guided by magma currents beneath them, have been crashing into one another and then breaking up again into different shapes for millions of years. They claim that before Pangaea, there were two other supercontinents that had formed and broken up, called Rodina and Gondwana. They say that this, of course, was a slow and gradual process that took place over several billion years. They provide no catastrophic mechanism for the fracturing of the continents but imagine it as a slow and gradual coming together and then a reshuffling into another form.

But this evolutionary mechanism is incapable of explaining the actual movements of the continents once the supercontinent was fractured. I have great difficulty believing that Antarctica would move directly toward the South Pole considering the indisputable fact that the centrifugal force of the spinning planet would tend to move all continents toward the equator. Unless it was thrust there by the impact of an enormous meteor strike, there is no way it would travel directly south in opposition to the centrifugal force of our spinning planet. Had this movement been controlled only by the magma currents below our plates, all free-floating continents would have by centrifugal force been forced toward the equator.

Our Judeo-Christian model not only rejects the long age of our Earth but also stipulates that the supercontinent that existed in the First Earth was, in fact, solidly intact. Something of great catastrophic power shattered our solid supercontinent and broke it into seven continents.

Something of great force must have driven Antarctica in that southerly direction toward the South Pole, something powerful enough to counter the centrifugal force of our spinning Earth. The same logic goes for the enormous islands of Greenland and Iceland in the extreme Northern Hemisphere that would have also been driven toward the equator by the centrifugal force of our spinning planet.

It makes more sense that the once whole landmass was cracked by giant meteor strikes and the continents were thus jarred into motion by the power and direction of the impacts. The direction of their motion, as we shall see, is due not only to the impact but to the events that followed the cracking of the crust in the formation of the Mid-Atlantic Ridge. Nevertheless, what can be said with great certainty is that long ago our planet had a much more stable environment than the planet we presently inhabit.

In contrast to the evolutionary gradualist history, our Judeo-Christian model stipulates that the First Earth was created by the Supreme Being to be an almost perfect habitat. There was a singular ocean composed of pristine water fit for drinking. The salinity level of the ocean obviously increased greatly during the titanic, hydraulic upheaval of the Great Flood that dissolved an enormous amount of minerals by the churning waters over the land as the fountains of the deep spewed the salt water, supersaturated with gases and minerals from the subterranean chambers or aquifers to the surface of our planet.

There was no rain, no storms, no hurricanes, and no tornadoes in the First Earth since the water vapor canopy kept the meteorological processes in homeostasis. The entire Earth was a veritable greenhouse filled with humidity and condensation ample enough to maintain an enormous variety of vegetation and animal life of which only a small fraction has survived until today.

For the former inhabitants of the previously serene antediluvian planet that survived the Great Flood in Noah's ark, the aftermath of this catastrophe must have been completely shocking, to say the least. The entire topography as well as the climate had become a completely foreign world to them. The mountains grew much higher; the divided continents, multiple seas, glaciers, deserts, thunderstorms, lightning, hurricanes, tornadoes, earthquakes, and tsunamis were all new as were the snow, sleet, and rain. The Second Earth had, indeed, become an inferior and more hostile planet for life.

To say that the Second Earth changed drastically would be an understatement. It would no longer be a safe and mild meteorological environment for humanity, animals, and plants. Now the ravages of storms would cause some areas to receive too much rain, creating local floods. Other areas would not receive enough rain and would turn into vast expanses of desert where lush forests filled with life once thrived. The North and South Poles would become frozen ice deserts, almost lifeless. Now there were vast expanses of icy tundra so cold that man would be hard put to find anything there to eat.

Much has changed, since the death of our First Earth, and much will continue to change until the death of our Second Earth. The harmful cosmic radiation of the Sun that was so effectively screened by the conditions in the First Earth now bombard the surface of our diminished or inferior planet. Three important barriers to cosmic rays were permanently altered. The water vapor canopy was no more. The strong magnetic field was now diminished by the alteration of the flow of magma due to the cracking of the crust by the enormous power of seven meteor strikes. The enormous ozone layer that effectively screened the cosmic rays was now greatly reduced.

Cosmic rays now bombard mercilessly upon the inhabitants of the Second Earth at a rate never before experienced. This inevitably causes the aging process to be accelerated and creates harmful mutations in the genetic structure of the cells, which could lead to cancer, premature aging, and other diseases. Were it not for the still existing though greatly diminished protection of the magnetosphere around our planet, cosmic rays would kill all life on the surface of the planet. Our Earth would be completely sterile.

The more hostile environment reduced the viability of many of the offspring of the creatures that once thrived abundantly in the First Earth. Our planet is a vastly inferior offspring of the world God designed for us. It is a testament to the falleness of man.

God's creation account of the primordial planet describes a very different biosphere than our present condition. As stated earlier, the First Earth contained an almost ideal climate throughout the entire surface of the landmass. The world that was, as depicted in the Scriptures, is nothing like evolutionary history claims. Let us now explore this in more detail.

Evolutionary history does not include the existence of a water vapor canopy on Earth. Some may think this is impossible. But it is not. Today we can view such a canopy on the planet Venus. This canopy serves in much the same manner as a greenhouse in the dead of winter. As the direct result of this water vapor canopy, the First Earth effectively maintained an almost uniform temperature with a high index of humidity globally.

> *Then God said "Let there be an expanse in the midst of the waters, and let it separate the waters from waters." God made the expanse, and separated the waters which were below the expanse from the waters which were above the expanse; and it was so.* God called the expanse heaven (emphasis added).
>
> —Gen. 1:6–7

It is clear in these verses that God separated the water vapor canopy above from the expanse of the sky. In other words, there was an expanse of air that separated the waters that were above the expanse of sky from the waters of the ocean.

Some have argued that the "waters which were above" is an allusion to clouds. But that makes no sense for the Genesis account also stipulates that rain did not begin to fall on the Earth until the day of the Great Flood. If clouds existed at the time of creation, then rain would have resulted. It is more likely that we had a thin water vapor canopy, only much smaller than that of Venus.

As stated earlier, according to Scripture, there was no rain on the Earth during the antediluvian period. Our biosphere was governed by an entirely different meteorological system.

> *For the Lord God had not caused it to rain upon the earth. . . . But there went up a mist from the earth, and watered the whole face of the ground.*
>
> —Gen. 2:5–6

Plants were watered daily by the morning dew created by the condensation of the humidity in the air during the cooling of the night. In effect, this humidity, uniformly sustained by the water vapor canopy, caused the entire Earth to become literally a lush paradise. Underground springs and streams and the morning mist created by the rich humidity amply watered our primordial planet.

This is a superior form of irrigation that does not cause undo erosion and avoids the problem of overwatering in low-lying areas and underwatering in higher elevations. Continuous watering by this mist evaded the problems of flash floods and arid areas where too little rain causes deserts.

The water vapor canopy worked in the same fashion as a greenhouse. It was a global temperature regulator. The net effect adequately kept the entire planet at a moderate and idyllic temperate climate over the entire surface of one single landmass. Although there were some minor variations in temperature, there were no frozen poles. There is no other explanation for the temperate weather in the extreme poles other than the water vapor canopy. In order for the temperature of the polar regions to be this moderate, the equatorial regions would have been blazing-hot deserts. They were, in fact, lush forest areas, as we shall now document.

The extreme northern and southern regions of the supercontinent had a temperate climate ideal for grasses, which gave ample food for large mastodons, rhinoceros, reindeer, musk oxen, horses, and other grazing animals. The lush vegetation that was initially thriving throughout the entire landmass provided ample food for an incredible variety of animals that grew much larger than their representatives in our diminished Second Earth. This water vapor canopy created an idyllic First Earth that was a veritable paradise compared to our present Earth.

The canopy was a marvelous benefit to our planet, acting in much the same manner as our ozone layer and magnetosphere. That is, it filtered the harmful cosmic radiation that batters us from our Sun but with the added benefit that it also moderated global temperatures and humidity levels exactly like a greenhouse.

I remember the first time I saw a greenhouse as a child. I was visiting my godfather in Princeton, New Jersey. Bill French was my mother's childhood friend and a veteran of World War II who had lost both his legs to a land mine while caring for the wounded as a medic. He regularly went on long walks in the morning, and I struggled to keep up with his pace, even with his prosthetic legs.

I grew up in a tropical climate and was used to seeing gardens in the open. Passing a greenhouse, I asked Billy why they built a glass house around their garden. He explained to me that the greenhouse had no heaters. The temperature inside was completely regulated by the light of the Sun. That a thin layer of glass could accomplish that was unimaginable to me. How could the air be so cold outside and yet be so warm inside?

He explained to me that light enters through the glass, and then the long wavelength infrared rays are trapped inside, creating heat inside the framework. As a consequence, the glass structure was able to maintain a uniform, temperate climate in the greenhouse in the dead of winter. I remember the wonder of learning that tropical plants could grow in the midst of winter while snow covered the ground outside.

How our planet has deteriorated! The First Earth had one large ocean with clear, pristine fresh water that supported an enormous variety of marine life. It was the Great Flood that turned our ocean waters salty. By the end of our Second Earth, the oceans shall become a cesspool. But fear not, my friends. The prophet Ezekiel informs us that in the future, the returning Messiah will once again turn our seas into fresh water (Ezek. 47).

This was our First Earth—a marvelously designed planet that kept a moderate temperature throughout its entire surface. Life grew abundantly, and the present extremes in weather, which often wreak havoc on our Second Earth, were not part of this ideal environment.

Diagram 14 - The Water Vapor Canopy

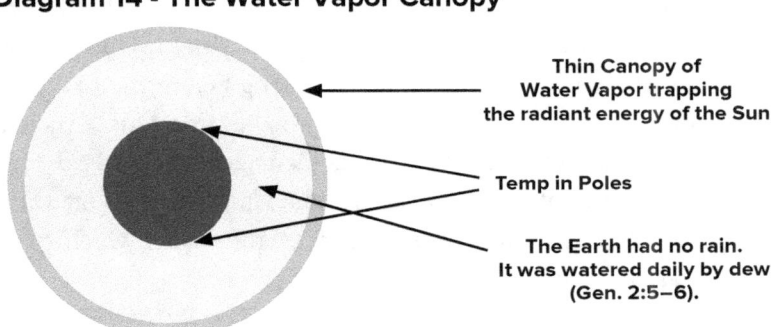

The idea of a water vapor canopy is therefore not some science fiction concept. As we have seen, there is such a canopy around our neighbor planet, Venus. However, the poisonous gases of Venus, the overwhelming thickness of the canopy, and its proximity to the Sun create an inhospitable environment for life. On Venus, the greenhouse effect is on steroids. The surface temperature is upward of 800 to 900 degrees Fahrenheit.

Moreover, the massive thickness of the Venetian canopy creates intolerable pressure on the surface of the planet. Earth's terrestrial water vapor canopy was much thinner, allowing just the right amount of light and heat to create an ideal habitat for life.

Our primordial First Earth, being just the right distance from the Sun, was an idyllic paradise that supported an enormous variety of fauna of which our present Second Earth is but a mere microcosm. Evolutionists call this serendipity that places Earth at just the right distance from the Sun to have water in the three phases of matter (solid, liquid, and gas). They have therefore dubbed it the "Goldilocks Zone." (Goldilocks, Papa Bear, Mother Bear, and Baby Bear had nothing to do with it. God made it so.)

This so-called Land of Mist may be exactly what the ancient Olmec traditions were referring to when they spoke of the fabled and venerated Tamoanchan. The chronicler Bernardino de Sahagún called the inhabitants of this ancient civilization the mysterious "rubber people." Ancient poems in Nahuatl speak of a legendary land associated with the memory of the Olmec, which they called Tamoanchan. This mysterious Land of Mist, they say, was located on the eastern shore of an ancient continent long before the founding of Teotihuacan—literally "place of those who became gods." Ancient Tamoanchan has been described as a golden age and could possibly be referring to the antediluvian civilization, which perhaps may also be what Solon referred to as the City of Atlantis from which some incredulous tales have evolved.

The reason I suspect the Mayas were speaking of an antediluvian civilization is quite simple. The name Tamoanchan in Maya means "Land of the Mist." This may very well be an allusion to the fact that a mist watered the antediluvian world every morning because prior to the Great Flood, there was no rain on the Earth. The following ancient poem in Na'huatl alludes to the antiquity of this land of mist and to the longevity of this civilization:

> In a certain era
> which no one can reckon
> which no one can remember,
> where there was a government for a long time (Coe and Koontz 1977, 70).

No doubt, in some respects the beginning of the antediluvian civilization was the golden age of man, for the First Earth was clearly superior to our diminished Second Earth. Not only was the cranium of the Cro-Magnon man (the Adamic race) larger than our modern man and their longevity seemingly impossible, but the environment of the First Earth was also much superior to our present planet.

Prior to the fracturing of Earth's crust, the surface of the Earth was an extremely stable environment. The solid granitic structure that supported the singular supercontinent of Arza provided a stable platform so life could flourish. The entire singular continent of the Earth was graced with gentle, rolling hills and fertile, luscious valleys. The thickness of the supercontinent was thinner than our present continents and spread out farther in the relatively shallower primordial ocean. There were no earthquakes, volcanoes, or tsunamis since the exterior plate of Earth's crust was still intact.

Land everywhere was full of thick, lush, fertile soil capable of sustaining an enormous variety and quantity of vegetation. Even evolutionists admit this. It is one of the reasons for the observed gigantism of that epoch, attested in the fossil record. In addition, the protection from the deleterious effects of cosmic rays that cause harmful mutations in our genes no doubt maintained a more perfect specimen of all the species. That was the reason for what scientists today call megafauna. In reality, that was the normal; today we are an inferior shadow of the world that was.

> Huge insects crawled, crept, and flitted across the earth. Two of them were the largest known insects of all time, the centipede *Arthropleura*, which grew to a length of more than eight feet, and the giant dragonfly *Meganeura*, which had a wingspan of some two and a half feet. These enormous dimensions were possible because at that time oxygen made up 35 percent of total air volume (rather than our current wimpy 21 percent) (Church and Regis 2012, 95).

All of this was changed in a single event that cracked the singular, supercontinent into the present seven continents. This catastrophic event subsequently drained the water vapor canopy, which had effectively regulated the temperature of the world fairly evenly over the entire surface.

Today, our wilting planet is but a shadow of the lush environment enjoyed by the inhabitants of the First Earth. Only a small fraction of our world enjoys such thick vegetation. It is on these few remaining forests that we desperately depend for our life-giving oxygen. If they die, so do we.

But man, who turned his back on the Creator, did not appreciate these idyllic climactic conditions. The early records of all ancient civilizations inform us that the world prior to the Great Flood eventually became filled with violence. That is universally attested by all the ancient Global Flood accounts that tell us God judged the planet for the violence humans perpetrated against each other. For example, the Mayas, separated by the Atlantic Ocean from the Old World, chronicled the same story.

But those that they had made, that they had created, did not think, did not speak with their Creator, their Maker. And for this reason they were killed, they were deluged. A heavy resin fell from the sky . . . and broke and mangled their bones and their nerves, and ground and crumbled their bones.

This was to punish them because they had not thought of their mother, nor their father, the Heart of Heaven, called Huracán. And for this reason *the face of the earth was darkened and a black rain began to fall, by day and by night* (emphasis added) (*Popol VuhI*, 90).

Modern man is naturally predisposed to reject such an account, for it would necessarily imply that if God judged us then, He should judge us now. None can deny that our world is once again filled with violence and our technology has provided lethal weapons for us that can create more destruction than ever before. The evolutionists would rather believe that natural changes are governed only by happenstance. But the Mayan description is quite accurate and in accord with our proposition that ejecta and tephra blanketed our planet and rained upon mankind as a thick black rain.

The Scriptures declare the antithesis of the evolutionary claim that man evolved from apes and was dispersed throughout the world, becoming human in multiple places with differing languages. It tells us that we were one people and spoke one language, but our greed led us into violence. Our ancient forefathers were destroyed by the judgment of God. It was not until after the Great Flood that our human family was separated into the present races and different languages.

Evolutionists generally believe that humans evolved from apes in different parts of the world and therefore our ancestral lineages are not supposed to be interconnected. In their minds, languages evolved independently in these various geographic locations. We have already discussed the empirical scientific evidence that discredits the idea that man evolved and specifically documented that all humankind today came from a single set of parents as documented by our mitochondrial DNA.

But the study of languages also points to a single place and time of origin. We can point to the origin of languages as the area of Turkey where the ark of Noah was said to have grounded after the Great Flood.

> Our work indicates that the protolanguage originated more than 6,000 years ago in eastern Anatolia (Gamkrelidze and Ivanov 1990, 110).

The Biblical narrative stipulates that the Earth's landmass was once united and that its inhabitants were one people who spoke one language prior to the judgment of the Tower of Babel, an event that took place sometime after the Great Flood, which transpired about 6,000 years ago.

> *Now the whole world had one language and a common speech.*
> —Gen. 11:1 NIV

The Hebrew Scriptures inform us that in the days of Peleg, whose name means literally "division," the Earth was divided. It was in his lifetime that the languages were confounded and the nations of the Earth were dispersed.

> *One was named Peleg, because in his time the earth was divided.*
> —Gen. 10:25 NIV

That means that until relatively recent times, all of humanity was united as a single people. The so-called races that we use to distinguish the different phenotypes of the human species are in essence superficial categories of no more significance than the grouping of human beings by the color of their eyes. We are in no uncertain terms brothers and sisters according to the Scriptures.

These variations developed in a relatively short period of time through the isolation of certain genetic traits, aided by the linguistic barrier and geographical dispersion stemming from the judgment of the Tower of Babel.

Just a few hundred years from the beginning of the Second Earth, something forced humanity to separate. It is therefore indirectly implied by the Scriptures that the climactic and geophysical changes that created our present condition have also taken place rapidly since the cataclysm of the Great Flood. We believe that at the time of the destruction of the Tower of Babel, the Earth's oceans had once again risen and inundated the region of the Land of Shinar, forcing the population to disperse.

Evolutionists have, of course, rejected these claims, insisting that climactic changes evolve slowly in gradual, minute steps that are almost undetectable through long periods of time as a product of their tenacious aberrant uniformitarian bias. The concept of sudden catastrophic upheavals is very antipathetic to evolutionists since it smacks too much of the biblical model.

Evolutionists do not deny that at one time the Earth was much warmer. They cannot deny the evidence of numerous pollen samples, flowers, and grasses found in frozen mammoths and rhinoceros in Siberia and Alaska that tell us these present tundra regions were at one time temperate grasslands, and the fossils indicate that mammals once roamed abundantly in these present tundra regions.

But since they tenaciously hold to the uniformitarian paradigm, they suppose that the temperatures varied at very slow rates, thus going from one Ice Age to another only after long periods of time had elapsed. In antithesis, we believe that the reason these thousands of frozen mastodons still had in their stomach flowers and grasses of a temperate climate signifies a sudden and catastrophic flood that rapidly froze into ice and entombed them until today.

If there was no water vapor canopy to regulate global temperatures, how could Siberia be warm enough to support vast prairies filled with grasslands that supported so many species? If the Earth had warmed that much to create temperate climates in the extreme northern regions of the supercontinent, then the equatorial regions would have been scalding deserts. But they were not.

Today, meteorologists are becoming more aware that drastic climactic changes can take place in relatively short periods of time. The global warming crisis has brought this awareness to the previously staunch uniformitarian-minded evolutionists. To no small extent, the realization that a single meteor strike could have caused the mass extinction of many species has begun to erode the previous dogma of their jaded view of uniformitarianism. But old misconceptions die slowly. Old paradigms die hard.

Sadly, the acceptance of the meteor strike as a mechanism that in one catastrophic event destroyed the dinosaurs has not changed much of their underlying uniformitarian presupposition. Incredibly, they therefore still resist the idea that this catastrophic event is responsible for precipitating the Great Noahic Deluge. Huge climactic changes can take place in very short periods of time. Soon they will find out that their uniformitarian bias has blinded them from this great danger that confronts us today.

However, as evidence mounts for the rapid change in our climate, I predict that soon they will be forced to concede that it was this singular event that destroyed the almost paradisiacal conditions that existed in the First Earth and threw our planet into a cataclysmic episode that had far-reaching ramifications, even beyond the time of the Great Flood.

There is good reason to suspect that these cataclysmic changes were precipitated by meteor strikes. The force unleashed by a single giant meteor strike such as the one they claim killed the dinosaurs is so immense that it could have easily cracked the crust of the Earth, destabilizing all previously stable meteorological processes.

The resulting massive volcanic eruptions created by the cracking of the surface of our planet caused the Second Earth to be blanketed with volcanic ash and debris that shot into the atmosphere. This injection of debris into the water vapor canopy would have been enough to cause it to precipitate. And as is customary after volcanic eruptions where tephra is shot into the atmosphere, black rain subsequently ensued. It is therefore no coincidence that all ancient cultures regarded comets and asteroids as portents of catastrophes and linked their Global Flood accounts to black rain.

But the water vapor canopy was not the only source of water that precipitated as rain during the Global Deluge. The thin water vapor canopy would not have been enough to flood the whole Earth, nor would it have been enough water to rain for 40 days and 40 nights. Where did all the water come from that flooded our First Earth? The argument that there is not enough water on Earth to make a global flood must be addressed.

The Scriptures claim that there were two connected mechanisms that brought the waters of the Great Flood upon the surface of our planet. Their sequence is important. The Scriptures insist that first was the breaking open of the fountains of the deep, and then came the opening of the floodgates of the windows of heaven. It is important to note that the Scriptures and the ancients do not describe this first mechanism as a single fountain spouting a singular stream of water. The fountains were numerous, and they were described as being located throughout the world and coming from the depth of the ocean, as we shall see.

The Underground Saltwater Aquifers

If Walt Brown's hydroplate theory is correct, and I suspect it is, then the First Earth had huge subterranean water chambers or aquifers that were interconnected throughout the planet. These subterranean chambers were located beneath the granitic substructure of our supercontinent Arza. The mechanism that caused the Great Flood would have had to be capable of releasing this enormous store of subterranean salt water.

Most of us are unaware that underground chambers and subterranean rivers run throughout Earth. Many of the freshwater sources for large population areas come from such subterranean aquifers. Today, shallow subterranean aquifers abound throughout the continents. In some places, it is the population's major source of drinking water. Some of these, called fossil aquifers, are unrenewable. That means they are not refillable by rainwater. They were created by ancient processes and cannot be refilled from surface rains that seep into the ground.

But these were chambers much deeper than the freshwater aquifers. They existed below the granitic superstructure of the single supercontinent Arza that alone jutted out of the singular antediluvian ocean, which I call Apsu. There is no denying that a great deal of water resides below the granitic continents even today. Volcanic eruptions today emanate enormous amounts of water vapor. Somehow during the formation of our planet, huge reservoirs of water were trapped below the crust.

Walt Brown's hydroplate theory has proposed that about half the volume of water that now resides in our oceans was once held in interconnected fossil aquifers, or chambers, about 10 to 16 miles below the surface of the planet. That would mean the pre-flood, solid, granitic composition of the supercontinent literally rested above a layer of super-compressed salt water. It effectively served as a giant cushion that kept the singular continent of Arza stable.

What physical evidence do we have for that? Modern-day deep drills have garnered vital evidence of these deep, underground, saltwater chambers. The deepest wells man has been able to drill in Russia and Germany have surprisingly shown that salt water abounds in those subterranean levels.

The world's two deepest holes are on the Kola Peninsula in northern Russia and in Germany's Bavaria. They were drilled to depths of 7.5 miles and 5.6 miles, respectively. (Such deep holes, when quickly filled with water or dense mud, will stay open.) Neither hole reached the basalt underlying the granite continents. Deep in the Russian's hole, to everyone's surprise, was hot salty water, flowing through *crushed* granite. Why was the granite crushed? In the German hole, the drill encountered cracks throughout the lower few miles. All contained saltwater having concentrations *twice that of seawater*. Remember, surface waters cannot seep deeper than 5 miles, because the weight of the overlaying rock squeezes shut even microscopic flow channels (Brown 2001, 94).

The well in the northern Kola Peninsula of Russia was a 24-year effort that began in 1970 to drill a 12-kilometer hole. It took five years to drill 7 kilometers and another nine years to drill the next 5 kilometers. In 1989, the drill got stuck, and eventually they restarted the hole. By 1994 it reached the 12,262-meter depth (7 miles), which is about a third of the way through the crust in that region. The target depth was 15 kilometers. The overall cost of the project was $100 million. The cost of the German project was $110 million for their shallower, 10-kilometer hole.

Both projects announced that the temperature they found exceeded what they had presupposed at that level. The Germans found it to be 118 degrees Celsius (they had expected 80 degrees Celsius), and the Russians found it to be a whopping 190 degrees Celsius, almost double the boiling point of water. Why is it so unexpectedly hot at that level?

Even more remarkable is the fact that the temperature gradient (the rate of temperature increase with depth) varies widely from one area to another. Variations in temperature gradients can exceed 600 percent, a characteristic that is incompatible with an old Earth.

In continental areas far from volcanoes, temperatures can differ from 10 to 60 degrees Centigrade for every kilometer. The typical geothermal gradient fluctuates from one area to another, but it always increases in temperature the deeper you go, so in diamond mines at 11,788 feet, for example, the temperature may be 90 degrees Fahrenheit.

The source of this heat is often attributed to two possible sources: radioactivity and primordial heat. If our Earth were billions of years old as the evolutionists claim, then why would the geothermal gradient fluctuate to such extremes? Heat radiates and seeks to find equilibrium. It would be a miracle of the first order, indeed, if after billions of years the Earth would not have found temperature equilibrium.

The second proposed idea, which stipulates that these temperature fluctuations are due to pockets of radioactivity, does not make sense either if the Earth had been molten for billions or even millions of years as evolutionists claim. Surely during these vast expanses of time, convection currents would have mixed all matter to a homogeneous state.

It is obvious that some recent event has created this heat and that there just has not been enough time for the heat to dissipate. This heat is simply the residual effect of the heat created by the rapidly shifting continental hydroplates (continents) once the supercontinent was cracked.

As we shall see, the overall physical evidence seems to support the hydroplate theory. Brown's brilliant theory stipulates that this subterranean salt water trapped between the granitic composite rock above and the basaltic composite rock below was thrust forth violently to the surface through cracks in the crust.

Although Brown does not hold to the idea that meteors were the actual mechanism that initiated the breaking of Earth's crust, it is hard for me to imagine anything else that would have that power. The stable crust of the First Earth would have looked somewhat like the following cross-section from Brown's book *In the Beginning*. (For a more in-depth study of the hydroplate theory, I strongly recommend this well-documented and clearly articulated book. Contact the Center for Scientific Creation, 5612 N. 20th Place, Phoenix, Arizona 85016.)

The subterranean saltwater chamber that existed perhaps 10 miles under the surface between the granitic composite supercontinent's landmass and the basaltic composite subterranean base below during the First Earth

(Courtesy of Walt Brown, In the Beginning)

The evidence of enormous stores of salt water below our continents is now mounting as science advances. On June 13, 2014, a scientific study by Brandon Schmandt et al. was published in the journal *Science*. Schmandt, a seismologist at the University of New Mexico, Steven Jacobsen of Northwestern University in Illinois, and their colleagues claimed to have found a giant subterranean ocean in the transition layer between the upper and lower mantles. "The transition zone can hold a lot of water, and could potentially have the same amount of H_2O as all the world's oceans," they stated (Schmandt et al. 2014).

The water is contained in a rare mineral called ringwoodite, which is formed under extremely high pressures from another mineral called olivine. Some reports estimate that this underground ocean may contain as much as three times the amount of water in our present oceans. This transition zone is found 250–410 miles below the surface of Earth and proves conclusively that large volumes of water could have been ejected as the biblical fountains of the deep that created the global inundation chronicled by all ancient civilizations. This is no myth.

The sudden pressurization created by several large meteor impacts was then followed by the subsequent depressurization created by the ejecting matter from these strike zones, which became the escape routes for the fountains of the deep. The almost immediate loss of all that weight in stone would have triggered an explosive outgassing of this underground ocean. The impact of seven giant meteors could have easily caused massive amounts of water to eject upward like a shaken soda pop bottle suddenly uncorked.

We can begin to better understand this process by studying the meteor strike under the Chesapeake Bay of Virginia, which is, in fact, relatively small compared to the seven largest meteor strikes that cracked the single supercontinent into seven continents. The Chesapeake Bay crater is about 85 kilometers across and spans the bay between the mainland of the United States and Virginia's Cape Charles with a depth of about 1.5 kilometers. The entire area of the crater is twice that of Rhode Island and almost as deep as the Grand Canyon.

Scientists first realized that a meteor impact had occurred when they discovered an 8-inch-thick ejecta layer in a drilling core taken off Atlantic City, New Jersey, in 1983. The ejecta layer contained glass beads called tektites and shocked quartz that are telltale signs of a high-energy asteroid impact. The massive power released by the impact can be readily seen by the distance it affected its surrounding vicinity since Atlantic City, New Jersey, is about 200 miles north of the actual crater. But it is the depth of the crack it created in Earth's crust that can more readily help us understand the enormous force exerted as it reached 8 kilometers down through the granitic rock.

More to our point, scientists recently discovered an enormous subterranean seawater aquifer below the crater that was created by that very impact. The giant aquifer contains some 3 trillion gallons of seawater that has a salinity content double that of the levels in our present oceans. That means this water did not come from our oceans but from the underground aquifers.

Evolutionists who always need great spans of time to make their theory of gradualism more plausible claim the impact that created this aquifer is 35 million years old. But I have great difficulty imagining how such a large asteroid impact would not leave the telltale trace of an iridium layer, which they claim is proof of the extraterrestrial nature of the Chicxulub meteor in Mexico.

This fossil ocean, they claim, is a remnant of an ancient and smaller Atlantic Ocean that had a much higher salinity layer than our present oceans. It is, however, hard to imagine how such an energetic impact would not have vaporized any water that would have been in that area from the tremendous heat and force of the strike. It is much more likely that this salt water did not come from the surface but from below where the salinity levels in the subterranean areas are known to be much greater than the surface oceans.

In fact, the prediluvian singular ocean Apsu was probably composed of fresh water with a very low salinity level. I suspect this because when the Lord returns, He shall bring our planet back to what it was originally intended. The prophet Ezekiel wrote that when the Messiah comes to rule from Jerusalem to return our world to its intended initial condition, a river will flow from the Temple of God that will turn the sea back to fresh water.

> *Then he said to me, "These waters go out toward the eastern region and go down into the Arabah; then they go toward the sea, being made to flow into the sea, and the waters* of the sea *become fresh. It will come about that every living creature which swarms in every place where the river goes, will live. And there will be very many fish, for these waters go there and* the others *become fresh; so everything will live where the river goes."*
>
> —Ezek. 47:8–9

THE DEATH OF THE FIRST EARTH

The First Earth had one landmass and one giant freshwater ocean that were fractured when Earth's crust was pummeled by several meteor strikes. When that Chesapeake meteor struck Earth, that area of the US coast was joined to Africa, and there was no Atlantic Ocean there. It was dry land. It was the very mechanism that created the fountains of the deep that broke up the singular landmass and brought up the much saltier water beneath Earth's crust that then mixed with the freshwater ocean as the floodwaters joined and created our present salinity levels.

The Atlantic Ocean was birthed by the fracturing of the singular supercontinent, Arza. As the fountains of the deep were cracked open, the broken continents separated, and the Atlantic basin was formed. None of this took place in slow, gradual millions of years. It was a catastrophic and rapid sequence of events triggered by the enormous energy of these meteors as they struck Arza.

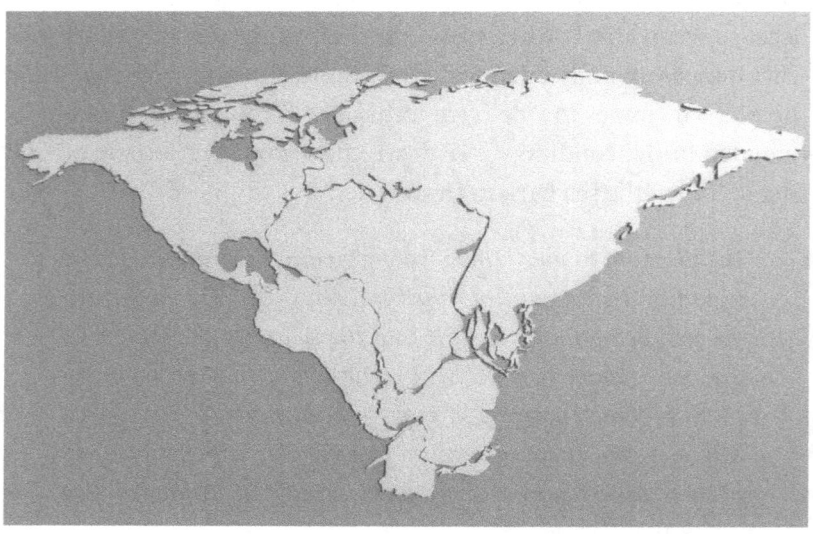

The continent of Arza during the First Earth

The huge cavity created by the massive force of the Chesapeake impact was then pressurized by rising water from below and then became sealed from above by the collapsing walls of the enormous crater, maintaining the original salinity level without the dilution that would have resulted from mixing with the aboveground ocean. The heavy sedimentation created by the hydraulics of the Great Flood would have added deep layers of sediment that were suspended in the enormous hydraulic forces of the Great Flood. These sedimentary layers helped further seal the subterranean aquifer from the waters above.

It is no coincidence that many of the sedimentary layers created by the Great Flood are filled with limestone and contain large quantities of olivine that quite likely originated in these deep subterranean aquifers connected to the ringwoodite area of the mantle.

The hydroplate theory, as we shall document from a scientific perspective, more adequately explains the Mid-Oceanic Ridge, the continental drifts, the shape of the continental shelves and slopes, the reason for ocean trenches, the large salt deposits, the seamounts and tablemounts, the magnetic variations recorded on the ocean floor, the development of the strata, the overabundance of limestone on our planet, and many more physical phenomena that are poorly explained by other evolutionary theories. We shall address all these individually.

However, for the moment, the point is that the scriptural narrative of the Noahic Flood reinforces the common universal references by most ancient cultures to the breaking of the fountains of the deep. It insists that the fountains of the deep were broken open first before the windows of heaven released the torrential rain that lasted 40 days and 40 nights.

The fountains of the deep did not subside until 150 days after commencing, long after the 40 days and 40 nights of rain stopped. That was the major source of water for the Global Flood. In other words, it was not a single fountain but rather a curtain of geysers spanning the globe all along the cracks of the new continents that were formed by the impacts of the seven meteors. As the curtain of geysers eroded the edges of the newly formed continents, removing the 10 miles or more of rock above the basaltic floor, the continents began to separate, and the pressure from the interior of the Earth began to lift the basaltic layer below the continents, which formed the Mid-Atlantic Ridge.

Even before scientists abandoned their uniformitarian dogma and accepted the catastrophic meteor strike scenario as the culprit that killed the dinosaurs, they concluded that the continents were once united in a singular landmass they called Pangaea. However, they simply assume that these continental shifts have been occurring since the beginning of the Earth. Their evolutionary hypothesis has these continental blocks coming slowly together like pieces of a puzzle and then falling slowly apart for eons. They have not yet abandoned their uniformitarian and gradualist bias.

We propose the opposite. We propose that all of this took place in one catastrophic meteor shower that fractured the previously stable and unified crust of the First Earth. In fact, we propose that the tectonic forces that they claim move the continents could not have been the mechanism that started the continents to shift. They may add some small component to the shifting motions of the plates today, but this magma flow below the continental blocks has very little to do with the direction and speed of the continental shifts, especially when they first began.

There is just not enough friction created by the molten magma that could move the massive weight of the continents, much less crack them into seven plates. Moreover, the direction of the continental movements does not align with the flow currents of magma that would be largely dictated by the direction of the spin of Earth. But let us begin at the beginning. The following is a historical list of the events that unfolded from the beginning of creation to the Death of the First Earth and the birth of our Second Earth.

We will first list them in a condensed form to give the reader a bird's-eye view of the entire story, and then we will provide the scientific evidence that substantiates our Judeo-Christian model.

The Hallmarks of the First Earth, Its Death, and the Birth of the Second Earth

1. The First Earth had a singular, solid supercontinent of granitic composition that remained intact. In other words, prior to the cracking of the Earth's crust, there were no continental plates. The crust was whole and stable.
2. Large subterranean chambers under the granitic suprastructure of the supercontinent of Arza were filled with saltwater aquifers that contained many dissolved minerals and gases such as limestone, olivine, and carbon dioxide. These sealed subterranean chambers, like a giant waterbed, provided a stable cushion for the granitic suprastructure of the landmass. Our present world is still riddled with these fossil aquifers but in much diminished form.
3. The Earth contained a singular ocean of pristine fresh water with a much-reduced mineral content compared to our present oceans. The present salinization of our oceans was caused by the swirling hydraulics of the Great Flood and the mixing with the much higher salinity of the deep underground aquifers below Earth's crust.
4. Mankind spoke one language, probably the same as ancient Sumerian.
5. There were no distinct races of mankind. We were one people. Our progenitors contained within their genes the variability

that brought forth the many superficial distinctions we observe in our present world. But not until the geographical divisions created by the judgment of the Tower of Babel were these distinctions realized. That was the catalyst that brought forth the different languages and the isolation that developed the many variations of the human race, as well as that of the animals.

6. The First Earth contained a thin water vapor canopy, similar but much smaller than that of the planet Venus, that provided for a more uniform climate throughout the entire world. The greenhouse effect this canopy created provided an ideal climate for many species to thrive throughout the entire landmass of Arza.
7. There were no frozen poles. Although there was a moderate temperature difference, the poles were not frozen over. Modern-day tundra regions were filled with prairies and grasslands that harbored a wide variety of animals. That is something evolutionists concede since the fossil evidence contains large numbers of animals that thrived in areas that today are under ice. The Earth's climate was stable and constant with only slight variations during the seasons.
8. There was no rain. There was no lightning. The Earth was watered daily by a morning mist that condensed the high humidity in the air and watered the ground everywhere.
9. There were no tornadoes, hurricanes, flash floods, tsunamis, or other hydrological disasters associated with our present unstable climate.
10. The vast majority of the prediluvian landscape contained deep fertile soil that was not washed away by torrential rains and storms.
11. As a result of the moderate global temperatures and abundant humidity, there were only a few deserts of limited size.

12. Prior to the cracking of the Earth's crust, there were no earthquakes.
13. There were also no volcanoes since the crust was stable and whole.
14. Due to the lush and temperate environment, every form of life on our planet thrived, providing a much greater variety of organisms with a wider character complex for each species.
15. The vegetation was so thick throughout much of the land area that the oxygen levels neared 37 percent compared to 21 percent in our present, much-diminished planet.
16. The extra oxygen saturation of our atmosphere due to the pressure created by the weight of the water vapor canopy, along with the plentiful food supply, stimulated gigantism in most species and was responsible for the megafauna.
17. As a result of this lush environment, mankind was largely a hunter-gatherer civilization that did not need to farm heavily for food. Yet from the earliest man, farming and the domestication of animals existed. Some of the population resided in a nomadic fashion, but many villages and some cities of several thousand inhabitants dotted the land.
18. From the sixth generation forward, the Nephilim were engendered in order to profane the bloodline of Adam and Eve and prevent the coming of the Deliverer through the seed of Eve promised in Genesis 3:15. The Earth took a violent turn toward the religion of the Nephilim. Man's rebellion toward God brought forth predation and great violence to this idyllic paradise. Human sacrifices through the shamanistic religion of the Mother Goddesses flourished. Ritualized cannibalism began to terrorize the world.
19. God took action to stop the violence, and in order to preserve the seed of Eve, He judged our First Earth. He gave Noah the design for an ark that would safely carry him through the watery judgment to come.

20. Something cracked the crust of our planet. We contend that seven giant meteors broke our crust open like a giant zipper that went around the entire globe, releasing the subterranean salt water in massive geysers that reached into space. Most of that water came back to Earth like a giant waterfall. Some escaped into space and formed comets.
21. As the curtain of geysers eroded the sides of the newly formed continents, massive amounts of sedimentation and debris became part of the process that flooded the whole world.
22. After the continents separated, the internal pressure from the interior of the Earth made the basaltic floor below the continents rise once the weight of the 10 to 16 miles of rock was removed above it and created the mid-ocean ridges.
23. Because of the force of these seven impacts, the nearly circular orbit of the First Earth around the Sun (like Venus, Mercury, and Mars) was made slightly elliptical at one end, pushing it outward from the Sun. Prior to the impact, the lunar calendar and the solar calendar were in perfect synchrony.
24. Our planet was tilted 23 degrees from the impact of the blow. The loss of the water vapor canopy, as well as the resulting tilt and the elliptical orbit, now caused the seasons to become more pronounced. Our solar calendar no longer matched our lunar calendar. The harmony and symmetry intended for the Earth was broken.
25. The impacts of these seven meteors were powerful enough to crack the crust and divide the singular landmass into our seven continents. The fracture reached the depth of the subterranean aquifers some 10 to 16 miles below the surface. That caused the fountains of the deep to burst open. The violent pressure waves sent by each striking meteor traveled all the way through the Earth and bounced back and forth several times, much like a stone thrown in a pool. These pressure waves agitated the dissolved gases in the

underground aquifers much like we do when we shake a soda pop bottle and then rapidly take off the cap. This agitation of the dissolved gases is what caused the violent outgassing eruption of the subterranean waters. Scripture says "the fountains of the great deep burst open" (Gen. 7:11 NIV).

26. The crack, like a giant zipper, then ripped across the entire face of the planet, breaking our once solid crust into the present fractured plates. The seven continents were formed.
27. This giant curtain of water under the immense pressure of the continents above them gushed out from these cracks at supersonic speeds, emptying the subterranean chambers. Salt water and dissolved minerals came up to the surface, and as a result, the contents of our pristine ocean were changed forever.
28. The erosion of the sides of the continents by the jetting water threw copious amounts of debris into the atmosphere, as well as the ejecta of the impact from the meteors. That caused the once stable water vapor canopy to precipitate and end the greenhouse effect. Evidence of this erosion is found in the V-shaped angles of the continental slopes.
29. Moisture in the form of overspray created by high-level winds alongside these walls of geysers through the Venturi effect oversaturated our skies. The debris thrust into our atmosphere by the jetting water and the tephra from erupting volcanoes became the cloud nuclei that caused the entire water vapor canopy to precipitate. Most of the jetting water fell back to Earth as a giant wall of water and supersaturated the atmosphere with moisture. Rain fell on our planet for the first time as black rain. Scripture says "the floodgates of the heavens were opened" (Gen. 7:11). It rained for 40 days and 40 nights.
30. As enough rock material was ejected by the eroding geysers, the release of all that weight above the underlying basalt floor caused it to push the floor upward and form the Mid-Atlantic

Ridge. The enormous pressure that caused the mountain ranges to rise in the Mid-Atlantic Ridge now caused the continents to slide away from the slopes of the rising ridges. Thus we believe that in a relatively short period of time, the continents separated to almost where they are today.

31. Volcanic activity and earthquakes abounded as a result of the pressure waves caused first by the impact and later by the moving plates. That intensified when the plates ground to a halt as the subterranean water was depleted. The sliding hydroplates created friction with the basaltic layer below and created massive amounts of magma as they came to a halt. In this process, the continents crunched into folds, which created the high mountains of our Second Earth. Many of these magma pockets became supervolcanoes as the sliding of the continents built up magma chambers below the surface.

32. Huge tsunamis would have circled the Earth, causing untold destruction on all the coastal regions from the motion of the continents sliding against the ocean and the impact of falling ejecta.

33. At first, global temperatures soared as the meteor strike and the reentry of ejecta heated the atmosphere. Our entire planet was ignited with fire, smoke, and searing heat. Fire first engulfed our planet as falling ejecta and volcanoes kindled numerous conflagrations that spread throughout the continents until they were doused by the rising waters. Were it not for the cooling rain of the floodgates of heaven, our planet would have completely perished from the global rise in temperature.

34. Nevertheless, this initial heat generated massive super hurricanes and powerful tornadoes of unimaginable power. Violent thunderstorms with lightning and thunder were seen for the first time. The storm of all storms buffeted our planet for 40 days and 40 nights.

35. The force of the meteor strike that traveled throughout the Earth in powerful pressure waves caused the ocean floor on the opposite side (the Pacific Ocean) to bulge outward, making the water and then the lava spill over onto the continents. These are what we presently call lava traps or provincial lava flows. The repeated pressure waves caused the characteristic steps of these provincial lava traps.
36. In time, the Pacific Ocean floor would once again find its former level through the centrifugal force exerted as the planet continued to spin, as well as through the rebound reaction to the rising of the newly created Atlantic Ocean floor on the opposite side of the world. But because of the large loss of lava in the formation of traps, the Pacific floor would, in fact, sink into deep depressions where it had previously bulged. These formed the deep depressions found in the Pacific Ocean.
37. Huge volcanic eruptions on the opposite side of the impact sites were precipitated by the pressure waves that caused the crust to initially bulge outward and crack. The molten magma was pushed by these pressure waves in unimaginable torrents of molten rock that spilled out on the surface of the planet.
38. The jetting waters of the fountains of the deep eroded the sides of the granitic suprastructure of the crust in the areas were the continents cracked. That eventually removed an enormous amount of weight along the areas where the crust had cracked. In this way, the opening between the continents was made wider. As the weight above it diminished, the negative pressure caused the basaltic layer underneath it to buckle upward. This rising basaltic lower layer then displaced the granitic upper layer of rock that had previously eroded and thus formed the Mid-Atlantic Ridge that rises above the Atlantic water level in Iceland and Greenland.

39. In turn, that caused the basaltic layer on the opposite side of the world to be subsequently sucked down, thus causing the many deep underwater trenches in that Pacific Rim area.
40. As the Mid-Atlantic Ridge rose even higher, the newly formed continents on either side slid down the elevated slopes. They glided on the water cushion still remaining inside the evacuating aquifers in the subterranean chambers between the basaltic layer and the granitic layer. The rise of the basaltic floor below picked up mounting speed as the continents slid sideways. This escalating motion caused a rapid separation of the continents that slowed down only as the water that lubricated their movement below emptied.
41. The emptying of the subterranean chambers caused the granitic suprastructure of the continents to grind to a halt through friction with the basaltic substructure. That cracked and fissured the continents and allowed the molten rock created by this friction to rise and spew into the surface as a second wave of volcanoes.
42. The grinding motion caused the continents to thicken and buckle, forming the present high mountain ridges observed on the Second Earth, especially in the distal coast of the sliding continents, which show the direction they were sliding.
43. Once the water vapor canopy was exhausted, the skies continued to be darkened by the erupting tephra spewing from the numerous new volcanoes.
44. The moderating influence of the water vapor canopy was no more. At first, heat simply escaped into space. But as the skies darkened, the Sun's energy was not able to reach the surface of the Earth. The relative temperatures of the polar regions to the equatorial regions now varied dramatically. The new tilt of the Earth, the elliptical orbit that sent the Earth farther from the Sun, and the destruction of the water vapor canopy that maintained the greenhouse effect all conspired to bring

a winter cold so fierce that ice began to form. As the ashes billowed into the atmosphere, sunlight was completely blocked from reaching the surface of the planet.

45. The darkened sky now filled with tephra from the volcanoes and the debris shot out by the fountains of the deep caused a dramatic drop in temperature. The global temperature plunged significantly. Snow, sleet, and winter storms raged throughout the polar regions and reached down with icy tendrils in giant glaciers toward the equator. The poles began to freeze solid, and the floodwaters that had covered the entire Earth began to recede. In the end, ice that was several miles thick covered our northern and southern latitudes. The First Ice Age blanketed our planet with gripping, cold fingers and threatened to make our planet a frozen world forever.

46. Gradually, normal precipitation cleared the skies. Sunlight filtered in, and our Second Earth was born in our First Ice Age. As the skies cleared, giant glaciers covered most of the Earth's landmass, except for a belt around the equatorial region.

47. Almost 95 percent of the species that thrived in the First Earth became extinct. The vastly diminished vegetation of the Second Earth now favored the smaller animals. The cold temperatures greatly curtailed the reptilian species.

48. Only a territorial band across the equatorial regions remained ice-free with a moderate climate. It is here where Noah disembarked on Mount Ararat and where his descendants settled in the Land of Shinar and created the Sumerian civilization. Farming became necessary more than ever to produce enough food. The domestication of animals became necessary for human survival because hunting was limited as the species began to slowly recover in numbers.

49. The enormous amount of decomposing animals and vegetation that were not buried in the mud layers caused by the turbulent waters of the Great Flood began to give off green-

house gases. Massive amounts of carbon dioxide released from the subterranean aquifers added to the greenhouse effect. The Second Earth began to warm up rapidly as the greenhouse gases blanketed the atmosphere. With every mile of white glacier lost, a darker Earth was revealed that absorbed ever more energy from the Sun. That caused a rapid runaway deglaciation, which made the oceans begin to rise again.

50. Within the short span of several hundred years, the Sumerian civilization became corrupted. The religion of the Serpent began to flourish once again. Cities became the center of corruption and immorality. Violence and human sacrifices again escalated. But mankind was yet one people with one language.

51. Mankind sought to usurp the place of God once again. They built a ziggurat called the Tower of Babel, which became the center of this counterfeit religion of the Serpent. Man sought to become gods and thought they could build a tower that would reach the heavens. They no longer looked to God for provision but trusted in the works of their hands. Nimrod sought to rule the world through tyranny.

52. God decided to judge mankind and disrupt the centralization of power that aided the demonic kingdom in the pursuit of the control of our Second Earth. Lightning from a mighty storm destroyed the Tower of Babel.

53. By this time, the oceans had risen more than 400 feet from the low point at the beginning of the First Ice Age. That inundated the area of the Land of Shinar and also aided in the dispersion of the people. God confounded the languages and forced humanity to disperse and decentralize power.

54. The melting glaciers interfered with the Atlantic conveyor belt and stopped the ocean currents that provide the heat exchange between polar oceans and equatorial waters. The Second Ice

Age began as a result of the melting glaciers interfering with these ocean currents. The poles began to freeze again. Once more the glaciers returned to cover most of the Earth. Today, we are now nearing the end of that Second Ice Age cycle as the Earth's polar ice caps continue to melt and the oceans continue to rise.

55. God instituted separate national governments as representatives of His law to ensure justice and provide protection for the people. Since then, the demonic hierarchy has dedicated itself to undo this judgment and once again reunite the world under one centralized global government. From that day forward, Satan has sought to bring all mankind under the rule of a global tyrant. The unifying motto of all secret societies became to gather that which was scattered.

This brief list includes the basic elements of our human history in those dark days that ended our First Earth and birthed our Second Earth. Something dreadful happened to humanity that brought on this horrific judgment from God. Few today know the details of this great tragedy.

Some think God is cruel for such a drastic judgment. They believe that because they are ignorant of the violence and injustice that marred our world. If they had suffered as victims of this injustice, they would not be so hasty to condemn God's just actions.

Our Western culture in particular has been sheltered from the horrors of terrorism. We of all people are the most naïve to the bloody and wicked nature of evil. That, however, shall not long remain that way. The political direction our world has taken shall open the door for the time of terror to begin again. We should have learned from the past, but few care to know truth.

For this reason, I shall begin this last volume of the *Machine or Man* series speaking not of scientific evidence but of the occult and its influence upon mankind that brought certain destruction upon the First Earth. I will address the scientific evidence afterward, but in order for us today to be prepared for the coming terror that awaits us at the end of the Second Earth, we must understand what happened that brought forth the Death of the First Earth.

The Time of Terror

> *Then God said to Noah, "The end of all flesh has come before Me; for the earth is filled with violence because of them; and behold, I am about to destroy them with the earth."*
> —Gen. 6:13

Argument 3 – How could a good God destroy all the inhabitants of the world?

Human nature is such that throughout the entire breadth of our history, we have witnessed over and over again the same pattern—civilizations rise to prominence, they become corrupted, and they fall. The abundance of the First Earth led many to forget God and turn to evil. It seems that when we are comfortable, we no longer sense a need for our Creator. We begin to rely on our own capabilities and gravitate toward the baser instincts.

The preponderance of human sacrifices evidenced by archaeology gives us a gruesome insight into that time. Evolutionists tend to categorize cannibalism as a sign of chronologically primitive culture, but it is nothing of the kind. It is a sign of a culture that has given itself over to the religion of the Serpent.

We can still find remote tribes in South America, the Far East, and Africa today who practice cannibalism, not because they have no other food available to them but because they have fallen for the religion of the Serpent that tells them they will inherit the ritual magic of those they eat. They are fooled into believing that the life force of their victims will be absorbed by them when they eat them ritually. In fact, there are those who still secretly practice such occult rituals even in the supposedly civilized Western world. They are not chronologically primitive peoples; after all, they have just as much history behind them as we do since they are our contemporaries. They are simply seduced by the shamanistic religion of the Serpent.

The preponderance of cannibalism found in Neanderthal man archaeological sites tells us that the First Earth was groaning with violence. The Book of Enoch says they ruled over mankind by the violent religion of the Serpent that taught man the art of sorcery and war. It was the religion of the Serpent that brought down the certain and sudden destruction of all mankind by a just and holy God. This rebellion was led by nine demon leaders of 10 but in particular by two fallen angels named Azazel and Semjaza. Mankind turned to cannibalism, sorcery, and debauchery.

> *And then Michael, Uriel, Raphael, and Gabriel looked down from heaven and saw much blood being shed upon the earth, and all lawlessness being wrought upon the earth. And they said one to another: "The earth made without inhabitant cries the voice of their crying up to the gates of heaven. And now to you, the holy ones of heaven, the souls of men make their suit, saying, 'Bring our cause before the Most High.'" And they said to the Lord of the ages: "Lord of lords, God of gods, King of kings, (and God of the ages), the throne of Thy glory (standeth) unto all the generations of the ages, and Thy name holy and glorious and blessed unto all the ages! Thou hast made all things, and power over all things hast Thou: and all things are naked and open in Thy sight, and Thou seest all things, and nothing can hide itself from Thee. Thou seest what Azâzêl hath done, who hath taught all unrighteousness on earth and revealed the eternal secrets which were (preserved) in heaven, which men were striving to learn: And Semjâzâ, to whom Thou*

hast given authority to bear rule over his associates. And they have gone to the daughters of men upon the earth, and have slept with the women, and have defiled themselves, and revealed to them all kinds of sins. And the women have borne giants, and the whole earth has thereby been filled with blood and unrighteousness. And now, behold, the souls of those who have died are crying and making their suit to the gates of heaven, and their lamentations have ascended: and cannot cease because of the lawless deeds which are wrought on the earth."

—Enoch 9:1–10

Our paradise became a place of horror. The children of Adam gave themselves over to the Neanderthal sorcerers and profaned the bloodline of Eve. A time of terror washed over our First Earth and stained our soil with the blood of innocents. At the appointed time, when the Pleiades reached their midnight culmination, Taurus struck with his two horns, and the Earth was cracked.

On the third day of the full moon of the second month, the month of Heshvan, on the 17th day, which was the 600th year of Noah's life, the judgment for the Second Insurrection that had begun in the sixth generation from Adam was pronounced and ended the First Earth. From that day forward, the Moon was waning. Darkness was ascending, light was descending, and the powers of the Dark Stars began their global plan while Gemini rose on the vernal equinox.

Sadly, our idyllic and almost perfect First Earth devolved into a living nightmare. The Second Insurrection of the rebellious angels brought forth a wave of violence that swept the world like wildfire. Our First Earth was filled with unrelenting violence. Peace fled our planet. The living things that had been made to flourish in peace were altered and profaned.

Giant meat-eating lizards now terrorized all living things within their habitat. The cruelty of predation became entrenched in the natural cycle of the animal kingdom. But predation was not limited just to the animals. Predation came to mankind. A breed of men was sired who were so powerful and superior to the sons of Adam that none could stand against them. They were bred for a single purpose: to destroy the world of men. Cannibalism became a ritualized ceremony to enhance the magical prowess of those involved in the occult craft.

We shall always expect the naturalists to scoff at anything that smacks of the supernatural. But I tell you unapologetically that this is nothing less than ignorance, for the supernatural is only the natural that we yet do not understand. Many may ridicule the existence of angels and demons, but ridicule proves nothing.

The idea that angels have rebelled against the Most High God is carried by all ancient cultures, and the existence of Satan has been caricatured likewise in every culture. The ancient cosmic battle between good and evil has been chronicled by every civilization in all human history, and it is, in fact, the narrative of the Zodiac.

Few today know the extent of the demonic involvement in the corruption of our human family and in the institutionalizing of violence against one another. Fewer yet understand the demonic attempt to derail the birthing of the Messiah. We must begin with the First Angelic Insurrection. It was Lucifer who led that insurrection in the Garden at Eden.

The most important battle for the Enemy of Man is the battle to discredit the authenticity and reliability of the Genesis record. In it is found the seven most fundamental axioms for the Judeo-Christian worldview. In it is found the root of the problem of evil and the curse over the living and nonliving that has plagued our universe. In it is found the reason for our broken world. In it is found the explanation of evil and the solution for mankind that was prophesied from the very day it entered our world by the very voice of the Creator.

This book is more than a scientific investigation of the claims of Genesis. It is also an investigation of the spiritual truths that provide a way for mankind to live in harmony and peace. The Word of God is truth. Hence, it is not just true about spiritual matters; it is also historically true. But that history would be meaningless if it were not in the wider context of the spiritual truths it contains. Genesis is the record of the ancient cosmic battle between good and evil.

Those who wish to allegorize the Genesis historical record fail to understand that they are rejecting God's words and making their minds the arbiter of truth. To deny the authority and authenticity of the Genesis record is to deny the Judeo-Christian worldview. It is no accident that the Enemy of Man has sought from the beginning to deny the record of Genesis. The following seven axioms are irreplaceable and uncompromisable if we are to maintain the core of God's divine revelation to mankind.

1. The first axiom is that there is a singular, personal Creator who is omnipotent and omniscient through which this finite universe was formed, which is eternal in existence (Gen. 1:1). The universe is not self-created. There are no other gods. The angels are created beings—finite beings. Demons are nothing more than rebellious or fallen angels parading as gods.
2. The second axiom is that God created man in His image to have infinite worth and value. Man was meant to live forever (Gen. 1:26). Human life is therefore sacrosanct.
3. The third axiom is that the Enemy of Man deceived mankind. The Great Opposer is real, and his plan has always been to take over the throne of God. For this reason he convinced man to partake of the esoteric fruit of the knowledge of evil, the forbidden fruit. He told them these three lies in the Garden: (a) "You surely will not die (Gen 3:4)," which corresponds to the occult doctrines of reincarnation and rebirth; (b) "Your eyes will be opened" (Gen 3: 5), which corresponds to the occult doctrine of illumination and gnosi, the doctrine of the esoteric wisdom; and (c) "You will be like God" (Gen 3:5),

which corresponds to the occult doctrine of correspondence—as above so it is below. It is the usurpation of God's place as King of the universe. The theology of the esoteric brotherhood to this day universally believes these three lies.

4. The fourth axiom is the fall of man. The acceptance of the knowledge of evil brought death upon mankind. For this reason, the curse of God was pronounced on man (Gen. 3:16, 19), the material universe (Gen. 3:17, 18), the animal kingdom (Gen. 3:14), and finally Satan (Gen. 3:15). Pain became part of our experience. Death entered the world on the back of selfishness. From that day forward, man could no longer eat of the tree of life. He was kicked out of the Garden at Eden (Gen. 3:22–24). He now has to labor to subsist. God could not allow evil to be eternal, and thus death became the only just solution.

5. From that day forward, man would be at war with the demonic hierarchy. This is the primordial prophecy spoken by the very voice of God in the Garden. It is the prophecy of the Dragon Doom. It is the prophecy that set in motion the ancient cosmic battle between good and evil. It is the prophecy that set at enmity the demonic hierarchy and their seed with the offspring of the woman (Gen. 3:15).

6. In spite of our rebellion, God's grace promised deliverance. The promise of the Messiah to conquer Satan would come through the seed of Eve. It is the prophecy that alluded to the virgin birth of the Messiah. The Dragon Sin, the central sin of Lucifer, is his desire to dethrone God. He wants to rule above all things in the universe. But in the end, the Messiah shall crush his head (Gen. 3:15). Hence, Genesis not only explains the problem but offers the solution that Satan so opposes.

7. God's grace was also promised as atonement for our sins. Thus God sacrificed an animal to dress Adam and Eve (Gen. 3:21). He accepted Abel's sacrifice because Abel understood that

without the shedding of blood there could be no redemption for our sins (Gen. 4:4). But He did not accept Cain's sacrifice of the toil of his hands (Gen. 4:5). Our redemption cannot come through our self-efforts. Thus God provided from the very beginning a picture of the redemption that would come through the virgin birth of the Messiah as our sacrificial Lamb. He is the Passover Lamb of God who alone can protect us from the Angel of Death.

These seven fundamental axioms are the backbone of True Truth. All further narratives in the Holy Scriptures serve to build upon, clarify, and illustrate these spiritual truths. Genesis is therefore the pivot upon which God's revelation to mankind turns. It reveals not only the message of salvation but also the tools of the Enemy of Man.

Selfishness, arrogance, and pride are the defining hallmarks Satan boldly peddles to mankind through the demonic hierarchy and the proponents of the esoteric occult religions and secret societies. From these are birthed all evil. From these all counterfeit religions are spawned. From these stem all wickedness. From these we have suffered all sorrows. And yet we blindly follow the Pied Piper to the cliff time and time again. But his tactic has long ago been described as the hallmark of the Enemy of Man. The reality of the Dragon Sin is then further defined and confirmed by the later prophets.

> *But you said in your heart, "I will ascend to heaven; I will raise my throne above the stars of God, and I will sit on the mount of assembly in the recesses of the north. I will ascend above the heights of the clouds; I will make myself like the Most High."*
>
> —Isa. 14:13

Lucifer abhors the idea of submitting his will to the moral dictates of the Creator. It was this sin with which he beguiled Eve and to which Adam later acceded. Three lies the Serpent told Eve form the three pillars of the occult tradition throughout all ages.

1. "You surely will not die!" (Gen. 3:4) – The quest for immortality is the denial of God's judgment. It is exemplified by the Eastern doctrine of reincarnation and the occult doctrine of rebirth. It is rebellion toward the just curse of death pronounced upon wickedness. It is the pushing back against God's judgment to fence evil in and keep it from becoming eternal.
2. "Your eyes will be opened" (Gen. 3:5) – The quest for esoteric illumination, the *gnosis* illusion is the rejection of God's grace for salvation and the promotion of the demonic doctrine that salvation can be attained by special knowledge. In occult circles, this salvation comes through their esoteric wisdom. In counterfeit religions, it comes through our self-efforts.
3. "You will be like God" (Gen. 3:5) – The quest for godhood (power) is the denial of God as Lord of the universe. It is the quest for absolute autonomy championed by the naturalists as well as the occult.

The quest for godhood is the central core of the demonic insurrection and the human rebellion that brought forth death and corrupted our human race. Satan's tactic has not changed much. This is the lie of naturalism, which makes finite man the arbiter of good and evil in the universe. Each man is his own god. This is also the lie of the esoteric religions that teach man that he is a god. The lies the serpent told Eve are alive and well even today, dressed in scientific jargon.

The doctrine of esoteric illumination is but a rewording of Lucifer's second lie to our Firstmother: "your eyes will be opened" (Gen. 3:5). The quest for immortality is nothing more than the quest to undo the curse of death. It is rebellion against God's judgment. But the curse shall not be lifted until the Seed of Eve comes to atone for what the Scriptures call the Indignation.

The serpent lied. Man believed him and partook of the esoteric "wisdom." Death entered our world, and God cast mankind out of the Garden because He could not allow evil to become eternal (Gen. 3:24). That was the birth of our First Earth, our first step in the downward spiral of the devolution of man and Earth.

But God did not just judge mankind and the Earth. He pronounced judgment on Lucifer for his sin. Since Lucifer chose the weaker vessel to corrupt mankind, God declared that through that weaker vessel His judgment would come. Through her seed would come the One who would deliver the mortal wound to Satan's head (Gen. 3:15). This is the prophecy of the Dragon Doom. It is alluding to the virgin birth of the Messiah since the doom would not come from the seed of Adam.

But Lucifer fought back. He devised a clever plan to derail this prophecy. It was the purpose of the demonic hierarchy to profane the bloodline of the coming Messiah through the creation of the Nephilim as described in the Torah. If the seed of Eve could be profaned, the Messiah could not be birthed. This was the Second Insurrection that brought forth the judgment of the Great Flood.

Long ago in the world that was, the demons successfully turned almost all humanity against God. It was in this antediluvian world that Satan and his brood of vipers devised one of the most heinous plans to undo the curse. They schemed to pervert the Adamic race through the creation of the dreaded and violent Nephilim.

After Satan deceived humanity in the Garden at Eden, God condemned him to be mortally defeated by the One who would come through the seed of Eve. The Serpent hatched a plan to pervert and profane the genetic pool of humanity in order to interfere with this prophetic sentence.

By cohabitating with humans, the demons interfered with the human genetic code designed by God and hoped to profane the entire human race, thus preventing the birth of the Messiah. So successful was this ploy that only Noah and his family remained faithful to the

Lord from the resulting violence perpetrated by this evil begotten brood of Halflings that Scripture refers to as the Nephilim.

These are the ill-fated Neanderthals who, along with the others who were profaned, were judged at the death of the First Earth. I have already documented in *The Descent of Man* that the genetic markers of the Neanderthals (Nephilim) have been eradicated from our human species. They cannot be found in those who colonized our Second Earth because Noah's family did not partake in the shamanistic plans of the Nephilim.

The naturalist would, of course, consider all this mythological rubbish. The supernatural power of deception is very real, indeed. It is imperative for the Enemy of Man to discredit God's record of the history of the First and Second Insurrections.

I have often been rebuffed even by Christians who say the idea that angels could engender a profaned human race is ridiculous. But, I ask you, if man, an inferior intellectual being, can through recombinant gene splicing create a completely new human race by adding genes not found in natural man, what makes you think that angels of superior intellect and power cannot? What, then, are Neanderthals? Did God create two Adams? Why do all the occult religions attest to this remarkable union between angels and man? Why is this unholy union recorded in almost all ancient cultures?

So much did their plan work that most of mankind was turned to the bloody religion of the Serpent. But God reserved a remnant. The generations of the patriarchs who preceded Noah remained righteous and unstained by the illicit blood of these mongrel Halflings. The Adamic race has been preserved for us today through the diligence and courage of this last man standing on our First Earth.

> *But Noah found favor in the eyes of the* Lord. *These are the records of the generation of Noah. Noah was a righteous man, blameless in his time; Noah walked with God.*
> —Gen. 6:8–9

THE DEATH OF THE FIRST EARTH

> *Then the LORD said to Noah, "Enter the ark, you and all your household, for you alone I have seen to be righteous before Me in this time."*
>
> —Gen. 7: 1

For this reason, Noah also became the first man standing on the Second Earth and the forefather of all who now breathe upon this third rock from the Sun. The profaned bloodline was utterly destroyed, but the evidence is still with us. This is no science fiction novel.

The remains of the Nephilim are with us today. We can touch them. We can see them. It is just that modern evolutionary science does not recognize the story of the Nephilim as historical. Their remains are those we call Neanderthals.

Naturalists prefer to think of Neanderthals as an extinct evolutionary appendage to modern man who evolved from apes. We have already covered the sham fossil lineage that evolutionists use to claim man has evolved from apes, but the historical evidence does not correspond with the naturalistic presupposition either. The historical records of our ancient ancestors have preserved for us their memory of the events that brought forth the judgment of the Great Flood.

Adamic man, whom we know as Cro-Magnon man, existed before the Neanderthals. This the archaeological record clearly substantiates. Even evolutionists admit that Cro-Magnon man preceded Neanderthals. (For further evidence that substantiates this, see my book *The Descent of Man*.) But man's historical record also attests to the prowess of this terrible race.

For example, the Egyptians clearly recognized that prior to the Flood, during the time they call Zep Tepi (the first time), a group of men were so superior to our human form that they were called gods. The Greeks called them Cyclops (the third eye of illumination is the symbol of esoteric magic), the Celts called them the Giants, and the Irish spoke of them as the race of gods called the Tuatha De Danann who now rule the underworld.

It was common knowledge for those who lived during the time of Christ—those who had received this knowledge as it was passed down through several generations through the children of Noah and their descendants. We can, for example, cite the writings of Flavius Josephus in the first century. Persuaded by friends to put together a history of the Jews for the Egyptians, he wrote, among other works, *The Antiquities of the Jews*. Speaking of the decline in the morality of mankind after the time of Enoch, he wrote:

> But for what degree of zeal they had formerly shewn for virtue, they now shewed by their actions a double degree of wickedness, whereby they made God to be their enemy. For *many angels of God accompanied with women, and begat sons that proved unjust, and despisers of all that was good, on account of the confidence they had in their own strength, for the tradition is that these men did what resembled the acts of those whom the Grecians call* Giants. But Noah was very uneasy at what they did; and being displeased at their conduct, persuaded them to change their dispositions and their actions for the better; -but seeing they did not yield to him, but were slaves to their wicked pleasures, he was afraid they would kill him, together with his wife and children, and those they had married; so he departed out of that land (emphasis added) (Josephus 1960, 28).

Even the occult authorities admit this to be true. Madame Blavatsky was perhaps the most influential esoteric authority in America who almost singlehandedly ushered in the New Age movement, and she wrote clearly of them.

> While in the Scandinavian legend *Buri* (the grandson of the cow *Audhumla*), a *superior* being, marries *Beisla*, a daughter of the depraved race of giants, in the Hindu tradition the first Brahman marries Daiteyī, also a

daughter of the race of the giants; and in *Genesis* we see the sons of God taking for wives the daughters of men, and likewise producing mighty men of old; the whole establishing an unquestionable identity of origin between the Christian inspired Book, and the heathen "fables" of Scandinavia and Hindostan. The traditions of nearly every other nation, if examined, will yield a like result (Blavatsky 1877, 148–149).

Of course, she puts the cart before the horse. It is to be expected. The occult lie claims unabashedly that their religion is the oldest. It may be the oldest counterfeit, but the oldest is the original religion of Adam, which is the religion of Noah, Abraham, Isaac, and Jacob.

The memory of this travesty (the Second Insurrection) is found in all the ancient civilizations. In every ancient civilization, the gods, which they worshiped, were reported to have sexual relations with the women of earth. They were no gods at all but demons that left their first habitation, their proper domain, in rebellion against the Most High God. They who abandoned their proper abode and mated with the daughters of Adam are now kept chained in Sheol until that day when they shall face the judgment of the Great Day when the Seed of Eve sits upon the Great White Throne. Jude, the half brother of Jesus said this:

> *And angels who did not keep their own domain, but abandoned their proper abode, He has kept in eternal bonds under darkness for the judgment of the great day.*
> —Jude 1:6

These are the purveyors of the occult counterfeit religions that have marred the human race. Their wicked offspring became the first shamans and sorcerers who brought great violence upon humanity. But their tactic has not changed in the Second Earth. We can see the clear reflection of this even in our modern history.

This was the goal when Hitler's occult Nazi group set up the SS Guards to bring a new race of men so superior to natural man that they would rule the world. This was the goal of the Vril Society that birthed the Thule Society that birthed the Nazi plan to gain global dominance. Those who study the occult know the importance of the religion of the Mother Goddesses in bringing forth the seed of Lucifer to war against the seed of Eve as prophesied in Genesis 3:15. God knew it would be so before it happened.

> *And I will put enmity between you and the woman, and between your seed and her seed.*
>
> —Gen. 3:15

God prophesied that the demons would engender a seed that would be in perpetual enmity with the children of Adam and Eve. The Book of Enoch tells us that 200 demons were involved in this Second Insurrection, but Lucifer remained aloof. He sent his lackeys to do the dirty work while he kept his hands clean.

> *And it came to pass when the children of men had multiplied that in those days were born unto them beautiful and comely daughters.* And the angels, the children of the heaven, saw and lusted after them, and said to one another: "Come, let us choose us wives from among the children of men and beget us children." *And Semjâzâ, who was their leader, said unto them: "I fear ye will not indeed agree to do this deed, and I alone shall have to pay the penalty of a great sin."* And they all answered him and said: "Let us all swear an oath, and all bind ourselves by mutual imprecations not to abandon this plan but to do this thing." Then sware they all together and bound themselves by mutual imprecations upon it. And they were in all two hundred; who descended [in the days] of Jared on the summit of Mount Hermon, *and they called it Mount Hermon, because they had sworn and bound themselves by*

mutual imprecations upon it. And these are the names of their leaders: Sèmîazâz, their leader, Arâkîba, Râmêêl, Kôkabîêl, Tâmîêl, Râmîêl, Dânêl, Êzêqêêl, Barâqîjâl, Asâêl, Armârôs, Batârêl, Anânêl, Zaqîêl, Samsâpêêl, Satarêl, Tûrêl, Jômjâêl, Sariêl. These are their chiefs of tens.

And all the others together with them took unto themselves wives, and each chose for himself one, and they began to go in unto them and to defile themselves with them, and they taught them charms and enchantments, and the cutting of roots, and made them acquainted with plants. And they became pregnant, and they bare great giants, whose height was three thousand ells: Who consumed all the acquisitions of men. And when men could no longer sustain them, the giants turned against them and devoured mankind. *And they began to sin against birds, and beasts, and reptiles, and fish, and to devour one another's flesh, and drink the blood. Then the earth laid accusation against the lawless ones.*

And Azâzêl taught men to make swords, and knives, and shields, and breastplates, and made known to them the metals <of the earth> and the art of working them, and bracelets, and ornaments, and the use of antimony, and the beautifying of the eyelids, and all kinds of costly stones, and all colouring tinctures. And there arose much godlessness, and they committed fornication, and they were led astray, and became corrupt in all their ways. Semjâzâ taught enchantments, and root-cuttings, Armârôs the resolving of enchantments, *Barâqîjâl, (taught) astrology, Kôkabêl the constellations, Ezêqêêl the knowledge of the clouds, <Araqiêl the signs of the earth, Shamsiêl the signs of the sun>, and Sariêl the course of the moon.* And as men perished, they cried, and their cry went up to heaven. (emphasis added).

—Enoch 6–8

The occult always presents two sides One side is those who teach "white magic," sometimes referred to as Luciferians whose main goal is to deceive that they are agents of good. The ancient religions of the world reflect this motif with the trickster gods, and it is the natural outflowing of the teachings of Semjaza (sometimes spelled Shemihaza). The Second Earth, which will be represented by the False Prophet, will come to cause all men to worship the Antichrist. Their weapon is deceit.

The second side is "black magic," promoted by the God of War and represented by Azazel who will be the main power behind the Antichrist. They do not hide their direct worship of Satanism. It was the demon Azazel who taught man the art of war and the instruments of death.

The religion of the Serpent is always the religion of war and sorcery. Azazel is the god of war whose role in bringing terrorism to the First Earth was pivotal. Violence became the norm in our human history, and the blood of the innocent soaked our fair soil. Their suffering rose to heaven in cries of anguish and pleas for justice. Peace fled our lands, for it was their dark religion that brought forth cannibalism and the drinking of blood.

> *And as men perished, they cried, and their cry went up to heaven.*
> —Enoch 8:2

It was their occult prowess that gave them such deluding power over human civilization and wholly turned to the enticements and lures of the shamanistic religion of the Serpent. The world was festering with such violence that God had to wipe them completely from the face of the entire planet. The seed of Eve, the lineage of the Messiah, was almost gone. The cry of the innocents rose unto heaven, and God ordained the death of the First Earth through the judgment of the Great Deluge.

THE DEATH OF THE FIRST EARTH

All the profaned creatures, both animals and humans, were wiped from the face of the Earth. The 200 demons who orchestrated the Second Insurrection were chained. Since that day, these demons have been kept in bonds within the bowels of Sheol until the time that their judgment shall be sealed. But they shall escape before the Great Tribulation to aid Lucifer in his war upon heaven.

> *And the angels who did not keep their own domain, but abandoned their proper abode, He has kept in eternal bonds under darkness for the judgment of the great day.*
> —Jude 1:6

The book of Revelation tells us that they will be loosed for a little while to help Lucifer in his Fourth Insurrection during the judgment of the fifth trumpet. In that day Lucifer shall free them from Hades to join him in his final attack on heaven and Jerusalem. This will be the Fourth Insurrection but not the last. It will mark the coming death of the Second Earth.

> *Then the fifth angel sounded, and I saw a star from heaven which had fallen to the earth; and the key of the bottomless pit was given to him. He opened the bottomless pit, and smoke went up out of the pit, like the smoke of a great furnace; and the sun and the air were darkened by the smoke of the pit. They have as king over them, the angel of the abyss; his name in Hebrew is Abaddon, and in the Greek he has the name Apollyon.*
> —Rev. 9:1–2, 11

Abaddon—the Destroyer, the God of War, Azazel—shall be released until the death of the Second Earth. Then will come the judgment of the Great Day. Then will come Yom Kippur, and the Messiah shall rule the Third Earth. In that day the meek shall inherit the Earth. In that day the lion shall lie down with the lamb, and Jerusalem shall at long last be at peace. In that day both the Antichrist and the False Prophet shall be the first to be thrown into the Lake of Fire along with Azazel and Semjaza and the 200 demons who aided them in the Second Insurrection. The rest shall be judged at the end of the millennium of Christ's rule at the Great White Throne Judgment.

Not only is Lucifer planning the overthrow of the throne of Jehovah in heaven, but he is also concurrently involved in the plan of taking over the throne of the Messiah on Earth. Have you ever wondered why Jerusalem is at the center of all political controversies? It is because the Evil One desires it for his global throne. All who seek a global government are doing his bidding, whether knowingly or not. His arrogance and greed are such that he covets the throne, which rightfully belongs to our Lord Jesus Christ.

Twice before, God has thwarted this Luciferian plan. The first time, in the nick of time, He wrested global dominion from him with the unexpected Great Deluge. In that single cataclysm, God completely wiped out the entire genetic components engendered by the demons. In that day, Noah became the Adam of the Second Earth and saved the seed of Eve for the birthing of the Messiah to come. The prophecy of the Dragon Doom was not foiled. Since then, Satan has been busy at work attempting to regain control of Middle Earth.

When Noah landed on Mount Ararat, the survivors thrived in the Land of Shinar. There they prospered and built a great civilization. They were one nation, one family, with one language, the Sumerian language. But once again, the occult religions gained dominance as humanity prospered in opulence. It was for that reason that God sent the judgment of the Tower of Babel.

Once again Satan was at the verge of global dominance when God divided the languages and divided the descendants of Noah's children into separate nations, making it much harder for Lucifer to coalesce the nations into a centralized global government through which he could rule mankind. God's judgment was to decentralize power. Ever since, Satan's goal has been to centralize power. Today, minions of the dark angels have managed to bring the nations once again to the verge of global union in rebellion to their God.

Hear my desperate warning, friend. If we do not understand the mechanism that brought forth the destruction of our human civilization in the First Earth, we shall not be able to oppose the same forces arrayed against us in the Second Earth. The story of Genesis is the story of the cosmic battle between God and Satan. The Enemy of Man does not want mankind to know the details of this battle.

There is more to Genesis than the story of our creation and the story of a Great Flood. It is the story of our fall, the horror that prevailed, the monsters that terrorized the innocent, and the terrible judgment that began our Second Earth. It is a map of our future as well. It is a window to the human soul and the spiritual warfare that rages about us.

So who were these Nephilim? It is difficult for humans of our age to receive this truth, so far has the veil of Satan's deception impinged on the minds of modern man. Our naturalistic paradigm has shielded the Evil One from the crimes of his past, for scarcely will anyone in our generation believe that a demon could sire a half-human to pander sorcery, the Dragon's device.

I am fully cognizant of the fact that such a claim will undoubtedly bring hisses and ridicule from our post-modern culture. Nevertheless, I am constrained to speak the truth in love and leave it to the Holy Spirit to convict people's hearts of the truth of what I here declare. One cannot fight what one does not believe to be there. But have they been here, and will they be here again?

Scripture tells us that demons actually mated with humans, creating a race of giants who were half-human and half-demon. To the normal person (including myself) with a decidedly Western outlook, which at the very least minimizes the supernatural, this is a hard thing to believe. Yet there are four reasons that I believe substantiate this unnatural union as an actual historical spacetime reality in the world that was.

1. First, the occult teachings speak of this as a reality, giving this account as the source of much of their occult knowledge of humanity. It is the gnosis they refer to as the Ancient Wisdom.
2. Second, Hebrew tradition has maintained that this was one of the overriding reasons God decided to end the First Earth with the Deluge. In the Qumran community, the spiritual leaders of this Essene Jewish sect thought it important enough that manuscripts in this regard were kept in their library. Thus, in the Dead Sea Scrolls, scholars have found manuscripts recording some of the conversations of these beings, even recording some of their names in a previously unknown work called *The Book of Giants*. *The Book of Jubilees*, which may have been written around the second century BC, states that this travesty took place in the sixth generation from Adam:

And he called his name Jared; for in his days the angels of the LORD *descended on the earth, those who are named the Watchers, that they should instruct the children of men, and that they should do judgment and uprightness on the earth*
—Jubilees 4:15

But unfortunately, some of these angels, or Watchers, chose to do otherwise. However, Enoch, the son of Jared, found grace in the sight of God, and the obedient angels of the Lord gave him the knowledge of writing and of astronomy, and he became a witness against the rebellious angels.

THE DEATH OF THE FIRST EARTH

And he was moreover with the angels of God these six jubilees of years, and they showed him everything which is on earth and in the heavens, the rule of the sun, and he wrote down everything. And he testified to the Watchers, who had sinned with the daughters of men; for these had begun to unite themselves, so as to be defiled, with the daughters of men, and Enoch testified against (them) all.

—Jubilees 4:21–22

And it came to pass when the children of men began to multiply on the face of the earth and daughters were born unto them, that the angels of God saw them on a certain year of this jubilee, that they were beautiful to look upon; and they took themselves wives of all whom they chose, and they bare unto them sons and they were giants.

And lawlessness increased on the earth and all flesh corrupted its way, alike men and cattle and beasts and birds and everything that walketh on the earth – all of them corrupted their ways and their orders, and they began to devour each other, and lawlessness increased on the earth and every imagination of the thoughts of all men (was) thus evil continually. And God looked upon the earth, and behold it was corrupt, and all flesh had corrupted its orders, and all that were upon the earth had wrought all manner of evil before His eyes. And He said: "I shall destroy man and all flesh upon the face of the earth which I have created. But Noah found grace before the eyes of the Lord.

—Jubilees 5:1–5

Therefore, God became wroth with these rebellious angels and sent destruction upon them.

> *And against the angels whom He had sent upon the earth, He was exceedingly wroth, and He gave commandment to root them out of all their dominion, and He bade us to bind them in the depths of the earth, and behold they are bound in the midst of them, and are kept separate.*
> —Jubilees 5:6

In chapter 7, the writer of *The Book of Jubilees* records the admonition of Noah to his sons before passing away.

> *And in the twenty-eighth jubilee Noah began to enjoin upon his sons' sons the ordinances and commandments, and all the judgments that he knew, and he exhorted his sons to observe righteousness, and to cover the shame of their flesh, and to bless their Creator, and honour father and mother, and love their neighbour, and guard their souls from fornication and uncleanness and all iniquity. For owing to these three things came the flood upon the earth, namely, owing to the fornication wherein the Watchers against the law of their ordinances went a whoring after the daughters of men, and took themselves wives of all which they chose: and they made the beginning of uncleanness. And they begat sons the Nâphîdîm, and they were all unlike, and they devoured one another: and the Giants slew the Nâphil, and the Nâphil slew the Eljô, and the Eljô mankind, and one man another. And every one sold himself to work iniquity and to shed much blood, and the earth was filled with iniquity. And after this they sinned against the beasts and birds, and all that moveth and walketh on the earth: and much blood was shed on the earth, and every imagination and desire of men imagined vanity and evil continually. And the Lord destroyed everything from off the face of the earth; be-*

> *cause of the wickedness of their deeds, and because of the blood which they had shed in the midst of the earth He destroyed everything.*
> —Jubilees 7:20–25

According to *The Book of Jubilees*, the Neanderthals may have been divided into three tribes—the Naphidim, the Naphil, and the Eljo. We can also find references to this travesty that defiled the First Earth in another second century BC book called *The Testaments of the Twelve Patriarchs*.

> *In like manner the Watchers also changed them order of their nature, whom the Lord cursed at the flood, on whose account He made the earth without inhabitant and fruitless.*
> —Testaments of the Twelve Patriarchs 3:5

3. Third, the DNA evidence shows that the Neanderthals had unique genetic markers that differentiated them from man. In *The Descent of Man*, I documented that the Neanderthals had at least 27 genetic markers that were not found in Cro-Magnon man or modern man. We know that God did not create two Adams; hence, where did these semi-humans come from?

   We know that the descendants of Adam (Cro-Magnon man) existed long before the Neanderthals. Abruptly they appeared in the sixth generation from Adam, and abruptly they ended in the Great Deluge. Why are there no descendants of Neanderthals alive today?

   The genetic interference bred into the Nephilim (Neanderthals) by the cunning demons has been completely eradicated from our present genes. The evolutionary model has no way of explaining how Neanderthal genes did not get passed down to us. We have evidence that the Neanderthals lived at the same time and mated with Cro-Magnon man. Hybrids have been found, and yet the Neanderthals and their hybrids were completely eradicated from the face of the Earth. Only the pure genetics of the Adamic race are present in our Second Earth. What global evolutionary mechanism can account for such definitive and surgical removal of their profaned genetic traits?

4. Fourth, many of our ancient church fathers believed it to be so and wrote about it. Julius Africanus wrote this:

> When men multiplied on earth, the angels of heaven came together with the daughters of men. . . . But if it is thought that these refer to angels, we must take them to be those who deal with magic and jugglery, who taught the women the motion of the stars and the knowledge of things celestial, by whose power they conceived giants as their children (*Extant Works* 1886, 2).

We have examples such as Clement of Rome (I Clement 19–20) and the author of the Epistle of Barnabas, Justin Martyr:

> But the angels transgressed this appointment, and were captivated by love of women, and begat children who are those that are called demons (*The Second Apology* 1886, 5).

Tertullian, speaking on the occult-corrupted version of astronomy we know as astrology and divination, writes:

> One proposition I lay down; that those angels, the deserters from God, the lovers of women, were likewise the discoverers of this curious art, on that account also condemned by God. . . . The astrologers are expelled just like their angels (Tertullian 1902, 9).

Philo, Clement of Alexandria, Athenagoras wrote:

> For this is the office of the angels ... Some, free agents, you will observe, such as they were created by God, continued in those things for which God had made and over which He had ordained them; but some outraged both the constitution of their nature and the government entrusted to them ... these fell into impure love of virgins, and were subjugated by the flesh, and he became negligent and wicked in the management of the things entrusted to them. Of these lovers of virgins, therefore, were begotten those who are called giants (Athenagoras).

5. And last but certainly not least, the Scriptures claim that it was so, and it is unapologetically and neutrally stated as a matter of fact in the sixth chapter of Genesis (the significance of the number six to the occult is providentially brought to bear upon this incident). The Scriptures claim that some of the fallen angels, or "sons of god" as they are called, married human women, creating the Halfling race of sorcerers called Nephilim, whom we have already mentioned.

> *The sons of God saw that the daughters of men were beautiful; and they took wives for themselves, whomever they chose. The Nephilim were on the earth in those days, and also afterward, when the sons of God came in to the daughters of men, and they bore children to them.*
>
> —Gen. 6:2, 4

The Hebrew word *Nephilim* means a bully or tyrant, a titan, a giant. Obviously, these individuals had a more robust form and were no doubt well advanced in the art of sorcery. The Neanderthal men were once thought to have been the ancestors of Cro-Magnon, but recently we have documented with certainty that (1) Cro Magnon preceded them; (2) they later lived at the same time; (3) both are fully human in every respect; and (4) they interbred and therefore in many places comingled. Yet there are some substantial differences between them. Evolutionists believe them to be an evolutionary dead end since their highly pronounced characteristics are not found in modern man.

The conundrum for the evolutionist is quite mystifying. If we have evidence of the hybridization of Neanderthal and Cro-Magnon (Adamic race), then why are there no genetic traces of the unique markers of Neanderthal man found in modern man?

The answer is that it was this very strain of genetically altered humans who God wanted to destroy from the planet for they were not part of the initial creation of God. These were humanoids expressly engendered by the demons to corrupt the very lineage of the Son of God who was prophesied to come from the seed of Eve. They were bred for the very purpose of stopping the fulfillment of the Genesis 3:15 prophecy of the Dragon Doom by corrupting the blood lineage of the future Messiah.

In almost all the Neanderthal archeological sites, evidence of cannibalism abounds, which shows there was indeed a distinct difference in their spiritual leanings. They were obviously bred for a single purpose. Their physical traits were designed to overpower, conquer, and assimilate the Adamic race.

In the final hour when victory for the demons was at hand, God intervened. Noah's progeny alone was left intact, and God took action to protect the lineage of the Son of Man. Had the First Earth not been destroyed, the Second Demonic Insurrection would have triumphed, and you and I would not be here today. The Messiah would not have been born, and salvation could not have been won upon the cross of Calvary. The Nephilim would have ruled our planet. Homo sapiens would have been genetically absorbed or completely eradicated by the Neanderthals.

Their physical superiority to the Adamic race was formidable. In 2008, the tooth of a young Neanderthal child discovered in the Scladina cave in Belgium was subjected to X-rays through a machine called a synchrotron, which provides an image with high resolution that enables us to see growth lines and stress lines in the growth of the individual. This three-dimensional hatch of daily and longer periodic growth lines in the teeth are like tree rings and provide a code with stress lines that enable scientists to analyze the age of the individual.

To their great surprise, this eight-year-old child was reaching puberty some four years earlier than modern humans. That means Neanderthals were capable of reproducing at a much earlier age, a decided advantage from a competitive standpoint. They reached maturity faster and were able to fight and reproduce far before the true children of Adam. Why, then, did they become extinct and not us? The evolutionary model, which touts their mantra of the survival of the fittest, has no answer for this.

It seems that they were genetically engineered to be an awesome force to reckon with for the Adamic race. Their musculature was structured more massively with huge shoulders and massive arms, which means they could easily manhandle us. They had larger flaring lungs with an astounding 60 percent greater capacity. That means they could outrun us and outlast us in a fight.

They undoubtedly had a superior intellect due to their larger brain. Add to this their knowledge of the craft of sorcery, and the Neanderthal was a formidable foe indeed. Their large brain, creating a greater need for nutrition, made them the perfect weapon against the Adamic race, which eventually led them to use humans as part of their diet.

Modern man has intentionally ignored this historical record, and the supernatural shroud that overshadows the truth has been almost complete. Few people really know why our First Earth was really destroyed. Cannibalism and the worship of the Mother Goddesses, instituted by the Nephilim to honor the women who gave themselves over to the procreation of these creatures, ruled our First Earth. This is precisely what ancient Hebrew tradition tells us in the Book of Enoch.

> *And all the others together with them took unto themselves wives, and each chose for himself one, and they began to go in unto them and to defile themselves with them, and they taught them charms and enchantments, and the cutting of roots, and made them acquainted with plants.* And they became pregnant, and they bare great giants, whose height was three thousand ells: Who consumed all the acquisitions of men. And when men could no longer sustain them, the giants turned against them and devoured mankind. And they began to sin against birds, and beasts, and reptiles, and fish, and to devour one another's flesh, and drink the blood. Then the earth laid accusation against the lawless ones (emphasis added).
>
> —Enoch 7:1-6

The last part of these verses seems to tell us that their genetic interference did not stop with human beings: "And they began to sin against birds, and beasts, and reptiles, and fish, and to devour one another's flesh, and drink the blood." I suspect that some of the fierce reptilian carnivores we call dinosaurs were the genetic products of demonic intervention.

Sadly, this practice of cannibalism and drinking the blood of the people they sacrificed did not end in the First Earth. The demonic hierarchy has taught man in all civilizations the same abominable practice that brought certain destruction on our First Earth. It seems likely that many of the giant carnivorous animals that wreaked havoc in the First Earth were genetically altered animals bred for the single purpose of destroying the world of men.

> *The notion that, by eating the flesh, or particularly by drinking the blood, of another living being, a man absorbs his nature or life into his own, is one which appears among primitive peoples in many forms.* It lies at the root of the widespread practice of drinking the fresh blood of enemies—a practice which was familiar to certain tribes of the Arabs before Muhammad, and which tradition still ascribes to the wild races of Cahtan—and also of the habit practiced by many savage huntsmen of eating some part (*e.g.,* the liver) of dangerous carnivora, in order that the courage of the animal may pass into them. The flesh and blood of brave men also are, among semi-savage or savage tribes, eaten and drunk to inspire courage (emphasis added) (Budge 1967, lxxxi).

It is not hard to imagine why God would want to obliterate the lawless ones from existence, for they were demonically engendered beings claiming to be gods whose sorcery and violence filled the world and marred the First Earth, bringing upon them certain judgment and utter destruction. This, contrary to the evolutionary claims, is what the ancient chronicles tell us.

Today, scientists shrouded by the naturalistic paradigm are blindly working to bring the Nephilim back into our world. You may think I am sensationalizing. Think again.

> A later technique under development in my Harvard lab will allow us to resurrect practically any extinct animal whose genome is known or can be constructed from fossil remains, up to and including the wooly mammoth, the passenger pigeon, and even Neanderthal man. One of the obstacles in resurrecting those and other long extinct

species is that intact cell nuclei of these animals no longer exist, which means that there is no nucleus available for nuclear transfer cloning. Nevertheless, the genome sequences of both the wooly mammoth and Neanderthal man have been substantially reconstructed; the genetic information that defines those animals exists, is known, and is stored in computer databases. The problem is to convert that information—those abstract sequences of letters—into actual strings of nucleotides that constitute the genes and genomes of the animals in question.

This could be done by means of MAGE technology—multiplex automated genome engineering. MAGE is sort of a mass-scale, accelerated version of genetic engineering. Whereas genetic engineering works by making genetic changes manually on a few nucleotides at a time, MAGE introduces them on a wholesale basis in automated fashion. It would allow researchers to start with an intact genome of one animal and, by making the necessary changes, convert it into a functional genome of another animal entirely.

You could start, for example, with an elephant's genome and change it into a mammoth's. First you would break up the elephant genome into about 3,000 chunks, each about 100,000 DNA units in length. Then, by using the mammoth's reconstructed genome sequence as a template, you would selectively introduce the molecular changes necessary to make the elephant genome look like that of a mammoth. All of the revised chunks would then be reassembled to constitute a newly engineered mammoth genome, and the animal itself could be cloned into existence by conventional interspecies nuclear transfer cloning (or perhaps by another method, the blastocyst injection of whole cells.)

> The same technique would work for the Neanderthal, except that you'd start with a stem cell genome from a human adult and gradually reverse-engineer it into the Neanderthal genome or a reasonably close equivalent. These stem cells can produce tissues and organs. If society becomes comfortable with cloning and sees value in true human diversity, then the whole Neanderthal creature itself could be cloned by a surrogate mother chimp—or by an extremely adventurous female human (Church and Regis 2012, 10–11).

It is no coincidence that this automated genome-engineering machine is called MAGE. It will be used to bring back those who first brought occult magic to our Earth. Little do these scientists know of the dark powers behind the bioengineering of Neanderthals during the First Earth. They will unleash a new race of men who will be superior to our own in every way. I am very well aware that I will be ridiculed for taking such a stance. I can only pray that God's Spirit will confirm the truth of which I speak to those who seek His face.

Certainly the naturalists will scoff at such claims, but sadly so shall many Christians. Anthropologists long used to seeing the paintings in the Neanderthal caves through naturalistic spectacles have no idea that the Neanderthals' entire purpose was to spread occultism and destroy the world of humans.

To ancient man, caves represented the entrance to the underworld. As such, they had special significance for those wishing to contact the demonic forces of the underworld. For this reason, most of the cave paintings that have survived for us are, in fact, the work of those who sought the contact and power offered by demons throughout the ages. For the most part, the concepts depicted in these caves are the views of those who follow the religion of the Serpent.

The art in these hidden and obscure caverns are therefore almost monolithically the work of those who are involved in the occult and do not represent the entire cross section of the population living at that time. The evolutionary minded archeologists who would like to paint a picture of an evolution of religion where none exists have intentionally overlooked this fact. The evidence of a Mother Goddess cult and of cannibalism abounds for this period. That did not represent the original religion of Adam but rather a profaned corruption brought forth in the sixth generation after Adam.

To make a first-hand study of this very important aspect of prehistoric religion the best centre is Les Eyzies on the banks of the Vézère in the Dordogne, within easy reach of which are a number of the principle examples, such as that known as Font-de-Gaume, less than a kilometre and a half from the village. A little further along the Sarlat road in the valley of Beune is a long subterranean tunnel called Les Combarelles with a number of engravings. Not far away at Laussel a rock-shelter contained a frieze depicting an obese nude female carved on a block of stone, apparently in an advanced stage of pregnancy and holding in her right hand what seems to be the horn of a bison. The figure had been covered with red ochre (*World Religions 1983*, 24).

The Mother Goddess of Laussel is an engraving of a nude pregnant woman holding the familiar horn associated with the cornucopia, which is offered by Satan to those who follow the religion of the "horned one."

The face of the woman depicted in the statue of Laussel seems to have a beard, and her thighs are so grotesquely depicted that one cannot help but associate her with the bearded Halflings of mythology called satyrs, which are supposedly composed of the legs of a goat and the body of a human. It is my contention that these are simply occult symbolic representations of the Nephilim that serve to obscure the obvious dualism from the uninitiated.

The red ochre is consistent with the occult choosing the color red as representative of the blood sacrifices made to Satan. The ritual of drinking the blood has been part of the occult religion of the Serpent from the beginning. Moreover, the nature of this engraving leads me to believe that the individual portrayed may be a graphic representation of the birthing of the Nephilim as we discussed previously.

The horn, a symbol of power and affluence, in the right hand clearly associates the woman with the horned gods and represents the opposition of the Impostor who has since his First Insurrection sought to usurp the authority of God. The horn is a symbol of power and dominion and has therefore been usurped by Satan. He has attempted to counterfeit the symbol portrayed by the horns of Taurus, who represents the One True God, the Lord Most High, and the Creator of the Universe.

For this reason, the many symbols of Lucifer contain horned depictions. The Goat of Mendes is but one of many such examples. The ancient Celtic horned god Cernunnos is therefore not surprisingly the consort of the Mother Goddess Gaia who is worshiped by those involved in modern Wicca. Sexual rituals abound between these two in many esoteric societies.

The esoteric brotherhood understands that many names from all sections of the world describe the same entity. This is true for Satan as well as for the Mother Goddesses. In a ritual called "drawing down the moon" described in *The Witches Bible*, the Great Mother Goddess is being evoked:

> High Priest: Listen to the words of the Great Mother; she who of old was also called among men Artemis, Astarte, Athene, Dione, Melusine, Aphrodite, Cerridwen, Dana, Arianrhod, Isis, Bride, and by many other names.

High Priestess: "Whenever ye have need of anything, once in the month, and better it be when the moon is full, then shall ye assemble in some secret place and adore the spirit of me, who am Queen of all witches. There shall ye assemble, ye who are fain to learn all sorcery, yet have not won its deepest secrets, to these will I teach things that are yet unknown. And ye shall be free from slavery; and as a sign that ye be really free, ye shall be naked in your rites; and ye shall dance, sing, feast, make music and love, all in my praise. For mine is the ecstasy of the spirit and mine also is joy on earth; for my law is love unto all beings" (Farrar and Farrar 1981, 42–43).

The second pillar of the occult is the offer of enlightenment into the deepest secrets of their arcane knowledge. Their call to freedom is the call to godhood when men and women claim absolute autonomy. To these the Enemy of Man offers many lures: sex, power, wealth, fame, and more.

That initiation into the secret knowledge is in essence the initiation into fellowship with demons. In the same esoteric volume, the High Priest of the order evokes Cernunnos, the horned god, the consort of the Mother Goddess.

High Priest says:

"Great god Cernunnos, return to earth again!
Come at my call and show thyself to men.
Shepherd of Goats, upon the wild hill's way,
Lead thy lost flock from darkness unto day.
Forgotten are the ways of sleep and night –
Men seek for them, whose eyes have lost the light.
Open the door, the door that hath no key,
The door of dreams, whereby men come to thee.
Shepherd of Goats, O answer unto me!"

High Priestess and High Priest together say: "Akhera goiti," lower their hand and say: "Akhera beiti!" (Farrar and Farrar 1981, 44).

The phrase *Akhera goiti, akhera beiti!* means "the He-Goat above, the He-Goat below." It is indicative of the demonic doctrine of correspondence that states "as above so below." In other words, men can be gods. It is one of the three lies that Lucifer told Eve in the Garden: "You can be like God" (Gen. 3:5).

The Great Rite of the sexual union between Cernunnos and the High Priestess as symbolic of the Mother Goddess celebrates the very birthing of the Nephilim sorcerers in the First Earth and establishes their goal to undo the curse of God levied in the Garden at Eden. I am referring to the prophecy of the Dragon Doom that would come through the seed of Eve—the Messiah. It is by profaning the bloodline of Eve that the demons sought to prevent His birth.

For this express purpose, the religion of the Mother Goddesses was established by the demons who led the second insurrection. They lifted to godhood those women who gave themselves over to the birthing of the Nephilim. Thus, the union of demon and mankind gave forth a race of giants who promoted the horned gods who usurped the place of God. Their remains are what we now call Neanderthal man.

Not only was it widely practiced throughout the end of the First Earth, but we also find the motif prevalent in all the occult religions of the Second Earth throughout the entire planet. We can cite, for example, the horns of the Divine Bull, supposedly killed by Nimrod as he placed the head of the slain bull over his own head. The religion of Mithras that was spawned by Nimrod taught the same basic occult doctrines of the Nephilim. That shamanistic motif is found in every continent in the Second Earth, but it began in the First Earth. The horned deer, the horned bull, and the serpents can be found in the ancient city we now call Catal Huyuk, perhaps 3,000 years prior to the Great Flood.

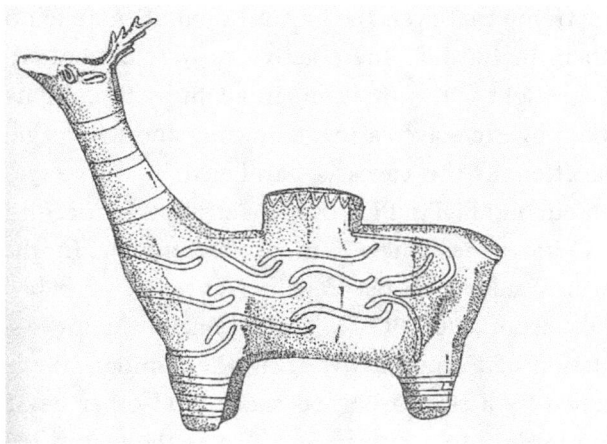

Horned deer with serpentine neck and riddled with serpents around its body, from Catal Huyuk

The names of these gods may differ from one nation to another, but their description and character betray their common identity. They are merely doctrines of demons that flower in many splendid colors to attract the ignorant who fail to look below the skin.

In Greek lore, Pan represents the horned god. He is depicted as a half-man, half-goat god who is associated with sexual lust, mischief, and things to do with nature. The Halflings' satyr motif is here an obvious allusion to the Nephilim Halflings of old, the goat being one of the animals that represent demons.

> He is now identified in modern witchcraft as a version of the Horned God. The Horned God is seen as a consort to the Goddess, and his annual birth at Yuletide and his symbolic death at the end of each summer mark the passing of the seasons, the cycle of birth, death, and rebirth in nature (Streeter 2020, 44).

Similar to Pan is the god Bacchus/Dionysus who is also often portrayed in the form of a satyr (half-man and half-goat). The drunken orgiastic activities associated with the rites of Bacchanalia were so extreme that even the pagan Roman Senate felt obliged to outlaw them in 186 BC. These activities were celebrated in secret meetings at night with initiation rituals lit by torchlights in caves and marked by excessive eating, drinking, and wild orgies. Again, the connection to the caves is paralleled in the religion of the Nephilim during the First Earth and betrays their occult origin.

The Celtic tribes knew him as Cernunnos. In the famous Gundestrup Cauldron, a decorated silver vessel probably made in the Danube around 100 BC, we find on one of the inner scenes the representation of Cernunnos wearing the familiar stag horns and accompanied by a stag, a horned snake, and other beasts, with a procession leading to a human sacrifice as the victim is sacrificed and drowned in a large cauldron. Their hatred for God for having drowned the Nephilim of old is vindicated by their ritualistic drowning of innocent human victims.

We know that these cauldrons were also used ritualistically to catch the blood of their victims of human sacrifices. From Irish traditions, we know that the use of these large cauldrons for ritual meals is abundantly documented. In modern Wicca it is called "the Cauldron of Cerridwen, which is the Holy Grail of immortality" (Farrar and Farrar 1981, 43).

This is the promotion of the esoteric doctrine of immortality to those who gain their secret wisdom—the gnosis. It is another of the three lies spoken to Eve in the Garden by the cunning Serpent. Do not underestimate the extent of their influence and power in our world. God tells us that Satan is the prince of the power of the air. He has divided our world into four quadrants ruled by four demon kings under his rule. He stands as the fifth ruler over the four quadrants. Thus the pentagram is the symbol of this demonic hierarchy.

Cernunnos, as depicted in the Gundestrup Cauldron, sporting the familiar horns and holding a serpent in his left hand and a torque in his right hand. The torque is a symbol of slavery or bondage to the god. The circle in the occult symbolizes global domination. For this reason the pentagram is often depicted within a circle, as is the swastika.

The pillars in the Gundestrup Cauldron with four identical faces carved on them and pointing to the four corners of the world represent the desire for the satanic dominion of the world and particularly allude to the Four Demon Kings charged over each of the cardinal points. The central figure in the cauldron is a Mother Goddess flanked by two crows and two other goddesses on either side of her.

Lying in front of her is a dead male, perhaps a soldier who died in battle or a sacrificial victim. These Mother Goddesses were seen as the harbingers of death in battle and are also known to be the consorts of the horned god. But this familiar motif of the triple Mother Goddesses is not peculiar only to the Celtic people. They are known throughout the world. Moreover, they are simply a later rendition of the Mother Goddesses of the First Earth.

Therefore, it is plain to see that the occult association with the horns also did not end with antediluvian man. The shamanistic religion of the Celtic Druids continued in the same motif of the familiar horned gods. And no doubt the worship of Cernunnos was carried out in probably the very same fashion as their prediluvian shaman predecessors. They, too, dressed with the antlers of the red deer and with the skins of wolves in their occult rituals while eating humans sacrificed to their gods. The name Cernunnos means "the horned one" and is derived from the root word *cerna*, which means "horn." In Paris there is a famous depiction of Cernunnos with the familiar horns of Nimrod and sporting a beard.

> A bronze statuette from Autun represents a similar figure, probably horned, who presents a torque to two *ram's-headed serpents*. Fixed above his ears are two small heads. On a monument from Vandoeuvres is a squatting *horned god, pressing a sack*. Two genii stand beside him on a *serpent*, while one of them holds a torque. . . . On the altar of Beaune are three figures, one *horned* with a *cornucopia*, another three-headed, holding a basket.
>
> Three figures, one female and two males, are found on the Dennevy altar. One god is three-faced; the other has a *cornucopia*, which he offers to a *serpent*.
>
> Another image represents a three-faced god holding a *serpent* with a ram's head (emphasis added) (MacCulloch 1992, 32–33).

The image of the cornucopia is, in effect, a symbol of material affluence offered in the horn of Cernunnos. It was his timeless bait. It is rather elementary; if you worship the horned god (Satan), he promises you prosperity, riches, and power on this Earth.

He is the "prince of the power of the air" (Eph. 2:2) and the "ruler of this world" (John 12:31), at least for a time. And make no mistake; he has the ability to persuade a great many in this regard, tapping into the endless well of greed intrinsic to the human soul. But his days are numbered, and in the end, the Messiah will rule the world. No doubt, numbered among the main reasons why people turn to Satanism is the ancient vice of avarice, the beguiling promise of wealth and power.

There can be no mistake in the symbolism of Cernunnos, whether the horns are depicted with the ram's head, the red deer antlers, or a bull, these are symbolic of Satan's' attempt to usurp the authority of Christ who is the Lamb who was slain for our sins. The horns turned up to heaven are the occult symbol of power vested against the heavens.

The ram is also a symbol for Israel (Aries), while the serpent and the goat are universally the symbol of Satan. The three-horned red deer in the background in the statuette from Autun are symbolic of Satan's unholy trinitarian godhead in which he counterfeits the divine, triune Godhead.

But as stated earlier, the horned gods are not exclusive to Europe, for similar horned gods are found in every corner of the world. Their beguiling influence extends the breadth of our planet from Europe to the Middle East and to China, India, Australia, Africa, and the American continent.

Their influence in the postdiluvian world began in the Middle East shortly after the Great Flood. Nimrod fathered the Babylonian people as well as the Akkadians, but unfortunately both he and his descendants strayed from the one true Lord, Elohim. Nimrod, beguiled by the old lie of the Serpent, attempted to usurp the authority of God, claiming to be the son of the sun god. Filled with self-importance, he arrogantly professed that he had by his own hand killed the Divine Bull, which represents the Messiah. Taurus is the symbol of God—Elohim or Jehovah—who was known by all ancient cultures through the Zodiac.

THE DEATH OF THE FIRST EARTH

Immediately before the death of the First Earth, the constellation of Taurus became the ruling house in the Zodiac. The constellation of Taurus represented a white bull coming to judge the world in righteousness. Hence, it represented the judgment that ended the First Earth. The twin horns represent the fountains of the deep and the windows of heaven that brought the Great Flood upon our planet.

Nimrod's audacious boast was symbolized by the cutting off of Taurus' head and placing it on his own head in triumph. For this reason, many of the depictions of Nimrod were made with him wearing the horns of the head of Taurus. In this fashion, he indicated symbolically that he had taken over the position of El, the God of the universe, claiming godhood for himself.

Of course, this is simply the same wish projection of Satan who instigates this same rebellious desire in mankind as he vainly desires to become the ruler of the universe, and it is for this reason that many of the depictions of Satan in all cultures have placed horns on his head. The horned gods then universally refer to the Great Impostor, which is corroborated in every ancient civilization. From Babylon through the Mediterranean area and into the land of the Vikings, this is the earmark of the gods that symbolizes Satan.

Bronze statue of the horned god found in Enkomi, Cyprus, dating to about 1200 BC

It is the intrinsic nature of every human culture to embellish and corrupt the truth due to the influence of the Great Deceiver. The truth of the original religion of Adam and Noah has been absconded by every culture as the work of the enemy of God continues to shroud the message of the salvation of the soul through the work of the Messiah by His propitiatory sacrifice for mankind. The goal of the occult has always been to usurp the throne of God and thwart the redemption of man. Their esoteric symbolism has for this reason always carried with it the horn of rebellion.

We can see many variations of this ancient motif throughout the occult world. For example, the mythical animal known as the unicorn and popular in all New Age shops is an occult symbol of this rebellion toward God as it represents magic and sports the horn upward toward the heavens.

But central to the religion of the Nephilim is the veneration of the women who gave themselves over to this travesty. The Mother Goddess depiction in Laussel is no isolated incident. The late Marija Gimbutas, formerly professor of archaeology at UCLA, is of the opinion that this figure of a fat woman is a representation of an archetypal Mother Goddess, which is universally found throughout this period in our human history.

Gimbutas, an evolutionist, believes it was the central religion widely practiced in that Neolithic time frame.

> *Gimbutas, who passed away in 2001, is one of the leading proponents of an intriguing hypothesis about who was who and what was what in prehistory. It concerns the distinctive carved and/or painted figures of enormously fat women that have been found in many European Neolithic sites (c.7000–4000 BC) and the almost equally numerous and virtually identical examples going far back into the world of Paleolithic cave art (the Venus of Laussel, c.30,000 BC; the Venus of Lespugue, c.25,000 BC, etc). According to Gimbutas and others who have entered this fray, these figures are the symbols and representations of an archetypal 'Mother Goddess' figure – simultaneously the Goddess of Fertility, the Goddess of Death and the Goddess of Rebirth – whose worship was ancient and must once have been extremely widespread. Whether*

we find her painted, carved in relief out of the rock wall of a cave (as in the celebrated example of Laussel), or in the form of a free-standing sculpture, the Goddess is usually represented as an imposing, hugely fat woman with dangling breasts, egg-shaped buttocks and bulging calves and forearms,. It is therefore noteworthy that many figures exactly matching this description have been excavated from Malta's megalithic temples, including two in repose – usually referred to as 'the Sleeping Ladies' – that were found in the Hypogeum itself.

"The Hypogeum", notes Gimbutas:

With its room painted liberally with red ochre wash, represents the Goddess's regenerative womb . . . An indication of the religious use of these womb-shaped chambers are the figurines of Sleeping Ladies lying stretched out on low couches, associated with two cubicles opening into the Main Hall. The more articulate one, known as "The Sleeping Lady of the Hypogeum", is a true masterpiece. This generously rounded lady with egg-shaped buttocks lies on her side, asleep, almost visibly dreaming. *Why is she sleeping in the tomb? One explanation is that this represents a rite of initiation or incubation. To sleep within the Goddess's womb was to die and to come to life anew. The Sleeping Lady could also be a votive offering of one who successfully passed through the rite of incubation in the Hypogeum* (emphasis added) (Gimbutas 2002, 345–346).

The rite of incubation is no doubt the ceremony that celebrates the birthing of the Halflings, which turned our First Earth into a world filled with violence. Just like today, the novice is required to undergo this incubation rite in order to become an initiate. Included in the ritual is usually a symbolic representation of death and rebirth. Sometimes they are required to sleep in cemeteries and at other times to even be placed inside caskets.

For this reason, their artistic depictions of the Mother Goddesses have grossly exaggerated representations of the female genitals. Their temples are often in the form of wombs. The Mnajdra Temple in Malta is such an example.

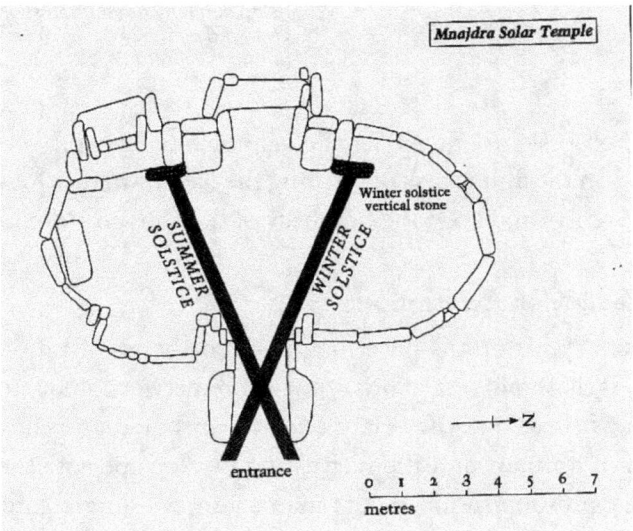

The womb-shaped Mnajdra Temple in Malta. The entrance symbolizes the cervix, and the positions of the two sunrays during the winter and summer solstices intersect and form a V, which has been traditionally the sign of the female sexual organ. The first sunrays entering through the eastern doorway on the summer solstice create a flag-shaped appearance on a stone monolith conspicuously placed to receive the effect at the rear of the temple, after which an almond-shaped eye appears at the right of the pole banner.

But this design is not particular to Malta. We find it scattered throughout all Europe and the Middle East.

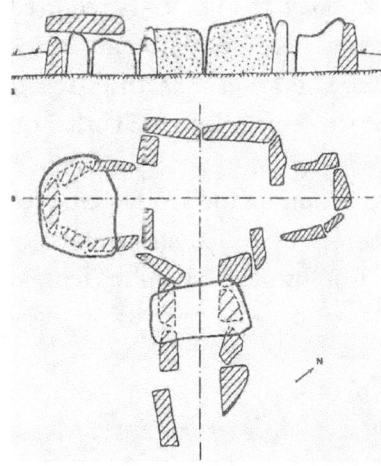

This prediluvian grave in Mendor, Locquettas, Brittany, is likewise designed to represent the womb and the cervix. Its orientation toward the rising sun may have been slightly changed by the tectonic movements during the Great Flood.

The obsession with the female genitalia and phallic symbols is centered on the divine task of birthing the Nephilim race to wipe out the seed of Eve and avert the prophecy of the Dragon Doom.

The Prediluvian Civilization

Evolutionary historians have long insisted that civilization began in the Tigris Euphrates plains somewhere between 4000 and 3500 BC. It was there that they claimed cities sprouted and the domestication of animals and the harvesting of crops began. Their evolutionary presupposition paints man as an evolving creature who slowly changed from primitive hunter-gatherers living in caves to a more evolved society of farmers and artisans living in homes. For this reason, since their reinterpretation of history was rooted two centuries ago during the Darwinian revolution, they believed that the domestication of animals and farming was a recent invention of man that appeared perhaps around 4000 BC in the fertile valley of Mesopotamia.

The Scriptures, on the other hand, state that Cain, the first man born upon the First Earth, "was a tiller of the ground" (Gen. 4:2).

His brother, Abel, was a shepherd who offered God a sacrifice, "the firstlings of his flock" (Gen. 4:4). Hence, both the domestication of animals and farming are as old as the first children of this Earth.

The Scriptures also claim that Jabal's brother, Jubal, was responsible for making musical instruments. It is from his name that we have the English word jubilee—to make joy (Gen. 4:21). But more importantly, it was their half-brother born from Lamech's second wife, Zillah, that man learned to forge metals.

> *As for Zillah, she also gave birth to Tubal-cain, the forger of all implements of bronze and iron.*
>
> —Gen. 4:22

Thus, from the seventh generation after Cain, man knew the art of forging iron. Tubal-cain, however, did not use this technological advantage for the furthering of humanity but for his lust, so says Flavius Josephus:

> Lamech; who had seventy-seven children by two wives, Silla and Ada. Of those children by Ada, one was Jabal: he erected tents, and loved the life of the shepherd. But Jubal, who was born of the same mother with him, exercised himself in music.; and invented the psaltery and the harp. *But Tubal, one of his children by the other wife, exceeded all men in strength, and was very expert and famous in martial performances. He procured what tended to the pleasures of the body by that method; and first of all invented the art of making brass* (emphasis added) (Josephus 1960, 27).

This no doubt was instigated by the urging of Azazel, one of the nine demons who were the leaders of the Second Insurrection. We can infer this from the comment made in the Book of Enoch, which I previously quoted.

> *And Azazel taught men to make swords, and knives, and shields, and breastplates, and made known to them the metals <of the earth> and the art of working them, and bracelets, and ornaments, and the use of antimony, and the beautifying of the eyelids, and all kinds of costly stones, and all colouring tinctures. And there arose much godlessness, and they committed fornication, and they were led astray, and became corrupt in all their ways. Semjâzâ taught enchantments, and root-cuttings, Armârôs the resolving of enchantments, Barâqîjâl (taught) astrology, Kôkabêl the constellations, Ezêqêêl the knowledge of the clouds, <Araqiêl the signs of the earth, Shamsiêl the signs of the sun>, and Sariêl the course of the moon. And as men perished, they cried, and their cry went up to heaven* (emphasis added).
>
> —Enoch 8:1–3

This was the last generation that God recorded of Cain's descendants. From that point forward, the children of Cain were mingled with the Neanderthals. God no longer recognized them as legitimate heirs of Adam and Eve to whom the management of Earth was given. Thus, their children are not recorded in God's book. That time was concurrent with the sixth generation from Adam through Seth.

In that fateful sixth generation, the Second Insurrection of the fallen angels engendered the Nephilim. The Mother Goddess religion of the Serpent became a blight and a cancer upon our people. Cult centers developed as cities spread outward from the Middle East. Cain's Adamic lineage was lost, but Seth's lineage lasted a bit longer to the 10th generation during Noah's time. At that crucial point, only eight people in the world remained faithful to God. This was no primitive cave-dwelling culture as evolutionary archaeologists are prone to insinuate.

Modern archaeology has shown conclusively that their previous, recent dates for the domestication of animals, farming of crops, and the building of elaborate homes have been time and time again pushed back by new archaeological discoveries. Long before the civilizations founded by the descendants of Noah in the Valley of Shinar, humans lived in homes, had domesticated animals, and farmed throughout their areas of colonization. In fact, the introduction of the Mother Goddess religion by the Nephilim created centers of cult worship around a temple that promoted the formation of large communities.

> Old Europeans had towns with a considerable concentration of population, temples several stories high, a scared script, spacious houses of four or five rooms, professional ceramicists, weavers, copper and gold metallurgists, and other artisans producing a range of sophisticated goods. A flourishing network of trade routes existed that circulated items such as obsidian, shells, marble, copper, and salt over hundreds of kilometers . . . Old European society was organized around a theocratic, communal temple community, guided by a queen-priestess (Gimbutas 1991, viii, xi).

In the rich plains of Thessalonica and Macedonia we have rich agricultural lands that had been centers of civilization during the First Earth. Recent excavations have shown that they were dotted with thousands of villages dating more than a thousand years prior to the Great Flood.

> The plains of northern Greece are dotted with mounds called *tells*, "Magulas" in Greek, which are mound shaped layers of settlement debris from the Neolithic and Early Bronze Age. Going west from the Bay of Volos and across the plain between the modern towns of Karditsa, Trikala,

and Larisa, one can easily count hundreds of them, standing five to fifteen meters high. These mounds hold the secrets of people who lived there for many centuries between 8500 and 4500 years ago. Mudbrick and layers of clay daub used for house walls crumbled in time and new houses were built over the old ones causing tells to grow higher, layer by layer (Gimbutas 1991, 13).

From Europe to as far away as Iran we find that animals had been domesticated and crops were being harvested some 3,500 years prior to the Great Flood.

> The dog had already been domesticated from the wolf in central Europe by the Magdalenean period of the Upper Paleolithic. Sheep were domesticated in the hilly flanks of the Zagros Mountains (Iran, Iraq) and in the Taurus Mountains (Turkey) before 7000 B.C. where they had previously been hunted in the wild Cattle and pigs followed between 7500 and 6500 B.C. in Anatolia and domestication continued locally in Europe from 6500 to 5500 B.C. The domesticated horse was unknown to the near east and east central Europe before the end of the 5th millennium B.C.
>
> There were domesticated grains on which early agriculture was based: einkorn wheat (Triticum monococcum), emmer wheat (riticum diococcum), and two-row barley (Hordeum vulgare ssp. distichum). These were domesticated during the 8th and 7th millennia in settlements between southeast Europe and Afghanistan. To this day, wild wheat, both einkorn and emmer, is found between Greece and Afghanistan and wild barley still grows between the Aegean basin and Baluchistan (Gimbutas 1991, 2).

THE MARVEL OF THE FIRST EARTH

Between 1961 and 1965, James Mellart undertook the excavation of an ancient town called Catal Huyuk in central Turkey. His findings completely overturned the previous dogma regarding the sophistication of our earliest civilization.

> The excavation of the 7th millennium B.C. town of Çatal Hüyük by James Mellart in 1961–63 and 1965 has revolutionized our views on the pre-history of Anatolia and the entire Old World.
>
> Çatal Hüyük consists of two riverside mounds situated on a dry plateau 1000 meters above sea level on the Konya plain in south-central Turkey. The larger mound occupies about 32 acres (16 hectares), one acre of which was excavated. The breathtaking discovery of thirteen building levels with houses, temples, murals, reliefs, sculptures, trade items, and other finds was an eye-opener to the level of Neolithic culture that existed in the 7th millennium BC. . . . it is estimated that up to 7,000 inhabitants could have lived there at one time. . . . Houses were timber framed and built of mud brick with flat roofs. There were no doors, and people entered their homes through openings in the roof. . . . Kitchens occupied about a third of a house's total floor space and ovens were set low in the walls. Storage rooms contained plaited baskets for grain, tools, and other supplies (Gimbutas 1991, 7).

It was incomprehensible to evolutionists that man, as many as 3,000 years before the Great Flood, could erect buildings of 13 levels and display the signs of an advanced culture. Certainly a population of more than 7,000 inhabitants must have had ample specialized workers in farming, carpentry, stone masonry, and metallurgy. The old idea promoted by evolutionary historians that farming was started around 4000 BC in lower Mesopotamia is simply another evolutionary fable.

The Scriptures clearly state that the first man born on this Earth was a farmer. It was from the produce in his field that he made the unacceptable sacrifice to God because it represented the works of his hands. In contrast, his younger brother, Abel, sacrificed a lamb and in so doing recognized that without the shedding of blood there could be no remission of sins. In this act he acknowledged the coming Lamb of God who would in the future come to shed His blood for our sins.

Catal Huyuk was no simple conglomeration of village huts. It was a complexly designed, interconnected structure that reached up to 13 levels and stretched for 32 acres: "The breathtaking discovery of thirteen building levels with houses, temples, murals, reliefs, sculptures, trade items, and other finds was an eye-opener to the level of Neolithic culture that existed in the 7th millennium BC" (Gimbutas 1991, 7).

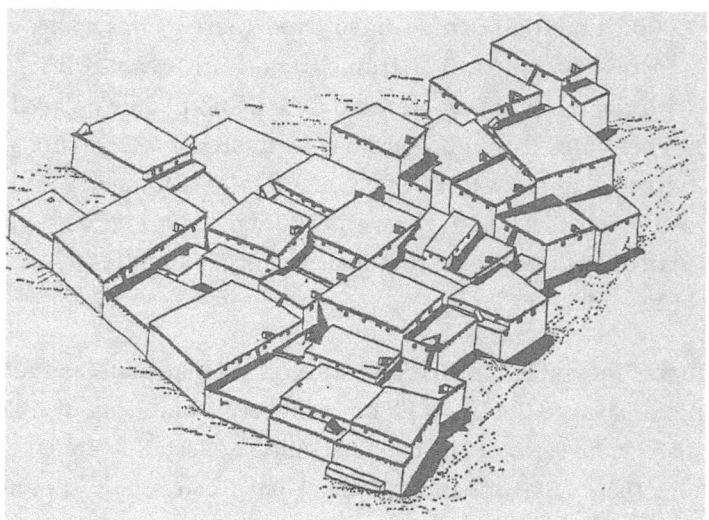

Catal Huyuk — *This is a very small section of the 30-acre city that existed in south-central Turkey some 3,000 years prior to the Great Flood. Some buildings were found to have 13 levels. The number 13 is a significant number in occult symbology.*

The high degree of this sophistication achieved 9,000 years ago is certainly greater than many of the shantytowns I have visited in Third World countries today. The archaeological evidence also attests to the moral degeneration in that civilization. It had by this time been seduced by the religion of the Mother Goddess instituted by the Nephilim for the procreation of their abominable race of Halflings whose purpose was the destruction of the seed of Eve.

> The main theme of these wall paintings and reliefs revolves around the Goddess of Regeneration portrayed as a frog-shaped woman giving birth. She is associated with animals, and around her are both the vulture, representing the death aspect, and the bull head, representing regeneration. There is also a myriad of accompanying symbols rhythmically lined out along the edges, framing the panels. Most of these symbols are abstracted representations of horns, triangles, rhombs or double triangles, or hourglass shapes and butterflies (Gimbutas 1991, 9).

One of the universal symbols of the Messiah figure throughout all cultures has been the eagle or hawk. They are, of course, the natural enemy of the serpent. Their occult counterfeit has been the vulture or the crow. The white bull is the symbol of Uru, a name for God that is symbolized by the Sun (uru). The constellation Taurus (Tau, the last; Uru, the Sun, which is the symbol for An (God) is the constellation of the avenging bull that came down to judge the First Earth. Taurus was the constellation rising on the vernal equinox when the seven stars (seven archangels) of An struck the First Earth and destroyed it with a Great Flood. These seven angels are represented by the constellation of the Pleiades riding on the back of the bull.

Like everything else, Satan always counterfeits the work of God. The red or black bull represents the Great Usurper with his horns turned up toward heaven. For this reason, depictions of gods with horns are always occult symbols of rebellion toward heaven.

The triangles or double triangles are symbolic representations of the union among man, the Nephilim, and their gods or annunakis (demons). The triangle is also simply a pictograph of the woman's genitalia and symbolizes the birthing of the Nephilim. The butterfly is a symbol of occult rebirth. The process of metamorphosis is a symbolic representation of the ritual rebirth into the occult.

Unlike the Judeo-Christian concept of resurrection and regeneration through God's propitiation, the occult initiates achieve their rebirth through the knowledge of their esoteric doctrines and initiation rites.

This temple in Catal Huyuk has the Mother Goddess with a frog head (or serpent's head) and serpentine limbs in a ready position to have sex (arms wide to receive their doctrine and legs wide to receive their seed) at the center of the temple. She is sitting on a skull of the aurochs bull, which symbolizes deity. She is thus revered as the sixth deity. Facing her are four bulls that symbolize the Demon Kings over the four quadrants of the Earth. Her four limbs likewise represent these four Demon Kings, while her head represents the fifth.

In the middle of her body is the navel that represents her womb and the reason for her being. These limbs that rotate around the navel become the Jaina Cross, or the Swastika, in occult symbols for global dominion. To her right is the fifth god, the quintessence, the point on the pentagram known as the Architect, the Great Breath, the Akasha, and Lucifer. She becomes the sixth deity by giving her body over to their plans and receiving their initiation rituals. The vulva at her navel represents her significance in birthing their Nephilim brood.

And thus the number six is representative of unregenerate man becoming part of the demonic plan for global control. The bull between her legs then represents the Nephilim brood she births. Notice that his horns are not the same shape as that of the demons. It is a diminished form.

For this reason we find phallic symbols in statuettes as well as symbols of the Mother Goddess pregnant or depicted with exaggerated female genitalia in cult centers and temples throughout the latter part of the First Earth. All of mankind, with the exception of Noah, had been seduced by the Mother Goddesses and their Nephilim shamans.

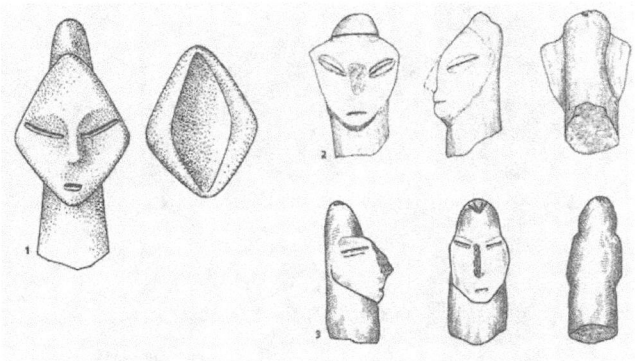

Figurines of phallic members with masks shaped like opened vulvas (second from left at top) abounded. The four points of the vulva also represent the four Demon Kings. From the rear (right top) they looked like flying serpents.

The importance to the demonic globalist plan executed by Hermetic sexual "magick" is here displayed by men living 9,000 years ago. Occultist theology is universal in time and place. In the Sumerian language, the Kundalini or Nagarajan of the Hindu was called Ningizzida. In Babylonia he is known as Tiamaz the dragon. It is the same as Rahu or Rahab of the Hebrew Scriptures. In Australia, he is known as Warramunga the Rainbow Serpent. In Chinese he is Fohi—half man, half serpent. In Fiji he is Ratumaibulu. In West Africa, he is Aidophedo. In the Voodoo of Benin, he is known as Dan. The Koreans know him as Eobshin. The Egyptians know him as Apep or Set. The Greeks know him as Typhon. The Celtics know him as Yormungand. The Gnostics know him as Ourobouros. The Central American Indians know him as Kukulcan.

THE DEATH OF THE FIRST EARTH

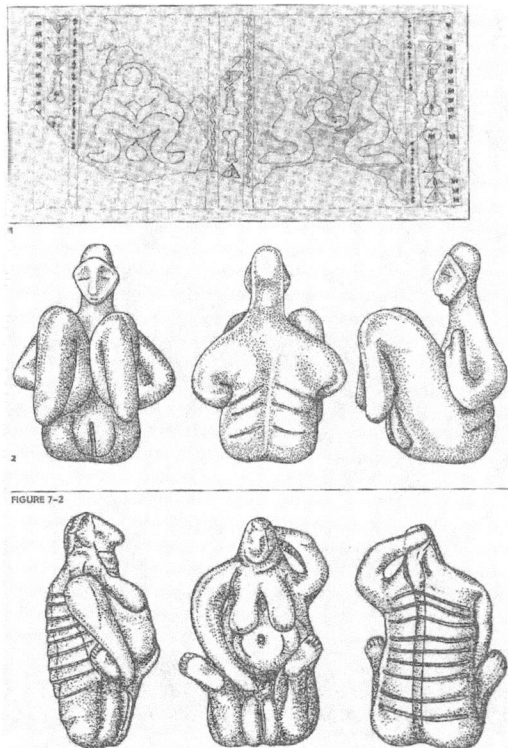

FIGURE 7-2

Frame 1 – In the frame at the top on the left we see the Mother Goddess giving birth. At the right, the Mother Goddess gives the child to the serpent god. Both are depicted in stylized serpentine fashion. Between the two scenes are drawings of male genitalia with a serpent's mouth open. These are pointed toward multiple triangles symbolizing the woman's genitalia. They depict copulation between the Neanderthal men and the women who gave themselves over to the religion of the Nephilim.

Frame 2 – The female's head, arms, and legs are drawn in serpentine fashion as she readies herself for conception. She has three stripes on her back symbolizing her apprenticeship as a novitiate.

Frame 3 – The female initiate form is now pregnant. Her hair is rolled into a single strand like a serpent coming to the head. She now has nine stripes signifying that she has reached her ninth level in initiation. The number nine is of immense occult importance because there were nine leaders of 10 who led the Second Insurrection of the fallen angels, according to the Book of Enoch. The left hand points to the head, and the right hand points to her genitalia. This symbolizes the occult doctrine of correspondence—above as it is below—which has multiple shades of meanings. Among them, it symbolizes that through the sexual act, humans will gain the wisdom of the gods. We find echoes of this motif in the nine chakras of Tantric Hinduism. The hair of the Mother Goddess in serpentine fashion symbolizes the Kundalini serpent force that ends at the head.

THE MARVEL OF THE FIRST EARTH

In every culture of the world, the religion of the Serpent has ever made its inroads and claimed much blood. But it was ever more prevalent toward the end of the First Earth when the Nephilim had conquered most of mankind. The violence visited upon mankind was pandemic. It shall become so again during the last days of the Second Earth when lawlessness shall bathe our ground in blood.

Cannibalism was central to their occult belief that eating the flesh of their victims would empower them with their life force. Hence, we find bodies that were decapitated and ritually excarnated, not only in Catal Huyuk but also throughout the entire breadth of the First Earth.

It was this violence, instigated by the bloody religion of the Serpent, that brought upon the First Earth the judgment of the Great Flood. This violence against humanity had so permeated mankind that God saw fit to end our first world. No descendent of the Adamic race was safe during those last days of the First Earth.

Enoch writes of the sad report given by four of the seven archangels of God, which I believe may be the four Princes of God who are responsible to watch over the north, south, east, and west of our Earth. This, of course, is counterfeited by the occult that universally acknowledge four Demon Kings who rule over the north, south, east, and west.

> And then Michael, Uriel, Raphael, and Gabriel looked down from heaven and saw much blood being shed upon the earth, and all lawlessness being wrought upon the earth. And they said one to another: "The earth made without inhabitant cries the voice of their crying up to the gates of heaven. And now to you, the holy ones of heaven, the souls of men make their suit, saying, 'Bring our cause before the Most High.'" And they said to the Lord of the ages: "Lord of lords, God of gods, King of kings, <and God of the ages>, the throne of Thy glory (standeth) unto all the generations

of the ages, and Thy name holy and glorious and blessed unto all the ages! Thou hast made all things, and power over all things hast Thou: and all things are naked and open in Thy sight, and Thou seest all things, and nothing can hide itself from Thee. *Thou seest what Azâzêl hath done, who hath taught all unrighteousness on earth and revealed the eternal secrets which were (preserved) in heaven, which men were striving to learn: And Semjâzâ, to whom Thou hast given authority to bear rule over his associates. And they have gone to the daughters of men upon the earth, and have slept with the women, and have defiled themselves, and revealed to them all kinds of sins. And the women have borne giants, and the whole earth has thereby been filled with blood and unrighteousness. And now, behold, the souls of those who have died are crying and making their suit to the gates of heaven, and their lamentations have ascended: and cannot cease because of the lawless deeds which are wrought on the earth"* (emphasis added).

—Enoch 9:1–11

It is abundantly clear in the archaeological record that the goal of this Second Insurrection was to corrupt the Messianic lineage to prevent the birth of the Messiah. By the time of Noah, this goal was almost complete. But God delivered Noah from certain death by destroying the First Earth. It was this act that saved the lineage of the Messiah.

It should not surprise us that Satan's goal has ever been to prevent the Seed of Eve from fulfilling the prophecy given by the voice of God in Genesis 3:15. Time and time again throughout history, this plan has been executed in various forms.

Most of us are familiar with Hitler's genocide campaign to eradicate every Jew from the planet. Some may even be aware of the same Islamic ideology that shall in the future attempt the very same thing yet once more. But few know how many times this has already happened in our history. It began in the First Earth with the birthing of the Nephilim race of men.

It continued in our Second Earth. When the occult astrologers of the Egyptian Pharaoh Thutmose III informed him that the constellations depicted a propitious sign indicating that a Messiah could be born from the Hebrew people, he was moved by Satan to kill every male child born during that time (Exod. 1:15–22).

And when all of Israel was trapped against the Red Sea, the Pharaoh Amenhotep, the son of Thutmose III, had determined in his heart to destroy the whole nation through which the Messiah was prophesied to come.

> *But Moses said to the people, "Do not fear! Stand by and see the salvation of the Lord which He will accomplish for you today; for the Egyptians whom you have seen today, you will never see them again forever. The Lord will fight for you while you keep silent."*
>
> —Exod. 14:13–14

It was not the efforts of the Hebrew nation that defeated the Egyptian Pharaoh and delivered them from certain destruction. In fact, they were commanded to stand by and be quiet. God's grace delivered them and brought salvation to the Hebrew people. He alone can accomplish our salvation.

Afterward, when the lineage was promised through David, several times did Satan conspire to eradicate His descendants through the Assyrians and the Philistines (1 Chron. 21:4, 22:10). When all Israel and Judah turned from God and turned to worship the religion of the Mother Goddess Ashtoreth, God brought Nebuchadnezzar to bring judgment upon their wickedness.

But as in Noah's day, God reserved a remnant that was led captive to Babylon, and the Temple of Solomon was destroyed on the ninth of the Hebrew month of Av. After the Medes and the Persians conquered Babylon, the capital of the Empire was moved to Susa. At that time, Satan, through a man named Haman, once again inspired another attempt to kill every last Hebrew.

> *When Haman saw that Mordecai neither bowed down nor paid homage to him, Haman was filled with rage. But he disdained to lay hands on Mordecai alone, for they had told him who the people of Mordecai were; therefore Haman sought to destroy all the Jews, the people of Mordecai, who were through the whole kingdom of Ahasuerus.*
>
> —Esther 3:5–6

And through God's providence and the faithfulness of the Jewess Esther, the gallows that were meant to claim the lives of Jews became the place of Haman's death (Esther 7:10). But this setback did not stop Satan from attempting it yet again. When king Cyrus of Persia commissioned Ezra and Nehemiah to rebuild the Temple of God, Satan sent adversaries to stop them since the Messiah is prophesied to rule from the Temple in Jerusalem. But God intervened, and Darius king of Persia overruled the previous order to desist from building (Ezra 6). The second Temple of God was rebuilt. In fact, Darius forced those who were trying to stop them to contribute financially to Israel.

And when the magi from Susa came to Jerusalem looking for the Messiah who was to be born, according to the constellations in the sky, they came to King Herod requesting His whereabouts.

> *Now after Jesus was born in Bethlehem of Judea in the days of Herod the king, magi from the east arrived in Jerusalem, saying, "Where is He who has been born King of the Jews? For we saw His star in the east and have come to worship Him."*
>
> —Matt. 2:1–2

Once more Satan conspired to stop the birthing of the Seed of Eve. Having been warned by angels from God, the magi never revealed the location where Joseph, Mary, and Jesus were. When Herod discovered that his plot to identify and kill the Messiah had not worked, he "became very enraged, and sent and slew all the male children who were in Bethlehem and in all its vicinity, from two years old and under" (Matt. 2:16).

And when the ruling class of Israel and the priests of the Second Temple rejected the Messiah, the Temple was once again destroyed on the ninth day of the Hebrew month of Av, the very same date the Temple of Solomon was destroyed for their unfaithfulness so all of Israel would know that it was an act of God. That day Rome also sought to kill every Jew but failed. Today, Iran includes in their constitution that their purpose is to kill every Jew and take over Jerusalem in order to facilitate the coming of their coming Mahdi. Islam teaches that the Mahdi will rule the entire world from Jerusalem.

Satan failed then, and he will fail again in the future when he sends the Antichrist, who I suspect is the Mahdi, into Jerusalem to enter into the Holy of Holies in the third Temple of God to declare himself the god of this world. He will try to annihilate all of Israel and kill every Jew. But God will provide a Chukka in the wilderness to protect them supernaturally underneath the eagle's wings for three and a half years (Rev. 12:1–15).

Then Christ and His angels will wage war with the Antichrist and his demons in the Battle of Armageddon. In that day, the Day of Judgment, the Day of the Lord, judgment shall come upon the Gentile nations, Christ shall rule the world from Jerusalem, and the Jews shall be His priests (Rev. 17:14).

In like manner, the demonic plan instituted in the First Earth by the Second Insurrection to foil the Prophecy of the Dragon Doom failed. The lineage of the Messiah was saved and carried by the womb of the ark of God into the Second Earth. Enoch tells us that the Archangel Raphael, along with the host of angels of the Lord, captured those 200 demons who participated in the birthing of the Nephilim.

In that day, they were unceremoniously cast into the darkness of Tartarus (Sheol) to await the Day of Judgment, the Day of the Lord, when the Messiah returns to claim His throne. In that day, those who participated in the Second Insurrection shall be cast into the Lake of Fire along with the Antichrist and his False Prophet at the end of the Second Earth. They will be the first to be cast into Gehenna, the Lake of Fire.

> *And the beast was seized, and with him the false prophet who performed the signs in his presence, by which he deceived those who had received the mark of the beast and those who worshiped his image; these two were thrown alive into the* lake of fire *which burns with brimstone.*
>
> —Rev. 19:20

Also in that day, Lucifer shall be cast into Tartarus to await his final judgment in front of the Great White Throne of God at the end of the Third Earth, which is the Davidic Kingdom that will reign for 1,000 years.

> *Then I saw an angel coming down from heaven, holding the key of the abyss and a great chain in his hand. 2 And he laid hold of the dragon, the serpent of old, who is the devil and Satan, and bound him for a thousand years; 3 and he threw him into the abyss, and shut it and sealed it over him, so that he would not deceive the nations any longer, until the thousand years were completed; after these things he must be released for a short time.*
>
> —Rev. 20:1-3

At the end of those thousand years, even with the Messiah ruling from Jerusalem with justice and righteousness, mankind will rebel one last time. Satan shall be loosed and lead a rebellion that will end the universe as we know it.

> *When the thousand years are completed, Satan will be released from his prison, and will come out to deceive the nations which are in the four corners of the earth, Gog and Magog, to gather them together for the war; the number of them is like the sand of the seashore. And they came up on the broad plain of the earth and surrounded the camp of the saints and the beloved city, and fire came down from heaven and devoured them. And the devil who deceived them was thrown into the lake of fire and brimstone, where the beast and the false prophet are also; and they will be tormented day and night forever and ever.*
> —Rev. 20:7–10

It is at the end of the Davidic Kingdom that God will make a new heaven and a new Earth, and all the wicked shall be thrown into the Lake of Fire. That will be the death of the Third Earth and the birth of the Fourth Earth, which shall be eternal. That will be the Omega Point when the children of God shall forever live with God, dwelling with Him in the Fourth Earth and the Second Heaven. In that day, sin will be remembered no more, and the curse shall be broken.

> *Then I saw a great white throne and Him who sat upon it, from whose presence earth and heaven fled away, and no place was found for them. And I saw the dead, the great and the small, standing before the throne, and books were opened; and another book was opened, which is the book of life; and the dead were judged from the*

> things which were written in the [books, according to their deeds. And the sea gave up the dead which were in it, and death and Hades gave up the dead which were in them; and they were judged, every one of them *according to their deeds. Then death and Hades were thrown into the lake of fire. This is the second death, the lake of fire. And if [anyone's name was not found written in the book of life, he was thrown into the lake of fire* (emphasis added).
>
> —Rev. 20:11–15

In that day Satan shall be judged and also thrown into the Lake of Fire. But prior to that, at the end of the Second Earth when the Messiah comes as the conquering Lion to battle the Antichrist, Israel shall once again stand by and watch the salvation of the Lord. The Lord will fight for us as we keep silent. The Lion of Judah shall roar, the mountains shall crumble to the ground, and every city shall be made into rubble. Our Second Earth shall die as the First Earth, though not by water but by fire and earthquakes, and the Third Earth shall resurrect from the ashes of the death of the Second Earth.

Close to 4,000 years after the death of the First Earth, the Apostle Peter wrote of that day when God imprisoned the rebellious angels of the First Earth. Writing from his prison, awaiting his execution, he warned us that the very things that brought our First Earth to destruction shall once again visit us at the end of the Second Earth.

> *But false prophets also arose among the people, just as there will also be false teachers among you, who will secretly introduce destructive heresies, even denying the Master who bought them, bringing swift destruction upon themselves. Many will follow their sensuality, and because*

of them the way of the truth will be maligned; and in their greed they will exploit you with false words; their judgment from long ago is not idle, and their destruction is not asleep.

For if God did not spare angels when they sinned, but cast them into hell [Hades – Tartarus] and committed them to pits of darkness, reserved for judgment; and did not spare the ancient world, but preserved Noah, a preacher of righteousness, with seven others, when He brought a flood upon the world of the ungodly.

—2 Pet. 2:1–5

The Intervention

The Lord sat as King at the flood;
Yes, the Lord sits as King forever.

—Ps. 29:10

God intervened and ordered Noah to build a very specifically designed ark of gopher wood and cover it with pitch. And at the appointed time, God brought forth the physical circumstances that created the Global Flood that ended the violence and the profane cannibalistic religion of the Nephilim. All the genetically profaned beings engendered by the Enemy of Man to destroy the seed of Eve were wiped from the face of the Earth. The cold-blooded, cold-hearted reptilian revolution was undone. But God's chosen were carried into the womb of the ark to bring forth the birth of the Second Earth.

God has always preserved a remnant of true believers and shall always preserve a remnant of true believers in the future until we reach the Omega Point.

Diagram 15 – The Continental Drift Theory

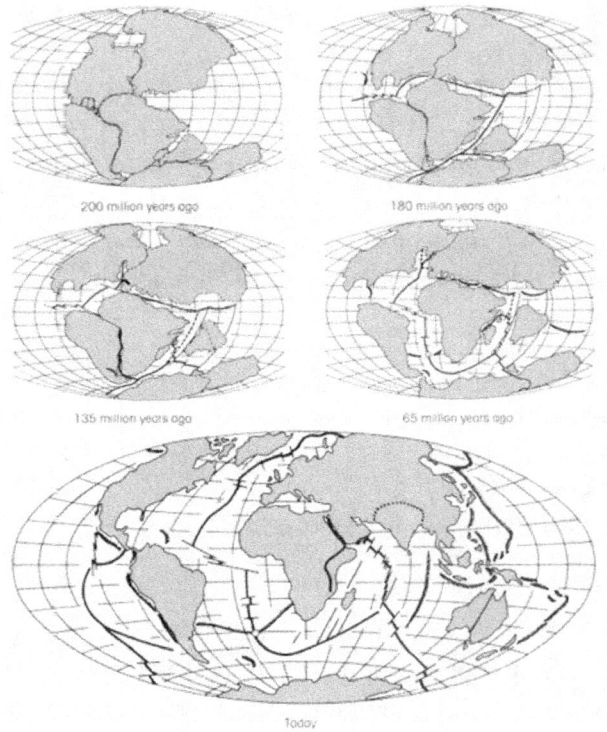

CHAPTER 2

THE PHYSICAL MECHANISMS THAT CAUSED THE GREAT FLOOD

You divided the sea by Your strength.

—Ps. 74:14

Scientists in the 20th century have come to understand that our ancient Earth once had a single supercontinent and a single, enormous ocean. The Scriptures have attested that for several millennia.

Scripture consistently refers to the "four corners of the land" or the "four corners of the earth" as encompassing the entire habitat for humanity.

And He will lift up a standard for the nations
And assemble the banished ones of Israel,
And will gather the dispersed of Judah
From the four corners of the earth (emphasis added).

—Isa. 11:12

> *"And you, son of man" thus says the Lord GOD to the land of Israel.*
> *"An end! The end is coming to the four corners of the land"* (emphasis added).
>
> —Ezek. 7:2

The psalms of David 1,000 years before Christ told us that God had divided the seas. Critics had in the past used such verses to ridicule the Scriptures. They are, in fact, poetic ways to speak of the whole of mankind, but they are rooted in the ancient memory that at one time during the First Earth our land was one—our ocean was one, our people were one, our language was one. And then the Earth was divided.

Space Rocks and the Continental Drift Theory

Argument 4 – No natural phenomenon can cause a Global Flood

It was in 1915 that German astronomer, geophysicist, and meteorologist Alfred Wagner proposed the now famous continental drift theory that confirms the oceans on our present planet were once united and the continents were once united in a single landmass.

Most modern geologists now accept that the Earth has a hardened crust on its surface that was broken into seven major pieces. Some have further subdivided these seven pieces and concluded that there are 12. Others have subdivided them into as many as 20. Nevertheless, there are seven continents that have historically been accepted throughout the history of mankind.

Geologists refer to these pieces of the crust as continental blocks or tectonic plates. These plates are floating on a sea of molten rock (mantle) called magma underneath the crust of the Earth. They believe this magma surrounds a central core of molten nickel and iron that, among other things, may be responsible for our magnetic umbrella (the magnetosphere) that protects us from the harmful radiation of the Sun. At the very center is the inner core, which is believed to be solid nickel and iron.

Evolutionists believe that tectonic forces slowly working over millions of years have separated our continents from this singular, primordial landmass. They believe, however, that the pieces were never unified in a solid crust. Instead, they believe the cracks have always been there and movement has always been going on at a snail's pace, sometimes crushing them together and other times pulling them apart.

There is no real scientific reason to support this oscillating scenario other than it is convenient for their long, evolutionary ages required in order for evolution to be plausible. A more logical analysis, which takes into consideration the fact that soil and rock samples across the boundaries of the plates where they were once joined were identical matches, should conclude that they were once really united in a solid, singular plate. Something very powerful and catastrophic had to have struck the planet with such force that it broke the singular landmass into seven pieces.

The tectonic plate theory stipulates that cracks between these plates form fault lines that are prone to slippage. As pressure is exerted between two grinding plates, the tension grows until it overcomes the friction, which binds them together. Every time there is a major shift between plates, we recognize the movement as an earthquake.

When earthquakes occur underwater between the plates, the rising plates can displace large amounts of water, causing a tidal wave that travels in every direction from the epicenter. When the wave approaches land, the sea floor rises and with it the wave, which upon striking the shore causes enormous damage. These are the feared killers known as tsunamis.

The upward shift of the Ninety East Ridge in the Indian Ocean was responsible for the devastating tsunami that killed more than 270,000 people in Sri Lanka and Indonesia on December 25, 2005. There are, however, other means of creating tsunamis such as large landslides into the ocean. The same feature from an underwater earthquake measuring 9.1 on the Richter scale brought a killer tsunami in 2011 to Japan's northeastern coast that destroyed three nuclear reactors and caused more damage than any other natural disaster in Japanese history.

Sometimes the magma pushes its way up to the surface through these cracks and spews into our atmosphere as a volcanic eruption. According to the tectonic plate theory, this release of magma in fault lines of the Mid-Atlantic Ridge under the ocean floor creates lateral stresses on these plates as magma rises, immediately cools, and solidifies as rock.

The solidified magma then exerts pressure on the plates, laterally pushing away from its source and consequently pushing that plate toward the opposite plate on its distal end. This lateral pressure on the plates causes it to crumble or wrinkle, creating overthrusts and upward movement that we recognize as mountains.

It is very difficult for me to imagine how soft, pliable magma could exert enough pressure to push an entire continent sideways. In addition to this mechanism, scientists also theorize that the rivers of molten lava below the continental plates exert frictional forces upon them as they float above. I have great difficulty believing that a current of magma could push a granitic continent some 10 to 16 miles in depth and thousands of miles wide with any great force.

Nevertheless, according to the plate tectonic theory, this horizontal pressure increases until the distal pressure generated on the plate becomes enormous and the moving plates slip under the opposite plate, causing what geologists call subduction. There is one glaring problem with this theory. The North American plate has no subduction in the distal end, and neither does the Asiatic plate.

Some of these tectonic plates are actually moving parallel to one another but in opposing directions. That means the swirling currents of lava below them would also be moving in two opposite directions next to one another. I have a hard time imagining how this could occur in a fluid environment without both forces cancelling each other through friction. I can picture ocean currents doing this when there is an energy gradient difference in the temperature of the water, but the currents would then be traveling at different depths and controlled by solid objects such as mountains and islands that channel their flow. In a completely viscous habitat, what could cause the swirling currents to travel at the same height in two opposite ways and remain so for long periods of time?

These magma currents could not affect the landmass above them if they were not in contact with the crust; hence, they could not be flowing at different levels. Furthermore, if there is an energy gradient difference between the two currents of magma, it would argue for a very young Earth. It would be inconceivable that an Earth 4 to 5 billion years old would not have reached homeostasis.

At any rate, what we can agree upon is that when the pressure between the two plates builds to a certain point, it exceeds the force of friction that holds them together, and slippage occurs along these fault lines. The slippage releases some of the energy stored up, and the terrifying result is what we call an earthquake, an event I unhappily witnessed in February 2001 when an earthquake measuring 6.8 on the Richter scale struck Seattle, Washington.

It was quite impressive to ride out one of these gigantic tremors on the 35th floor of a hotel while my wife and I held on for dear life. My wife is a flight attendant and was scheduled to work on our anniversary. I decided that if she had to work, I would go with her, and we could at least be together for our anniversary. After arriving in Seattle, we were pleased to see that the weather was sunny and cool. Wasting no time, we immediately set out to go sightseeing and then have a nice dinner at the wharf. We explored the famous fish market there and had a delightful time visiting the beautiful city.

The next morning we were preparing to meet the limousine that would take us to the airport. My wife was still applying her makeup while I was waiting and gazing out the floor-to-ceiling window that overlooked the picturesque bay. All of a sudden, the windows began to creak, and a deep, guttural roar came up from below. Carmen turned and looked at me with a wild look in her eyes. "What was that?" she asked. As I looked out the window, I saw tall buildings undulating like writhing snakes, and our building began to sway back and forth wildly. "Oh! It's just an earthquake," I responded as calmly as I could.

The TV flew off the dresser and crashed to the floor. Carmen was screaming at the top of her voice. The bed and all the other furniture in the room began to roll back and forth from one side of the room to the other. The toilet water splashed up onto the bathroom ceiling, and I pushed my wife into a corner of two load-bearing walls. On the 35th floor, it seemed as though our building was swaying a good 10 to 12 feet from one side to the other.

Although the tremor lasted less than one minute, it seemed like an eternity. At any moment I expected the building to begin to collapse, but it did not. When the earthquake subsided, I grabbed my wife and took off out of our room like a bat out of hell.

When we arrived at street level, the sounds of car alarms filled the air. Bricks and other falling debris had damaged almost all the cars parked on the street. Glass from broken windows above and from the cars littered the streets. People who had evacuated the buildings crowded into the middle of the streets, stepping on the crunching glass. Most of them were smoking nervously in a state of adrenaline overdose. The shocked survivors were jabbering a million miles per hour, each retelling their horrible two minutes.

Our limo driver, pale-faced and wide-eyed, puffed furiously on a cigarette. The middle-aged gentleman told me that the tremors hit when he was only a block away from our hotel. As the old guy told his story, he puffed on his cigarette as if it were Valium. "I was driving calmly," he said, "when a brick fell on the hood of my car. At first I thought some idiot had thrown a brick from one of the buildings. I stuck my head out the window and looked up, but then I saw the street in front of me rise like a wave. I could not believe my eyes. The street was undulating, and I was riding wave after wave in my limo like a bucking bronco. I did not know that waves could bend stone and concrete like water."

On the way to the airport, we saw several highway overpasses that had collapsed, and traffic was snarled everywhere. Arriving at the airport, we found a mass of people stranded, standing in endless lines by the security desks. The airport was closed; it had lost electricity so all the computers were down. Wires and tiles from the ceiling were hanging down, and nobody knew what to expect next.

We walked through the grumbling masses of stranded travelers to the operations headquarters for my wife's airline, and there we waited to see what would happen. I struck up a conversation with one of the employees who happened to be an air traffic controller. He said he was in the tower when the earthquake hit. The tower's thick glass window "shattered into a million pieces like a grenade had hit it," he said. The ceiling began to fall down on them, and the tower swayed back and forth violently. Everyone took off down the stairs, afraid that at any moment the tower would collapse. The supervisor valiantly stayed behind and proceeded to announce to the airplane pilots in the air to "please circle around because we are presently experiencing an earthquake." I doubted seriously that I could have responded with such calmness.

Needless to say, the airport did not open until the next day. That meant we had to spend another night in Seattle, a prospect my wife and the rest of her crew did not appreciate. So we set out to find a two-story hotel that was low to the ground and also near the airport. We got a room on the ground floor with an immediate door to the outside. Fortunately, there were no appreciable aftequakes.

As terrifying as this experience was, it is nothing compared to the devastating earthquakes that have killed hundreds of thousands of people many times over. As I looked at the stars that night, I pondered how different the First Earth was.

The reality of the Fall is embedded in the very fabric of our universe and evidenced by the second law of thermodynamics all around us. Death entered our universe, and it has been slowly dying ever since. Stars and galaxies are dying. Galaxies are turning into black holes.

Our planet is also dying. In each epoch we traverse, the Earth is less the ideal planet that it was meant to be. It has been fractured, and the consequences of this catastrophic event have ramifications that continue to plague us even today. The oceans, our atmosphere, and our rivers and lakes are all dying as time goes by. The ideal paradise of the world that was is invariably becoming more and more hostile to life. Unfortunately, mankind has been the chief antagonist in this ongoing drama that began in the Garden at Eden. It makes perfect sense to me that our world began with a solid crust underneath our singular supercontinent Arza.

Although originally scientists derided Wagner's theory, with the advent of modern computers and satellite technology, we have been able to compute the present movement of the continents, thus verifying his theory.

Today, computers have neatly pieced together the continents into a single mass with matching soil and sedimentary deposits of the corresponding continents, which convincingly proves the major points of the theory to be factual. As we shall see later, this fit of the continents is even better explained through the hydroplate theory. Through global positioning satellites, we see that the American continent is presently moving away from Europe and Africa at a variable rate of 1 to 6 inches per year.

Evolutionary scientists, of course, tell us that this movement has been slow and gradual, evolving over hundreds of thousands and even millions of years because they need long periods of time in order for their evolutionary process to be plausible. Creationists have long insisted that the continents were formed from a singular landmass, but they believe the timetable and mechanism that caused their shifting are completely different from what evolutionists believe.

According to the plate tectonic theory, the currents of the magma below the plates are responsible for the shifting of the tectonic plates. That is, the flow or currents of the magma beneath the plates is suspected of being the force that causes the floating plates to move in different directions.

The movement of these plates is then considered by them to be slow, perhaps similar to the rate at which our fingernails grow. But that is not the only explanation for how our continents arrived at their present position. The hydroplate theory provides a viable mechanism for these continental plates to have moved great distances in a rather short amount of time, as we shall see.

Although the Bible is not a science textbook, it is a book of truth. Therefore, we believe that when it divulges historical information, it is possible for us to scientifically support the historicity of its narrative. To this end, Walt Brown's hydroplate theory provides solid scientific understanding for the fracturing of the singular landmass and at the same time corroborates the historicity of the biblical narrative in that regard. But it does so through a completely different mechanism than the plate tectonic theory. Moreover, it provides for a completely different timeline.

This hydroplate mechanism, which is responsible for the formation of our present continents, is completely consistent with the biblical account of the Great Flood. Most creationists are convinced that the very mechanism that created the Great Flood is the one responsible for splitting the surface of the crust of the Earth. Well-respected creationist scientists have for years proposed that the mechanism needed to trigger this process could have been a giant meteor strike.

The idea of a catastrophic event of this magnitude, of course, was previously flatly rejected by uniformitarian-minded evolutionists since the geological mechanisms of their preference by necessity required long periods of time in order to give the theory of evolution a chance to be plausible.

However, the near miss of a meteor in the latter part of our last century has become the catalyst that is awakening evolutionists to the reality of cataclysmic events that create major changes in short periods of time. They, of course, continue to insist that this movement of the tectonic plates has always been very slow and gradual, taking millions and even billions of years to reach its present state.

Our Judeo-Christian model, on the other hand, believes that the initial impact of seven meteor strikes is the most plausible mechanism that could have cracked the crust of the Earth and triggered a series of geologic events that eventually led to the Global Flood. You may ask, "Why seven meteors?" Your question will be answered with empirical data, but for the moment, let us focus on the nature of the kind of impact that that kind of force would have upon our First Earth. Let us first examine what the Scriptures declare.

The Catastrophic Impacts – The First Horn of Taurus

> *In the six hundredth year of Noah's life, in the second month, on the seventeenth day of the month, on the same day* all the fountains of the great deep burst open, *and the floodgates of the sky were opened. The rain fell upon the earth for forty days and forty nights.*
>
> *On the very same day Noah and Shem and Ham and Japheth, the sons of Noah and Noah's wife and the three wives of his sons with them, entered the ark* (emphasis added).
>
> —Gen, 7:11–13

The first horn of Taurus was the opening of the fountains of the deep. "All the fountains of the deep burst open," says the Genesis account in the New American Standard version of the Bible. The King James version says, "the same day were all the fountains of the great deep broken up." The Hebrew word translated *broken* is *baqa*. It comes from a primitive word that means "to cleave." It means "to rend, break, rip open, to make a breach, to burst, to divide, to hatch (as a chick hatches from an egg), to tear." No clearer description than the process of the crust ripping open and uncorking the underground aquifers could be found. Each one of these meanings corresponds to a literal rendition of the process that actually occurred.

Notice that it is not one fountain but all the fountains ("all the fountains of the great deep burst open"). In other words, they were *ripped open* as the crust of the Earth was *cleaved*. The *rending* crust created the mid-oceanic ridges and allowed the waters of the subterranean aquifers to *hatch*. These *burst* with great intensity into the stratosphere.

Make no mistake; these were no gentle flowing fountains as those we are accustomed to seeing in public parks and town squares. They were literally geysers on steroids that reached up into the stratosphere and came back down as waterfalls of epic proportions that were thousands of miles long, twisting around the entire planet along the cracks that formed the seven continents.

Have you ever experienced the power of pressurized water? Every year I have to clean my tile roof due to the mold that builds up after the rainy season in Florida. I use a pressure cleaner, and if I carelessly hit my toe, it will literally blow the skin off. When I was a firefighter, I rode on a ladder truck with a 100-foot reach. At the top in the bucket was a nozzle that could put out a stream of 1,000 gallons of water per minute. Each morning we took inventory of all the supplies on the truck, and I set out the outriggers and tested them. The power of the water canon bent the ladder backward and reached from our Station 3 across Collins Street into the middle of the Intercontinental Waterway. It was, indeed, a powerful force.

Imagine a jet of water filled with rock and debris, an abrasive traveling at supersonic speeds. Now imagine that powerful geyser like a wall of water as far as the eye can see from horizon to horizon.

It stretched like a serpent all the way around the Earth, following the contours of the broken continents. That was the secondary result of the multiple meteor strikes.

The primary result was the immediate explosion of the seven enormous impact zones. It must have seemed to them that all hell had broken loose when this rapid-fire series of meteors struck, sending millions of tons of dust into the stratosphere as giant mushroom clouds and initiating volcanic eruptions of an enormous magnitude throughout the entire planet. When that wall of water rose into the heavens as far as the eye could see from horizon to horizon, the wrath of God was made clear to all who lived in that day. The inhumanities and terrorism perpetrated against the innocent brought forth God's just recompense for their unbridled violence.

The end of the First Earth would have been announced by the loudest sounds ever in the history of our planet. Each of these giant rock missiles would have created an enormous boom as they entered our atmosphere and an even louder boom when they struck the surface of the planet. Because of their great speed, the sounds would have seemed almost simultaneous for the seven meteors. The third boom would have come from the explosion of the water from the underground chambers at supersonic speeds. Those three loud booms that were heard around the world like three trumpets of God signaled that destruction was coming upon the First Earth.

But the roar of the third boom did not quickly end. The continuous roar of the jetting fountains would have been millions of times louder than the roar of Niagara Falls and the Iguazu Falls together as the ripping crust circled the entire Earth. All mankind heard the roar of God's judgment upon the terrorists who ruled our planet with unrelenting violence.

The Floodgates of the Heavens – The Second Horn of Taurus

Seas of lava covered the landscape at the opposite point of impact on the far side of Earth. Huge super-volcanoes as well as normal volcanoes triggered by this seismic wave would have blown millions of tons of tephra into the atmosphere. The sky darkened, and the fine dust, injected into the water vapor canopy, became the cloud nuclei that collected the water vapor in the sky and caused it to precipitate. Tons of poisonous gases and acid rain began to assault our planet.

In addition, the curtain of water released from the underground chambers would have escaped at supersonic speeds, thrusting enormous chunks of rock and eroding debris as it shot upward. Some of them would have reentered the atmosphere like falling meteors, adding to the heat and destruction below. Our atmosphere was under direct assault as temperatures around the falling ejecta skyrocketed. The Prince of the Power of the Air was powerless to do anything about it. Judgment had come.

The jetting curtain of water and the tephra that shot into the stratosphere would have quickly destabilized the protective, thin, water vapor canopy, destroying the delicate meteorological balance the Earth had previously enjoyed. The blanket that provided protection and created a uniform climate was literally ripped away.

The once stable water vapor canopy that had encircled our Earth and protected it from cosmic radiation now began to precipitate as black rain. The ocean and the atmosphere began to dramatically rise in temperature as the skies darkened to pitch black. At first the dark clouds acted like a blanket, trapping the heat inside our atmosphere.

This in turn must have produced enormous hurricane-force storms beyond Category 5 that pelted the entire planet with black rain and winds of unimaginable destructive power. For the space of 40 days and 40 nights, our First Earth was buffeted by multiple super-hurricanes that brought enormous destruction along their path. Here and there as lightning ripped through the sky, a brief snapshot of the cataclysm could be seen by those who may have managed to survive thus far.

The jetting curtain of water thrusting upward from the underground chambers along the rips in the crust would have produced high, violent winds. Functioning like a giant Venturi pump, the winds would have been sucked upward into the stratosphere and super-cooled in space. The super-cooled air becoming denser would have then dropped back down to Earth, forming zones of impact on the surface of our planet where super-cold air flash froze everything it hit.

Huge hailstones would have buffeted everything within the area of their influence. That would have taken place all along the jetting curtain of water. Today, those flash-frozen animals preserved by the polar ice caps remain as silent testimony of the awesome power of the fountains of the deep.

Millions of tons of dust and gravel would have eroded from the sides of the continents as the jetting water thrust them into the stratosphere. Fine water droplets would have saturated the entire atmosphere, adding more fuel to the torrential rains and hurricanes. Some of the droplets entering the stratosphere with dust particles would have frozen at these high altitudes and blanketed our planet as dirty hail. Missiles of stone and ice fell from the sky and pummeled our planet.

But God was still in control. Were it not for this cooling effect from the fountains of the deep, the quickly heated atmosphere created by the energy of the seven meteor impacts, the falling ejecta, and the massive volcanic upheaval would have completely cooked all life on Earth. There would have been no survivors. Our Earth would have been a sterile cinder rotating in empty space. God's judgment was measured and mixed with grace.

The downward movement of the continuous flow of torrential hail also generated downdrafts, bringing the super-cold air from the upper atmosphere toward the surface of the planet. That also helped create dramatic and sudden changes in the surface temperatures in those areas impacted within a matter of a few short hours.

Walter Brown has convincingly pointed out that this is the only mechanism that adequately explains the quickly frozen animals that have been found with fresh food in their mouths, stomachs, and digestive tracks, not yet broken down by the stomach's acids and by the natural process of decomposition after death.

If these giant animals had fallen in a frozen lake or river as some evolutionists have conjectured, the internal heat of their massive bodies would have been enough to decompose the material in their stomachs, even if they were frozen on the outside. At normal body temperatures, the acids and enzymes found in the stomach can break down the vegetation within an hour of ingesting it. The stomach would have had to cool to a temperature of about 40 degrees Fahrenheit within a period of about 10 hours in order to stop this process. Since the huge body of the mammoth insulates the stomach, the sudden drop in temperature must have been extreme to accomplish this feat.

If we estimate that the mammoth's body temperature is comparable to that of modern elephants (96.6 degrees Fahrenheit), then the outer layers of the skin would have to be in contact with air at least -175 degrees Fahrenheit. The temperature difference needed to freeze them internally would have been much greater than the climate of that area could possibly have produced during that time. How else can you explain a drop in temperature to -175 degrees Fahrenheit that flash-freezes thousands of mammoths as they are eating fresh grass and flowers in an obviously warm savannah?

The evidence found in the stomach contents of these creatures categorically proves that this area was temperate. How then can evolutionists explain the flash-freezing of an enormous mammoth in a climate where flowers were blooming? How do you go from flowers to -175 degrees Fahrenheit in a few hours? The evolutionary mirage of mammoths trudging through deep snowdrifts is without any scientific basis. These giant herbivores could not have survived tundra conditions any more than modern elephants could. But the cooling was just beginning.

From the shock of the initial suffocating rise in heat, the Earth now plunged into unimaginable cold as it had never experienced before. Once the water vapor canopy was depleted, heat readily dissipated into space. Once the fountains of the deep subsided, the torrential storms eventually stopped. But the plumes of tephra continued to plague our atmosphere for some time. The skies remained relatively darkened.

As the darkened skies blocked the sunlight, the temperature on the surface of the Earth plummeted as much as 115 degrees Fahrenheit in some places. To get an idea of the massive scale of such an event, consider what modern scientists think happened with the eruption of just one supervolcano.

Michael Rampino, a biologist and geologist at New York University, has suggested that the tephra of the Toba supervolcano alone could have reduced the overall global temperatures by 21 degrees Fahrenheit. In fact, he concedes that our human lineage was reduced to just a few thousand human beings as a result of such a catastrophe. He is at least getting closer to the truth. A few decades ago such a catastrophic scenario would have been utterly ridiculed by the entrenched dogma of uniformitarian evolutionists.

The Ancient Chronicles

The turbulent floodwater would have initially encased all living things in wholesale sheet-flooding events continental in width. Massively wide rivers of mud would have dragged trees, boulders, animals, and all objects in its path into runoffs until the waters covered the entire surface of our planet.

The Babylonians describe the Global Flood in similar terms. In the following verses of Tablet XI of *The Epic of Gilgamesh*, it is clear that the land was broken like a pot and became completely darkened. All men were covered with clay. The whole world was embroiled in mud. The raging fountains reached to heaven. The flowing geysers reached the stratosphere.

> The raging of Adad reached unto heaven
> *And turned into darkness all that was light*
> *The land he broke like a pot*

no man could see his fellow
the people could not be recognized from heaven
In truth, the older time has turned to clay
and all mankind had turned to clay (emphasis added)
(*Gilgamesh* Tablet XI, lines 105–107, 111–112, 118, 133).

It is this clay that has encased for us the many fossils that give us a glimpse of the wide variety of living things that once roamed our First Earth. In every part of our planet, we can find branded in the memory of its human survivors the same telltale signs of this cataclysmic event that ended our First Earth. The common elements found in all the cultural chronicles around the entire planet are proof that these are realistic depictions of such a catastrophic force and show that there is a historical spacetime event behind all these accounts.

The Greek historian Hesiod, considered by many evolutionists to be the father of history, wrote of this cataclysm in terms that completely concur with the hydroplate theory. The fountains of the deep were, in fact, streams of ocean in the abyss of Earth. The planet groaned with earthquakes. The sonic booms of the striking space rocks and the refalling ejecta must have made a cacophony of terrible sound that seemed to reecho around the Earth. The megastorms thrashing out with rapid, furious lightning and howling hot winds filled with projectile debris pelted our planet. Red-hot magma rose from the ground, swallowing all things in its path like a gulping monster from the deep.

Once the surface of the planet was completely inundated and the fountains had slowed somewhat from their initial ferocity, the ejecting waters of the subterranean chambers that were filled with sediment would have caused the once pristine clear sea to seem as though it were boiling and dark in color. We can still see the remnants of these geysers in the dark smokers ejecting super-hot, mineral-rich salt water in the Mid-Atlantic Ridge. Listen to the story remembered by the ancient Greeks.

> *Harshly then he thundered, and heavily and terribly the earth re-echoed around; and the broad heaven above, and the sea and streams of ocean, and the abysses of earth.* But beneath his immortal feet vast Olympus trembled, as the king uprose and *earth groaned beneath. And the heat from both caught the dark-colored sea, both of the thunder and the lightning, and fire from the monster. The heat arising from the thunder-storms, winds, and burning lightning. And all earth, and heaven, and sea, were boiling* (emphasis added) (Hesiod).

This was no gentle rise in sea levels as we experience today. Are you not yet convinced? Do you need more examples? The Sumerian account in a tablet found at Nippur speaks also of the fountains of the deep stopping at the end of the Global Flood. It is understood in this tablet that the source of the waters from the Great Flood was not rain but the fountains of the deep.

> Above [Adad made scarce his rain];
> Bel[ow] (the fountains) were stopped, [so that the flood did not rise at the source]. (*Gilgamesh Epic*, 112).

Still not convinced? Let us then travel to the New World and see what the Mayas thought of the reason for the Global Flood.

> And instantly the figures were made of wood. They looked like men, talked like men, and populated the surface of the earth.
>
> They existed and multiplied; they had daughters, they had sons, these wooden figures, but they did not have souls, nor minds, *they did not remember their Creator, their Maker* . . .
>
> *They no longer remembered the Heart of Heaven and therefore they fell out of favor* . . .

THE PHYSICAL MECHANISMS THAT CAUSED THE GREAT FLOOD

Therefore they no longer thought of their Creator nor their Maker . . . These were the first men who existed in great numbers on the face of the earth.

Immediately the wooden figures were annihilated, destroyed, broken up and killed.

A flood was brought about by the Heart of Heaven; a great flood was formed which fell on the heads of the wooden creatures . . .

But, those that they had made, that they had created, did not think, did not speak with their Creator, their Maker. And for this reason they were killed, they were deluged. *A heavy rain fell from the sky . . .*

This was to punish them because they had not thought of their mother, nor their father, the Heart of Heaven called Huracán. And for this reason the face of the earth was darkened, and a black rain began to fall, by day and by night (emphasis added) (*Popol Vuh*, 89).

Local floods by swollen rivers do not create black rain. That is the result of the ejecta plumes and the volcanic tephra instigated by the meteor strikes. The reference to the wooden men is no doubt a reference to the Nephilim sorcerers who began the religion of the Mother Goddesses and turned humanity to cannibalism and the blood oath of the demons. God judged mankind with a Global Flood. The ancients all declare the same story. It is the evolutionist who must ignore the archaeological evidence to maintain their uniformitarian dogma in spite of the historical and geological facts.

We shall deal with the historical evidence for the Global Flood more completely later on, but my purpose is to illustrate the catastrophic nature of the cataclysmic event that brought the demise of the First Earth and fractured our supercontinent Arza.

Most modern evolutionists simply dismiss all these historical records as mythological and relegate them to superstitious fables.

But when the records of all the ancient civilizations concur, rational people must conclude that it is our modern naturalist thinkers who are tinkering with fantasy. I have listed some of these ancient traditions in Chapter 10 for the reader to make their own conclusions.

Some creationists have suggested that the majority of the water that caused the Great Flood came from the water vapor canopy that surrounded our planet. But for the amount of water needed to cover the whole Earth, the water vapor canopy would have had to be immense.

That would have resulted in drastic atmospheric pressures at the surface of our planet, which would have been very limiting to life and also would have created a drastic rise in temperature that would have been incompatible with human life. I do not think the water vapor canopy could alone account for the majority of the floodwaters. The Scriptures clearly tell us that the water came from two primary sources: the fountains of the deep and the windows of heaven. As we shall see, the first added to the second. Now let us discuss where that water came from.

CHAPTER 3
THE UNEXPECTED SPACE VISITORS

Perhaps the most common argument against the biblical narrative concerning Noah's Flood is the claim that there are no known natural phenomena that could create a worldwide flood. Moreover, the uniformitarian bias against global catastrophes leans them toward scenarios of only local potentialities. But global catastrophes have occurred in our past, and they will again occur in our future.

We know for a fact that cosmic accidents in our past have caused catastrophic consequences by the force of their impacts on our Earth. The evidence for this has been staring us in the face for a very long time since we have gathered the scientific data of craters on our planet that were formed by such powerful impacts. But it seems like the uniformitarian blinders have kept eyes shut from the horrendous specter these craters represented.

Only recently has modern science become aware that a catastrophic total extinction potential really exists. Evolutionists have for the last several centuries ridiculed the scientific model of catastrophism since the advent of uniformitarianism and Darwinism. The biblical account of the Flood was simply swept into the dustbin and relegated to superstition. All geologic processes were declared dogmatically and unequivocally to be of a gradual and slow rate occurring over millions of years. The influence of Lyell's uniformitarian dogma during Darwin's time made deep inroads in the scientific community. But their bias has now been scientifically exposed and refuted by reality. Global catastrophes do take place and have taken place in our human history.

The fact is that our planet speeds around the Sun at about 70,000 miles per hour along a path that is not exclusive to the Earth. Other inhabitants of our solar system such as comets and asteroids cross our elliptical solar highway during their own orbits around the Sun. These asteroids traveling at speeds averaging 60,000 miles per hour and likewise comets traveling at speeds averaging 140,000 miles per hour cross the very same area of space that our planet inhabits. The immense energy released by any collisions from these extraterrestrial neighbors would be catastrophic to all living things on our planet.

It would seem that such collisions would have been obvious to scientists looking at our neighbor the Moon with a simple telescope. Its surface is scarred by such collisions. But due to the uniformitarian horse blinders, modern scientists had a glaring blind spot in their ability to see reality that would in any way smack of catastrophism and give credence to their much-despised biblical narrative.

Much to their chagrin, in 1989, two astronomers working for the Palomar Asteroid Comet Survey (PACS) discovered an asteroid about half a kilometer in width a few hours after it swept by Earth at a mere distance of only 600,000 kilometers. That is only one and a half the distance to the Moon. They didn't discover it until it had already passed us.

The nail in the coffin came in 1996 when an asteroid approximately one-third mile in width came so close to hitting our planet that for a while scientists were very worried. The asteroid, named 1996 JE1, shot past Earth, missing us by only 280,000 miles, which is about the same as the distance to the Moon.

An asteroid that large would have caused the near extinction of the human race. This near miss was the final wake-up call for modern-day scientists. Curiously, all of a sudden catastrophism became vogue. Evolutionists finally came to grips with the insurmountable evidence that there was a sudden and catastrophic end to an enormous number of animals and fauna by a catastrophic event of a global magnitude. Quite reluctantly, they finally consented to the obvious, which had been staring them in the face all along.

As they began to calculate the massive energy that would be released by these space rocks striking Earth at such incredible speeds, they were utterly amazed. Then they discovered that the giant Chicxulub crater in the Yucatan might have actually been a nearly total kill impact. So powerful was the release of energy that our Earth was almost completely sterilized by this one meteor.

Almost overnight, evolutionists credited the sudden disappearance of the dinosaurs to the Chicxulub asteroid strike. No slow, gradual, uniformitarian process brought the catastrophic end of the dinosaur age. It happened suddenly and dramatically in an immense flash of astronomical proportions.

Now, albeit grudgingly, they admit that the dust generated in the air by this strike could have blackened the Sun around the entire Earth for months or even years and would have therefore caused the extinction of a great variety of flora and fauna. Large animals dependent on huge amounts of vegetation would have naturally perished without the rich vegetation of the prediluvian world. This impact was utterly cataclysmic in nature.

But their self-imposed horse blinders have not yet been completely removed. Although the evidence for a worldwide flood is overwhelming, they have not been able to bring themselves to admit it due to the obvious biblical implications so abhorred by the naturalists. These naysayers and history deniers would rather believe in UFOs and an imaginary, parallel universe than concede that God exists and we are not morally autonomous beings.

Every year, some 18,000 meteorites hit the Earth. Most of them are so small that they burn up as they speed through the atmosphere. The relatively few that survive the entry into our atmosphere create craters of varying sizes. The threat of a large meteor strike such as the one that caused the Chicxulub crater in the Gulf of Mexico has now caused Hollywood to produce several movies that depict this possible, life-ending event.

There are presently more than 200 such space rocks that we know of that are sailing in trajectories so close to Earth's orbit that they are considered by scientists a very real threat to life on our planet. The truth is that most certainly there are many more we have not yet discovered.

Finally, in response to the obvious danger of a near-Earth asteroid (NEA) strike, the United States Congress asked NASA to examine the impact potential. The international effort known as Spaceguard was thus born.

> *The idea was to have a network of dedicated telescopes, which jointly could track over a hundred thousand main-belt asteroids per month, as well as rarer Earth-crossing comets,* way before what we can do with current technology (but no more than about a year or two before impact) . . . Under the original plan, Spaceguard could reduce to a couple of decades what would instead take centuries with current search tools. *In the meantime, an organization called Spaceguard Foundation, with headquarters in Rome Italy, was established by the international astronomical community to integrate observations and data analysis from observatories around the world. The goals set by Spaceguard are ambitious: to have 90 percent of all near-Earth asteroids (NEAs) larger than one kilometer, tracked by 2010.* This requires an eightfold increase over present rates.

THE UNEXPECTED SPACE VISITORS

> *As of August 2000, we know of about 1,050 NEAs of which 400 are large ones, that is, wider than 1 kilometer* (emphasis added) (Gleiser 2001, 104–105).

The tide has turned so much toward catastrophism that some scientists are now claiming that the Moon was actually accreted from the space debris created by the giant meteor strike that caused the extinction of the dinosaurs. Others claim it was another planet almost the size of Mars. The evidence, however, does not in my view clearly substantiate that conclusion. The nearly circular orbit of the Moon seems to contradict that theory. The probability of ejecta creating an elliptical orbit is infinitely greater than a perfectly circular orbit.

Nevertheless, the majority of the modern public is now becoming aware that there is grave danger looming in the skies. On February 15, 2013, at 19:25 Universal Time, an asteroid named 2012 DA14 streaked between us and the Moon about 17,239 miles from the surface of the Earth. The 150-foot diameter rock with an estimated mass of 40,000 metric tons flew past us closer than geosynchronous satellites. Its closest point was directly over Indonesia.

I will never forget watching the television monitor as the satellite hit the marker where it reached the closest point to the surface of the Earth. According to the data obtained, it will pass again on February 15, 2046, and later on February 16, 2123. Scientists calculate that it will not strike the Earth during the next two passes if the present orbit is not perturbed along the way.

Ironically, just 16 hours prior to the event on February 15, 2013, another asteroid some 49 feet in diameter and weighing 10,000 metric tons entered our atmosphere and exploded over Chelyabinsk, Russia, with an enormous blast that shattered glass and injured several people over that town. The largest chunk made an 8-foot-wide hole in the ice and sunk in a lake. But these asteroids are small potatoes and do not have the capacity to create the catastrophic damage that ended the First Earth.

Scientists have become aware that most asteroids travel in pairs and often in a cluster. Likewise, comets are often broken into pieces as they pass near the gravity of a large planet such as Jupiter. That was observed in my lifetime in the Comet Shoemaker-Levy 9 that struck Jupiter and split into 21 pieces. From that comet we learned that multiple impacts can create massive damage of cataclysmic proportions.

The small asteroids usually explode as they disintegrate during entry into our atmosphere. But the Chicxulub meteor was 6 to 9 miles in length. When it struck the Earth, its tail was higher than the altitude our modern airlines fly. It cracked our crust and made a hole 200 miles wide to a depth of 40 miles. But as it turns out, the Chicxulub crater is not the only giant crater that has been found on our planet.

The Big Seven

Interestingly, there are at least seven craters formed by such gigantic meteor strikes that are each large enough to have the energy necessary to crack and shatter the crust of the Earth. I propose that this was the mechanism that answers the first objection of the naturalists. It is the mechanism that brought forth the Great Flood. It unleashed the highly pressurized, underground aquifers that the Scriptures call the fountains of the deep and the Greeks called the ocean streams from the abyss that precipitated the water vapor canopy that surrounded our early Earth. It is surely the mechanism that broke open the fountains of the deep and the opening of the floodgates of heaven referred to in Scripture. I will deal with these two propositions later, but for now, I would like to continue with the seven largest meteors that have struck our planet.

According to the Earth Impact Database at the University of New Brunswick, Canada, there are five craters whose enormous size makes them stand in a league of their own. However, this database does not include two even larger craters found more recently. Of the

180 or so craters found on Earth, most are small and insignificant compared to the overwhelming heavyweights.

Of the 180 known craters listed in the database, 22 of them are smaller than 1 kilometer from rim to rim. Between 1.13 kilometers and 5 kilometers, there are 42 craters. Between 5 kilometers and 10 kilometers in diameter, there are 44 craters. Between 10 kilometers and 20 kilometers, there are 24 craters. Between 20 kilometers and 45 kilometers, there are 30 craters. Then the list gets thin. There are four craters between 52 kilometers and 55 kilometers in width. There are two craters between 60 and 65 kilometers in width. There is one that is 70 kilometers wide called the Morokweng crater in South Africa, and there is one 85 kilometers wide called Manicouagan in Quebec, Canada.

Then there are the Big Seven that range from 90 to 600 kilometers across. I will address them one by one from north to south as they are found on our planet. But there are two new finds not yet contained in that database from the University of New Brunswick. They are the absolute largest of them all, leaving the rest behind. The largest is the northernmost crater in Maniitsoq, Greenland, and the second is the southernmost crater in Wilkes Land, Antarctica.

1. The Maniitsoq Crater

Recently, a giant crater was discovered quite accidentally in Western Greenland. Geologists looking for nickel and other ores stumbled on the evidence of a giant meteor strike. Evidence of broken-up, contorted, melted, and hydrothermally altered rocks could be explained with only one conclusion: a high-energy impact and the influx of seawater. No terrestrial geologic processes could explain the enormous size of the affected zone. Both Greenland and Iceland have been driven upward from the floor of the Atlantic Ocean as the Mid-Atlantic Ridge has literally come up out of the water from its previous depth.

But when the Mid-Atlantic Ridge was first formed, the present surface layer of the strata in Greenland and Iceland lay 10 to 16 miles below the surface of the Earth. An enormous amount of rock was instantly evaporated, and the rest of it was shot into space by the enormous impact of perhaps the largest meteor to ever strike the Earth. Some of that continental granitic rock has eroded during the years, but most of it was instantly shot out into space as ejecta by the massive force of the strike and by the angle it struck the Earth.

> Until recently, the Vredefort crater in South Africa, with its 300 km in diameter and an age of just over two billion years, was considered to be the largest and oldest documented crater structure on Earth.
>
> In September 2009, however, an even larger and much older crater structure in West Greenland was "found" in an office in Copenhagen – at the offices of the Geological Survey of Denmark and Greenland (GEUS). . . .
>
> Boris A. Ivanov, of the Institute of Planetary Science in Moscow has conducted a series of provisional model calculations, which suggest that the Maniitsoq meteorite had a diameter of more than 30 km – at least twice that of the Vredefort meteorite, and with a mass of at least ten times greater.
>
> Had this meteorite hit the moon, the resulting crater would have a diameter well above 1,000 km and would be easily visible from Earth with the naked eye.
>
> But since the Earth has a much stronger gravitational force than the moon, the original Maniitsoq crater will probably have had a diameter of "only" 500–600 km (Vinther 2012).

The Maniitsoq crater is today 100 kilometers from rim to rim, but when it was first made, it would have been as large as 500–600 kilometers from rim to rim. Today, it is only 100 kilometers from rim to rim because some 16 miles deep and 500–600 miles in diameter of the granitic rock below the surface of Greenland before the impact was either instantly vaporized or jettisoned as ejecta from the force of the impact. And no wonder, the space rock that created such a deep and powerful impact was estimated to be more than 30 kilometers wide. I think that is even an underestimate of the size of the meteor.

Imagine the force of an impact that could vaporize or destroy and eject a column of granitic rock 16 miles deep and 500–600 miles wide. Most of it was instantly vaporized, and the rest was catapulted into space by the giant ejecta mushroom cloud it created. The impact was so powerful that some of the rocks ejected hit our Moon with a barrage of smaller asteroids. Some of it rained down on the First Earth as smaller asteroids that superheated the air as they reentered our atmosphere. Some of it, the dust and smaller pieces, fell back into orbit around our Earth and darkened the skies globally. If the impact of the Chicxulub meteor was so powerful that it caused the extinction of the dinosaurs, imagine the annihilation potential of a meteor four to five times that size.

The impact was so powerful that it shattered the northern part of the supercontinent of Arza into a thousand islands. Evolutionists have come up with different names for this singular continent according to the timetable in which they think it came together. Since they view this as a cyclical event where the continents, like a giant jigsaw puzzle, haphazardly come together and fall apart time and again, their names for their imagined supercontinents will therefore not match our model.

We believe that God created the Earth initially as a single landmass that was stable and solid. It began to separate only after the crust was cracked by the meteor strikes that brought forth the Great Flood. I chose to call this singular supercontinent Arza because it is the Hebrew word for Earth.

The northern part of Arza was shattered into Iceland, Greenland, England, Ireland, and the many smaller islands that surround them. It cracked open the Scandinavian countries like fingers from mainland Europe. It helped split North America from Europe and North Africa. It was an absolutely massive strike that crushed the crust of the Earth and, along with the other massive meteor strikes, split the supercontinent into seven smaller continents.

The area around the town of Maniitsoq in Greenland where the remains of the meteorite impact were discovered. (Graphic: GEUS)

The pressure wave created by this giant meteor traveled through the Earth and bounced back much like ripples in a pool when a diver strikes the surface of the water. I suspect that the Siberian Traps were formed as this pressure wave pushed the crust outward in the opposite end of the trajectory of the Maniitsoq strike.

The returning pressure wave quite likely caused the rebound of the surface of the Earth near the impact zone in the basaltic layer to rise dramatically from its previous depth to the surface of the Earth. Once the weight of the 16 miles of granite rock was removed, the internal pressures inside the Earth pushed the basaltic floor upward. This is quite likely the reason the Mid-Atlantic Ridge rises out of the water in this area where the largest meteor that ever struck our Earth landed.

2. The Popigai Crater in Siberia

The second crater of the Big Seven as we come down from the north is the Popigai crater in Siberia, Russia. The powerful impact created the many Siberian islands, breaking them off from the mainland of Arza in that region and pushing them northward toward the Arctic.

It no doubt also helped in the formation of the rips in the crust that we know as the Siberian Traps that flowed unimaginable amounts of lava to the surface of the Earth.

The 100-kilometer-wide crater is about 300 kilometers east of the outpost of Khatanga, Russia. For years scientists were unable to explore this impact zone because Stalin declared the entire area off limits. The giant impact created a rich deposit of diamonds. Gulags were established in that area so the political prisoners of Stalin could mine the diamonds.

It was not until 1997 that a major investigatory expedition was undertaken. Russians announced in September 2012 that the massive diamond reserves contained hundreds of thousands of tons of industrial-grade diamonds. Those diamonds are not made by the constant steady heat and pressure of 75 miles of rock above them as is customary but by the immense pressure and heat generated from the impact of a meteor and are therefore called impact diamonds. Realizing the power of such enormous meteor strikes, scientists are now claiming that it could have caused a mass extinction event.

> The new age, which is later than other estimates, means the Eocene extinction — long blamed on climate change — now has another prime suspect: an "impact winter." Meteorite blasts can trigger a deadly global chill by blanketing the Earth's atmosphere with tiny particles that reflect the suns heat (Oskin 2014).

Of course, every mass extinction event evolutionists propose is millions of years ago. If every one of these giant meteors caused a mass extinction event, there would be no life left on our planet. It is possible that the Popigai meteor may have been flying in tandem with the Maniitsoq meteor and could have contributed to the eruption of the Siberian Trap.

3. The Sudbury Crater in Ontario, Canada

The third enormous crater coming from the north is the Sudbury Crater in Ontario, Canada. The crater is 130 kilometers from rim to rim, but it is estimated to have been 250 kilometers wide when it was first formed.

> The **Sudbury Basin**, also known as **Sudbury Structure** or the **Sudbury Nickel Irruptive**, is a major geological structure in Ontario, Canada. It is the third-largest known impact crater or astrobleme on Earth, as well as one of the oldest ("Sudbury Basin").

A view from a real photo or map shows how the enormous impact cracked a huge chunk of Canada from the main body of the North American continent and created the Great Lakes between the United States and Canada. The rock that plowed into North America was estimated to be between 10 kilometers and 15 kilometers cubed. Therefore, I do not agree with Wikipedia that this was the third-largest meteor, but it is possible that this meteor may have broken apart and a splinter from it landed in the area of Virginia, causing the 85-kilometer-wide crater underneath Chesapeake Bay. It may also be possible that this meteor was flying in tandem with the Chicxulub meteor that struck Mexico.

4. The Chicxulub Crater in the Yucatan Peninsula

The fourth crater as we travel south is the Chicxulub crater in the Yucatan Peninsula measuring 150 kilometers from rim to rim. The impact of the 6.2–9.3-mile-wide meteor (10–15 kilometers) that struck the Yucatan Peninsula was so powerful that it penetrated Earth's crust with a hole 200 miles wide and some 40 kilometers deep.

> Two samples from depths of 1.2 and 1.3 kilometers in one of the boreholes into the structure were re-examined and found to contain diagnostic evidence of an impact origin.

The melt rocks and breccias within the structure are not the produce of magmatic intrusions and extrusions as previously interpreted, but rather the consequences of an impacting near-Earth asteroid (or possibly comet) with the kinetic energy equivalent to ~100 million magatons of TNT. The breccias covering the upper Cretaceous elsewhere on the Yucatán Peninsula were neither volcanic or debris eroded from tectonic uplifts as previously presumed, but products of more than ten thousand cubic kilometers of debris ejected from a crater. That discovery was reported by Kring, Hildebrand, and Boynton at the 1991 Lunar and Planetary Science Conference. At that same meeting, Glen Penfield and Antonia Camargo Z. described the geophysical elements of the subsurface structure. The results in both those papers were integrated with an additional geophysical analysis by Mark Pilkington and an isotopic analysis by Stein Jacobsen in a paper published later that year by Hildebrand et al. (Geology 19, 867–871, 1991). Additional geochemical details linking the Chicxulub impact melt rock to the K-T boundary deposit in Haiti followed (Kring and Boynton, *Nature* 358, 141–144, 1992), showing that the Chicxulub crater was produced precisely at the K-T boundary ("Chicxulub Impact Event").

Such a powerful impact by itself could have easily precipitated the evacuation of the underground saltwater chambers and the resulting volcanic activity responsible for causing the Great Flood. We will speak more of these subterranean aquifers later.

The ejecta of any one of these meteors alone could have been enough to precipitate the water vapor canopy. Scientists believe that the ejecta from this meteor reached a quarter of the way to the moon and then fell back as thousands of smaller asteroid strikes that superheated the atmosphere as they reentered our planet. The debris that also shot out into space by the sudden and violent expulsion of the subterranean water as it was released from their subterranean chambers would have also been significant.

5. The Vredefort Crater in Southwest Johannesburg, Africa

The fifth impact crater traveling south is found in the northwest province of South Africa at the southern tip of the continent. The Vredefort crater is southwest of Johannesburg and measures from rim to rim 160 kilometers. It is estimated that when it first formed, it may have been 300 kilometers wide. It is larger than the Chicxulub crater, and its impact would have penetrated more than the 40 miles the Chicxulub meteor reached into the Earth.

With an estimated original diameter of 300 kilometers, the Vredefort Impact Crater is the largest asteroid impact structure that still has visible evidence at Earth's surface. It is also the second-oldest impact structure with visible evidence at Earth's surface (King).

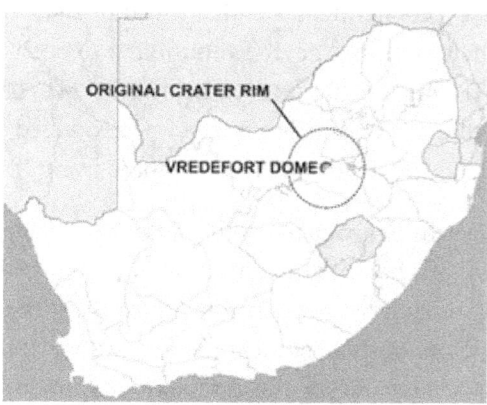

Map of the Vredefort Crater showing its approximate footprint in the country of South Africa. The dotted line marks the approximate location of the original crater rim, which has been obscured by erosion in the northwest and covered by sediment in the southeast. The feature marked Vredefort Dome is an area of uplifted strata in the center of the crater. This image was created by Oggmus and is used here under a Creative Commons license.
(King)

No doubt this massive impact contributed to the fracture of Africa from Antarctica and South America and quite likely also fractured India and Madagascar from the eastern coast of Africa. It may have been flying in tandem with the Wilkes Land meteor in Antarctica and perhaps even the Acraman meteor in Australia. We must remember that Africa, Antarctica, and Australia were united before the meteors cracked the supercontinent into seven continents.

6. The Acraman Crater in Australia

The sixth crater traveling south from Africa is the Acraman crater in Australia. It is perhaps the smallest of the Big Seven with a diameter of 90 kilometers from rim to rim but with some outer arcuate features at 150 kilometers in diameter.

> Acraman is a complex crater. Rather than the simple bowl shape we often associate with craters, Acraman has a complicated surface with variations in elevation. Geological studies have found that, over time, Acraman's surface eroded several kilometers below the original crater floor. Studies of the current land surface and debris ejected by the collision suggest that the impact produced an uplifted ring spanning roughly 40 kilometers (25 miles) in the crater's center. The rim surrounding the inner ring may have spanned 85 to 90 kilometers (53 to 55 miles), and the total area of disturbed rocks might have been as wide as 150 kilometers (95 miles) ("Acraman Impact Structure" 2010).

The center of the crater contains a dry, salt lake 20 kilometers in diameter that is in a peculiar hexagonal shape. The impact may have caused the ripping of Tasmania and New Zealand from the mainland of Australia.

7. The Wilkes Land Crater in Antarctica

The southernmost crater is perhaps the second-largest behind Maniitsoq at the opposite end of the supercontinent of Arza. It is called the Wilkes Land crater on the eastern side of Antarctica. No doubt this enormous crater, in combination with the relatively close Vredefort crater in Africa, was responsible for fracturing Australia from Antarctica and likewise South America and Africa, as well as India on Africa's eastern side along with the island of Madagascar.

> An apparent crater as big as Ohio has been found in Antarctica. Scientists think it was carved by a space rock that caused the greatest mass extinction on Earth, 250 million years ago.
>
> The crater, buried beneath a half-mile of ice and discovered by some serious airborne and satellite sleuthing, is more than twice as big as the one involved in the demise of the dinosaurs.
>
> The crater's location, in the Wilkes Land region of East Antarctica, south of Australia, suggests it might have instigated the breakup of the so-called Gondwana supercontinent, which pushed Australia northward, the researchers said (Britt 2006).

The enormous size of this crater, which is the size of Ohio, is mindboggling, and the ejecta of this meteor no doubt also reached the Moon. I will agree with the evolutionists that this crater is tied to the worst mass extinction event ever in our Earth's history, even if I do not agree with their evolutionary timetable. Our Judeo-Christian model proposes that the combination of these seven meteor strikes is what broke our supercontinent of Arza into our present seven continents. Their combined impacts would have utterly sterilized our planet had it not been followed by the Flood to mediate the dramatic rise in global temperatures initially generated by these massive meteors.

The relatively close triple impact may have resulted from the meteors rotating around one another and traveling as a cluster with the Acraman meteor being the smallest. As stated earlier, this may also be true for the Maniitsoq and the Popigai meteor that landed in Siberia and the Sudbury meteor on the border of the United States and Canada with the Chicxulub meteor that struck in Mexico.

According to evolutionists, it was the Chicxulub crater that ended the age of the dinosaurs. That impact, however, was not even close to being the largest impact. It is greatly overshadowed by the huge impacts of the Maniitsoq crater in Greenland, the almost comparable Wilkes Land crater in Antarctica, and the Vredefort Crater in East Africa, which were three to five times the size of the one in the Yucatan Peninsula.

Let us examine the powerful effects of the smaller Chicxulub meteor that evolutionists claim killed off the dinosaurs in order to get a better grasp of the immensity of the power of the impacts these combined seven strikes would have had on our planet.

The Chicxulub Crater

Certainly, the Chicxulub crater in the Yucatan Peninsula is a formidable giant crater. It is large enough by itself to have been the trigger that emptied these two water reservoirs (the underground aquifers and the water vapor canopy). A hole 40 kilometers deep and 200 kilometers wide would certainly provide the mechanism for the sudden breaking of the fountains of the deep. The size of this crater is so great that it was not recognized as such until satellite pictures were taken of the area. Subsequently, scientists traced the great zenotes (sink holes in the limestone bedrock) in the Yucatan Peninsula and realized that they form a perfect ring that is consistent with the shape of the underwater crater formed by this meteor strike on the floor of the Gulf of Mexico.

Producing a crater some 110 miles across (150–170 kilometers), the devastating impact from this meteor, estimated to have been

10–15 kilometers in diameter, must have been unimaginable to the inhabitants of the First Earth who were unfortunate enough to have witnessed it. The name *Chicxulub* means "tail of the devil." Scientists estimate the magnitude of the impact to be somewhere in the neighborhood of 10 billion atom bombs of the size that destroyed Hiroshima in World War II. How can we even begin to appreciate the awesome destructive power of 10 billion atom bombs?

Evolutionists believe that the Atlantic Ocean was already in existence when this meteor struck. We propose that the Atlantic Ocean was, in fact, created by the multiple strikes that broke our supercontinent of Arza into the seven continents of our Second Earth. Therefore, we maintain that when this meteor struck, New York was attached to northern Africa. The impact zone on the supercontinent of Arza would have been on the western edge. The combination of the Maniitsoq meteor, the Sudbury meteor, and the Chicxulub meteor ripped North America from Africa and Europe and sent the continent spiraling counterclockwise toward the west.

The subsequent separation of the continents and the braking of the fountains of the deep then birthed the Atlantic Ocean. The Gulf of Mexico was probably created by the very blast of ejecta from this meteor that was 10–15 kilometers long. Nevertheless, let us hear the description of the power of this meteor from the eyes of an evolutionist.

> Again the memory of the rocks came into play. The impact, it was later found, happened either very near or just within the waterline of the Yucatan Peninsula in the Gulf of Mexico. The enormous violence of the collision caused a tsunami estimated to have grown at least fifty and possibly a few hundred meters in height. Such a gigantic wave wiped out most of the Gulf Coast of the United States and Mexico, as well as the Caribbean, carrying with it all sorts of debris. Working backward, geologists found the sediment layer

brought by the giant tsunami right on the KT boundary, at sites in Texas and Haiti. If the tsunami carried sediments to Texas and Haiti, they reasoned, the impact must have occurred in the Gulf of Mexico. Sharing information with geologists from Petróleos Mexicanos (PEMEX, the Mexican oil company), the American geologist Alan Hildebrand and collaborators located the site of impact: the Chicxulub Crater, from the Mayan word meaning "tail of the devil," with a diameter of roughly 170 kilometers. It took a 10-kilometer-wide object, traveling at roughly 20 kilometers per second to dig such an enormous hole. It is hard to imagine a more horrific event on a planetary scale. . . .

The extraterrestrial killer, estimated to have been about 10 kilometers wide, approached Earth at about 20 kilometers per second, crossing most of the atmosphere in less than two seconds. The air in front of it was so severely compressed that it reached temperatures four to five times that of the Sun's surface, creating a blinding flash of light and a sonic boom the likes of which has not been heard since then. . . . The energy released by the impact was equivalent to an absurd 100 million megatons of TNT, ten thousand times more than all the thermonuclear bombs available at the height of the Cold War detonated together.

The consequences of dumping such an enormous amount of energy in so short a time are terrifying; the celestial killer carved into the ocean floor a hole about 40 kilometers deep and 200 kilometers wide, immediately vaporizing all the water and rock it found in its way. Waves of boiling water and rocks rushed into the gigantic hole as 100-meter tsunamis propagated outward. Earthquakes of unheard of strength, reaching 10 on the Richter scale, shook the ground for hundreds of kilometers, causing the coastline to crumble, while feeding further tsunamis. . . . The impact was so violent that vaporized rock, debris, and water were thrust upward in a plume that went halfway to the Moon, only to fall back again, causing an umbrella of destruction thousands of kilometers wide. Rocks behaved literally like fluids, ground zero marking the site of a giant bull's-eye surrounded by circular undulations that were imprinted on the boiling bedrock.

Any living thing within many hundreds of kilometers from the point of impact was immediately vaporized. Farther out, at a few thousand kilometers, animals saw a blinding flash of light followed by an uncontrollable shaking of the ground, as the seismic waves passed one after another. The ejecta falling back on Earth from space caused the next wave of devastation. They reentered the atmosphere with such fury that the sky was literally set ablaze, igniting continent-size fires that broiled anything in their path. Giant tsunamis completed the immediate devastation. Most parts of the United States and Mexico were completely destroyed in a matter of hours. The heavens brought hell to Earth. . . .

An astonishing amount of dust was lifted into the atmosphere by the impact, as if a million volcanoes had erupted together. As this dust spread through the upper atmosphere blocking the sunlight, Earth turned cold and dark for months. Very cold and dark. So dark that you could not have seen your hand in front of you, and so cold as to reach subfreezing temperatures. The plants and animals unlucky enough to survive the near-instant death from the impact faced agonizing hunger because of the food chain's collapse. Still, there was more to come. As rains washed down the dust, the temperature started to increase (Gleiser 2001, 94–96).

THE UNEXPECTED SPACE VISITORS

It is quite difficult for modern man to imagine the devastation created by such enormous rocks traveling at 20 kilometers per second pummeling Arza. By the time the leading edge of the meteor was touching the Earth's crust, the tail end was still 6–9 miles high at the edge of our atmosphere, clearly past the height our modern airlines fly. The telltale evidence of the vast expanse of its destructive power is preserved for us today in what geologists call the KT boundary.

Above the KT boundary, geologists claim to find no dinosaur fossils. It seems to mark the extinction of most of the flora, fauna, and species that existed before the Great Flood. The KT boundary was one of the major telltale signs that this destruction was caused by meteorites due to the concentration of iridium found in this layer of the deposit in the strata. Iridium is an extremely rare element on the surface of our planet, yet it is found in much higher concentrations in space rocks. In its layer, the KT boundary has 1,000 times the amount of iridium normally found on our planet.

Here is the curious thing. According to evolutionists, one of the smallest of these seven giant impacts created a KT layer that is not found in any other layer of our geological strata. Yet evolutionary geologists insist that these seven meteors struck on very different dates.

The enormous 30-kilometer-wide meteor that struck the Wilkes Land area of Antarctica was three times larger than Chicxulub. Evolutionists claim it struck during the Permian Triassic boundary, but there is no observable layer of the ejecta or iridium that would have come from such an enormous impact. In fact, none of the other meteors, which were much larger than Chicxulub, can be traced by the kind of broadband evidence on a global scale marked by the KT boundary. Their dating is more wishful thinking than fact. It is reflective of their underlying bias to create vast spans of time in order for evolution to have any chance at all.

To be fair, their thinking is tempered by the fact that each of these meteors by themselves would have destroyed most life on Earth, and hence they cannot imagine them striking anytime during the history of life evolving on our planet without completely destroying it, thus forcing evolution to restart all over again. If it is unlikely that life evolved from nonliving matter once, how unlikely is it that it would do so seven times over?

Because they reject the biblical narrative of the Great Flood, they reject the cooling mechanism that would have mediated their destructive power and brought our Second Earth into existence. Let us continue to examine the effects of these impacts.

Some of the initial ejecta thrust into space by the powerful seven blasts would have reentered the atmosphere as smaller, burning meteors, effectively heating the immediate atmosphere globally as hot as an oven. The overall global temperatures may have initially risen by 20–30 degrees Fahrenheit by the multiple impacts.

The much smaller multiple impacts of the reentering ejecta also caused many more smaller tsunamis as they landed in the ocean. Earthquake swarms of unimaginable force that reached more than 10 on the Richter scale and were caused by the impacts ripped the crust and shook the entire planet with such power that they would have decimated most of the manmade structures in their paths. Animals hundreds of miles from the point of impact would have had their legs forcibly jammed into their bodies by the power of the ground tremors, killing them in a horrible death.

To date, we have discovered at least 180 impact craters around our planet, although most of them are much smaller. A large portion of the 180 impact craters we have now documented may probably have come from the returning ejecta of the seven giant meteors, although it cannot be denied that many smaller meteors have continued to fall on Earth sporadically and do so even today.

If the Chicxulub strike created a kill zone thousands of kilometers wide from the point of impact, how large would have been the kill zone for all seven of them put together? "The impact was so violent that vaporized rock, debris, and water were thrust upward in a plume that went halfway to the Moon, only to fall back again, causing an umbrella of destruction thousands of kilometers wide" (Gleiser 2001, 94).

The falling superheated debris reentering our atmosphere from the ejecta of the seven meteors started continent-size conflagrations throughout the thick and luscious forests of Arza, burning the rich vegetation that once thrived throughout our First Earth. The ejecta were further aided by the burning hot lava spewing out of the newly formed volcanoes and super-volcanoes initiated by the enormous pressure waves of the seven impacts traveling throughout Earth's interior. The second wave of volcanism came as the continents began to move, especially throughout the edges of the shifting plates. Here they were cracked and more so on the distal ends as they ground to a halt. The sliding continental plates would have created massive volcanoes by the friction with the underlying basaltic rock as they eventually ground to a halt.

Then the torrential black rains began to come down. Those who managed to survive this initial fiery furnace would have at first welcomed this rain until they realized the inferno was becoming a watery, muddy hell that would soon overrun them.

It had never rained before. The First Earth was watered by morning dew every day. But this was no normal rain shower. It was a thick, black, sooty rain containing debris from the ejecta as well as tephra from the volcanoes. The fear and horror that filled the bosoms of those who first experienced this phenomenon must have been incalculable.

The tons of ejecta that spewed into the sky just by the initial blast of these giant meteors would have by itself filled our atmosphere with dust and debris that would have lasted years had it not been for the cleansing rains. But if we add the millions of tons of tephra that spewed into the sky from the resulting super-volcanoes and countless other smaller eruptions, the scenario intensifies exponentially. Daytime was like the middle of a moonless night.

Our planet would have been shrouded by a thick layer of tephra throughout the entire atmosphere, completely blocking the life-giving light of the Sun from reaching Earth's surface. At high noon, it was totally dark on the First Earth. The evolutionists admit all of this, describing only one of the seven big ones. Little do they know that it shall be so again at the end of our Second Earth. But that is another story.

Those who survived the initial volcanic blasts, both animals and humans, filled their lungs with this deadly ash falling from the sky and suffocated long before they were burned by the conflagrations that ensued. The tiny particles of tephra became like cement in their lungs. In that day, darkness ruled the day, and the fear in those who witnessed such a cataclysm must have been unparalleled.

Much of this dust dispersed with the rain, and today we only see the familiar black rain after volcanic eruptions. In fact, were it not for the cleansing rain, no life could have survived in the Second Earth. This is the mechanism that evolutionists ignore as the great mediator that stopped our planet from burning into a blackened cinder.

The waters cleansed the Earth of the defilement and buried beneath mud and ash the profaned and violent world that rebelled against God. It should serve as a warning to us that a just and holy God will not long tolerate violence. The seven Shepherds that struck our Arza and split it into seven continents and seven seas released God's wrath in a single day. But the ordeal did not end when the black rain stopped after 40 days. It was not until 150 days after it started that the fountains of the deep finally stopped and the waters no longer rose any higher. However, the volcanic storm that ensued was catastrophic and lasted even beyond that time.

There are 21 super volcanoes in the world. It is quite possible that the impacting meteors and the destabilization of the Earth's crust caused all 21 of them in a single catastrophic volcanic upheaval that helped end our First Earth. Can you imagine the hell that 21 super volcanoes would have brought on our planet? One super volcano has as much destructive power as 100,000 volcanoes like the one at Mount St. Helens. The number 21 is significant. It is three sets of sevens. It seems to me a parallel sign that these super-volcanoes were, in fact, part of the judgment of God upon the First Earth. It ended the world in a manner that shadows the coming death of the Second Earth.

In the Book of Revelation, we are told that God's judgments upon our Second Earth shall come in groups of seven. To be exact it will come in three groups of seven judgments (21): the seven seals, the seven trumpets, and the seven bowls of wrath.

It would not surprise me if these 21 monster super-volcanoes were triggered by the powerful impacts that cracked the Earth's crust and the events that unfolded because of them in the day God judged the First Earth. But volcanoes were not the only forces of destruction brought upon our First Earth.

The rising temperature of the ocean that received superheated salt water from the pressurized underground aquifers, along with the initial rising atmospheric temperatures created by the impacting meteors and their ejecta, turned the First Earth into a fiery hell. The latent moisture compounded by the high winds brought forth by the jetting aquifers birthed raging hurricanes of unimaginable power.

There is no way to know how many super-hurricanes ravaged the Earth during that time, but I am willing to conjecture that there were seven, or perhaps three sets of seven. We do know that the singular crust of the Earth that was once whole and steady broke into seven continental hydroplates that began to slide away from each other as the Mid-Atlantic Ridge lifted up, and due to their massive weight, they slid down the slopes of the ridge. In a single day, Arza was no more.

But the veil of deception created by the Great Deceiver has shrouded the truth from most of modern humanity. Modern man did not even discover that the continents were once united until the middle of the 20th century.

It is also not a coincidence that the singular landmass broke into seven continents—North America, South America, Africa, Europe, Asia, Antarctica, and Australia. The single ocean was divided into seven oceans—the North Pacific Ocean, the South Pacific Ocean, the North Atlantic Ocean, the South Atlantic Ocean, the Indian Ocean, the Arctic Ocean, and the Antarctic Ocean. God's judgment comes in sevens.

This is not a modern convention. In fact, long before we circumnavigated the world, ancient man had the notion that a sailor who had been around the world had sailed the seven seas. For instance, the Phoenicians charted the Mediterranean with seven seas—the Alboran Sea, the Balearic Sea, the Ligurian Sea, the Tyrrhenian Sea, the Ionian Sea, the Adriatic Sea, and the Aegean Sea.

The Arabs and Persians know them as the seven seas one must cross to reach China—the Persian Gulf (the Sea of Pars); the Gulf of Khambhat (the Sea of Larwi in Gujarat, India); the Bay of Bengal (the Sea of Harkand); the Strait of Malacca (the Sea of Kalah between Sumatra and Malaya); the Singapore Strait (the Sea of Salahit); the Gulf of Thailand (the Sea of Kardanj); and the South China Sea (the Sea of Sanji). However, the real seven seas are, indeed, the seven oceans.

Can we call this universally held notion of our Earth being divided into sevens just sheer coincidence? Could it be that it stems from the ancient memory of the judgment over the First Earth that Noah recalled and that passed down generation to generation to his descendants until it was eventually forgotten?

Those who learn not from the past are doomed to repeat the same mistakes. There are many things in our past that man ought not to have forgotten, things that as memory faded passed into legends. Those legends passed into myths, and now, none live who know the secrets of the lost knowledge. All we are left with are the clues found within the ancient chronicles, clues that universally recount a paradise lost, a world marred by violence, and a catastrophe that almost killed all life on Earth were it not for the faith of one man, a single ark, and the grace of God. Those who see without eyes will understand God's whisper in the midst of the world's deafening clatter, and they shall see, even in the midst of the veil of the coming darkness. We are children of the light.

> *When you pass through the waters, I will be with you;*
> *And through the rivers, they will not overflow you.*
> *When you walk through the fire, you will not be scorched,*
> *Nor will the flame burn you.*
> *For I am the* LORD *your God,*
> *The Holy One of Israel, your Savior.*
>
> —Isa. 43:2–3

It is hard for us today to understand the magnitude of this global cataclysm. We have little in our modern experience to compare it with. Thus far, all catastrophes in our modern experience are localized. Evolutionists use that to rationalize their aberrant uniformitarian faith in gradualism. Terrible as those disasters may be, they are comparatively miniscule, local phenomena. That, however, will not remain so. At the end of our age, the three sets of seven judgments in the Apocalypse shall be global in nature.

Some of us are want to dismiss such talk as superstitious, and many regard them as allegories to train the ignorant. Such is the power of deception that we believe our own lies. Such is the lure of selfishness that looking in the mirror we cannot see our real self. Do not be deceived. The great darkness will come again when violence terrorizes our planet through the religion of the Serpent.

But those who turn to God shall inherit the Third Earth. In that day, God shall make an everlasting covenant of peace with Israel, and mankind shall prosper in the Age of Aquarius when the Water Giver, the Life Giver, rises over the vernal equinox. Isaiah the Hebrew prophet saw it.

THE DEATH OF THE FIRST EARTH

> *Ho! Everyone who thirsts, come to the waters;*
> *And you who have no money come, buy and eat.*
> *Come, buy wine and milk*
> *Without money and without cost.*
> *"Why do you spend money for what is not bread,*
> *And your wages for what does not satisfy?*
> *Listen carefully to Me, and eat what is good,*
> *And delight yourself in abundance.*
> *Incline your ear and come to Me.*
> *Listen, that you might live;*
> *And I will make an everlasting covenant with you."*
>
> —Isa. 55:1–3

The Apostle John wrote these words of Jesus:

> *And He who sits on the throne said, "Behold, I am making all things new." And He said, 'Write, for these words are faithful and true." Then He said to me, "It is done. I am the Alpha and the Omega, the beginning and the end. I will give to the one who thirsts from the spring of the water of life without cost."*
>
> —Rev. 21:5–6

But that day, which births the Third Earth when the lion lies down with the lamb, shall not come until the time of terror brings forth the coming night. The time of terror shall return. Few shall be prepared for the coming night. Nevertheless, if we consider the magnitude of the force of this impact that ended the First Earth, it may bring some measure of appreciation and perhaps give us some measure of preparation for what is in store for mankind at the death of the Second Earth.

In an instant, our planet was changed forever. The force unleashed by the seven meteor impacts was so great that at ground zero in every impact zone, what was not vaporized was immediately liquefied.

"Rocks behaved literally like fluids, ground zero marking the site of a giant bull's-eye surrounded by circular undulations that were imprinted on the boiling bedrock" (Gleiser 2001, 96). Those waves, frozen in stone, are set for our eyes to behold today the raw power of God's judgment on the violence that ruled our planet. Take heed, my friends. God is not mocked. Little does the writer of that statement understand how appropriate his reference to these meteor strikes is to "the site of a giant bull's-eye." As we shall later see, Aldebaran, the eye of Taurus, was, in fact, involved in this cataclysm.

The impact of the seven meteors was nonetheless powerful enough to shatter the crust of the Earth, creating a structural weakness of the crust from pole to pole. The 40- to 70-kilometer-deep cracks made by each of the meteors reached and passed the area of the subterranean aquifer chambers some 10–16 miles below the surface of the granitic supercontinent. The pressure waves exerted from the impact points would have generated outward from the line of trajectory it took, penetrating the crust.

This downward push from the impact zone would have come in a series of pressure waves that severely agitated the gases held in solution in the deep reservoirs of the underground aquifers by the extreme pressure that exists deep below the ground. The many cracks throughout the Earth would have provided an exit path for the trapped saltwater chambers to empty outward through the newly formed fissures created by the impact force in all the adjacent areas of the impact zones.

The sudden outgassing would have created explosive geysers of unprecedented force. That process was repeated and magnified by the larger space rocks that struck our planet from the northernmost part of Arza to the southernmost point. The crust simply ripped like a giant zipper between the impact points where the meteors struck, and the rip in the crust then circled the entire Earth.

One single impact by itself could have precipitated the uncorking of the pressurized subterranean saltwater layer below our continental granite base. But it is doubtful that a single meteor could have fractured our entire singular supercontinent of Arza into the seven current continents. There was not one but seven impacts that would have had the power to form cracks radiating between the impact zones. The direction of the incoming meteors would have affected the subsequent motions of the newly cracked continental plates.

For that reason, Antarctica was driven south, and Australia was fractured from Antarctica, driving it eastward and separating both from South America and Africa. The smaller strike in the Yucatan Peninsula and the huge one in Greenland together fractured North and South America from Europe and Africa. The direction of the two impacts drove North America in a counterclockwise motion (north and west).

The Maniitsoq impact was so powerful that it fractured the area into many islands, including Iceland, Greenland, England, and Ireland. It no doubt opened the North Sea and caused the peninsulas of the Scandinavian countries to open like fingers. The impact in Siberia fractured the land and created the many islands in Siberia that stretch into the Arctic Circle from the force and direction of the impact.

In the south, the combination of the Wilkes Land meteor that hit Antarctica and the Vredefort meteor that hit the tip of Africa resulted in breaking off India from the eastern side of Africa and sending it northward toward Asia. The larger Wilkes Land meteor struck the east side of Antarctica, breaking off Australia and sending it eastward. The Acraman meteor that struck Australia broke off the islands of New Zealand and Tasmania from the mainland.

As the aquifers uncorked, the force of the ejecting stream of water literally ripped a jagged seam along the crust of the Earth where the continents cracked. That is the line of the Mid-Oceanic Ridge that circles the entire planet.

As water evacuated from the underground aquifers, it became like a super-geyser. The almost simultaneous strikes broke the once singular supercontinent of Arza into the presently observed seven major hydroplates and instigated massive volcanic eruptions throughout the edges of these newly formed plates.

Tsunamis of enormous size and destructive power, along with fiery conflagrations created by the reentering ejecta, brought down repeated waves of death and utter destruction to all living things throughout the First Earth. The chain of events that this multiple impact triggered caused radical and immediate changes in global temperatures, which eventually resulted in a complete and permanent change in our geological and meteorological systems. From that fateful moment on, our planet was changed forevermore.

The immense shock waves generated by the initial impacts traveled through the magma under the Earth and through the core of the Earth to the opposite side of the planet. The almost unimaginable internal pressure caused the crust on the opposite side to bulge and crack outward.

Enormous plumes of magma pushed up through the newly created faults in the crust. That was the mechanism that probably initiated the enormous lava flows generated by the Siberian Traps in the Northern Hemisphere as well as the Deccan Traps found in India in the Southern Hemisphere. India would have been attached to Africa at that point.

Let us now examine the giant Wilkes Land meteor in Antarctica.

The Wilkes Land, East Antarctic Crater

The fact is that a single meteor of the gargantuan size that struck either Antarctica or Greenland could have probably triggered most of this cataclysm. The meteor that struck the Yucatan Peninsula was a mere hiccup compared to the giant craters found in Greenland and Antarctica. So large were these craters that man did not recognize them as such. They were discovered accidentally through other observations. It is difficult to see a crater that is 100 kilometers across, but imagine one that spans 500–600 kilometers. That is like trying to see the border of Georgia and Florida from the city of Miami. Our modern satellite observations have become indispensible to detect these giant craters.

In March 2002, a twin satellite system called GRACE (Gravity Recovery and Climate Experiment) was placed in a polar orbit. The twin satellites orbit parallel to one another with about 137 miles between. These sophisticated satellites that orbit about 310 miles above the surface of the Earth can detect minute gravitational shifts on the surface of the planet. The gravitational differences alert scientists to varying densities in the crust of the Earth.

> In January 2005, for example, Ohio State University geophysicist Ralph von Frese and his colleagues noticed a concentration of higher-than-average-density material in the rock about a mile under the surface of the East Antarctic ice sheet. Mass concentrations like this often accumulate when giant impacts from space pound the crust. When the rock rebounds, it carries higher-density mantle materials up towards the surface and holds them there. Comparing the GRACE data with radar imagery of the icebound bedrock, von Frese found it was centered perfectly inside a ring some 300 miles wide—just what you'd expect from an impactor 30 or so miles across. "It just jumped out at us," he says.
>
> An asteroid that big would be about four to five times the diameter of the object that killed off the dinosaurs 65 million years ago [the impact in the Yucatan Peninsula]. The crater is much older, arguably dating back to a time, some 250 million years ago, when something—perhaps a projectile from outer space—wiped out the majority of the species on Earth, including most reptiles, sponges, corals, starfish, clams, sea scorpions, and fish, thereby clearing the evolutionary decks for dinosaurs to become

dominant. That was the greatest mass extinction in history, and thanks to GRACE, paleontologists and evolutionary biologists now have an idea of how it may have happened (Flamsteed 2007).

Of course, evolutionists must place this huge meteor strike far in our past in order for evolution to have enough time to give rise to life after such a cataclysmic event. A meteor strike of this size without some moderating influence to cool down the atmosphere afterward would have left our planet almost sterile. But I have a hard time understanding how a projectile from outer space "wiped out the majority of the species on Earth, including most reptiles, sponges, corals, starfish, clams, sea scorpions, and fish, thereby clearing the evolutionary decks for dinosaurs to become dominant" (Flamsteed 2007). If the reptiles were wiped out, how did the dinosaurs pop into existence? If the smaller meteor in Mexico killed the dinosaurs, how could this one that was four to five times more deadly clear the deck for dinosaurs? That seems to be an irrational conclusion.

Seven sterilizing impacts would have been impossible for any life to overcome through their imagined and speculative evolutionary process of natural selection. For this reason, evolutionists must spread them millions of year apart to have time for evolution to rebound. But as we have seen in the previous four books of this series, evolution has yet to provide a viable mechanism to change one species into another. The truth is that the Earth would have been completely sterile after any one of these impacts unless there was some other mechanism such as the Global Flood to cool the planet down immediately after.

It would be utterly improbable that life could simply begin evolving anew after such catastrophic global effects. The possibility of life evolving in the first place is so remote to begin with that to state it fortuitously happened seven times in a row is absolutely irresponsible from a scientific perspective.

We have already documented that most evolutionists have admitted the high improbability of chance chemical reactions evolving into the complicated structures of even single-celled organisms. For those readers who have not read the first four volumes, let me provide a quick review of the statistical chances for random chemical reactions to create a single living cell.

> Since the odds of developing one cell of 600 proteins are 1 to *an astronomical* $10^{99,999,999,873}$, but the largest number of potential physical interactions since the beginning of time in the entire universe is 10^{140}, it is literally impossible to conceive that chance could have randomly formulated a single cell of just 600 proteins within the time frame of our universe. To assert otherwise cannot be construed as objective scientific reasoning. It is nothing more than simple blind faith.
>
> *Given the fact that Murray Eden has proposed that the number of protein molecules that could have ever existed in the presupposed 15 billion years of evolutionary history is 10^{52}, one can readily appreciate the seriousness of this number. Eden is a retired engineering professor at Massachusetts Institute of Technology and was one of the participants at the now famous Wistar conference in Philadelphia.*
>
> The odds that chance could have produced even the simplest living entity are so remote that it should be recognized as realistically impossible by anyone who is considered an objective observer. These are the odds for just one small cell to form. If all of life were to evolve from this single ancestral forefather, the cell would then have to survive the hostile environment envisioned by the reducing atmosphere of the evolutionists (emphasis added) (Patiño 2019, 97).

How many times have I heard their standard cop-out? "We just got lucky. The fact that we are here means that it must have happened." But if it is so improbable the first time, how could it have happened seven times in a row? What are the chances of that? It is the definition of subjective bias of the first magnitude.

Moreover, their age estimate of 250 million years for this giant crater is based on their uniformitarian assumption that the ice sheet above the surface of Antarctica came only through the slow process of precipitation. Our model proposes that the freezing of the Deluge waters caused the First Ice Age. As the ice melted, the seas rose again, although not to the first maximum extent. Nevertheless, the seas encroached into large sections of land.

The Second Ice Age was probably caused by the failure of the thermohaline conveyor belt due to rapid deglaciation and runaway greenhouse gases. Each Ice Age came from the rising sea levels that froze afterward, and thus there was no need for millions of years of precipitation. We will explore this in more detail when we cover the two Ice Ages.

Once the heat distribution currents of the world stopped, the planet began to freeze again. The seas froze a second time, creating the Second Ice Age. It may be possible that the eruption of super volcanoes helped trigger this scenario, or it may have been triggered by another meteor such as the 70-kilometer-wide impact called the Morokweng crater in South Africa or the 85-kilometer-wide impact called Manicouagan in Quebec, Canada. The dust canopy they would have produced could have lasted several years and would have dropped the temperatures once again to subfreezing levels at both poles.

Today, we are nearing the end of the melting process of the Second Ice Age. The immense ice caps created by the Second Ice Age were, of course, aided by the precipitation of snow afterward, but the bulk of it came from the freezing of the global floodwaters.

The long ages that evolutionists pander are quite convenient to give the improbability of this evolutionary restart at least a wishful chance. But such powerful impacts as the ones in Antarctica and Greenland, without some mediating force to counter them, would have most certainly created a complete extinction episode on the entire Earth. Even if evolution were possible, it would be impossible for it to bounce back from seven separate assaults of that magnitude, no matter how much time we gave it.

It is my suspicion that these seven largest craters were formed simultaneously with the judgment of the Great Flood that broke up our single continent and ended the First Earth. The evidence is in the rocks. Evolutionists claim that the crater in Mexico created an iridium layer in the strata that proved conclusively that it was created by an asteroid impact. This rare metal is quite rare on the Earth but commonly found in comets and asteroids. Why is it that no other iridium layer exists for the much more massive impacts we have just documented? It does not exist because they all impacted at the same time, and the magic evolutionary wand cannot explain it otherwise.

If these much larger impacts cannot produce an even larger iridium layer than the meteor that supposedly killed off the dinosaurs, then evolutionists' entire dating system must be seriously flawed. It is my belief that not only were the dinosaurs killed by this series of impacts but the Great Dying they claim happened millions of years before that killed 90 percent of all living things are one and the same event as the Global Flood.

The combined effects would have then been responsible for the devastation that precipitated the uncorking of the underground aquifers and the precipitation of the water vapor canopy that together caused the Global Flood. Had this not happened, no life could have survived the massive volcanic upheaval and intense heating of our atmosphere created by the combined impacts. It was the water that cooled down the intense furnace created by the massive impacts. Hence, water is both the giver and the taker of life—another symbol of God.

The precise locations of the meteor impact zones created the stress necessary for the crust of the Earth to initially rip between

THE UNEXPECTED SPACE VISITORS

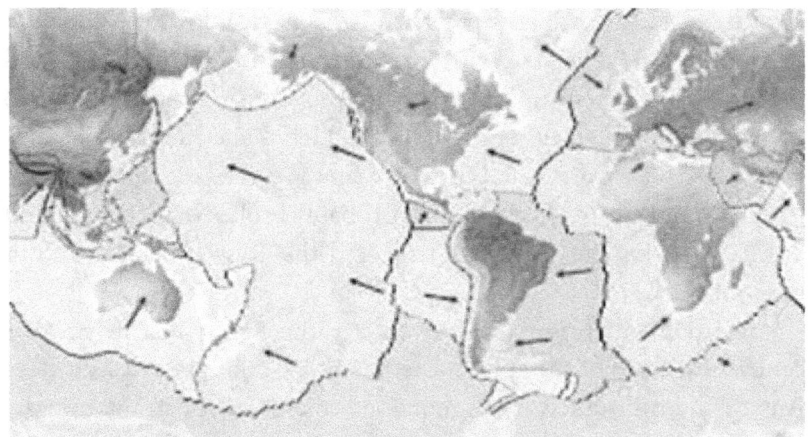

The direction of the movement of the continents after being separated shows that their motions were moving away from the Mid-Atlantic Ridge that rose up into the present heights after the rocks above them were eroded by the fountains of the deep. That made the continents slide down their slopes away from the original cracks made by the seven meteors that fractured Arza.

these points from the Arctic to the Antarctic, causing the Mid-Atlantic Ridge we observe today. That precipitated a rip in the crust that literally went around the world like a giant zipper opening up.

The South American and North American continents moved westward toward Asia and the Pacific Islands. At the same time, the European continent moved eastward, and the African continent moved north and east, showing that all of them were moving from their initial position where the Mid-Atlantic Ridge marks the place they were when they once connected as the single supercontinent of Arza. We see as well the Asiatic continent moving eastward toward the Americas, which would have quite likely created further stress points as the plates collided with one another at their distal ends that formed the Pacific Ring of Fire all along the distal ends of the sliding new continents with the Pacific plate.

Although not shown in the above map, Antarctica was previously attached to South America and Africa. Australia was attached below Antarctica. The force of the impact fractured this area of Arza into the present continents and thrust Antarctica downward toward the southern pole by the power of both the Land Wilkes meteor and the Vredefort meteor in Africa. The tremendous power of these two meteors so close together created a spider-shaped crack that also broke Australia from Antarctica and sent it eastward. No doubt the Acraman meteor in Australia that probably broke New Zealand and Tasmania from Australia also triggered the Toba super-volcano in the process.

Because Antarctica reached exactly the South Pole where the centrifugal force of the spin of the Earth does not affect it as it does Australia, for instance, it has remained stationary. Australia initially moved east but is now moving northward toward the equator. In the same manner, Africa is going northward toward the European continent. India as well is moving northward and crunching into the Asiatic continent, forming the spectacular Himalayan Mountains. None of these movements can be adequately explained by magma currents as the evolutionists describe. But they are easily explained by both the direction of the impacts that broke them from the supercontinent and the centrifugal force of the spinning Earth that drives them toward the center of the planet where it bulges from the centrifugal force.

The full impact of such a multilayered global catastrophic upheaval is staggering. But for those who have eyes to see, the empirical evidence is there to examine. We have witnessed in our recent history local catastrophes on a much smaller scale, but they can scarcely help us project the consequences of such a large-scale multilateral global event.

The Earth's crust was simply broken into shards like a pot crushed by a hammer. The survivors would not easily forget an event of that magnitude. In fact, we find that ancient man everywhere chronicled this as historical reality, which many evolutionists today try hard to ignore in order to evade the historicity of God's judgments on mankind and rationalize their subconscious drive for absolute autonomy.

The Land Was Broken Like a Pot

Ancient man universally chronicled this Great Flood that wiped out all of humanity except a small remnant protected by God. In Chapter 12, we will document many of these accounts. But I would like to focus here on the specific description found in the Babylonian *The Epic of Gilgamesh* that describes exactly the expected results of a meteor bombardment.

> The . . . land shattered like a . . . pot. (*Gilgamesh* Tablet XI, line 107).

How does a local flood shatter the land like a pot? If we are to believe the evolutionary version, how does a mere local flood have the power to break the land like that? No better accurate description can be given by modern man than the effects of multiple meteor strikes on Earth's crust.

If the smaller Chicxulub meteor that hit the Yucatan Peninsula penetrated our crust with a hole more than 40 kilometers deep and 200 kilometers wide, then it is logical that the much larger ones in Antarctica and Greenland would have probably been at least three times that depth and twice the width. Imagine a series of holes in the ground that vary from 70–80 kilometers deep and 300–600 kilometers wide. The amount of ejecta thrown back into the sky by the seven impacts would have been staggering.

The Earth literally trembled as earthquake swarms radiated outward from all the impact zones, cracking the once-solid supercontinent into our present seven continents. These enormous holes gouged out by the impacting meteors provided the escape route for the underground aquifers. The now highly agitated underground aquifers exploded upward by the enormous pressure of the weight of the continent above them. The supersonic geysers shot upward through all the cracks that fractured the supercontinent. The sound of cracking rock for thousands of miles must have been terrifyingly loud. They stretched along the entire length of the supercontinent, eventually connecting with all seven impact zones and creating our smaller seven continents.

That would have created a continuous wall of water gushing heavenward at supersonic speed around the entire Earth with a force much mightier than the Iguazu Falls. But unlike the Iguazu Falls, this wall of water had so much force that it initially went up into the stratosphere and beyond. The pressure and power of the geysers would have been highest when the opening between the continents first cracked. Some water may have escaped into space and formed comets. As the sides of the continents began to erode and the opening widened, the force of the geysers lessened, and water cascaded back down to Earth as a giant waterfall extending the entire breadth of the now fractured supercontinent.

Ancient men, and certainly the Sumerians, were well versed in irrigation canals. The term used in Scripture refers to opening the floodgates of a canal to redirect the water into another irrigation canal. They are, in essence, small waterfalls. Since the waterfall was literally coming from the heavens as this powerful wall of water reached the stratosphere, it seemed to men that the floodgates of heaven had literally opened.

These seven catastrophic impacts would have sent giant shock waves throughout the center of our planet, causing the distal crust at the opposite end of the Earth to bulge in various places that corresponded to the direct angle of the meteors when each of them struck. The pressure waves pushed up lava from the interior magma through these bulging cracks. They formed provincial-sized traps with enormous beds of lava sometimes 2 miles thick. As the shock waves bounced back and forth through the interior of the Earth, each returning pulse formed the familiar and unique steps observed in all these provincial magma flows.

By looking at the position of the crater in the Yucatan Peninsula and its relation to the Gulf of Mexico, it is evident that the force of the impact of the meteor was so great that it probably gouged out the Gulf. The soil that occupied the region of the Gulf was sent upward in a giant mushroom cloud as an expanding pressure wave of dust and rocks radiating from the point of impact. The water in the Gulf of Mexico came afterward as the sliding continents separated from the Mid-Atlantic Ridge and formed the Atlantic Basin.

On the surface of the planet at each of the strike zones, the initial shock wave of each impact traveled outward in circumference, vaporizing anything in its vicinity and leveling everything in its path for several thousand miles. The very large impact in Antarctica would have similarly affected the area of Argentina and Africa where Antarctica and Australia were previously connected to the supercontinent, causing an enormous amount of rock to be thrust into the sky as ejecta and spilling mammoth-sized magma flows to the surface. We find that South America as well as Africa are made of the exact same composition.

The western edge of Africa has been rising as the continent now slowly slides northeastward. The area of the Vredefort meteor in the east has caused the continent to dip lower in the east. Surely this was the culprit that broke India from east Africa and sent it northward. But we know that the African continent was connected to South America in the supercontinent of Arza by the matching soil samples of the two continents.

While the supercontinent was intact, Greenland, Iceland, England, Ireland, and all the islands in that area were connected solidly to Europe on their eastern sides, along with the northern part of Canada on their western sides. The massive Maniitsoq meteor smashed into the supercontinent and fractured that area into hundreds of islands. The impact was so powerful that the North American continent was literally ripped from Europe and, in combination with the Chicxulub meteor strike, was ripped off the northern part of Africa and sent in a counterclockwise motion.

The direction of the approaching meteors caused the North American plate to swing north and west after it cracked from Europe and Africa. Prior to the impact, the coast of New York was touching what is today the African plate by Spain. The whole North American continent swung counterclockwise from the combined force of the three impacts. The highly fragmented North Canadian border and the creation of many islands such as Iceland, Greenland, England, Ireland, and the Siberian islands, as well as the fracturing of the Scandinavian nations from northern Europe, are all the result of the these powerful impacts in the Northern Hemisphere.

We can see by matching the continents with the Mid-Atlantic Ridge that the fit is far superior to the coastal fit. That is because the coastal area has been eroded unevenly by the action of the ejecting fountains of the deep. In addition, the present higher levels of oceans hide the true continental borders that existed at that time. Our oceans are currently more than 400 feet higher than they were during the First Ice Age. The level of the singular ocean Apsu during the First Earth before the Great Flood was probably even lower than that.

By looking at the shape of the continents as they fit along the line of the Mid-Atlantic Ridge, we find two V-shaped areas where the erosion of the granitic suprastructure is the greatest. These V-shaped areas are probably due to the general direction of the meteor strikes that probably came at an oblique angle.

It is obvious that the areas where the meteors struck are the most eroded between the two continents from the ejecta blown away by the initial impacts. Prior to the impacts, the continents of South America and North America were joined together without the isthmus of Central America.

This separation and the resulting isthmus were created by the gouging impact of the meteor strikes and the ejecta cloud that sent millions of tons of debris into the sky. The V-shaped area in the Southern Hemisphere was probably caused by both the Vredefort and the Wilkes Land impacts.

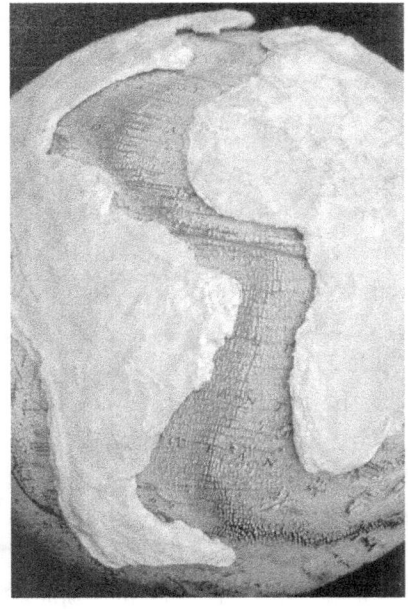

The continental fit with the Mid-Atlantic Ridge is superior to the fit between the coasts.

The two largest areas of continental erosion are where meteors would have struck the singular landmass, precipitating the tear of the crust along the ridge. The V-shaped area shows that the general trajectories of the asteroids came from the same direction.

(Courtesy Walt Brown, *In the Beginning*)

The direction of the Vredefort impact in Africa would have traversed the interior of the Earth and impinged with the relative position of India where it was at that time connected to the eastern side of Africa. As the cracked supercontinent fractured, the impact of the Vredefort meteor was so great that it literally ripped India and Madagascar from the eastern side of Africa and sent them eastward and northward. Initially as it fractured from Africa, India had also become an island continent. But eventually, the centrifugal force of the Earth's spin caused it to go farther toward the equator and crash into the Asian plate, forming the Himalayan mountain range in the process.

The combination of the two relatively close impacts in the south fractured that area into what we now know as Antarctica, Australia, South America, Africa, and India. Australia was actually connected to Antarctica at the tip of Africa before the shattering impacts broke them apart.

The trajectory of the pressure waves into the interior of the Earth from the Wilkes Land impact and the Vredefort impact can be traced to the Deccan Traps in India. The Pacific deep ocean trenches were caused by the rebounding pressure waves that caused the Atlantic Ridge to rise on one side of the world and suck down the ocean floor on the opposite side.

So powerful was the southern Wilkes Land impact that it broke the landmass in that area into the two huge island continents of Australia and Antarctica and fractured South America from Africa. Antarctica drifted south, and Australia drifted south and eastward. Australia is still moving eastward at the rate of 5 inches per year, but like India, it is now moving upward toward the equator due to the centrifugal forces of the Earth's spin. That coincides with the angular momentum expected by the direction of the two southern impacts.

This multiple impact scenario, along with Brown's hydroplate theory that we will cover later, explains the motion of the continents better than the tectonic plate theory. It is simply inconceivable that floating tectonic plates would move toward the poles without some enormously powerful force to drive them there. The magma currents in the mantle do not travel north and south but rather east and west due to the spin of the Earth. The rotation of the Earth with its centrifugal force would cause the continents, if they were really free-floating and only affected by the magma currents, to all initially move toward the equator. But that is not what we have observed. The modern evolutionary plate tectonic mechanism does not have the power to do that.

If these continents were truly floating on the magma of the mantle, the centrifugal motion of the rotation of the Earth would tend to move all the landmasses toward the center of the Earth. Moreover, the magma currents, precipitated by the rotation of the Earth, would not be capable of moving Europe eastward while at the same time moving North America westward in the opposite direction.

The fact that Antarctica moved from a more central position between South America and Africa toward the area we find it today in exactly the South Pole shows that a tremendous force would have had to counter the natural propensity to move upward to the equator in reaction to the centrifugal force created by the Earth's spin. This is only possible to understand from the power of the impacts and from the mechanism of the hydroplate theory, as we shall soon see. The predominantly laterally directional rivers of magma in the mantle could not possibly generate the kind of downward force that would move a continent against the angular momentum of the spin of the Earth.

The Bulging Crust and Provincial Magma Traps

The pressure waves generated by these seven gigantic meteor strikes traveled through the entire diameter of the Earth, causing magma flows of biblical proportions immediately around the area of the impact and also at the opposite end of the Earth where the crust bulged outward as the initial pressure wave traveling through the interior of the Earth struck the opposite side. The combined energy of these giant meteors generated enormous pressure waves by the sheer force of the impacts that traveled through the Earth's molten core and impinged on the opposite side of the world. That caused the distal end of the trajectory line to bulge outward in the crust and precipitated enormous basaltic magma eruptions.

These gigantic magma flows, or traps, are so large that they are sometimes called igneous provinces. The term *traps*, or sometimes *trapps*, comes from the Swedish word for stairs (*trappa*). It refers to the unique step-like formation of these enormous basaltic magma flows that were pushed out by each rebounding pressure wave of the meteor impacts as they traveled back and forth through the interior of the Earth and bounced back, pushing the magma in pulses.

So large is this igneous province that it is almost equal to the entire area of Western Europe, or around 2 million square kilometers.

THE DEATH OF THE FIRST EARTH

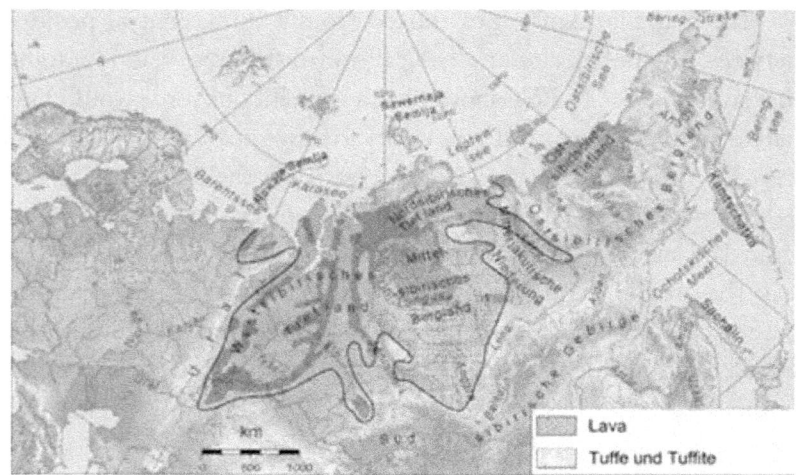

The map shows the enormous extent of the Siberian Trap. The Siberian traps are by themselves large enough to have brought about the end of the dinosaurs, as some evolutionists speculate. So impressive is this evidence that many scientists who have not accepted the meteor strike theory credit these traps alone for the extinction of the dinosaurs.

Scientists estimate that its original span may have reached as much as 7 million square kilometers, holding an estimated volume of lava of 4 million cubic kilometers. No doubt, this was the work of the enormous Maniitsoq meteor.

Surely this event by itself would be impossible to explain without an impact pressure wave by an enormous meteor that forced a magma plume to gush out from the bulging crust. Scientists are now proposing that normal volcanoes, due to the immense evidence left behind, could not have caused these enormous lava beds.

Russia is not the only place in the world that harbors the evidence of this titanic volcanic upheaval. We have already mentioned the Deccan Traps in India. Here we find the indisputable evidence of magma eruptions of truly biblical proportions. We find more than 0.5 million square miles of lava, in some places as much as 8,000 feet thick. This large igneous province is found on the Deccan Plateau in west-central India and was no doubt precipitated by the enormous

Vredefort asteroid that hit Africa while India was still connected to the eastern side of Africa.

The lava plume created by the pressure wave impinging on the crust and bulging it forced the flood basalt magma to cover an area of 500,000 square kilometers with an estimated volume of 1 million cubic kilometers of lava. Scientists estimate that the original extent of the Deccan Traps may have been close to 1.5 million kilometers square.

If we travel to the northern border of Argentina in South America between Brazil and Uruguay, we find a wondrous marvel of nature known as the world-famous Iguazu Falls. It is surely one of the grandest spectacles of nature as the largest waterfall in the world.

The enormous Iguazu Falls dwarfs the grandeur of the Niagara Falls on the border of the United States and Canada. The thunderous sound of the waterfalls is breathtaking. I cannot begin to imagine what thunderous sound the fountains of the deep would have made as they circled the world.

This breathtaking waterfall is known for its spectacular beauty and grandeur, but most people are not aware of an even more spectacular secret it holds. It cascades over an enormous bed of lava that is more than a mile thick. But what is even more astounding is that this lava bed covers an area twice the size of the state of Texas.

Iguazu Falls on the Argentinian side (https://www.naturalworldsafaris.com/latin-america/argentina/iguazu-falls)

The magnitude of the volcanic upheaval necessary to cover 250,000 square miles 1 mile deep in lava is astronomical. But even more astounding is the fact that the lava flow of this very same incident continued across the Atlantic and into Africa.

Samples of this basalt rock were chipped from the bedrock in Argentina and compared to the bedrock of Namibia in Africa, and they were found to be exactly the same composition, proving these three things:

1. The continents of South America and Africa were once joined.
2. The volcanic eruption that created the basalt bedrock found on the surfaces of both continents was contemporary to or prior to the splitting of the continents.
3. The separation between Africa and South America was not a slow, gradual bumping together of continents that were already broken, as the evolutionists insist. A catastrophic event capable of producing such enormous lava flows broke them apart.

The presence of so much lava at this breaking point speaks against the slow, imperceptible, eternally oscillating, peaceful scenario envisioned by the evolutionists who love to invent various jigsaw puzzles of the continents through eons of years, giving each new iteration a new, fancy name. Instead, it points to a single, massive cataclysm that violently broke up the supercontinent of the First Earth.

It is around this area where the continent of Antarctica was severed from the Americas and Africa and violently shoved southward toward its present location. We can see the Mid-Oceanic Ridge making a 90-degree turn going eastward under the horn of Africa, heading up toward the Indian Ocean at the east end of Africa and going the opposite direction under the Cape of Good Hope below South America as it went westward and then up toward the Pacific Ring of Fire. It is in this relative area that the initial impact of the Wilkes Land meteor and the Vredefort meteor hit and brought forth all this mayhem.

The cracks created under the immediate area of the impacts would have weakened the granitic plate, allowing the pressurized salt water beneath it to break and escape through the cracks as the fountains of the deep. The rebound pressure waves returning from the opposite side of the world would have further agitated and aided this expulsion process of the underground aquifers as they exploded upward.

Soon the cracks from each of the meteors came together and broke apart the seven continents. It was not a slow, peaceful bump and go as imagined by uniformitarian evolutionists. It was a dramatic rupturing with thunderous sounds louder than man had ever heard before as rocks cracked for thousands of miles and earthquake swarms shattered all of Arza. It was an apocalyptic scenario of deafening sounds.

When fitting the continents of South America, Antarctica, and Africa together with the base of the Mid-Atlantic Ridge, we see that the areas of most erosion by the jetting streams are in this southern region where the larger meteor struck and in the north where the enormous Maniitsoq meteor shattered everything to pieces, which we see now as islands, and in the middle where the Chicxulub meteor impacted.

The combined energy of these seven giant meteors would have been enough to crack the entire surface of our First Earth, ripping the crust between the impact zones and then circumambulating the entire globe like a giant zipper that busted loose.

That these asteroids could have struck at the same time is not as far-fetched as some may think. In fact, it may be more probable than most people imagine. Astronomers have been surprised to find that many asteroids fly in tandem with another asteroid. Sometimes they are found in small clusters; that is, two or more asteroids may sometimes fly in tandem, each with a moon. In fact, stars more often than not come in pairs, circling each other and sometimes traveling in clusters of three or four.

THE DEATH OF THE FIRST EARTH

The naturalistic argument that there is no mechanism to bring forth a global catastrophe as described in Noah's Flood account in Scripture can no longer be considered a credible scientific argument. The undeniable, empirical physical evidence of these seven giant craters created by seven giant meteors is the apocalyptic power to bring forth a global flood.

Moreover, when considering the large number of Apollo asteroids and comets that threaten Earth today, it is no longer possible for humanity to ignore the catastrophic account of the Global Flood, which may bring another apocalyptic catastrophe upon us.

The scientific evidence that substantiates the cataclysmic and global description found in the biblical record of the Great Flood can no longer be ignored and trivialized as folklore. As a matter of fact, it would behoove us to know the prophetic message of the book of Revelation, which predicts one and perhaps two more such strikes in the future. But that is a story for another book, *The Coming of the Prince of Peace*.

The evidence for the simultaneous strikes is forever etched in the continuous rip created in our Earth for those who have eyes to see. It is called the Mid-Atlantic Ridge, and it still has remnants of the fountains of the deep that we have filmed with underwater robots, allowing us to see spouting water 4 miles deep, about 700 degrees Fahrenheit, and laden with minerals. They are called smokers.

It would be impossible to explain the present

The remnants of the fountains of the deep (Geology for Today, http://www.geologyfortoday.com/restless-oceans.html*)*

configuration and movement of the continents if the seven meteor strikes had not happened in relative succession.

The Seven Shepherds of the Pleiades

We cannot claim dogmatically that exactly seven meteors struck at the same time, but there are many reasons we suspect there were seven.

1. The constellation of the Pleiades, whose stars number seven, and their historical involvement in the story of the Great Flood chronicled by ancient man
2. The physical data observed on our planet—seven giant asteroid impacts in a category that dwarfs all other impacts on Earth
3. The fact that each of them could have been an extinction event and that it is hard to believe that life could have survived without the Global Flood to mediate the firestorm that each one would have brought on our planet
4. The fracture of the continents and the direction of their movements relative to the meteor strikes
5. The creation of the Mid-Atlantic Ridge that was produced by the separation of the cracked continents of Arza
6. God's pattern of using groups of seven judgments as declared in the Book of Revelation
7. An ancient Sumerian Planisphere found in the Library of Ashurbanipal in the Assyrian capital of Nineveh that may have recorded the very seven asteroids' trajectory through the constellations prior to the Great Flood

You might wonder what the Pleiades have to do with the Great Flood. The Mayas called the constellation of Pleiades the Tzab, which, when translated, means "rattle," having the same function as that of a rattle snake since it warns of an impending strike. We can then understand the significance of Pleiades in warning us of the coming judgment of Taurus. This particular function as a warning sign of an impending judgment was not peculiar only to the Mayas. The fact that the destruction of the antediluvian world may have been heralded by the midnight culmination of Pleiades seems to be preserved in other cultures of the world as well.

> In the same way *they are intimately connected with the traditions of the Flood found among so many and widely separated nations, and especially in the Deluge-myth of Chaldea.* . . . they were pictured in the New World on the walls of Palenque temple upon a blue background; and certainly were a well-known object in other parts of Mexico, for Cortez heard there, in 1519, *a very ancient tradition of the destruction of the world in some past age at their midnight culmination* (emphasis added) (Allen 1899, 385).

The universal assignation of this phenomenon is another inevasible and vital evidence of the historicity of the Great Deluge. The constellations symbolized a new beginning or the entrance into a new epoch as God judged the previous epoch and instituted a new way. Richard Hinckley Allen documents the immense importance given to these stars by ancient cultures when he quotes from *The System of the Stars* by Agnes M. Clerke:

> With November, the "Pleiade-month," many primitive people began their year; and on the day of the midnight culmination of the Pleiades, November 17, no petition was presented in vain to the ancient Kings of Persia; the same event gave the signal at Busiris for the commencement of the feast of Isis, and regulated less immediately the celebration of the fifty-two year cycle of the Mexicans. Savage Australian tribes to this day dance in honor of the "Seven Stars," because "they are very good to the black fellows." The Abipones of Brazil regard them with

pride as their ancestors. Elsewhere, the origin of fire and the knowledge of rice-culture are traced to them. They are the "hoeing stars" of South Africa, take the place of a farming-calendar to the Solomon Islanders, and their last visible rising after sunset is, or has been, celebrated with rejoicing all over the southern hemisphere as betokening the "waking-up time" to agricultural activity (Clerke 1963 in Allen 1899, 401).

The ancient Mayas would gather on a particular night at midnight to observe the movement of the Pleiades during the culmination at the end of the 52-year cycle. All the fires in the community were turned off as they waited in darkness. If after the stroke of midnight the constellations continued their movement, then there was great celebration, for the world was not yet to come to an end.

At that time, a new fire was lit to symbolize a new beginning; that was their Festival of the New Fire. There can be no doubt that this ancient ceremony is, in fact, a memory of the new beginning of the postdiluvian civilization that developed after the Great Deluge when Noah made an altar unto the Lord to celebrate the deliverance of the survivors.

The New Fire ceremonies of the Celts on the other side of the Atlantic were uncannily similar and celebrated at the same time, clearly establishing the fact that these were nothing less than a universal memory of the same event.

The Celtic Samhain Festival, or Festival of the New Fire, was supposed to be a festival that celebrated the survival of the long night of winter that descended upon the Second Earth after the Great Flood. The New Fire commemorated the return of warmth and the beginning of a New Earth, the Second Earth, and it was a time for reflection to remember those departed in the Great Flood and consider the judgment or consequence of the rebellion of the First Earth.

The Hebrew calendar begins the New Year to correspond with the autumnal equinox that roughly coincides with this phenomenon; Genesis tells us that the destruction came on the 17th day of the second month of Heshvan. The Mayas divided their time cycles in similar fashion to the Hebrews, but instead of every 50 years, they divided them into every 52 years.

The 50th year in the Hebrew calendar is the Year of Jubilee because it represents the beginning of the Millennial Kingdom of God and is therefore a time of great celebration as the witness in the sky predicts that the coming Taurus shall destroy Satan's kingdom, ushering in a time of Jubilee. In the day that Aquarius rises on the vernal equinox, Taurus shall rise on the winter solstice to mark the end of the ascension of darkness over light. In that day, swords shall be turned into plows.

The Sumerians called the Pleiades the Plow. It is no coincidence that seven meteors plowed through the Earth and turned it into seven continents. It is also not insignificant that from that day forward, man had to plow the Earth with more vigor in order to survive since the paradisiacal First Earth was destroyed and the planet was bereft of wild animals to hunt and wild fruits to forage.

CHAPTER 4
THE SUMERIAN PLANISPHERE

Postmodern man arrogantly believes that our modern minds are superior to our ancient ancestors' minds. Due to their erroneous evolutionary presupposition, they routinely interpret history through their pink evolutionary lens, which leads them to assume that ancient men had no deep knowledge in the areas of astronomy, engineering, or mathematics. For that reason they insist that Noah could not have built a ship of such sophisticated engineering prowess. They likewise could not imagine someone like Noah writing an astronomical Planisphere that far back in history when men were supposed to be less evolved.

Western culture thus does not understand that ancient men long ago discovered many things that were later forgotten and once again rediscovered. What history really tells us is that man is a fallen creature prone to self-destruction. Knowledge is not always successfully passed on from one generation to another due to a wide variety of reasons. Wars, famines, pestilences, and many other human calamities often bury discoveries under the sands of time. Can you name one scientist who knows the entire true recipe for Greek fire?

Our modern age has progressed so rapidly that we tend to subliminally accept the evolutionary assumption that our minds are superior to our ancestors' minds. Turn to any modern textbook in college, and it will tell you that Pythagoras was the first to discover the Pythagorean theorem. But this is simply false.

In the ancient city of Larsa, a curious tablet was found that dates back to the Old Babylonian Empire right after the Tower of Babel. It is called the *Old Babylonian Geometry Tablet* and dates to the beginning of the second millennium BC, several thousand years before Pythagoras was born. This ancient tablet not only taught the Pythagorean theorem but also taught students geometric problems of varying degrees of difficulty. It was in essence a geometry textbook that also involved the construction of equilateral triangles and displayed several geometry problems in increasing complexity.

You probably thought calculus was invented 700 years ago by Europeans. At least that is what our universities teach.

> Looks like it's time to rewrite the history books again — and the math books, while we're at it.
>
> An elementary form of calculus thought to have been discovered some 700 years ago may be three times as old, analysis of ancient Babylonian astronomical artifacts shows. Scholars as early as 350 B.C. appear to have calculated the area under a curve (an operation known as taking the integral) in order to determine the distance traveled by Jupiter over a period of time.
>
> Mathieu Ossendrijver, of Berlin's Humboldt University, studied certain clay tablets covered in cuneiform writing stored at the British Museum for more than a decade. He knew they had calculus-like work on them, but it wasn't until he was shown photos of some even earlier, undocumented tablets that he made the astronomical connection.
>
> "These computations predate the use of similar techniques by medieval European scholars by at least 14

centuries," wrote Ossendrijver in his paper describing the discovery, which was the cover story of the journal Science on Friday.

The revelation could seriously affect the timeline of the history of mathematics, propelling the Babylonians — already advanced for their time — to the head of the class for having anticipated European scholars by more than a millennium in this foundational technique (Coldewey 2016).

This should not be a surprise to students of history who have an inkling of the engineering skill necessary for ancient men to build mammoth buildings such as ziggurats like the Tower of Babel or the Great Pyramids. It is doubtful that these massive and precisely engineered works could have been built without an understanding of geometry at a sophisticated level. In fact, the very earliest finds of the Sumerian people evidence an extremely advanced knowledge of architecture and engineering, and I would not be surprised if the Babylonians inherited their knowledge from the Sumerians.

We have been taught that it was the Roman civilization that invented the arch. No doubt it gave them a great advantage in their engineering skills that surpassed their contemporaries. But they were not the first to discover this engineering marvel. Thousands of years before the Romans, the Sumerian civilization had long mastered these engineering skills. They were known to man before the Great Flood and later forgotten.

> It is astonishing to find that at this early period the Sumerians were acquainted with and commonly employed not only the column but the arch, the vault, and (as may be argued from the apsidal ends of the chambers) the dome, architectural forms which were not to find their way into the western world for thousands of years.

That the general level of civilization accorded with the high development of architecture is shown by the richness of the graves. Objects of gold and silver are abundant, not only personal ornaments but vessels, weapons, and even tools being made of the precious metals; copper is the metal of everyday use. Stone vases are numerous, white calcite (alabaster) being most favoured, but soapstone, diorite, and limestone also common, while as rarities we find cups or bowls of obsidian and lapis lazuli; lapis and carnelian are the stones ordinarily used by the jeweller. The inlay technique that was illustrated by the Kish wall-decoration, carried out in shell, mother-of-pearl, and lapis lazuli, occurs freely in the graves at Ur (Woolley 1965, 37–38).

Their knowledge of astronomy was no less impressive. Josephus Flavius, writing around the time of the destruction of the Second Temple in Jerusalem, tells us that the children of Seth, the son of Adam, were experts in the science of astronomy, even before the Great Flood. In fact, he states that their deep concern was that future posterity might, through the corruption of our society, lose this precious knowledge. Their fear was actually well-founded.

Now this Seth, when he was brought up, and came to those years in which he could discern what was good, he became a virtuous man; and as he was himself of an excellent character, so did he leave children behind him who imitated his virtues. All these proved to be of good disposition. They also inhabited the same country [the Land of Elda] without dissensions and in a happy condition, without any misfortunes falling upon them till they died.

They also were the inventors of that peculiar sort of wisdom, which is concerned with the heavenly bodies, and their order. And that their inventions might not be

> lost before they were sufficiently known, upon Adam's prediction that the world was to be destroyed at one time by the force of fire and at another time by the violence and quantity of water, they made two pillars, the one of brick, the other of stone: they inscribed their discoveries on them both that in case the pillar of bricks should be destroyed by the flood, the pillar of stone might remain, and exhibit those discoveries to mankind (emphasis added) (Josephus 1960, 27).

Some of you might balk at the idea that Noah could create an astronomical chart depicting this coming cataclysm in the night sky with such sophistication. If we set aside the evolutionary bias for a moment and listen to the record of our ancestors, we might think otherwise. It was the long age of man during that early period that allowed mankind to accumulate such deep knowledge in the areas of astronomy and geometry.

> God afforded them a longer time of life on account of their virtue, and the good use they made of it in astronomical and geometrical discoveries, which would not have afforded the time of foretelling [the periods of the stars], unless they had lived six hundred years; for the Great Year is completed in that interval (Josephus 1960, 9).

Imagine the amount of accumulated knowledge a man could accumulate if he lived for those spans of years and maintained a clear and insightful mind during that long period. Ancient man was well aware that God had placed the stars in the heavens for the measuring of time, not in the corrupted form of modern astrology that uses the constellations and the positions of the planets to profane God's purpose and turn it into divination. The Mazzaroth tells the story of the ancient cosmic battle between God and Satan. It marks the ages of our human history.

Because of a slow wobble in the Earth's rotation, the view from our eastern horizon changes 1 degree every 72 years. Hence, the constellation rising over the eastern horizon during the spring equinox changes approximately every 2,160 years because each of them is roughly 30 degrees wide (30 x 72 = 2,160).

However, it must be noted that the rate of our present wobble is not necessarily the rate of the wobble of the First Earth prior to the meteor strike that precipitated the changing of the original orbit of our planet around the Sun. Certainly the year was shorter than it is today, and I strongly suspect that the constellations at that time may have shifted at a much faster pace that was slowed down by the impacts.

In our Second Earth, it now takes roughly 2,160 years to shift from one constellation to the other. For example, the constellation Pisces began to rise over the vernal equinox when Christ was born. The two fish of Pisces thus represent the Jewish and Gentile branches of God's people—the Church.

The sign that preceded that was Aries, the ram. It began to rise over the vernal equinox when Abraham was born. The Akkadians called this constellation Lu Hun Ga, "the Hired Man." An (God) hired the Seed of Eve to end the rule of the Serpent. Hence the symbolism of the ram as the sacrificial substitute for man is quite in line with this symbolism.

The Sumerian Planisphere calls it "UDU SUB DI," which translated means "the sheep casts judgment." This was the age of Israel. It was a ram that God provided for Isaac when Abraham offered his son to God. He did so on top of Mount Moriah, the same place the Temple Mount sits where the Holy of Holies of the Temple of God was built. Through Israel would come the Seed of Eve who would become our sacrifice upon the cross, and therefore on this same mountain He was crucified as An's hired man for our propitiation.

Prior to Aries, Taurus was the ruling house; that is, it rose on the vernal or spring equinox. It would have begun to rise over the vernal equinox circa 4000 BC if there had been no change of the Earth's orbit from the time of Abraham up to 4000 BC. That is the time I presume to be the judgment of the Great Flood (see *A Witness in the Sky*). But the severe impacts of the meteors that broke our singular continent into seven continents also changed the orbit of the Earth and its tilt, and it probably slowed down our tottering.

Prior to Taurus, Gemini was the constellation that was rising over the vernal equinox when the Nephilim ruled the Earth. Gemini speaks of the Adamic lineage and the Nephilim, or Neanderthals, which were totally eliminated at the rising of Taurus on the vernal equinox. As I have previously stated, it was during the time that Gemini rose on the vernal equinox that the seed of Cain became party to the birthing of the Nephilim.

The problem is that between the time Gemini rose on the vernal equinox and the time Taurus rose on the vernal equinox, there was not the typical 2,160 years that span one constellation and the other. The reason is that the meteors that slammed into Earth when Taurus rose on the vernal equinox and Scorpio rose on the autumnal equinox knocked Earth away from its near circular orbit into an elliptical orbit. Therefore, the time of the precession of the equinoxes in the Second Earth is much longer than it was in the First Earth.

It also probably caused our 23-degree tilt. It may have also greatly slowed down the wobble of the Earth and therefore the length of time of the precession of the equinoxes. That also changed drastically the angle from which we view the stars. Hence, I believe that the period between Taurus and Aries was drastically shortened compared to our typical time to change from one constellation to the other in our Second Earth by the tilting of the axis.

It is my contention that the men of the First Earth understood the precession of the equinoxes and had a very advanced knowledge of astronomy. Hebrew traditions state that it was Seth and Enoch who revealed the Mazzaroth (Zodiac) to mankind. That is, ancient man even before the Great Flood knew the story of the Zodiac, the Bible of the First Earth.

The discovery of the Library of Ashurbanipal at his royal palace in ancient Nineveh during the latter part of the 19th century sent shock waves throughout the archaeological community. There, Henry Layard discovered an item called a Planisphere that had baffled scientists for almost 150 years until it was recently deciphered. The extent of the careful calibration of the astronomical data recorded is utterly astounding.

The tablet is probably a copy of the original work from many years before. We know that from the position of the stars the astronomer recorded and from the ancient Sumerian language it used. That particular night sky dates all the way back to the earliest Sumerian civilization. It may very well be that it dates back to the moment the Great Flood destroyed the First Earth.

The most remarkable data recorded is found in the lower quarter. The bottom half of the Planisphere carefully marked the path of a group of seven meteors that began in the constellation of Gemini and traveled through the constellation of the Pleiades before striking Earth.

There have been several attempts to match the sky recorded on the Planisphere with dates where the night sky matched our ancient past. The use of computers to turn back the clock and simulate night skies were not available when this ancient tablet was first unearthed in Nineveh.

However, although Bond and Hempsell's interpretation is on the right track by acknowledging that it is a sky chart of an ancient Sumerian night, their star chart does not fit quite correctly yet. Unless the change in our Earth's orbit and axis precipitated by the meteor impacts are included in the computations, the computer will not be able to match the sky to the right date. I suspect that this star chart may be the record of the asteroids that struck Earth and broke open the underground aquifers that brought on the Great Flood.

There is a possibility that this very star chart was recorded by none other than Noah. Certainly Noah was forewarned by God a week before the coming disaster, so he may have prepared well for the coming cataclysm.

> *For after seven more days, I will send rain on the earth forty days and forty nights; and I will blot out from the face of the land every living thing that I have made.*
> —Gen. 7:4

Noah might have been the Sumerian astronomer who traced the night sky in this ancient tablet. If my suspicion is correct, the present computer programs cannot arrive at a proper star chart because of the effects of the powerful impacts of these meteors.

A look at the orbits of Venus and Mercury show that all the internal planets are in an almost circular orbit around the Sun. I suspect that Earth had a similar orbit when it was created. The slightly elliptical orbit that it has now at one end of the ecliptic was probably created only by the massive impacts of these meteors. I also highly suspect that our 23-degree tilt came as a result of those impacts.

I suspect that when God created the Earth, it was near perfect in every way. The lunar calendar and the solar calendar were in complete harmony. The solar calendar was subsequently elongated because of the elliptical orbit created by the massive impacts. Something very powerful struck Earth and made it move 5 million miles farther from the Sun than in its previous orbit at one end of its ecliptic. The strike happened at the time Genesis says this event took place, on the 17th day of the second Hebrew month. Modern star charts in computer software do not take that variable into account. Hence, any star charts beginning with our present elliptical orbit and tilt cannot produce a copy of the night sky as it was seen on the First Earth prior to the cataclysmic impacts.

To properly correlate the night sky to that date on the 600th year of Noah's life on the second month, the month of Heshvan, and the

17th day, corrections must be made to simulate the position of the Earth when it was in a nearly circular orbit around the Sun such that the lunar calendar and the solar calendar were in perfect harmony and the axis was less tilted.

If my suspicions are correct, we will find that the date the flood began would correspond to somewhere close to the time when Taurus began rising in the vernal equinox and Scorpio began rising on the autumnal equinox while the Earth's orbit was circular. Had the meteors not changed our orbit, we could backtrack our night skies through the present computer programs to the date circa 4000 BC and watch Taurus begin to rise in the vernal equinox.

The movement of the precession of the equinoxes would have been decelerated by the shifting position of our planet due to the impact event. The change in the wobble cannot be accurately known prior to the impacts. Thus, before the impact, the typical 2,160 years would not have lapsed between Gemini rising on the vernal equinox and Taurus rising on the vernal equinox. The shift in the Earth's orbit not only elongated our year but also changed our axis and the rate of the wobble by slowing it down. The precession now has increased the time it takes to shift the 30 degrees between one sign and the next after the impact.

It is my suspicion that the rise of Virgo in the vernal equinox during the time of the Garden at Eden and the shift to Leo, Cancer, and Gemini would have transpired during the time of the 10 patriarchs of the First Earth and the Great Flood. I suspect the constellation of Gemini marks the time of the Nephilim when mankind was introduced to war, sorcery, and cannibalism as the demonic plan to profane the lineage of the seed of Eve in order to prevent the birthing of the Messiah prophesied in Genesis 3:15. But the prophecy of the Dragon Doom could not be undone since God vanquished from our world the illegitimate seed of the Neanderthals. Only Noah's family survived, and the legitimate seed of Eve was saved from the demonic plan to avert the prophecy of the Dragon Doom.

Because the Earth shifted positions, from our viewpoint the background stars also changed positions. In order for us to find the night sky on the 17th day of Heshvan when Scorpio was rising on the autumnal equinox, we need to compensate for the Earth's change in tilt and trajectory. We need to place the Earth back in its original, circular orbit.

As astounding as that may sound, there is a possibility that we may have in our possession an ancient Sumerian tablet that has actually recorded that particular sky, and that tablet may have recorded the seven meteors and their trajectory across the constellations before striking Earth. If that is so, then the astronomer who made that momentous star chart could have very well been Noah or, at the very least, one of his three children. Since they were the only survivors, it is safe to conclude that one of them must have been the astronomer who made this magnificent star chart of our ancient sky recorded in the Sumerian Planisphere.

Much has been learned of our ancient forerunners through the treasure trove of information contained in the Library of Ashurbanipal whose name shows a connection to the biblical patriarch Asshur, the grandson of Noah through Shem who had many children, but five are most notable.

The sons of Shem were Elam and Asshur and Arpachshad and Lud and Aram.
—Gen. 10:22

Of these, Arpachshad may have been the oldest for he was born two years after the Great Flood. The Scriptures also seem to indicate that the three sons of Noah begat all their children after the Great Flood (Gen. 10:1). These eventually coalesced into tribes that produced different nations after the Tower of Babel. But prior to the division of the languages, all the grandchildren and great grandchildren of Noah for six generations were Sumerians. It is my belief that the Sumerian language was the language of the First Earth.

In the sixth generation during the time of Peleg, the Earth was divided. After the dispersion, Elam became the father of the Elamites, who were later known as Persians. Asshur became the father of the Assyrians. Arpachshad became the father of the Chaldeans. From him came the messianic lineage. From him came Abraham of the city of Ur of the Chaldees. Lud became the father of the Laudians, who later became Lydians. Aram became the father of the Aramites, who later became Syrians.

The Scriptures tell us that Shem's son Asshur founded the city of Nineveh. It was in the Assyrian capitol of Nineveh that Ashurbanipal's royal library was found. Among this list of many clay tablets in varied forms was found the curious artifact shaped like a round plate, which today we call the Sumerian Planisphere. It is presently held in the British Museum as item no. K8538.

The Sumerian Planisphere

The Star-Planet Sent by An

The Planisphere, a map of the ancient Sumerian sky, seems to record seven meteors that struck the Earth. Seven dots are marked by the constellation of Pisces in the trajectory that originated from the constellation Gemini and then passed through the right arm of Orion, through the eye of Taurus (Aldebaran), and then through the Pleiades. These then passed through Pisces to Pegasus and Sagitta and finally to Ophiuchus, where they intersected the path of the Sun and crashed into Earth.

In the Pisces sector of the Planisphere, these Sumerian words are written: ANEN LIL A TES IGI MUL [AN (God) and EN (planet) are written together]. The Sumerian word *AN* is the name of God, the Great Father and Creator, who is symbolized by the Sun. The title AN LUGAL means "Sky King" and refers to the "Sky God" we know as the Heavenly Father. That title for the Supreme Being is found in almost every ancient culture.

The word *EN* can be translated "planet." For example, it has been used as a prefix in the names for Mercury and Venus. Although Bond and Hempsell's final interpretation of the Planisphere is not in accord with mine, they agree in their book that deciphers K8538 (the number assigned to the tablet by the British Museum) that this passage may be referring to celestial objects that are neither stars nor planets.

> Turning to EN, the use of EN (B99) meaning "planet" was discussed under the Cancer sector. As with some other signs in places on K8538 the AN and EN have been run together indicating a moving star-like object which the observer is having trouble identifying (Bond and Hempsell 2008, 46).

Credit must be given to Bond and Hempsell for having first seen that this is, in fact, the work of an ancient Sumerian astronomer whose calculations are amazingly accurate and whose knowledge of astronomy is highly sophisticated. I am indebted to their work and to those who translated the MUL APIN for most of the translation of this incredible tablet. As previously noted, I disagree with their final conclusion, but their work is admirable. Few people today know how to think outside the box. For this, I am extremely grateful to them.

The Sumerian word *EN* has also been used in the MUL APIN (constellation of the plow) Sumerian star chart as a prefix for the constellation of the cross, Crux. Additionally, it is used as a prefix for EN LIL, which translated means "God of the Air" and, as EN KI, when translated means "God of the Earth." LIL means "wind" or "air." KI means "earth." It is quite possible that EN KI is a special appellation to the Son of God and EN LIL is their name for the Holy Spirit.

The word *EN* comes from E = wall and N = high. The high wall is intended to represent protection from attack; hence, the title insinuates God the protector and can be translated as "Lord"—one who protects. The ancients customarily associated planets with God or prominent figures in the cosmic battle between God and Satan.

For example, Jupiter is considered the king planet and symbolizes the Messiah, while Saturn symbolizes God the Father. Mars represents the warring Messiah. Mercury represents the Messiah in His priestly office. Venus symbolizes Eve, the mother of mankind, but also her Seed, who is the Messiah.

Of course, the occult has profaned these symbols and adopted them for themselves. Mars is seen as the symbol of Satan as the opposer—the war god, black magic, and also a symbol for Azazel, the demon who taught mankind the art of war. It is also the symbol of the Antichrist. In Celtic lore, it is associated with Odin, the usurper of Thor, the Son of God.

Mercury, on the other hand, represents the role of Lucifer, the deceiver and magician. In Celtic lore, it is Loki the trickster god. It represents white magic, Luciferianism, the False Prophet, and Shemihaza, the demon who taught mankind the art of sorcery.

In profaned occult circles, Venus has been robbed from Eve and given to the fertility goddesses. Their role is to birth the impostors of Christ who call themselves gods. The Moon has also been profaned in the same fashion as a symbol for the fertility goddesses that began during the rule of the Nephilim and continues to this day in modern occult circles such as Wicca. But we can see the original meaning in Scripture as Christ is referred to as the Morning Star, which is Venus.

The Moon was known by the ancient Sumerians as EN ZU. It is also almost universally considered by ancient cultures as the symbol of the Messiah and Eve. Through Eve's Seed comes God in diminished form to light our path during the darkness. The light of the Moon is no less the light of the Sun, who is AN, the God of the universe. In the book of Revelation, Israel is described as "a woman clothed with the sun, and the moon under her feet, and on her head a crown of twelve stars" (Rev. 12:1).

Israel is clothed with God (Sun) and stands upon the Great Redeemer (Moon). Her crown of 12 stars represents the 12 tribes of Israel, and each tribe no doubt has an angel protector. The Sun is not God; it is the symbol of God. The Moon is not the Messiah; it is the symbol of the Messiah. Likewise, stars are symbols of angels.

Taking all the meanings of AN and EN into consideration, it is evident that the writer of this Sumerian tablet was trying to describe a special heavenly body that did not fit exactly as a planet or a star and was sent by God. A probable translation of the text in the Pisces sector would thus be "Star-like object sent by An passes this way before the constellations."

The Path before the Constellations

The significance of this specific trajectory through the constellations is quite revealing. As we shall see later, the Sumerian Planisphere seems to indicate that these meteors were first seen in the sky coming from Gemini through the constellation of Orion. It is the only constellation named twice in the Planisphere. It is drawn in the Gemini sector and the Taurus sector, thus connecting these two constellations through the medium of Orion's purpose. The name for this constellation of Orion in Sumerian is the Loyal Shepherd of Heaven. This is known from the MUL APIN star charts in Sumerian as SIPA ZI AN NA.

Orion is a constellation that depicts the Messiah. The name Orion is derived from UR AN NA. UR is the symbol of God, the Sun. It is from UR that we derive the name Urusalem (Jerusalem). With His mighty right arm, the Messiah bashes the head of the impostor lion who comes to take His sheep. His right foot stands on the head of Lepus the rabbit, which symbolizes the fertility cults of the Mother Goddesses. It is a star picture of the Genesis 3:15 prophecy that states that the Seed of Eve shall strike the lethal blow on the head of the Enemy of Man. In ancient Egyptian culture, the constellation of Orion was known as Horus, the Son of God who would vanquish Apep the Serpent.

The constellation Orion is also depicted in the Sumerian Planisphere within the sector of Gemini, below the twins. The constellation of Gemini is called in Sumerian MAS TAB BA GAL GAL (the Great Twins). The Twins are Castor and Pollux. Castor has been historically associated with Cain, the first born on Earth, and Pollux with Abel or Seth (his replacement), which became the lineage of the Messiah. The symbolism of Cain killing Abel is repeated in the story of the Nephilim. The attempt to wipe out the lineage of the Messiah is as old as the first man born in this world.

But a curious deviation from the normal arises in the Sumerian Planisphere. The astronomer who drew the stick figure of the twin constellations purposely avoided tracing the brighter stars of Pollux and instead drew the stick along a set of much dimmer stars. That choice has baffled modern astronomers as they try to imagine why the Sumerian astronomer chose such a configuration that is more difficult to see with the naked eye.

This was no accidental choice. The dimming stars represent the near extinction of the Adamic lineage and the line of Seth through which the Messiah was to be born. It represents the dire condition at the time of Noah when all mankind had gone the way of the Mother Goddesses and our human bloodline was almost completely profaned by the Neanderthals.

But there is another curious item in the Planisphere that further tells the story of this star chart. A line is drawn through those dim stars toward the eye of Taurus, the star called Aldebaran (the Captain that Cometh). That line drawn through the dim stars of Pollux has an arrow that points to Aldebaran.

There is another line coming from the right shoulder of Orion that also intersects at Aldebaran. The meaning of the connecting line is quite clear. The purposes of all three constellations are intertwined. The purpose of the Shepherd is to protect His flock and kill all predators. The horns of Taurus are also pointed toward the impostor lion in Orion's left hand. Aldebaran is the Captain that Cometh to destroy the lion who is destroying His sheep. Both the horns of Taurus and the club on Orion are aimed at the head of the impostor lion in Orion's left hand. Again, this is a reference to the Genesis 3:15 prophecy of the Dragon Doom.

This symbolism is continued in Scripture with Samson killing a lion with the jaw of an ass, the colt upon which the Messiah would enter Jerusalem. It also continues with the shepherd, David, killing a lion with his bare hands defending his sheep. In fact, it is that story that wins him the chance to fight Goliath who is symbolic of the Nephilim.

But in the Planisphere, there is a third line that also transects Aldebaran and traces its path between the line from Gemini and the line from Orion. The line between these two lines from Gemini and Orion is the path of the meteors. There are also three similar lines in the sector called the Path Sector that create the same angles and pattern depicted in the Gemini sector of the Planisphere.

The top line from left to right travels through the dim stars of the bottom section of Gemini, the sector of Seth that ends in Aldebaran. The bottom line travels from the star Beatlegeuse on Orion's right arm and also intersects with Aldebaran in the eye of Taurus. The name Beatlegeuse is Arabic for "the House of the Twins." The connection shows that Orion comes through the lineage of Pollux (Seth). Orion is from the House of Seth. Hence, the interconnection between the two lines is made obvious. Orion is the Faithful Shepherd, the Seed of Eve who comes through Seth to fulfill the Genesis 3:15 prophecy of the Dragon Doom that will defeat the Nephilim of the line of Castor. The twins shall be no more.

In the middle, dividing the upper and lower lines, is the third line that is quite likely the path of the meteors. It also crosses through Aldebaran and splits the difference between the upper line and the lower line almost exactly.

I also believe that the significance of uniting the two sectors of Gemini and Taurus with Orion is tied to the precession of the equinoxes. This event took place when Taurus began to rise over the vernal equinox to mark the end of the age of Gemini. It was when Gemini rose over the vernal equinox that in the sixth generation from Adam the Nephilim came upon this Earth. The lineage of Cain thus did not reach beyond the seventh generation and was therefore not recorded in Genesis.

There is no record of Cain's lineage after that. The reason is clear; God did not recognize the union of the Nephilim with mankind as legitimate. Thus, his line ended when they turned to the comingling of Neanderthal shamans with man. Taurus then marked the end of the two lineages. Only Noah of the lineage of Seth entered the Second Earth. Thus the stars of Pollux were dim indeed for only eight remained to populate the Second Earth.

In the sector of Taurus, a statement of Orion is made that gives purpose to the meaning of this constellation. The phrase "Orion stands in knowledge" is written MUL SIPA ZI AN NA GUB ZU. What does that mean? I believe it is a twofold message.

First, the very crux of the occult message is what they refer to as the "esoteric knowledge." It is often phrased in terms such as Arcane Wisdom, Gnosticism, Illumination, and so on. It is what the Serpent offered Eve in the Garden—the knowledge of evil. This the religion of the Nephilim expounded with dire consequences to humanity. In stark contrast, God is telling us that the real knowledge is not found in the occult but in the Messiah, the Faithful Shepherd of the heaven—Orion.

Orion knows the end from the beginning because He is the Alpha and the Omega. This tablet is thus depicting the end of the rule of the

Nephilim from the very beginning. The path of the meteors shall end the rule of the Nephilim. Hence, this sector sets forth the end of the story at the beginning of the path.

Secondarily, Orion stands on the constellation of Eridanus, which in the Sumerian tablet is called AN NI NI AB SITA, "the Sea Channel of Heaven." Perhaps this is alluding to the fact that the meteors shall bring down the water vapor canopy that surrounded the First Earth. It may be referring to the breaking of the floodgates of heaven spoken of in Genesis.

Therefore, these three lines in the Sumerian Planisphere that cross at a definite point—in my opinion, the eye of Taurus, Aldebaran—represent the work of the Messiah whose number is also three. The line from Gemini that points to Aldebaran is transected by the line from the right arm of Orion in Aldebaran. The line in the middle must therefore be the line of the path of the meteors.

The sequence of lines 1 and 2 then reads, ***SUKKAL AN NA AN SAKKAR SILA. The first three symbols before SUKKAL are badly damaged and unreadable. But the MUL APIN (constellation of the plow) refers to a PAPSUKKAL, which is translated "the first envoy." PAP means to lead. From its location in this sector, it is probably referring to the constellation of the Pleiades where the line of the meteors' path connects next after leaving Aldebaran.

Hence, the paths of the meteors now travel beyond Aldebaran to the back of the Bull where the Pleiades are perched. These seven stars represent the seven eyes of God, the seven spirits of God, the seven archangels of God—"the First Envoys of God." The word *angel* means "messenger" or "envoy." Angels are the instruments of leadership that God uses to rule the heavenly hosts. They are also the instruments of judgment to mankind. In the book of Revelation, all the judgments are carried out by God's angels.

The prominence of the Pleiades in Sumerian astronomy is documented by Bond and Hempsell:

> It is proposed that the Pleiades cluster was used by the Sumerians as the starting reference for angular measurements along the Celestial Equator and not the Vernal Equinox as used today. Their name in the MUL APIN text, MUL MUL, (the "constellation of constellations") is suggestive of some special prominence. Thus when the Pleiades are at their Zenith the "King" point is on the eastern horizon and the "Queen" point is on the western horizon, setting over, "foreign lands" (2008, 51).

The evidence of the Pleiades' special prominence as the envoys of God is found throughout all the ancient cultures. The Mayas were engrossed in the observation of the Pleiades and believed this constellation was directly linked to the end of this age. They were quite right in this regard for Taurus is the symbol of the returning Messiah who will bring an end to the rule of the Antichrist and usher in the Age of Aquarius at which time Aquarius shall cleanse the ocean waters and heal our dying planet. In that day, Taurus will be rising in the winter solstice, but at the end of the First Earth, it was rising in the vernal equinox.

The importance of the Pleiades is held universally by almost all ancient cultures and associated with the judgment of the Great Flood.

> Often doorways or roof-combs, which are a particular feature of Classic Maya temples, were placed in such a way that they could mark the rising, culmination or setting of particular stars. They were especially interested in the movements of the Pleiades star-cluster as well as those of the wondering planets Mercury, Venus, Mars and Jupiter. Needless to say they made close observations

of the sun and moon, and this enabled them to predict eclipses accurately (Gilbert and Cotterell, 1996, 38).

The Mayans called the constellation of Pleiades the Tzab, which when translated means "the rattle," having the same function as that of the rattlesnake since it warns of an impending strike. The sight of seven meteors traveling across the sky cannot be more accurately represented than as a serpent flying through the sky. The warning rattler, Tzab, is exactly what the First Envoys of An did during the midnight culmination of that night on the 17th of Heshvan in the 600th year of Noah's life.

We can then understand the significance of Pleiades in warning us of the coming judgment of Taurus. This particular function as a warning sign of an impending judgment was not peculiar to the Mayas. The fact that the destruction of the antediluvian world may have been heralded by the midnight culmination of Pleiades seems to be preserved in other cultures of the world as well.

> In the same way *they are intimately connected with the traditions of the Flood found among so many and widely separated nations, and especially in the Deluge-myth of Chaldea* . . . they were pictured in the New World on the walls of Palenque temple upon a blue background; and certainly were a well-known object in other parts of Mexico, for Cortez heard there, in 1519, *a very ancient tradition of the destruction of the world in some past age at their midnight culmination* (emphasis added) (Allen 1899, 385).

The universal assignation of this phenomenon is another inevasible and vital evidence of the historicity of the Great Deluge. The constellations then symbolized a new beginning or the entrance into a new epoch as God judged the previous epoch and instituted a new way. Richard Hinckley Allen documents the immense importance given to these stars by ancient cultures, as he quotes from *System of the Stars* by Clerke:

> With November, the "Pleiade-month," many primitive people began their year; and on the day of the midnight culmination of the Pleiades, November 17, no petition was presented in vain to the ancient King of Persia; the same event gave the signal at Busiris for the commencement of the feast of Isis, and regulated less immediately the celebration of the fifty-two year cycle of the Mexicans. Savage Australian tribes to this day dance in honor of the "Seven Stars," because "they are very good to the black fellows." The Abipones of Brazil regard them with pride as their ancestors. Elsewhere, the origin of fire and the knowledge of rice-culture are traced to them. They are the "hoeing stars" of South Africa, take the place of a farming-calendar to the Solomon Islanders, and their last visible rising after sunset is, or has been, celebrated with rejoicing all over the southern hemisphere as betokening the "waking-up Time" to agricultural activity (Clerke 1963 in Allen 1899, 401).

The Hebrew calendar also begins the New Year (Rosh Hashanah) in correspondence with the autumnal equinox. It was in the second month (Heshvan) on the 17th day that the Great Flood began. That was the day the Pleiades signaled the coming judgment. The fact that ancient nations considered the 17th of November this crucial day cannot be viewed as a simple coincidence.

The Mayans divided their time cycles in similar fashion to the Hebrews, but instead of every 50 years, they divided them into every 52 years. The 50th year in the Hebrew calendar is the Year of Jubilee because it represents the beginning of the Millennial Kingdom of God and is therefore a time of great celebration as the witness in the sky predicts that the coming Taurus shall destroy Satan's kingdom, ushering in a time of Jubilee. On the Year of Jubilee in the day Aquarius rises on the vernal equinox, Taurus shall rise on the winter solstice to mark the end of the ascension of darkness over light.

The ancient Mayas gathered on a particular night at midnight to observe the movement of the Pleiades during their midnight culmination at the end of the 52-year cycle. All the fires in the community were turned off as they waited in darkness. If after the stroke of midnight the constellations continued their movement, then there was great celebration for the world was not yet to come to an end.

At that time, a New Fire was lit to symbolize a new beginning. That was their Festival of the New Fire. There can be no doubt that this ancient ceremony is, in fact, a memory of the new beginning of the postdiluvian civilization that developed in darkness after the Great Deluge when Noah made an altar unto the Lord to celebrate the deliverance of the survivors.

The New Fire ceremonies of the Celts on the other side of the Atlantic were uncannily similar and were celebrated at the same time, clearly establishing the fact that these were nothing less than a universal memory of the same event. For this reason, many of the ancient chronicles speak of the great darkness that accompanied the judgment of the Great Flood. But the dawn rose as the tephra was cleared by rain, and the Second Earth was born.

The Celtic Samhain Festival, or Festival of the New Fire, was supposed to be a festival that celebrated the survival of the long night of winter that descended upon the Second Earth during the Great Flood. The New Fire thus commemorated the return of warmth and the beginning of a New Earth, the Second Earth. It was a time for reflection, remembering those departed in the Great Flood as well as considering the judgment or consequence of the rebellion of the First Earth. Unfortunately, as in the First Earth, mankind later corrupted that original meaning. But that is another story.

The path of the meteor depicted in the Planisphere now enters into the Aries sector. This sector is badly damaged but appears to have contained 10 identical sentences saying, "UDU SUB DI," which translated means, "The sheep casts judgment." Although our constellation is pictured with a ram, the Sumerian may have been a lamb. This, of course, is none other than the Lamb of God who was slain for our sins and the same person depicted in Orion and Taurus—the Messiah. Although the MUL APIN calls this section of the sky the "Hired Man," the symbolism remains the same as previously noted.

The path of the meteors now crosses the Pisces sector, which, as we noted earlier, is where the astronomer named the meteors as coming from An (God). Pisces was known to the Sumerians as the constellation of the plows. The significance of this is that because of our expulsion from the Garden, man had to plow the earth in order to live as part of the judgment in the Garden at Eden. This, of course, was essentially a message to the people of the First Earth that was more prominently made for those who would survive in the Second Earth. From this point forward, man was forced to till the ground in order to survive in our much-diminished Second Earth.

Nevertheless, the MUL APIN, or "constellation of the plow," effectively represents God's people through Cain and Seth. The shorter plow represented the shorter line of Cain that was severed by the path of the meteors and separated from the longer plow that stretched toward Aquarius and represented the line of Seth that continued.

In the Second Earth, this constellation also represents the household of God. The two fish of Pisces represent the two components of the church—Jews and Gentiles. The Jews are the natural branches of the olive tree, and the Gentiles are the wild branches grafted to the tree.

The left fish represents the Jews who first received the gospel. That is strengthened by the fact that it is superimposed on the constellation of Andromeda who is chained by Leviathan. She will be freed by Perseus and shall then sit on the throne as Cassiopeia, reigning next to Cepheus, the Messiah. In that day, all the nations of the world will be gathered against Israel. Then Israel shall recognize the wounds of the One whom they pierced, and there shall be a fountain of grace showered upon Israel.

> *And all the nations of the earth will be gathered against it. "In that day," declares the* LORD, *"I will strike every horse with bewilderment and his rider with madness. But I will watch over the house of Judah, while I strike every horse of the peoples with blindness." And in that day I will set about to destroy all the nations that come against Jerusalem.*
>
> *I will pour out on the house of David and on the inhabitants of Jerusalem, the Spirit of grace and of supplication, so that they will look on Me whom they have pierced; and they will mourn for Him, as one mourns for an only son, and they will weep bitterly for Him like the bitter weeping over a firstborn.*
>
> *In that day a fountain will be opened for the house of David and for the inhabitants of Jerusalem, for sin and for impurity.*
>
> *"It will come about in that day," declares the* LORD *of hosts, "that I will cut off the names of the idols from the land, and they will no longer be remembered; and I will also remove the prophets and the unclean spirit from the land."*
>
> —Zech. 12:3, 4, 9–10, 13:1, 2

The larger fish on the right represents the Gentiles who received the gospel next, and it points to Aquarius when the Messiah shall take His throne on Earth. Just as Joseph was rejected by his brothers and sent to Egypt (Gentiles), it will be the One they rejected who shall save them from the seven years of famine during the Great Tribulation at the end of our Second Earth. And so the day of recognition shall be a day of rejoicing and weeping at the same time.

Curiously, unlike any other constellation in the Planisphere, the constellation of Pisces is drawn as a stick figure without the dots that mark the stars. This could be that the constellation was obscured by clouds and the ancient astronomer drew it from memory, or it could be done for a specific purpose. It could be that it is symbolizing the fact that this constellation, being opaque, represents the end of life on the First Earth—the death of mankind in the coming judgment.

There is a line drawn in this sector connecting Pisces to a closed triangle that reads in Sumerian MUL AS KAR, which means "constellations the one encircles." That could mean one of two things: the One is An who is symbolized by the Sun, and hence this probably means it is the path of the Sun; or, as Bond and Hempsell suggest, it could be a constellation that encircles the pole star. But it cannot be the pole star because the pole star at that time was Thuban in the constellation of Draco the Dragon. It is just too far away from this point. It must therefore be pointing to the path of the Sun.

If the mathematical compensation for the change in Earth's orbit and the change in tilt could be made, a comparison of this path of the Sun and the peculiar angles of the constellation of Pisces could bring us to the particular night sky on the 17th day of the month of Heshvan in the 600th year of Noah's life. Since the shape of the constellations vary slightly as time passes, the peculiar angle portrayed in the constellations of the Sumerian Planisphere may bring us to an exact moment in time.

There is also a planet inside the constellation of Gemini recorded in this star chart that is probably either Mars since it represents the Messiah at war or Jupiter, the king planet. There are also two planets just outside Gemini, probably Mercury and Venus. Their particular positions in the Planisphere could also narrow down the particular night of this observation.

The place of observation where the astronomer was located is also important in coming to a proper interpretation. Although we may not be able to come to an exact place, I believe it can be roughly calculated to an area to the east of the city of Shuruppak, although we have no way of knowing if Shuruppak was rebuilt in the same area as it was prior to the Great Flood. Nevertheless, it must be somewhere east of Mesopotamia and west of Shushan, Persia.

Genesis says they traveled from the east to settle in the valley of Shinar. Hence, their original home prior to the Great Flood must have been east of Mesopotamia. The position of the observer would be some distance from Shuruppak, for Josephus tells us that Noah fled the city because of the danger to his family. My guess is that he fled eastward away from the more populated areas toward Shushan.

That is perhaps the clue given to us from the position of the magi who read the constellations and knew the time of the birth of the Messiah. God's patterns in the intricate web of His providence are there for us to see if we look through eyes of faith.

In the lower boundary of the Path sector is a text that says BA BA BUR DIM, which translated means "bright white stone bowl coming toward." Perhaps no better description of a meteor can be made. Another annotation is found in this sector that reads AN BANDA SI, which translated means "AN vigorously swept along." Remember that the meteor was previously called ANEN. Hence, the two observations by the astronomer make it clear that it is neither a planet nor a star because it moves much more quickly than other celestial bodies. That could only describe comets or meteors.

I will speak more about the Sumerian Planisphere in a later book, but for now, the point I want to make is that these seven meteors I previously described are so much larger than all the other meteors that they are in a class by themselves. It is hard for me to conceive that these meteors struck at seven different times and that life managed to miraculously recover from the catastrophe every time. There had to be a counter event to the extinction event created by each of the massive impacts in order for life to survive. Only a scenario that includes the Global Flood to mediate the catastrophic effects of each of these impacts could explain the survival of life on Earth.

It is my contention that these seven meteors plowed through the Earth and broke up the continents in one single catastrophe that created the Great Flood of Noah. For this reason, it is recorded in the Planisphere as having passed through the constellation of the plow (Pisces).

It is also no accident that the constellation that represents God's people is also known as plows, for it is also God's judgment after the Fall that man would have to earn his living by tilling the Earth through the sweat of his brow (Gen. 3:17-19). Thus, the meteors were responsible for the twofold judgment that ended our First Earth (i.e., the fountains of the deep being broken and the floodgates of the heavens being broken). Their passage through Aldebaran, the eye of Taurus, symbolized the time of this judgment for Taurus began to rise over the vernal equinox after Gemini.

Hence, it is symbolic of the age of Gemini ending and the age of Taurus beginning. When Taurus began to rise over the vernal equinox, becoming the dominant house of the Sun, His two horns brought an end to the First Earth. The first horn thrust into the Earth and broke open the fountains of the deep. The second horn broke open the floodgates of heaven, and our First Earth drowned. All the profaned perished, and God began anew with Noah as the second Adam.

There were five major cities that existed before the Great Flood—Eridu, Badtibira, Sippar, Larak, and Shuruppak. No doubt these became centers of occult worship by the end of the First Earth. Flavius Josephus tells us that God told Noah to leave the city of Shuruppak for his safety. "So he departed out of that land" (Josephus Chapter III, vs. 1). He feared for his family because after addressing the Nephilim, they did not heed to his warning of the impending doom.

At this point, the reader might be skeptical. Scientists date the meteor strikes as separated by millions of years. In fact, they believe the Chicxulub strike in the Yucatan Peninsula was 65 million years ago at the time the dinosaurs became extinct. But I would like to remind the reader that they also believe that the dinosaur tissue discovered by Mary Higby Schweitzer in 2004, which is still elastic and belonged to a female *Tyrannosaurus* rex, is 65 million years old.

> Schweitzer gazed through a microscope in her laboratory at North Carolina State University and saw lifelike tissue that had no business inhabiting a fossilized dinosaur skeleton: fibrous matrix, stretchy like a wet scab on human skin; what appeared to *be supple bone cells, their three dimensional shape intact; and translucent blood vessels that looked as if they could have come straight from an ostrich at the zoo.*
>
> *By all the rules in paleontology, such traces of life should have long since drained from the bones* (emphasis added) (Yeoman 2006, 37).

Such soft tissue could perhaps in certain extreme cases (where they remain frozen) last several thousand years. But to believe that this tissue specimen has survived 65 million years is absolutely ludicrous. No living tissue could survive 65 million years without decomposing, and to believe that is scientifically irrational. If you don't believe me, stick a steak in the dirt, and leave it for six months.

Argument 5 – There is not enough water on the Earth to cover the mountaintops as described in Scripture

Naturalists claim that it is physically impossible to flood the entire world. There is just not enough water to cover all the mountains, they say, even by melting all the water frozen in the ice caps. They are right. There is not enough water in our world to cover our present mountaintops. But they are assuming that our present mountaintops achieved their height prior to the Great Flood. That is an enormous error based on their failed slow and gradual uniformitarian assumption. Cataclysms by their very nature create sudden and drastic changes within relatively short time periods.

In our Judeo-Christian model, we maintain that most mountain formations were a byproduct of the mechanism that caused the Great Flood. Prior to the cracking of Earth's crust, there were no shifting continents. The crust of the Earth was whole and stable. There was but one landmass and one ocean. The supercontinent of Arza was wider in area than the combined areas of our present seven continents.

It is the shift in the tectonic hydroplates that caused the protrusion of large chunks of landmasses skyward. The First Earth had a stable and whole crust. It was, indeed, a more ideal world than the one we inhabit today. But the seven continents were thickened as they dragged to a crawl by friction with the basaltic layer below. That not only shortened the total area of land but in doing so also made the continents buckle and thicken.

The prediluvian landscape contained some small mountains but not the giant rocky peaks we are accustomed to in our Second Earth. These prediluvian mountains were nothing more than large hills that were not thrust upward by tectonic movement and sculpted into craggy peaks by ice, water, and melting snow like our modern counterparts.

As we shall see later, it is the movement of these continental hydroplates that thrust the mountains into the sky as they ground to a halt. Others have doubted that rain alone could account for such an inundation that would cover the world. They are also right. It was not rain alone.

Two sources of water are recorded in Scripture. As we have already stated, the first is referred to as the fountains of the deep, and the second is the floodgates of heaven. The biblical narrative tells us that it took 40 days and 40 nights of a continuous, torrential downpour, which as previously explained were of mega-hurricane proportions throughout the entire Earth.

But it took 150 days to stop the fountains of the deep. That is to say that after the water vapor canopy was exhausted, the waters continued to rise by means of the first mechanism, the fountains of the deep, for 110 more days until they finally reached their zenith and topped every mountain of the First Earth by 15 cubits.

> *The water prevailed fifteen cubits higher, and the mountains were covered.*
> —Gen. 7:20

But prior to that, on the 40th day, the elevated waters of the ocean reached a level that was high enough, and the continents drifted far enough apart to create a much wider opening for the subterranean waters to be released. That reduced the force of pressure in the escaping salt water from the underground chambers and the curtain of water that reached into space at the beginning. As a result, the once-mighty geysers were effectively reduced to a rolling, bubbling, boiling ocean along the Mid-Oceanic Ridge and the Pacific Rim where the continents ripped apart.

We can observe this phenomenon by reducing the size of the tip in a fire hose with a constant water pressure. The smaller the diameter of the tip, the farther the stream of water is projected. Conversely, the larger the diameter of the tip, the less distance the water is projected. For five months the water rose until it reached its apex (five is the number of Satan). Every mountain of that First Earth was covered by at least 15 cubits of water (Gen. 7:20, 8:2).

Enduring the Ark

It is quite difficult for us to imagine the horror of a cataclysmic event such as what ended our First Earth. We can begin to appreciate such matters in a very minute way when we experience the fear of things such as volcanoes, tsunamis, earthquakes, tornadoes, and hurricanes. But we cannot begin to fathom the combined effects of all the things that came together at one single point in time and brought the death of the First Earth.

Imagine Noah's family inside the ark as the storm raged. Of course, there was no air-conditioning then. At first, the heat and humidity must have been terrible. The sounds must have been terrifying. The sonic booms created as the meteors entered the atmosphere announced the commencement of God's judgment. They were the loudest sound ever made on Earth until they made impact. The explosions created by the sudden impact then became the loudest sound ever in the history of the world. They would have been heard around the entire supercontinent of our First Earth.

The impact of the seven meteors was so powerful that it sent millions of tons of rock as ejecta into the sky. The rocks, heated by the force of the impact and later by friction as they fell back through the atmosphere, glowed in the sky like a global fireworks display, visible as glowing, red objects in the dimness of the darkness.

The initial heat generated by the returning red-hot, glowing ejecta of the rocks and debris sent into space must have heated the atmosphere globally by perhaps 20–30 degrees Fahrenheit within a very short period of time, producing the hot winds recorded by Hesiod. The sights must have been quite sensational and the thousands of sonic booms from each of the ejected boulders reentering the atmosphere absolutely frightening.

Deep, thunderous sounds rumbled from below as the crust of the Earth ripped with earthquakes so powerful that all things in the entire world shook violently. But this was not the only source of such terrible sounds. Loud booms heard for thousands of miles came from exploding volcanoes that sprouted everywhere from the ripping crust.

Together they must have filled the world with a deafening array of terrible sounds never before heard. Billowing plumes of smoke with lightning discharges inside the enormous ash clouds would have struck fear in the hearts of Earth's inhabitants. At night against the dark, the electrical discharges would have created an eerie, red glow flashing in the skies. Man had never experienced anything like that before.

People had never seen lightning or volcanoes. They had never experienced earthquakes. They had never experienced hurricanes or tornadoes. It had never even rained on the First Earth. All things were watered by the morning dew, so perfect was the controlled environment. Our First Earth had been a global greenhouse with moderate temperatures all over its surface. Now, all hell seemed to break loose, and our planet was being cooked by the heat.

Temperatures in the immediate vicinity of the returning ejecta would have equaled that of a modern oven on high at around 450 degrees Fahrenheit. Forest fires raged in all areas where the ejecta landed. Flowing magma from volcanoes added to the fires and the overwhelming heat. The verdant luscious forests went up in flames and turned to ash and smoke. Firestorms raced through the land, generating fire tornadoes.

Where the meteors had penetrated the crust deep in its interior, gushes of water now spurted from the underground aquifers. They jetted upward into the stratosphere with such force that they traveled at the speed of sound.

The enormous force of the water ripped around the entire length of the boundaries where the plates had been cracked by the seven impacts. Think of what happens to a soda bottle when you shake it violently and then open it quickly. The agitation combined with the sudden pressure drop from the fissure created by the meteors caused the violent outgassing of these underground aquifers. That happens to be the same mechanism scientists claim cause the high-energy explosion reactions of supervolcanoes that make them 100,000 times more violent than regular volcanoes. The agitation of the magma caused by earthquakes, which has dissolved gases pressurized in them, causes a sudden outgassing that hurls the magma into the atmosphere at an unprecedented force compared to normal volcanoes.

All along the ruptured plates, a thick curtain of water would have jetted upward, thrusting rocks and everything else it eroded from the sides. The roar would have been deafening all along the length of the rip around the entire planet. Imagine the power of Niagara Falls in reverse. As terrible as this gushing curtain of water would have been, had it not been for this injection of water, our Earth would have burned to a cinder.

Not only the blasts from the two meteors but also the falling ejecta and massive volcanic eruptions would have immediately changed the global temperature of the Earth's atmosphere. That heat radically changed our world in a very short period of time. Meanwhile, the jetting water was injecting moisture into the air and cooling it down. Volcanoes were also sending water vapor into the air. But more critically, millions of tons of ash were being jettisoned into the upper atmosphere, becoming the cloud nuclei that allowed the water vapor from the canopy and the jetting fountains to condense into raindrops.

Then came the rain—black rain. The thin water vapor canopy began to precipitate. Without the input of moisture high into our atmosphere by the gushing geysers of the fountains of the deep, the water vapor canopy would have quickly been exhausted. But for 40 days and 40 nights, the gushing fountains continued to inject moisture into the atmosphere, and it rained nonstop with an intensity that no one has ever witnessed in our time.

Torrents of flowing rivers of lava and the glowing hot falling ejecta heated during reentry into our atmosphere would have ignited firestorms in the densely wooded areas of the planet. They would have raced unchecked until succumbed by the floodwaters. The First Earth was roasting, and all life was in imminent danger of complete extinction.

Two things saved the Earth:

1. The jets of water that streamed up from our subterranean depths saturated our atmosphere with an enormous amount of moisture and helped remove the heat generated by the impact, the volcanoes, and the falling ejecta.

2. The water vapor canopy and the latent moisture injected into the atmosphere by the curtain of water thrusting upward from the subterranean chambers began to condense around the dust particles ejected into the sky by spewing volcanoes. Black rain fell all over the entire planet and cooled the superheated atmosphere.

It was that canopy, like a blanket, that had initially trapped the heat and kept the Earth safe from cosmic radiation. But now the once-protective canopy became a death sentence to our planet as it trapped all that heat like a broiling cauldron. If it had not dissipated, the planet would have roasted. Were it not for the copious amounts of water streaming through the air by both the spray of the fountains of the deep and the rain from the precipitating canopy, our atmosphere would have heated beyond what life could have endured. It would have become a sterile, lifeless, burnt rock.

Once the water vapor canopy completely disappeared through precipitation, the heat further dissipated into space. But the accumulating tephra and debris from the ejecta slowed down this process and turned the day into night. Darkness swallowed the planet. Eventually, the lack of sunlight penetrating into the atmosphere made the temperatures plunge and brought forth the First Ice Age.

We find references to this darkness that accompanied the Flood in many supposedly mythological accounts of the Great Flood. We can cite the Book of Jasher as one example that although not accepted as part of the Hebrew canon has great antiquity and is part of the Hebrew tradition.

> *Two and two came to Noah into the ark, but from the clean animals, and clean fowls, he brought seven couples, as God had commanded him.*
>
> *And all the animals, and beasts, and fowls, were still there, and they surrounded the ark at every place, and the rain had not descended till seven days after.*

> And on that day, the Lord caused the whole earth to shake, and the sun darkened, and the fountains of the world raged, and the whole earth was moved violently, and the lightning flashed, and the thunder roared, and all the fountains in the earth were broken up, such as was not known to the inhabitants before; *and God did this mighty act, in order to terrify the sons of men, that there might be no more evil upon the earth.*
>
> *And still the sons of men would not return from their evil ways, and they increased the anger of the Lord at that time, and did not even direct their hearts to all this.*
>
> *And at the end of the seven days, in the six hundredth year of the life of Noah, the waters of the flood were upon the earth.*
>
> And all the fountains of the deep were broken up, and the windows of heaven were opened, and the rain was upon the earth forty days and forty nights (emphasis added).
>
> —Jasher 6:9–14

I find the following descriptions of the opening of the fountains of the deep to be particularly accurate: "the Lord caused the whole earth to shake," "the fountains of the world raged," "the whole earth was moved violently," and "all the fountains of the earth were broken up, such as was not known to the inhabitants before."

Clearly, some catastrophe of an unprecedented global force must have caused the Earth to move so violently that the crust was cracked. So we see that in our Judeo-Christian model, the events that triggered the Great Flood also caused the continents to crunch and in some cases crush against each other. What other mechanism could have caused "the whole earth to shake" so that "the whole earth was moved violently" and "all the fountains of the earth were broken up"? That is not the description of some gently spouting geyser. It is a description of catastrophic global tectonic forces that broke the crust of our Earth and released the fountains of the deep by a process of "breaking."

For 40 days the entire Earth was embroiled in a torrential storm the likes of which no one had ever seen and no one has seen after. That greatly helped diminish the suspended tephra and ejecta debris. The number four is the number of the Earth, and the number 40 is the number of testing.

During those 40 days, monstrous thunderstorms borne from the sudden increase in atmospheric temperatures and the rising temperature of the ocean receiving the heated salt water from the underground aquifers ravaged the planet. The skies lit up with ferocious lightning bolts from cloud to cloud and from land to cloud. The ark, floating blindly in the ocean, was protected by God's merciful hand in the midst of utter chaos. The latent energy was such that mega hurricanes of Categories 5 and 6 savagely ravaged our world, ripping like a bulldozer through what forests managed to survive the fires. Monstrous tornadoes with even more powerful winds ripped all things from the face of the Earth, leaving a swath of bare soil like a plow through a meadow.

Monstrous waves and howling winds rocked the ark like a cork floating on angry water. The billowing, mega-hurricane storm of all storms must have made everyone on board seasick for at least the duration of a month and 10 days. The eerie sound of the intense, howling winds spawned by the enormous rise in ocean and atmospheric heat would have sent chills down the spine of the hardiest of men.

Most of us have not had the unfortunate experience of living through a hurricane. I have seen them more than a few times while living in South Florida. Rain has come down so violently that the noise of it hitting the roof drowns out our voices. The huge, thick drops flow sideways in the wind like a waterfall flowing horizontally. The power is so strong that the raindrops sting and hurt when they hit your skin. The winds are so strong that you cannot stand. I have seen couches from living rooms whose walls were torn apart deposited several blocks away after being lifted into the air.

The combination of the wind and water is so powerful that it can knock you off your feet and drag you down the street. Flying debris, like missiles through the air, slams into homes and shatters doors, windows, and walls. The eerie sound of the howling wind in the night strikes fear in all hearts. Giant trees with stout limbs are shredded and uprooted. Wooden homes are splintered and blown away like chaff in the wind. Storm surges dig huge gullets in some places and deposit several feet of sand in others.

And yet these are relatively mild storms compared to the Category 6 or more storms that plowed through the Earth during the Great Flood. Their powerful winds are almost unimaginable today. Thus our First Earth was baptized in fire and water to cleanse from it the profaned and the corrupt.

After some time, the heat dissipated, and the storms abated. The loudness of silence now brought an eerie, still peace to the strange, new world. The skies were still dark. The sun glowed with a strange, red luminescence. The blood moon ruled the night. The bright stars that once adorned the heavens were gone from the night sky. Darkness enveloped the Earth in a funeral shroud. The time of the shadow spelled the death of the First Earth.

Cold came, and it was the first great winter of our people. Deep darkness swallowed the light. Blackness filled the world from horizon to horizon. The sickle of retribution brought justice to the wicked. The stench of death—the smell of violence at its natural end—lingered in the wind. There were no more chants or sky-clad dances around the midnight fires, no more ghastly rituals and shedding of innocent blood, no more orgies while eating human flesh, and no more drinking of blood.

The howling demons were chained and silenced in the yawning darkness of the Great Abyss. The line of Cain was no more. The spawn of demons who had brought the time of lawlessness to the

First Earth were no more. Ophiuchus had wrestled the Serpent and prevented him from attaining Corona Borealis, the global crown over our planet. All this was heralded by the midnight culmination of Pleiades. Behold, the Eye of Taurus sends the seven eyes of God to make an end of the Indignation, to make all things new.

Saggita, the arrow of God, sends forth judgment from the night sky. Broken is the land of Arza. Washed away is the land of Nod. But God reserved a remnant from the Land of Elda. The Seed of Eve was carried safely in the womb of the ark of God, the Living Ark who makes the staff of Aaron bud though it be dead. Thus our Second Earth was birthed from the death of our First Earth.

The icy fingers of the cold drew in the freezing waters toward the poles. The oceans began to subside. Except for the equatorial regions, the temperatures plummeted to levels never experienced by our planet. With the cold, the death of the First Earth was almost complete.

Imagine Noah's family peering out their window over a shoreless ocean worldwide, finally floating peacefully after enduring the world's worst series of terrifying storms. At night the skies were completely dark without a single visible star in the heavens. During the day the sky was pitch black. Day turned into night.

It took months before the darkness began to fade by the now normal meteorological schedule of intermittent rains. In the meantime, the blood moon ruled the night sky. It had a weird, crimson glow. Except for the occasional red haze of the spewing volcanoes in the distance, no night lights could be seen, no campfires in the distance, no village lights on the horizon. All of mankind had been washed away. All the monsters had been buried in the ash and mud of death.

During the day, the Sun was a reddish hue and hardly visible. A few volcanoes that were still active spewed billions of tons of tephra into the atmosphere. The tephra had brought the entire globe into a deathly pale shadow. It was the shadow of the death of the First Earth. There were no birds in the sky and no shores in the distance.

All was a deathly silence except for the sounds of the waves against the boat. The roar of the volcanoes finally gave way to a cold silence that settled over the entire globe. The pungent stench of rotting flesh and decaying plants was overwhelming.

They had never experienced a bitter, chilling cold like this. It penetrated to the marrow of the bone. The warmth of the glowing Sun upon their shoulders was no more. It was a distant memory, almost like a long-lost dream, one that Noah did not know if he would ever feel again.

Then sounds came back—howling bitter winds, hailstorms, and later snowstorms. And the seas churned once more. Within a few months, a new shore was visible on the horizon in the grey haze of noon. But it was not land. It was ice floating on the ocean. The cold, the snow, and the icebergs floating on the ocean were a marvel Noah and his family had never known before. The winter solstice of that fateful year marked the height of the cold shadow. And as the ice grew, the waters receded.

Eventually, the winter storms died down. Daylight began to pierce delicately into the shadow. In due time, the first spring of the Second Earth brought forth a new hope. And on the 17th day of the month of Nisan (Gen. 8:4)—the very same day and month Moses had crossed the Red Sea to mark the resurrection of Israel from the slavery of Egypt, the very same day and month our Lord would be resurrected to mark the redemption of mankind, on the spring equinox when daylight begins to ascend over the darkness of the long night—the ark came to

The Scriptures record that Noah's ark landed on Mount Ararat in modern-day Turkey.

rest on dry land on Mount Ararat and touched the ground of the Second Earth. From that day forward, the daytime grew longer than the nighttime. Light gained preeminence over darkness. It was the birth of our Second Earth.

The Scriptures say that on the 17th day of the seventh month (Nisan), the ark came to rest on Mount Ararat in present-day Turkey, but the waters continued to recede until the 10th month. And on the first day of that month, the tops of the mountains became visible (Gen. 8:4–5). That was the summer solstice when daylight reached its maximum and nighttime reached its minimum.

We witness here a marvelous example of God's providence, for on precisely the same day of the year that Christ would resurrect from the dead, exactly 33 hours after He would die on the cross of Calvary, on the 17th day of the month of Nisan, our Earth also resurrected. On that day Moses would pass through the Red Sea on dry ground and step into Sinai. The army of the Pharaoh would be washed away and drowned in judgment, and the Chosen of God would be miraculously preserved just like Noah and his family.

And in the summer solstice, light gained preeminence over the darkness of the First Earth, and the mountain peaks were first seen. The providential hand of God is ever in control. Those who wish to know His face can clearly see that He is not without power to protect His children when all human hope is lost. Hopelessness is the failing of faith in the sovereignty of the Creator.

The Genesis record is not an allegorical myth for our spiritual edification. It is a real, spacetime, historical account that shows us that God is, in fact, the Creator of the universe and Lord of all. Every historical event has deeper spiritual significance, but they are real, spacetime events. Even when the Earth had dried enough to disembark, Noah had to wait to step onto the ground. He could not disembark until the proper time. God asked him to stay inside the safety of the ark. The reasons for this are manifold, as we shall see.

THE DEATH OF THE FIRST EARTH

On the first day of the seventh month, the Month of Tishri, Noah first saw dry land. The Second Earth was ready to be colonized. This is also the same day the Lord created the heavens and the earth, according to Hebrew tradition. So the symbolism is clearly that the resurrection of Christ on the 17th day of Nisan, the same day the ark ran aground, is that the firstfruits open the door for us to enter into the heavenly creation. God is the Living Ark that brings us through death into the Promised Land. He went through the punishment of death on our behalf, and when we belong to Him, He keeps us safe within forever. Our Second Earth was ready to be inhabited on exactly the same day our First Earth came to be. But Noah could not step out onto dry ground.

And so we see that in accordance with His providential will, it was on that same fateful day that Christ resurrected and brought forth a new order—the Church, composed of both Jew and Gentile. And so in this manner He made it possible by this resurrection to begin a new covenant between God and man on the anniversary of when He also made it possible to begin a new covenant between Him and Noah and a new covenant between Him and Moses.

But we shall not inherit the Earth until the day God returns to atone it. He shall come in the month of Tishri on the 10th day during Yom Kippur to atone and end the Second Earth. On that day, the armies of the Gentiles shall gather at Megiddo and assemble an army greater than has ever been assembled to oppose the Prince of princes. This is the Day of Vengeance when God shall atone for the sins of the Earth and cleanse it in preparation for the establishment of His Davidic Kingdom that shall also begin in the month of Tishri.

> *Now it came about in the six hundred and first year, in the first month, on the first of the month, the water was dried up from the earth. Then Noah removed the covering of the ark, and looked, and behold, the surface of the ground was dried up. In the second month, on the twenty-seventh day*

of the month, the earth was dry. Then God spoke to Noah, saying, "Go out of the ark, you and your wife and your sons and your sons' wives with you."

—Gen. 8:13–16

So we see that Noah could not step forth to claim the new kingdom of the Second Earth until the 27th of the month of Heshvan (the second month). The Scriptures tell us that he built an altar and sacrificed unto the Lord.

Then Noah built an altar to the LORD, and took of every clean animal and of every clean bird and offered burnt offerings on the altar.

—Gen. 8:20

In like manner, the Lord as High Priest shall atone for the Third Earth in the Day of Vengeance when He returns to claim His Earth. That day is the 10th day of Tishri. It is Yom Kippur when God atones for the sins of man on Earth. None shall be able to stand against Him as He brings judgment upon those who have oppressed His people and profaned the Promised Land. In that day, Israel shall be saved, and Jerusalem shall become the City of Truth. But although the victory has been won, the effects of that judgment will not finish until the 27th day of the second month, the month of Heshvan. On that day, we shall be able to step into Jerusalem to begin the reign of Christ upon the Third Earth.

The fountains of the deep were cracked open on the 17th of Heshvan.

In the six hundredth year of Noah's life, in the second month, on the seventeenth day of the month, on the same day all the fountains of the great deep burst open, and the floodgates of the sky were opened. The rain fell upon the earth for forty days and forty nights.

THE DEATH OF THE FIRST EARTH

> *On that very same day Noah and Shem and Ham and Japheth, the sons of Noah, and Noah's wife and the three wives of his sons with them, entered the ark.*
>
> —Gen. 7:11–13

Hence they were inside the ark for the space of one year and 10 days. Why those 10 days extra? Nothing in Scripture is written without significance. Why would the Lord not allow them to step onto the land on Rosh Hashanna, the first day of Tishri, when the ground had dried up?

> *Now it came about in the six hundred and first year, in the first month, on the first of the month, the water was dried up from the earth. Then Noah removed the covering of the ark, and looked, and behold the surface of the ground was dried up.*
>
> —Gen. 8:13

Or if the judgment was to be for the space of one year, why did Noah not disembark on the same day they entered, which was the 17th of Heshvan? God did not allow Noah to disembark until the 27th day of the second month (Gen. 8:14).

God does nothing by accident. From that day forward would be the change in time it takes for the Earth to circle the Sun since the meteors struck the Earth and elongated its nearly circular orbit into an elliptical one. First, the original lunar year and the solar year prior to the Great Flood would be offset by a 10-day period every year. Thus they stepped out of the ark the same moment the Earth circled the Sun since they entered the ark. Now it took the Earth 10 more days to reach that same position in space.

From that day forward, the alignment of the stars would be different than it had been before the Earth was knocked off its original orbit. The 23-degree tilt would make the stars that rose over the eastern horizon shift from the position they had prior to the Great

Flood. No longer would the lunar calendar harmonize with the solar calendar. Our Earth was now less perfect than it had been before the seven "shepherds" struck our planet.

Second, at the end of the Second Earth, man will not be able to come out of the place of hiding to repopulate the Third Earth until after the Chukka in the desert that lasts three and a half years. In other words, after Rosh Hashanah (the 1st of Tishri) is the anniversary of God's creation and the Hebrew New Year, which is the same time Noah saw dry land. But not until 10 days later is the atonement of Yom Kippur (the 10th of Tishri). That is the Day of Atonement when the High Priest atones for the sins of the world. In that day, the Lion of Judah shall end the Indignation. After Yom Kippur comes the Feast of Tabernacles that symbolizes the divine protection from the Antichrist and the Serpent, which the Apostle John speaks of in Revelation.

> *Then the woman fled into the wilderness where she had a place prepared by God, so that there she would be nourished for one thousand two hundred and sixty days.*
>
> *And when the dragon saw that he was thrown down to the earth, he persecuted the woman who gave birth to the male child. But the two wings of the great eagle were given to the woman, so that she could fly into the wilderness to her place, where she was nourished for a time and times and half a time, from the presence of the serpent. And the serpent poured water like a river out of his mouth after the woman, so that he might cause her to be swept away with the flood. But the earth helped the woman, and the earth opened its mouth and drank up the river which the dragon poured out of his mouth. So the dragon was enraged with the woman, and went off to make war with the rest of her children, who keep the commandments of God and hold to the testimony of Jesus.*
>
> —Rev. 12:6, 13–17

The woman who gave birth to the male child prophesied in Isaiah 7:14 is Israel. The time this happens is in the very middle of the seven-year tribulation period when simultaneously Lucifer attacks the Temple of God in heaven and the Antichrist attacks the Temple of God in Jerusalem (Rev. 12:7–9).

The place of hiding is the Chukka of Israel where the true manna from heaven, the Bread of Life, and the water that pours forth from the Rock of Ages is the Living Water. In that day, Israel will know that those who hold to the testimony of Jesus are her offspring.

Thus the meek shall inherit the Earth but not until after the Feast of Tabernacles, or Chukka, which is from the 15th through the 22nd of Tishri. This is the feast that recognizes the time God's chosen were kept under the Eagle's wings for three and a half years. This succoth shall be the ark of the Third Earth. On the 23rd of Tishri there will be a great celebration for that divine protection.

It is the day that the Lion of Judah celebrates His harvest, the priests of His kingdom, who have been kept safe during the wrath of God in the last part of the Great Tribulation. The 23rd of Tishri will be a day of rejoicing.

It was in the 33rd year of His life that the Messiah (whose number is 3) died on the cross on Passover to redeem mankind. He died on the afternoon of the 13th of Nisan, and 33 hours later, He resurrected on the morning of the third day.

It was 73 days after the ark was grounded on the mountain peak before the peaks of the mountains became visible (7 = the number of God the Father; 3 = the number of God the Son). Considering that the height of the ark was approximately 45 feet high, its draft was probably some 15 cubits. That means it took 73 days to effectively lower the level of the water worldwide some 15 cubits.

We do not know how long it took after that for the world to reach the final ocean level since it was not recorded. But we do know that at its apex, the water level of the Great Flood cleared the mountain peaks by at least 15 cubits so the ark could float safely above the peaks. The sedimentary deposits present in the mountains of every continent amply attest to the veracity of this claim today.

It is quite probable, as previously stated, that the primordial mountains were more like gentle rolling hills, perhaps only several hundred feet high, creating an ideal and more habitable environment than the ragged rocky peaks of the mountains that are so hostile to inhabitants today. The Global Flood, therefore, did not have to top our present mountain ranges that have steadily risen in height since that fateful day the crust of the Earth was cracked.

The evolutionary charge that there is not enough water in our world to cover the mountaintops is based on ignorance of the terrain in the First Earth and on the tectonic forces that drove the mountains to their present height after the Great Flood. Our mountaintops were driven skyward by the very mechanism of the crunching of the sliding hydroplates during the Great Flood.

That these mountains were once under water cannot be disputed, for the marine evidence even in the Himalayan range abounds. This assumption also neglects the major player in the inundation event—the fountains of the deep. As we shall see, it was this event that caused the seven tectonic hydroplates to separate and crunch, forming the mountain ranges of our Second Earth. We shall also later document that this mechanism was actually known to the ancients who wrote clearly about it in their respective flood accounts.

It is quite probable that the topography of our antediluvian planet was composed of gentle, undulating hills and fertile plains as far as the eye could see. There were no deserts or bleached out wastelands in our antediluvian planet. Dense tropical forests abounded in the equatorial regions. And in the polar regions, wide, open steppes with fertile grassland provided sustenance for an incredibly wide variety of roaming animals. Only roughly 5 percent of the species that abounded in the First Earth managed to survive and adapt to the much harsher conditions of the Second Earth. Most of the Second Earth was covered with ice, and only a swath across the equator was habitable for life.

CHAPTER 5

THE FOUNTAINS OF THE DEEP WERE BROKEN OPEN (THE HYDROPLATE THEORY)

We have already established that the granite composite layer of rock upon which our continents are formed was once a single and unbroken superstructure that formed the supercontinent of the First Earth. This granitic substructure of the supercontinent lay over a basaltic layer that under this high pressure and heat is somewhat the consistency of silly putty. As we stated earlier, between the granitic substructure of the supercontinent and the basaltic rock below were enormous underground aquifers.

These interconnected subterranean saltwater chambers formed a honeycomb layer between this granitic suprastructure and the deeper basaltic floor at its base. No matter the weight of the granitic structure above it, as long as the chamber was intact it could sustain the pressure of the denser rock above in the same way a waterbed can sustain a concrete slab as long as the waterbed lining remains intact. Water does not change very much in volume, even when it is highly compressed. However, it will hold vast amounts of gas and minerals in the solution when it is under extreme pressure.

Walt Brown proposes that under this huge pressure, the saltwater layer in these subterranean chambers contained enormous amounts of limestone, olivine, and dissolved carbon dioxide gas. Imagine driving a nail into the lining of a waterbed that is filled with carbonated water (water with dissolved carbon dioxide gas) before a stone slab is dropped on it. The weight and impact of the stone slab would agitate the pressurized gas inside the waterbed, and the action of sudden outgassing would send a violent squirt of water from the rupture in the lining. Imagine if the bed had been shaken violently before the rupture. That is the effect violent meteor impacts would have had on the subterranean aquifers filled with carbon dioxide and under pressure.

A sudden crack in the granitic rock from a striking asteroid that reached even close to the subterranean chambers would have breached the seal. The powerful and successive returning pressure waves striking the aquifer would have continued to agitate and release the contents of the underground aquifer with violent outgassing through the weakened fissure in a magnitude that is almost unimaginable. We can observe this violent outgassing in carbonated bottles of soda pop when shaken before opening.

As long as the granitic structure above it remained intact and the saltwater layer below was undisturbed, it would remain stable. But if a crack developed that could weaken the granitic rock above it and release the pressure, the sudden depressurization would be released in an indescribably violent eruption.

However, the crack could not come from below; it had to originate from the top. Rocks at that depth are under enormous pressure and temperature and thus have the consistency of stiff putty. They could not crack the granitic substructure of the supercontinent since they are elastic, and the enormous pressure would not allow space between the crammed molecules. The pressures are just too great to physically allow it. The crack had to come from above.

That is the fundamental reason the cracking of this supercontinent could not have been caused by any geologic processes on the Earth. It had to be broken by a high-impact scenario that had enough energy to reach 10–16 miles below the surface of Arza and would be capable of providing an escape route for the super-compressed saltwater aquifer below it.

This sudden and violent outgassing is the same physical phenomenon believed to be responsible for the gigantic eruptions of supervolcanoes from magma pockets. If the depressurization is slow and the contents are *not shaken or agitated*, the gases are released in a controlled fashion. But if the depressurization is *sudden and the contents are agitated by a series of previous earthquakes*, the abrupt release is extremely violent, making supervolcanoes 100,000 times more violent than a regular volcano.

What do you think would happen if seven gigantic meteors cracked the Earth and agitated the subterranean saltwater layer with repeated seismic shock waves of unprecedented energy?

The First Earth Ripped

If we assume, as evolutionists have confirmed, that the speed and mass of the Chicxulub meteor created a crack some 40 miles deep and 200 miles wide in our crust by the force of its impact, then certainly the two larger 30-mile meteors must have penetrated at least twice as deep. These are the likely culprits that initiated the ripping of our crust. The violence of the two larger impacts along with the other five large meteors would have severely agitated the saltwater layer through the repeated shock waves generated by the multiple violent strikes and their pressure waves returning from the opposite side of the Earth. Each strike zone made an opening for the evacuation of the underground aquifers. Each of the impacts would have caused the supercontinent to fracture along fissures that connected all seven strike zones.

In this way, it is easy to see how our singular supercontinent of Arza was fractured into seven pieces by the seven gigantic meteors recorded in the Sumerian Planisphere. Enormous earthquakes generated by the impacts would have cracked the continental plate and spewed out unprecedented flows of lava. These spilled over the land and covered an estimated area of 400 million cubic miles from the Northern Hemisphere to the Southern Hemisphere.

We can see the enormous deposits of lava in opposing continents that correspond to the area where they were once connected. New York was once connected to North Africa, and the area of the Iguazu Falls in South America was once connected to Western Africa. Matching magnetic readings imprinted on the basaltic rock when it cooled and rock compositions show that they were neighbors and that the incident that separated our continents was instigated by the same event that created an enormous lava flow. This was no gradual reshuffling of continents. It was a dramatic and destructive cataclysm that cleaved our supercontinent into seven shards.

In New York are basaltic structures that show the lava flow in this area was close to a mile deep. In the Palisades on the western shore of the Hudson River are the remains of this magma flow as the basaltic cliffs reach almost 1,000 feet high today. But that was just the beginning

The sudden, deep cracks in the granite superstructure would have resulted in an explosive outgassing of unprecedented force from the extremely pressurized and hot salt water in the subterranean chambers. Stretching from impact site to impact site through the cracks that now circled the world, a curtain of ejecting water from the deep aquifers shot into the sky, thrusting water, eroding rocks, and perhaps even flowing lava into the stratosphere and beyond.

Once the cracks in the crust reached a critical depth, the enormous pressure of the overlaying rock above the water in the aquifers thrust the pressurized water upward at supersonic speed through the openings created by all the fissures between the new, smaller continents. The evidence left behind of this enormous crack in the supercontinent of Arza is what we recognize today as the

Mid-Oceanic Ridge that circles the Earth. Smokers, the remnants of the fountains of the deep captured in photos taken by underwater robotic submarines, still spew out superheated water mixed with rich minerals and gases from the depths of the ocean floor.

The violent outgassing that was triggered by the uncorking of these fossil aquifers released vast stores of salt water, carbon dioxide, olivine, and limestone sediments from the subterranean chambers and propelled it upward through the cracks at supersonic speeds, carrying eroded material from the edges of the continents with it. These jetting geysers thrust skyward at such enormous pressures that they severely eroded the landmass all along the so-called zipper.

Prior to the meteor strikes, there was no Atlantic Ocean. The continents were united in a single landmass roughly square in shape. As the process developed, the rip began in the mid-Atlantic region primarily from the two points where the larger asteroids struck. Like a giant zipper it literally traveled around the world through the path of least resistance. Water, magma, steam, gases, and eroded debris thrust into space at an enormous pressure and speed. The overwhelming sound would have been utterly deafening as a giant curtain of water from horizon to horizon jetted high into the sky.

The Mid-Oceanic Ridge circling the Earth
(Courtesy of Walt Brown, *In the Beginning*)

This curtain of water traveling at supersonic speeds reached up to space along the ridge as the continents unzipped between the multiple strike zones. Then the crack circled the entire globe, creating the seven great hydroplates and fracturing the supercontinent into the seven continents of our Second Earth.

Initially, some of this material would have fallen back to Earth, but some was catapulted beyond our gravitational pull into space. The water and debris launched into space would have given birth to many icy comets and asteroids that are now circling our Sun.

Vast amounts of the long curtain of water sprayed upward and then came down as the largest waterfall in Earth's history, arching over both sides of the long wall of geysers that circled our planet. Anyone who has witnessed a waterfall, especially one that is high, sees that some of the water fragments into droplets that create a mist around the waterfall. That mist supersaturated our atmosphere with moisture globally and eventually fell back down as rain.

The small water vapor canopy that existed was overwhelmed with moisture, and the strong air currents formed by these geysers filled the air with particulate matter that formed the cloud nuclei in order for droplets to form. Besides the action of the jetting geysers, the ejecta from the initial strikes sent billions of tons of dust and rock into the atmosphere.

This dust and debris in our atmosphere helped "open the floodgates of the windows of heaven." The "windows of the heaven" created by the cascading waterfall, as well as the water vapor canopy precipitating, was supercharged by the infusion of small water droplets into our atmosphere by the jetting geysers. That is the source of the water that brought upon the First Earth a deluge that covered the entire Earth. Rain fell upon Earth for the very first time.

Even after the water vapor canopy was exhausted, the curtain of water continued to supersaturate our atmosphere with more moisture, thus causing even more rain. In other words, the water vapor canopy did not contain all the rain that fell for 40 days and 40 nights. A good portion of it would have come from the overspray as the fountains reached their maximum height.

These supersonic jets of water thrusting into space would have also spawned enormously powerful winds through the Venturi effect. For 40 days and 40 nights, torrential rains with super-hurricane winds pummeled the Earth continuously as never before or ever after.

This action created by the continuous stream of water ejecting from below eroded the sides of our present continents on both sides of the 46,000-mile rupture in the crust, gouging an average of 400 miles of rock some 10 miles in depth and thrusting it either into space, or into the muddy waters of the Global Deluge. This massive hydraulic process left the familiar V-shaped pattern in the continental shelves and created an enormous amount of sediment that saturated and darkened the once clear and pristine ocean of our First Earth. The dark waters broiled with anger, as Hesiod wrote.

According to Brown's assessment, about 35 percent of the sediment suspended in the floodwaters were eroded from the subterranean basalt below as the escaping salt water gouged its way between the granite structure above and the basaltic floor below. An enormous amount of suspended limestone in the salt water of the subterranean chambers was in that way thrust upward to the surface of our planet.

The limestone later precipitated from the water once it reached the surface, and the pressures that kept it in a solution abated at the surface of the planet. This mixture of the many types of rocks produced the thick, muddy consistency of the floodwaters, which eventually settled in the stratified layers we now recognize as the strata formations. It was this process that gave us our enormous fossil beds that record forever in stone the destruction of the First Earth.

The temperature of the escaping subterranean salt water, which was already hot at that depth, typically increased 50 degrees Fahrenheit as it was forced from the high-pressure, superheated, subterranean chamber through the rupture. At the beginning, when the diameter of the crack was relatively small, the pressure of the spouting fountain was great. Most of the water thrust high into the stratosphere cooled and turned into small, medium, and giant muddy hailstones that pummeled whatever survivors remained after the initial blast.

The downward drafts created by the falling hail brought the cold air of the upper atmosphere in powerful downdrafts to the surface of the planet and in short order lowered the temperatures in those specific areas to -150 degrees Fahrenheit. These super-cold air downbursts were particularly strong along the edges of the jetting curtain of water. As stated earlier, this literally flash-froze animals while they were grazing. There is no other physical explanation for the way the frozen mastodons were preserved in situ with their stomach contents undigested and their mouths filled with food that had not decomposed.

Their flesh was frozen in such a way that their cells did not erupt, which invariably points to a flash freeze that took place within only a few hours. That would have frozen their bodies completely through, preserving even the food in their mouths. Falling into a river or lake could not have preserved the food in their mouths. Slow freezing as in the case of animals falling into frozen rivers and lakes causes the cells to explode. These cells were perfectly preserved as in the case of modern food facilities that flash-freeze foods. The food in their stomachs would have decomposed had the freezing process not been as quick.

Once the diameter of the crack increased enough in width, the continents slid apart and began to slide down the slopes of the rising Mid-Oceanic Ridges rising between the continents. Because the continents were literally gliding on the subterranean aquifers, the movement at first was quite rapid. But as the cracks widened, the reduction of the fountains' pressure could no longer thrust them high into the sky. The wall of geysers slowly declined in height as the Atlantic Ocean was born.

The newly created Atlantic Ocean began to broil. The hotter subterranean water of the flood naturally rose to the top of the ocean and tended to evaporate faster, creating even more rain and instigating mega-hurricane storms. The contrast of the warm waters and the cold air brought furious clashes in warm and cold fronts that spawned tornadoes, hurricanes, and winter blizzards, depending on the area of the planet.

Were it not for these mediating forces that dissipated the heat in the planet, the Earth would have either burned to a cinder or frozen all together. Each step of the catastrophe brought wild fluctuations in temperature that were mediated by the next process, and in that way God was able to maintain the delicate balance that gave birth to our Second Earth and protect the inhabitants inside the ark. We will speak further on this, but let us first examine the effects of these fountains of the deep on our continents.

The ejection of the subterranean chamber would have caused the continents to bow as the water at the end of the continents was the first to be depleted. The continents began sinking at the tips. That would have caused many fissures from top down in the granitic suprastructure throughout the length of its surface.

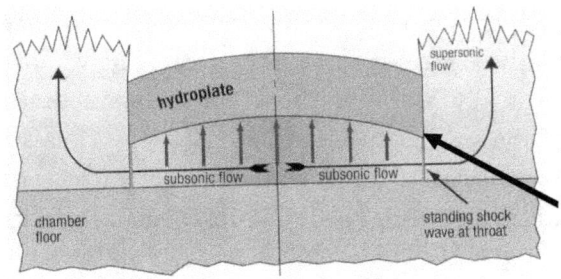

Salt water ejected with supersonic force through the ripped crust caused the continents to bow as the water subsided in the subterranean chambers, and the tips were heavily eroded by the ejecting salt water.
(Courtesy of Walt Brown, In the Beginning)

As the water evacuated the subterranean chambers, the tips of the continental blocks eroded at a much more furious pace, thinning out the tips of the newly formed continents and causing the familiar gradual sloping in the continental shelves. Hence, the hydroplates initially flexed in convex form.

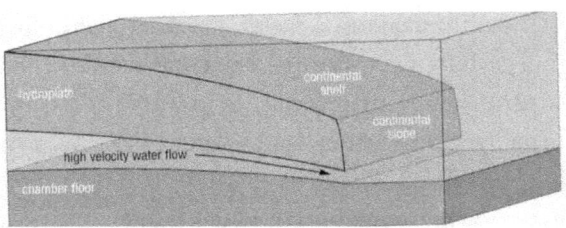

Erosion pattern of the hydroplate caused the familiar continental shelves and slope that we encounter.
(Courtesy of Walt Brown, *In the Beginning*)

The following three forces caused the continents to migrate from their original position after the Earth was cracked:

1. The first force was due to the direction of the meteor impacts. The trajectory of several twin meteors spinning around a common center of gravity would have made slight differences in the direction of the force created upon impact. All of them were traveling west to east. For example, one of the smaller ones in a northeast trajectory struck the area we now know as the Yucatan Peninsula. That, along with the Maniitsoq meteor, pushed North America in a counterclockwise motion. One of the two larger asteroids, the Land Wilkes asteroid, that struck in the Southern Hemisphere hit the area we now know as Antarctica in a southeast trajectory but with five times the intensity of the smaller meteor that struck the Yucatan Peninsula. It fractured Africa from South America, sent Antarctica south to the South Pole, and broke Australia from Antarctica, sending it eastward.
2. The second force that helped move the floating continents was the upward force of the water that created a lateral force as it eroded the sides of the newly formed continents in the familiar V-shaped slopes. As the water was evacuating through the rips in the Earth, the upward movement of the water began to force the continents to slide laterally from the point of ejection. The continents tended to glide away from the force of the ejecting

water in the same way a balloon moves away from the force of the ejecting air (for every action there is an equal and opposite reaction). However, this force was not enough to alone cause the drastic movements that followed immediately.
3. The third force was the physical rise of the Mid-Oceanic Ridge. The catastrophic erosion of the sides of the continents by the plumes of jetting water reduced the material that was over the subterranean basalt bedrock below. As the weight of the 10–16 miles of rock above the sight of impact and along the ripped crust was forcefully ejected, the pliable basaltic bedrock below bulged upward from the internal pressure of the Earth, reaching some 7 miles above its pre-flood position. The downward pressure that existed previously from the overwhelming weight of the 10–16 miles of bedrock completely disappeared as it was catapulted into the sky. That negative pressure caused the highly pressurized basaltic layer below to be shoved upward by the pressure exerted on it from the interior of the Earth. In that way, the Mid-Oceanic Ridges bounded upward and were birthed from the depths of the Earth. The continents on either side, aided by gravity and gliding on the water below the continents, slid sideways away from the Mid-Atlantic Ridge.

This bulge of the basaltic floor was also probably aided by repeated returning shock waves from the opposite side of the world that were generated by the initial impacts. As the Mid-Atlantic Ridge rose higher, it lifted the tips of the continents on both sides, and with the help of gravity, the hydroplates slid downward and away from the slopes of the basaltic ridge created from the upwelling of the basaltic floor.

The enormous weight of the sliding continents caused lateral stresses that forced them to buckle in the opposite direction as they were first bending down at the tips. As the continents slid away from the rising Mid-Atlantic Ridge, they buckled upward. Now, the bending of the continents was concave, creating fissures in the bottom of the continental hydroplates.

The bulging basalt bedrock pushed up through the rip in the continents, and the edges of the basaltic mound cracked as it expanded, creating the deep canyons we observe at the Mid-Atlantic Ridge today. We can see these fractures all along the mid-oceanic ridges created by the rip in the continents.

For this reason, the floor of the Atlantic Ocean is today what once was the subterranean bedrock of the supercontinent of Arza in the First Earth.

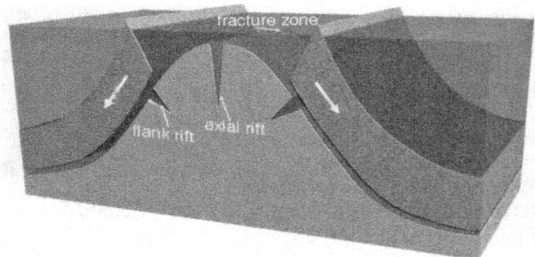

The basalt subterranean bedrock bulged, causing the continents to slide outward in a lateral direction and causing the basaltic mound to form fissures.
(Courtesy of Walt Brown, *In the Beginning*)

Because the tremendous weight of the newly fractured continental plates was so great, the continents slid down the sides of the buckled basalt bedrock and thus moved laterally, gliding on the lubricating, subterranean salt water below it. Eventually, as the aquifers evacuated enough water, the granitic continents come in contact with the subterranean basaltic floor. This grinding created an enormous amount of lava that went up the fissure created by the bending continents and formed numerous volcanoes.

Once the continents began to slide, the inertia created by the enormous weight of the plates caused them to move laterally at a great pace in short time, reaching almost their present state. But the hydroplates have not stopped grinding. They have, however, slowed down considerably.

This process of sliding and braking to a crawl caused three major geophysical effects:

1. First, the continents crunched together and thickened, developing in a relatively short period of time the deep undulations in the crust we call mountains.
2. Second, the continents eventually began to grind to a halt on their glided path when the water underneath was substantially depleted. Subsequently, the bottom layer of the granitic continental superstructure was crushed as it slid against the subterranean basalt block below. That produced enormous amounts of magma when the heat of the friction melted the rocks. And the magma escaped through the fissures created by the bending continents, forming numerous volcanoes.
3. Third, during this process of coming to a halt, many of the deep compression fissures continued to develop in the continental granite suprastructure below or on the understructure of our continents. These fissures were created from the bottom up rather than from the surface downward as initially experienced when the fountains of the deep first vented. These deep fissures were the same fissures encountered by the deep drill in Bavaria that allow the transport of the underground magma to the surface as volcanoes. Therefore, much of the volcanic action experienced at the end of our First Earth was precipitated in two stages, first when the meteors struck and second when the sliding hydroplates came into friction with the basaltic rock below.

As stated previously, some surface fissures were already created during the first phase when the continents sagged at the tips (convex shape), causing cracks at the surface of the plates. As the bulging basaltic substructure began to rise, creating the Mid-Atlantic Ridge, the continents slid down the slopes, and the granitic hydroplates were bent the other way (concave shape), causing fissures in the deeper or lower layers of the plate.

That contortion of the continent caused the tips in the distal end of the direction of movement to bend downward and come in contact with the basaltic underfloor. Once the subterranean chambers evacuated enough of its contents, the distal tips of the sliding hydroplates began to come in contact with the basaltic rock underneath. In this last phase, the grinding of the granitic rock with the basaltic substructure not only caused massive amounts of magma from the friction but also caused stress cracks that tended to be in the deeper layers of the granitic suprastructure and on the distal ends.

That is the fairly recent geological mechanism that created the physical condition we encountered in the deep-hole drills. It is what caused the crushed granite with hotter-than-expected, supersaturated salt water. It is through these fissures that the magma created by the friction of the gliding plates thrust upward in the forms of volcanoes and supervolcanoes all over the planet during the death of the First Earth. The strike force of the meteors instigated the first volcanic phase. The friction of the gliding plates as they ground to a crawl instigated the second volcanic phase.

For this reason, the Ring of Fire around the Pacific today marks the most active volcanic area in the world. It is the consequence of the North American and South American continents sliding westward and the Asiatic and Australian plates moving eastward. The ring literally forms the connection between the distal ends of the sliding hydroplates.

And since all this took place roughly 6,000 years ago, it provides a rational explanation for the wide underground temperature gradients we still find today. Had these processes happened in the imagined uniformitarian fashion that evolutionists dogmatically claim lasted billions of years, these temperature gradients would have long ago found equilibrium.

The Crunching Lateral Forces That Formed Mountains

When most of the subterranean chambers finally evacuated through the ruptured crust, the movement of the plates slowed to a crawl by the immense friction between the granitic superstructure of the newly formed continents and the basaltic understructure. The sides of the continents eventually sagged enough at the tips that they subsequently sealed the chambers once again. That marked the 150th day since the fountains of the deep were broken open.

Today these subterranean chambers contain a much-reduced remnant of the saltwater reservoir that once was. But that salt water is still there. The deep-hole drills still find hotter-than-expected salt water at those enormous depths where groundwater could not possibly reach from the surface. The pressure at that depth is too great to allow for surface water to reach those levels. That salt water has been there from the creation of the Earth.

The process of continental thickening caused by the gliding of the continents as they crunched into a near halt caused the land to rise higher as it buckled, forming long mountain ranges near those distal ends of the grinding plates. The crunching or thickening of the continents caused them to shorten in width but rise in height. That process, along with the freezing of the poles, is what seemed to reduce the overall ocean levels.

Some of the water of the Great Flood froze in the two polar regions due to the darkened skies filled with tephra and ejecta debris from the meteors. But the thickening of the continents also helped raise the land above the water. Dry land slowly appeared above sea level as the giant ice sheets began to form over the poles.

But these volcanic areas are not limited to the Ring of Fire around the Pacific. Anywhere continents moved, we also find evidence of powerful impacts in the form of massive magma flows in their distal ends at the opposite side of the Earth.

The water that inundated our First Earth thus did not have to rise above the peaks of our present-day mountains that were, in fact, created by the sliding and crunching of the continental hydroplates. The evolutionary argument that there is not enough water to cover the entire Earth is therefore based on ignorance of the mechanisms that brought forth the splitting of our continents and the crunching of the sliding continents that formed our modern mountains, a process that continues even today.

For example, we can point to the ridge between the Indian continent and the Asiatic plate that created the Himalayan Mountains. Do not imagine for one moment that this Global Flood had to exceed the present height of Mount Everest. We must remember that the topography of the First Earth was radically different than our present Earth. It was the impact of the Indian plate with the Asiatic late after the cracking of the Earth that crunched the land and buckled it upward, creating the enormous Himalayan mountain range. Today, this area poses one of the greatest earthquake hazard zones in the world.

The relentless and gargantuan physical force of the moving plates as they slowly grind on the basaltic floor below them literally bends the plates into wrinkles, pushing the land upward, a process we recognize as mountain formation. The high mountain ranges we currently have on our planet continue to reach ever higher into the sky with every second that passes. But it was not always at this crawling rate. Before the Earth's crust was cracked, there were no high mountains.

The mountains today continue to grow as the continents continue to move, albeit in a much diminished fashion. As the Earth spins, it creates centrifugal forces that cause the continents to glide further. The spin of Earth is slowly changing the direction of the movement of the continents through the centrifugal force exerted upon them.

A careful inspection of the geologic evidence leads us to conclude in the study of our geologic formations that the stresses that birthed mountains were not all upward in thrust. There were lateral stresses created by the grinding continents that greatly affected the geology of our Second Earth. It is this lateral stress that causes the upward thrust of mountains in a relatively short period of time. Once the fresh, sedimentary deposits cemented, the mountain formation slowed down to its present crawl.

Mountains in British Columbia, Canada, show evidence of lateral compression created by the shift in the sliding continents.
(Courtesy of Walt Brown, *In the Beginning*)

We can observe the familiar undulations of our crust in areas where canyons have been dug by erosion to reveal the internal structure of mountains. The above picture of undulating sedimentary rock near the Sullivan River in southern British Columbia, Canada, evidences the obvious lateral compression necessary to create these undulations that were caused by the sliding continents. So we can clearly see that at one time, our continents were thinner and wider.

It would be hard to explain how these undulations developed in hardened rock without causing cracks and fissures. If instead the sediments were fresh and pliable, then the lateral pressure forced upon it by the gliding and crunching continents could easily mold them into these smooth, undulating patterns we observe in the mountains of British Columbia. Such would have been the conditions if these sedimentary layers were recently deposited, being yet wet and pliable as they were laterally stressed through the grinding forces that halted the movement of the continents. That is precisely the physical evidence that would be predicted by the Great Flood.

They say a picture is worth a thousand words, and I think that is right. Lateral pressures on hardened rocks would not create these

The peak on the left is Mount Everest, the highest point on Earth at 29, 028 feet above sea level. Although the right peak looks higher, it is only an illusion because it is closer to the camera.

smooth undulations but would instead create great fissures and overthrusts instead of smooth, unbroken undulations as we see here so clearly.

If the biblical model of the Great Flood is correct, then we can assume that mountains did not reach their present heights until after the Flood. There should be ample evidence of sedimentary rock in the crests of even the highest mountains since they were once submerged under the waters of the Great Flood.

That is precisely the evidence that was found. Even in the highest mountains of the Himalayas, seashells have been found. Undulating deep deposits of sedimentary rock abound in the highest mountain ridges of all the continents.

The Indians know the Himalayas as *Sagarmatha*, or Summit of Heaven. With the use of our modern-day positioning satellites, scientists have undeniably confirmed that the Himalayas are presently being pushed upward (higher) at the rate of 10 millimeters per year. They are also moving north, crushing into the plate where China rests at the present rate of 15 millimeters per year, in spite of the fact that the mountains have now hardened into solid rock.

But this rate is nothing compared to the enormous shifts that occurred during the year of the Great Flood. We can also see evidence of this titanic upheaval in the rocks of western California. As the North American plate slammed into the Pacific plate, it lifted huge sections of the Pacific Ocean floor and stacked them like dominoes in vertical positions. The intense pressures generated between the stacked chunks of sea floor caused the rocks to melt and form huge fissures of quartz that run vertically. It is inside these quartz veins that we find so much of California's gold that leached out of the rocks when melted and then coagulated when the veins eventually cooled down.

It may very well be that the magma currents underneath the plates have some minimal influence on the movement of the plates. But these forces are not strong enough to crack the continents apart from a single landmass. The magma currents underneath could not have caused the cracking of Earth's crust. The chronicles of the ancients seem to favor not a slow and imperceptible process but a cataclysmic event that literally shook the world and moved it violently in one single, catastrophic event.

Some powerful impact of catastrophic force had to shatter the crust before the continents could move apart. The proponents of the tectonic plate theory insist that the crust has always been fractured and that the continents have been migrating for billions of years. There is, however, no physical evidence that can substantiate that assumption. It is an assumption predicated on their failed uniformitarian bias. Moreover, the historical records of the ancients certainly soundly contradict that assumption.

The melting of the ice caps also causes the continents to change positions as the balance of the weight of the ice cap melts. But there is no good reason to think that the present rate of motion has been uniform all along as the evolutionists blindly assume.

The very mechanism of the Great Flood could have caused the newly fractured continents to glide outward at an incredible speed compared to modern processes. Once the waters were sufficiently depleted from the underground aquifers, the grinding friction would have crunched the continents with enormous lateral forces that would have created the higher mountains in a relatively short span of time.

Hence, the global nature of the geophysical forces created during the Great Flood is what gave rise to the towering mountains we observe today, and the height of the floodwaters did not need to exceed more than perhaps several hundred feet above the sea level of the First Earth. Moreover, we must remember that the sea level has already risen some 430 feet since that time as the glaciers slowly melt.

The amount of water presently frozen at the poles is a miniscule amount compared to what was there shortly after the time of the Great Flood when these gigantic glaciers extended to the southern areas of Europe and North America. It is scientifically well documented that the ocean levels have risen 12 feet worldwide in just the last 100 years. As a matter of fact, the newest evidence is that the rise in sea level is beginning to increase in pace again.

It stands to reason, then, that the water in the ice poles would have sufficed to cover all the prediluvian landmass. Today, after thousands of years of constant juxtaposition between the hydroplates, these mountain ranges continue to grow taller but at a much reduced rate. It is also reasonable to conjecture that this wonderment with the new mountains of the Second Earth is what spurred the almost universal fascination for pyramids in all the ancient cultures after the Great Flood.

The evolutionary misconception that the Global Flood had to exceed the height of modern mountains, an idea that is often given as the reason they doubt the historicity of the Noahic Flood account, is simply due to the false assumption that our mountain ranges during the Flood were as high as they are today. The idea that a global flood could cover all the landmasses as claimed by the Holy Scriptures is thus not some mythological, fairy-tale idea but rather a very plausible, historical event that can be scientifically explained through realistic physical phenomena that correspond magnificently with the evidence left behind.

That grinding friction created by the sliding continents thus became the catalyst for the second enormous volcanic upheaval that, if it had been left unchecked, would have ended all life on Earth.

Volcanoes and Supervolcanoes

The movement of enormous areas of crust caused friction, heating, and the melting of rock that found its way to the surface through the cracks created by the contortions and motion of the crust. Hundreds, perhaps thousands, of volcanoes would have simultaneously been spewing water vapor, poisonous gases, and tephra into the sky.

One sentence does not do justice to the impact of such an event. It is hard to imagine such an all-encompassing and terrifying scenario. Human nature is such that we would rather believe that global catastrophic events don't happen. But if the reader would humor me for a moment, I would like to now recount the impact of just one ordinary volcano in our recent history. Simply multiply the effect of this historical account of one simple, run-of-the-mill volcano's impact on our planet by several hundred thousand times, and perhaps it then might be possible to begin to imagine the grand scale of the catastrophic upheaval that ensued when many supervolcanoes were erupting simultaneously.

Of course, evolutionists insist that these events did not take place at the same relative time but were separated by eons. The uniformitarian-gradualist paradigm is an essential cog of the necessarily long, evolutionary timetable. Nevertheless, we have witnessed catastrophic events of such scale that evolutionary-minded scientists should take notice of their failed uniformitarian hypothesis. Certainly the catastrophic impact of the Levy-Shumaker comet on Jupiter should warn rational people that grand-scale catastrophes are a reality in our solar system.

THE DEATH OF THE FIRST EARTH

The eruption of the volcano on the Indonesian island of Krakatau was certainly a catastrophic event, albeit subdued compared to the eruption of a supervolcano. That single volcanic eruption thrust such an enormous volume of tephra into the atmosphere that the temperatures around the entire planet tumbled by half a degree. The volcanic ash that spewed into our atmosphere caused the sunsets in London to be redder for months after.

In 1883, a small island between Sumatra and Java peacefully existed, uninhabited by man and hosting a dormant volcano. On the 20th of May, the volcano began erupting with loud explosions that shook walls as far as 100 miles away. For six years, a series of severe earthquakes had preceded it.

On the 22nd of May, a column of dust and water vapor erupted from the volcano to a height of 7 miles. The pyroclastic flows resulting from such volcanic explosions sent a wall of deadly superheated gases some 2,800 feet high, traveling at 200 miles per hour, engulfing all and roasting all living things along the way. But the victims did not die from asphyxiation. They were literally cooked instantaneously in the superheated suspension.

The gray pyroclastic cloud contains poisonous gases, ash, and superheated air that scorch the lungs completely upon the very first breath, killing all living things in its path. The temperature is so high that skulls have been known to explode like popcorn from the expansion of the cranial fluids into steam. Water expands in volume 1,700 times as it turns into steam. All living things caught in that pyroclastic flow would be instantaneously charred.

Volcanic ash from the plumes would have entered the water vapor canopy and precipitated as black rain.

The ashes or tephra that fell from the volcanic explosion in Krakatau clouded the skies as far as 300 miles away, causing what observers termed black rain. On the 26th of May, six days after it began erupting, a black, billowing cloud of smoke and water vapor rose to a height of 17 miles. A series of violent explosions boomed, and lava began to pour out over the sides of the caldera.

On May 27, four stupendous explosions blew the top of the volcano as high as 50 miles into the sky. The third boom was so loud that people heard it on the islands of Rodriguez some 3,000 miles away. That is like someone in Los Angeles hearing an explosion that happened in New York. As the giant caldera below the summit evacuated all its contents, the crust of the Earth collapsed into the magma chamber and created an enormous caldera 4 miles long from north to south and 3 miles wide from east to west. The ocean water that rushed in created giant tsunamis, the largest of which were some 120 feet high, and sped out in all directions, destroying anything that had not been destroyed by the pyroclastic flow.

Tephra fell for 12 days as far away as 3,300 miles from the volcano. The surrounding cities were totally destroyed, and 36,380 people died from the ensuing tsunamis. As far away as the English Channel, a rise in tide was recorded. The entire northern end of the island completely disappeared. Where there were once three mountain peaks now stood only one. That was Krakatau, a single, normal volcano. What would have been the damage of several supervolcanoes some 100,000 times as strong as a normal volcano?

The evolutionary timetable ascribes vast amounts of time between the eruptions of the many volcanoes that dot our planet. But the mechanism of the Great Flood would have triggered massive volcanic upheaval in a concentrated space of time. Today, as the spin of the Earth causes the hydroplates to continue to glide due to gravitational imbalances, the friction continues to cause earthquakes and volcanoes. But these occur at a much reduced pace than the huge movements of the crust during the cataclysm created by the striking meteors.

The idea that mountains and volcanoes take thousands of years to produce is simply not supported by our known facts. In 1952, the volcano El Boqueron on San Benedicto Island in lower California built a cone more than 1,000 feet high within just a few weeks. The rate of mountain formation and volcanic mountain formations were much more furious during this hyperdynamic period as the plates were sliding at an incredible rate compared to our modern-day rates. The heated granitic suprastructure would have become more pliable and would have lent itself toward molding more than it does today. And yet today we can still catch a glimpse of the fury of such power in the much more subdued volcano called Paricutin in Mexico.

The Mexican volcano Parícutin is shown here spewing tephra, water vapor, red- hot glowing rocks, and lava. The ejection of the tephra billows up like a column of black smoke into the atmosphere. The red-hot rocks are shot thousands of feet into the air and come back down, starting fires wherever they land.

Scientists tell us that there are 21 major supervolcanoes around the world. A supervolcano is in a completely different order of magnitude than the regular, run-of-the-mill volcano. It qualifies as a supervolcano when it has a mega caldera that produces an ejecta volume greater than 1,000 cubic kilometers (240 cubic miles). In other words, it is a volcano that erupts 240 cubic miles of magma in a single explosion.

Besides our nation's largest and most famous Yellowstone Caldera in Wyoming, the United States has the not-so-coveted distinction of having three more supervolcanoes. In California is the Long Valley Caldera that is 200 square miles in size. In New Mexico is the Valles

Caldera that is 175 square miles. There is also the La Garita Caldera in Colorado, a monster of a supervolcano.

Scientists with the U.S. Geological Survey use the Volcano Explosivity Index (VEI) to measure the magnitude of volcanic blasts. It's a logarithmic scale that runs from 1 to 8. A magnitude 1 eruption spews less than 350,000 cubic feet (10,000 cubic meters) of volcanic tephra, which consists of ash and rocks; a magnitude 8 eruption puts out more than 240 cubic miles (1,000 cubic kilometers) of the stuff. To help grasp that scale, the recent eruptions at Mount Merapi and Eyjafjallajokull in Iceland were both 4s. The 1980 eruption of Mount St. Helens was a magnitude 5.

> By studying rock samples, geographical features, and layers of ash in ice core samples, scientists can reconstruct some— though certainly not all—of the most epic volcanic eruptions, including ones hundreds of millions of years ago.
>
> The most energetic of those occurred in the San Juan Mountains in southwestern Colorado around 27 million years ago. That explosion formed what is known as the La Garita Caldera and spewed more than 3,107 cubic miles (5,000 cubic km) of lava — enough to put down a 40-foot layer on all of California. La Garita Caldera's ignimbrite, or volcanic deposit, is known as the Fish Canyon tuff and consists of dacite, an igneous rock formed by lava.
>
> According to the USGS, it is the largest known eruption since the Ordovician era, between 504 and 438 million years ago. It was so large, in fact, that in a 2004 report in the Bulletin of Volcanology, scientists recommended adding a ninth level to the VEI scale, and declared the La Garita eruption a magnitude 9.2. Although this ranking is of some debate – the scale of any ancient volcanic activity is partly based on estimates, after all – La Garita is the only known magnitude 9 eruption (Melina 2010).

But La Garita is not without competition. The Lake Toba Caldera in Sumatra covers an area of 1,080 square miles, and the Pastos Grande Caldera in Bolivia, which is comparable, covers 1,000 square miles. Not far from Lake Toba is the Lake Taupo Caldera on the north island of New Zealand with a size of 485 square miles. These are massive volcanic monsters that dot our Earth in areas where the sliding continents left large pockets of magma underneath areas where the land above was stretched thin.

The grinding continents churned up magma that was thrust upward through the fissures created by the bending of the continents, but in some cases, the lava did not make it to the surface. Instead, it pooled into large magma chambers just below the surface of the planet. These so-called hot spots are fissures that traverse all the way down to the basaltic layer below us. When they are not capable of reaching the surface, they form giant magma lakes under the surface that can explode with incredible power if earthquakes destabilize them with agitation that causes explosive outgassing.

Volcanologists tell us that the magma lakes are saturated with gases that, if disturbed or agitated by earthquakes, can cause an eruptive outgassing that supercharges the explosion and breaks through the thin crust above them into a supervolcano. These terribly dangerous magma pools are found all over the planet. In New Zealand, the Oruani eruption of the Taupo volcano was rated at level VEI-9, the highest level volcanologists give to such eruptions that have global consequences. Just one supervolcano eruption can send the world into a mini ice age by the amount of tephra it spews into our atmosphere. There are many supervolcanoes that are extremely dangerous in their potential for destruction on a global scale.

For example, scientists predict that if the Yellowstone supervolcano were to erupt, it would instantly kill more than 87,000 people in the immediate vicinity of the pyroclastic flow and would make two-thirds of our country completely uninhabitable by the finely suspended tephra that turns into cement inside our lungs. The estimated ash fall would be three meters thick. But the tephra that blocks the sunlight would not be the only problem. The impact would be global in nature since the atmosphere would be injected with massive amounts of sulfur dioxide gas that forms into a sulfur aerosol that not only reflects but also absorbs the sunlight, thus adding to the problem that would radically cool temperatures worldwide.

It has become popular for some volcanologists to suggest that the bottleneck in the human population that is evidenced by the mitochondrial DNA may have been caused by the eruption of the supervolcano that formed Lake Toba in Sumatra. The idea that the Global Flood was a spacetime, historical catastrophe that wholly changed our Earth by the creation of these monsters has not dawned upon them.

> The explosion of this Indonesian supervolcano 75,000 years ago is regarded as one of the world's most explosive volcanic events.
>
> Palaeontologists thought Toba's eruption plunged our planet into a volcanic winter, pushing our species through an evolutionary bottleneck and putting our ancestors on the brink of extinction.
>
> Recent research suggests otherwise – that even though Toba's tantrum did cool the climate as ash spread across most of the Indian Ocean – it didn't cause the near-extinction of the human race.
>
> No evidence has yet been found in the sediment record that suggests that East Africa – a hub of human settlement at the time – was affected by the volcano. So while the eruption's timing coincided with the human bottleneck, it didn't cause it (Howden 2016).

Well, I agree. It did not cause it by itself. It had many other partners in crime.

Below are the 21 supervolcanoes around the world:

1. Yellowstone Caldera – Wyoming, United States
2. Long Valley Caldera – California, United States
3. Valles Caldera – New Mexico, United States
4. Lake Toba – North Sumatra, Indonesia
5. Taupo Volcano – North Island, New Zealand
6. Aira Caldera – Kagoshima Perfecture, Kyushu, Japan
7. Pastos Grandes Caldera – Bolivia
8. Laacher See – Germany
9. La Garita Caldera – Colorado, United States
10. Kikai Caldera – Ōsumai Islands, Japan
11. 11-Mount Aso – Island in Kyushu Japan
12. 12-Mount Tambora – Sumbawa Island, Indonesia
13. Campi Flegrei – Naples, Italy
14. Paekdu Mountain – Border of China and North Korea
15. Whakamaru – North Island, New Zealand
16. Snowdonia – Wales, United Kingdom
17. Lake District – England
18. Glen Coe – Scotland
19. Cerro Galan – Catamarca Province, Argentina
20. Bennet Lake Volcanic Complex – British Columbia–Yukon border, Canada
21. Macauley Island – Kermadec Islands, New Zealand

The destructive power of 21 supervolcanoes erupting over a relatively short period of time is almost unimaginable to us today. Modern man has not experienced an event of such magnitude. The amount of ash, carbon dioxide, and sulfur dioxide gas spewed into our atmosphere would have been enormous. The Sun would have been completely occluded by this triple combination. In addition, firestorms created by their magma explosions, as well as the reentering ejecta of the meteor impacts, would have whipped up their own hurricane-force, superheated winds that spawned fire tornadoes that would have raced unchecked throughout the lush primal forests of our First Earth.

The entire planet would have initially burned as if it were hell itself. Anyone who has ever witnessed a giant forest fire can testify of the unparalleled fury of firestorms. The rising heat spurs on hurricane-force winds as flames spread up canyons faster than anyone can run. Many firefighters have lost their lives fighting these unpredictable and treacherous firestorms. Our planet was on the brink of total sterilization. Were it not for the cooling effect of the storms that followed, Earth would have completely burned into an ashen cinder.

CHAPTER 6

THE WINDOWS OF THE HEAVEN WERE OPENED

In the six hundredth year of Noah's life, in the second month, on the seventeenth day of the month, on the same day all the fountains of the great deep burst open, and the floodgates of the sky were opened. *And the rain fell upon the earth for forty days and forty nights.*

On the very same day Noah and Shem and Ham and Japheth, the sons of Noah, and Noah's wife and the three wives of his sons with them, entered the ark (emphasis added).

—Gen. 7:11–13

We have already discussed that the opening salvo of God's judgment upon our First Earth was the impact of seven giant meteors. The mushroom clouds jettisoned from the impact zones reached into space. Our Earth was cracked, "like a pot" (*Gilgamesh: Man's First Story*). The second salvo was the bursting of the fountains of the deep as the continents were divided. The rip stretched around the entire Earth, and a curtain of geysers shot at supersonic speed into the stratosphere. The fountains of the deep were open for 150 days. The third salvo came when "the floodgates of the sky were opened" (Gen. 7:11).

Never before had the Earth experienced so much as a raindrop coming from the heavens since the First Earth was watered by the morning mist. But on that day, a torrential downpour began that set in motion a series of calamities. It rained for 40 days and 40 nights, but this was no gentle April shower. The ocean became a violent maelstrom as huge boulders slammed into it from the ejecta. The geysers that tore apart the coastlines of the newly formed continents rained down a barrage of hail and stones that smashed everything underneath them. Giant boulders landing on the ocean from nearly outer space would have created a terrifying slew of tsunamis.

Tsunamis

The death of the First Earth was announced by those three salvos in a single day, and now the great calamity would render judgment for the space of one year and 10 days in ways man had never dreamed possible. It is not hard to conceive how tsunamis of differing intensities from reentering ejecta striking the ocean, as well as earthquakes and the pyroclastic flows of volcanoes and not to mention the enormous impact on the ocean by the sliding of the continents, would have followed for days and perhaps weeks after the initial impact. These killer waves would have completely devastated all the coastlines.

Tsunamis in the First Earth overran most of the coastal villages and traveled deep inland with no real resistance from high mountains. Underwater earthquakes throughout the ocean floor would have created many other tsunamis of differing magnitudes as the plates lifted upward or downward, displacing huge areas of ocean water. Some were created by the splash of returning ejecta from the initial blast and others by boulders heaved into the stratosphere by the eroding crust as the ejecting water catapulted them into the sky.

Other much more intense tsunamis were created by the physics of displacement as hills cleaved and were cast into the sea. Some of these mega-tsunamis would have been traveling at the speed of modern commercial jets through the ocean until they reached the shore. Once they reached the shallow shores, the repeated waves would have slowed down and risen as battering rams several hundred feet high.

The sliding hydroplates would have also created giant worldwide tsunamis that devastated the coastlines and drowned every island as the waters washed over them. Once the planet was under water, the unimpeded waves would have circled the Earth, bouncing off of each other. Consider the tumult of the "boiling ocean" described by the Greeks as the fountains of the deep brought forth God's judgment on our human depravity.

The tsunami that struck Japan on March 11, 2011, was created by an underwater earthquake that caused plate displacement. Cars, boats, houses, and even buildings were carried miles inland by the numerous waves as they completely destroyed the coast of Ōarai, Ibraraki Prefecture, and decimated a nuclear plant (Sim 2017).

It is hard for most people to imagine the enormous raw power of such waves unless they have seen it with their own eyes. Even when the fountains of the deep weakened and no longer jetted into the stratosphere, they still caused enormous waves, unimpeded by coastlines that circled the Earth in an endless series, as the ejecting water boiled up along the rifts. The long and short of it is that the devastation that came upon our planet was total and incomparable to anything mankind has ever witnessed before or since. And then came the storms.

The Storm of All Storms

The new moon was a dark moon. It was completely eclipsed by the great shadow that enveloped the First Earth. And so it marked the beginning of the Second Earth in the darkness of the shadow that ended the First Earth. Darkness enveloped our planet not only from the ejecta of the crashing meteors but also as tephra jettisoned into the atmosphere by the numerous volcanic eruptions. It was the black rain that eventually broke the shadow.

But do not make the mistake of thinking that during those initial 40 days and 40 nights the rain fell softly from the sky as a gentle spring shower that feeds the flowers. The initial rise in global temperatures would have triggered horrendous megastorms. Hurricanes and tornadoes are nature's way of burning excess energy as it tries to reach meteorological homeostasis. They are the natural air conditioners of the world that burn up the energy of the heat in the oceans and the atmosphere. As a matter of fact, the entire planet would have been a giant superstorm.

The temperature of the ocean would have increased dramatically by the infusion of superheated water from the subterranean aquifers. The heated air would have held much more moisture, making it ripe for these mega-hurricanes to spawn. The potential energy released by such titanic forces would have created many huge, powerful, Category 6– hurricanes stronger than any we have ever encountered since. On land, it would have also spawned swarms of immensely powerful super deadly Category 5 tornadoes. These tornadoes are so powerful that they can rip up the tar from streets and leave a strip completely bare as they pass over it.

We can actually see the impact of this rise in temperature with the intensity of storms on our planet today, albeit on a more moderate scale. The rise of ocean temperatures by only 1 degree Fahrenheit today has already created a marked increase in the intensity of the hurricanes in our time.

> A team of scientists that included Curry and Holland published a study in the journal *Science* that surveyed global hurricane frequency and intensity over the past 35 years. On the whole they found the number of Category 1, 2, and 3 storms has fallen slightly, while the number of Categories 4 and 5 storms—the most powerful ones—has climbed dramatically. In the 1970s, there were an average of 10 Category 4 and 5 hurricanes a year worldwide. Since 1990, the annual number has nearly doubled, to 18. Overall, the big storms have grown from just 20% of the global total to 35%....
>
> In a study published in the journal *Nature* last month, he [Emanuel] surveyed roughly 4,800 hurricanes in the North Atlantic and North Pacific over the past 56 years. While he too found no increase in the total number of hurricanes, he found that the power—measured by wind speed and duration—had jumped 50% since the mid-1970s (Kluger 2005).

Can you imagine the meteorological impact on our planet of a rise in temperature of 20–30 degrees in a much shorter time span? It is hard to imagine the raw power of hurricanes unless you have lived through them. The power of wind is absolutely awesome, but the power of water is significantly more lethal.

Living in South Florida most of my life, I have witnessed the immense power of wind and especially water. I have felt the fury of hurricanes more times than I care to remember. I have seen

THE DEATH OF THE FIRST EARTH

monstrous waves devastate buildings, bridges, roads, and any other structures that stood in their path as they were lifted to new heights by the tidal surge of hurricanes. It is an awful and destructive force that often surprises unaware victims.

Even relatively weak hurricanes such as Hurricane Opal that struck the city of Destin in the Florida Panhandle in October 1995 can cause great damage by the strength of their tidal surges. As one of the original members of the South Florida Search and Rescue Task Force II team, I was able to see firsthand the power of water tearing through buildings. Wave upon wave hammered everything in its path. The city of Destin was filled with beautiful, seaside homes on this barrier island off the Gulf of Mexico. The tidal surge that went through this island devastated homes and buildings. Lovely, stately homes were splintered into pieces like matchsticks.

This buoy I'm leaning on with my left foot was in the middle of the Gulf of Mexico before it was ripped from its anchor and deposited on the beach by Hurricane Opal. The home behind us was shredded by the waves and the tidal surge.

This picture was taken three blocks inland. If you look carefully, you will see the top of a fire hydrant at our feet by my shovel. The surge buried the street with more than 2 feet of sand.

Pictured is the leeward side of the island. The lamppost on the right marks where the dock (4 feet below the sand) was prior to the storm. I am standing in front of a car that smashed into the boathouse that was buried in the sand. At the bottom right, the 5-foot high fence is barely visible. The surge built a brand new peninsula that jutted into the bay.

Hurricane Opal was only a Category 1 hurricane. In 1992, Hurricane Andrew ripped through South Florida and caused major havoc. The night before it struck, it was forecast to remain a Category 2 hurricane, but by the time it made landfall in the middle of the night, it had surged to a strong Category 4. Concrete telephone poles more than 2 feet thick broke like twigs. I would not have believed it had I not seen it with my own eyes.

This huge, concrete telephone pole broke in four places. The base was about 2½ feet in girth. It was kept together only by the reinforcing iron rods.

A Miami-Dade fire rescue helicopter was skewered through its engine by a steel I-beam while it docked inside the building that was supposed to shelter it. The steel beams were contorted, bent, and twisted like spaghetti.

A view from a helicopter over the damaged swath where the cone of the hurricane passed through looked like a nuclear bomb had blasted the area. All the street signs were ripped away by the wind. Trees were flattened, looking like they had been plowed down with a giant steamroller. Houses were shattered.

Gas pumps were literally sucked out of the ground by the force of the winds.

I was on duty with the Miami Beach Fire Department during Hurricane Andrew and worked five days straight. When I was finally released, I hopped in my trusty red Jeep with a portable generator and took off to South Miami where my college friends Bobby and Donna MacAnn were living with their two children. The cell phone towers had all been knocked down, so I had received no notification of their condition. I had learned earlier from headquarters that the area had been hit hard, so I raced there to check on my friends.

On my way I stopped at a local hamburger joint and told the manager of my mission. There was no electricity so there was no refrigeration for the hamburgers. The manager gracefully donated several hundred hamburgers and buns to me, packed in cartons that were thawing out. The young man was even nice enough to help me load the cartons into my Jeep, and then I headed south.

In spite of the fact that I had grown up in Miami most of my life and knew the area quite well, I found myself not knowing where I was. All the familiar landmarks were gone, and everything looked different. The streets were blocked by fallen trees and power lines. I meandered back and forth, gradually going forward. After moving some trees out of the way and running over others, I managed to finally reach Bobby and Donna's neighborhood.

At the entrance, a soldier with the National Guard met me and said, "No one is permitted to enter this area." They were deployed to stop potential looters. Fortunately, I was still in my uniform. I pulled out my Fire Department ID and showed him the supplies I was bringing for the neighborhood. The young soldier snapped to attention, gave me a salute with a smile, and called to some of his men to assist me.

The rest of the way into the neighborhood was impassable for my vehicle. It was completely blocked with heavy tree trunks that had fallen. The soldiers helped me haul all the food to the neighborhood on foot.

As I approached Bobby and Donna's house, the total devastation made me sick in the pit of my stomach. I glanced at Bobby who was sitting on a sofa with his wife in the street in front of their house. For four days they had been sitting there, not knowing what to do. They did not want to abandon to looters the few things they had left.

"Why do you have the sofa out in the street?" I asked stupidly.

"It had blown away," replied Bobby. Then pointing west, he said, "I had to retrieve it from three blocks away."

"What?"

"Yeah, the entire north end of the house simply ripped away, and it took the couch along with it. We had been sitting on it just minutes before."

Poor Donna was crying as I hugged her.

"When the north wall began to rattle," Bobby continued, "I told Donna, 'I think that wall is going to go. We need to move farther inside.'" They took both kids and their dog and went into the bathroom off the hallway. As Bobby was about to enter last, he looked through the corner of his eye as the north wall tore away.

"I watched the sofa we had been sitting on get sucked out as if a giant vacuum cleaner had snatched it from the living room."

"The north wall of the house just flew away?" I asked, in shock.

"Yeah, let me show you," said Donna.

Donna's standing in the area that used to be their living room. Bobby is where the kitchen used to be. Directly behind Donna is the hallway to the master bedroom. The makeshift drape in the middle of the picture is over the first bathroom they entered after leaving the couch.

Looking at the missing bathroom walls in the hall bathroom, which now had a bed sheet draped over part of it, I asked, "You made it through the storm in that bathroom?"

"No," said Bobby shaking his head, "I told Donna, 'This is an outer wall. We need to move into our master bathroom.'"

Each of them grabbed a kid and crawled through the hallway into their master bedroom and on into their interior bathroom.

"So then you made it through in your master bathroom?"

"Nope, not there either. By now the ceiling was beginning to tear away."

"How did you know that?"

"I could hear the screws popping as the plywood in the roof tore off one at a time," said Bobby. "We became afraid the whole house was going to crumble around us."

"What did you do?"

"We decided to try to make a run for the neighbor's house, hoping theirs had fared better."

"You went out into the storm?"

"Yup. With one kid each in tow, we crawled to the neighbor's house through a foot of rushing water that flowed like a river between the two houses."

"Were you hurt by the flying debris?"

"Donna scraped her knees pretty good, but we stayed low in the water."

"What did you do then?"

"We knocked desperately at the door, but the neighbor thought it was debris hitting the walls. Finally, I called out to him, and he opened the door."

"Thank God," I said, "At least you guys were safe there."

"Safe?" he said with a wince. "Not long after we arrived, the entire middle of his roof simply ripped off and flew away."

"What?"

"Yup. We were back at square one again."

The neighbor's roof tore away, forcing both families to abandon this home also.

"It occurred to me that none of these houses were going to be able to withstand the force of this storm. But we couldn't just give up. So I simply said, 'We must move again to the next neighbor's house.'"

The two families braved the storm on their knees and crawled to the third neighbor's house. There, all three families finally found shelter inside a homemade gun vault of reinforced concrete that was large enough to accommodate them and sturdy enough to make it through the storm. When Bobby finished the story, I wondered how many similar horror tales had transpired that night. Not all of them ended as well as Bobby and Donna's story. Some people did not make it through the night.

Bobby remained stoic for the sake of his family, but Donna was heartbroken for all she had lost. All the family pictures and wonderful decorations she had so expertly used to make her house a warm home that was beautiful to the eye and pleasant to the soul had simply blown away. She had that special woman's touch to make her home a nest of comfort. Now it lay in utter ruin.

Trying to boost her spirits, I said, "At least you made it through alive, and your kids are unhurt. Things can be replaced."

"I know, silly," she replied with a half smile and hugged me.

I turned to view all the broken houses in the neighborhood. In a single day, their lives had been changed forever. All they had worked for and accumulated in a lifetime was literally gone with the wind. Thirty-nine people lost more than that. They did not make it through the night.

That day I caught a glimpse of what it must have been like for the survivors in the ark when they stepped into the radically different Second Earth. The overwhelming destruction of all things as far as the eye could see and beyond was total and complete. The smell of death no doubt saturated the air with its acrid, pungent odor, a smell that in my profession I have come to know all too well.

But as dramatic as these present-day catastrophic experiences are, they are utterly insignificant in scope when compared to the cataclysm that ended our First Earth. The hurricanes that smote our First Earth were even more intense due to the enormous excess of potential energy harbored in the air and sea at that time. Winds of more than 200 miles per hour would have been the smaller hurricanes in that day. There is nothing in our Second Earth that can be compared to that cataclysm in all its various forms.

Many times I have witnessed the furious power of strong storms, and I feared that Hurricane Andrew was going to take a grim toll. Fortunately, it veered south just before landfall and missed the barrier islands that form Miami Beach. Had it hit head-on, we would have been burying people for weeks. Andrew claimed relatively few lives in spite of its power because the worst of the storm passed through a rather undeveloped area of Dade County. The tragedy could have been much worse.

It is the tidal surge packing huge maverick waves that is the real killer. The area where Hurricane Andrew landed was, to our great fortune, mostly inhabited by mangroves on the shore that served to minimize their destructive power. Had it veered north about 20 miles, Miami Beach would have been under water 15–20 feet with waves striking the second- and third-floor windows of hotels and other tall buildings. In spite of our best efforts to evacuate these low-lying regions, many people unwisely chose to stay. The death toll would have been horrific.

THE DEATH OF THE FIRST EARTH

I do not think most people can truly understand the real power of a wave unless they are surfers. In my youth I had the bright idea of going with a few friends to surf the large waves that were coming in before a hurricane. We walked all the way to the end of the pier in South Beach, threw our surfboards over, and jumped in the water. The waves were averaging about 12 feet, which to Floridians is a lot but to Californians is nothing. They were really choppy and not ideal for surfing. But when you are young and stupid, you do mighty crazy things.

You cannot judge the awesome strength and power of a wave unless one of these monsters has struck you and made you roll over and over like you were in a washing machine, causing your back to scrape against the seafloor several times. I held my breath as long as I could, but the water was so murky I did not even know which way was up until fortunately I was unceremoniously spit out of the water. I crawled out onto the sand, gasping for air with my shorts halfway down my legs, my back completely scraped, and my ego quite shaken. The power of hydraulics is almost unimaginable. Storms have claimed the lives of many who ignorantly stood in their way.

Typhoon Nina struck China in 1975 and claimed more than 100,000 victims. But even this staggering number pales against the toll claimed by the Bhola Cyclone of 1970. On November 12, 1970, I was in my first semester of college when I heard the news that Bhola had struck the area of East Pakistan, which we now know as Bangladesh.

The storm was the equivalent of only a Category 3 hurricane, but the tidal surge penetrated deep into the low-lying land and literally washed entire villages into the sea. Estimates of the casualties ranged from 300,000 to 500,000. The horrific aftermath of the storm left behind a sea of bloated, floating corpses blanketed by thick clouds of buzzing flies. That day, I caught my first glimpse of what the immediate aftermath of the Great Flood must have been like.

Although hurricanes cover a larger expanse and carry an overall greater amount of destructive energy, they do not reach the higher wind speeds of tornadoes that specialize in concentrating their destructive force. Bangladesh has the not-so-desirable distinction of experiencing the deadliest hurricane in modern history and also the deadliest tornado.

On April 26, 1989, at about 6:00 p.m. local time, the Daulatpur-Salturia tornado tore into Bangladesh, gouging a 1-mile-wide path. Within a matter of a few minutes, it killed 1,300 people, injured 12,000, and left 80,000 people homeless. The tornado left a strip of barren land 1 mile wide and 52 miles long as if a giant bulldozer had cleared the land.

If the storm clouds are energetic enough, they often produce not one but swarms of tornadoes that sometimes merge later into larger components of terrible power and destruction. Often hurricanes spawn tornadoes in their wake. It is quite likely that the volatile meteorological conditions at the end of the First Earth created many super-hurricanes of unprecedented power that repeatedly gave birth to many destructive super-tornadoes. Their combined forces shredded everything in their path. For 40 days and 40 nights, our planet endured a global barrage of mega-storms the likes of which man had not experienced or ever will.

Before that fateful day, the inhabitants of the First Earth had never seen so much as one raindrop, much less a thunderstorm. All of it was as foreign to them as a gamma ray burst from a Quasar would be to us today. All hell literally broke loose on them. The overwhelming and unrelenting judgment on the profaned world was complete and total in scope.

Yet without those storms to mediate the heat created by the impacts, the meteor strikes, and the volcanoes, our Earth could not have survived. Initially, the First Earth was in danger of overheating to the point of sterilization, but fortunately the copious amount of water streaming through the air and evaporating cooled the atmosphere. Those monstrous storms fed on that energy and in due time depleted it.

For 40 days and 40 nights, Noah's family survived inside the ark. The heat outside was lethal at first. Inside the ark it was a sweat lodge. I suspect the Native Americans duplicated this with their sweat lodges to celebrate the survival of the Great Deluge. On the third day before the end of the third month on the first day of the new moon, the floodgates of the sky were closed, and the rain stopped. The torrential tempests ceased.

But the fountains of the deep continued to pour forth water. It did so for a total of five months. God chose to bring judgment according to the number that represented the Great Instigator. The number 5 is the number of the Serpent who beguiled Eve in the Garden. The one and only holy God sat as King over the Flood and atoned for the transgressions of the Earth.

When the billowing tempests were silenced, the Sun dawned a reddish hue, and the howling winds were no more. A strange silence spilled over the still Earth. Fire had been conquered by water. Inside the ark it was now comfortable. But the oceans were still angry from the action of the broiling fountains of the deep.

The skies had begun to be cleansed of the darkening ash by the billowing storms. The torrential rains caused by the fragmentation of droplets from the curtain of ejecting water and the precipitation of the water vapor canopy saved the Earth from burning up into a cinder. It was the work of those super-hurricanes that effectively cooled the atmosphere during the first critical phase of the cataclysm that ended our First Earth. That kept the planet from soaring to temperatures that would have completely killed all higher life.

The torrential rains also washed much of the air from the particulate matter that had been thrust into it by the many factors of the same cataclysmic event. In that way, it saved mankind from complete and utter extinction. Were it not for the jets of water thrusting into the atmosphere to clear out the dust, our Earth would have been completely void of light, the air would have been unbreathable, and no life, at least the higher forms of life, could have survived at all. The only things that could have survived were extremophilic organisms that draw energy from chemosynthesis.

The air eventually became crisp and cool. The warming blanket of the water vapor canopy had completely precipitated. But the Earth was now without the protective canopy that regulated global temperatures. The excess heat that still remained escaped, unhindered, into space. It was the eye of the storm—the long breath before the plunge.

The judgment was not yet complete. Now came the second death, the icy death. The continents began to grind to a halt in their rapid movement beneath the floodwaters. Friction between the sliding continents and the basaltic floor below began a new barrage of volcanic activity as millions of metric tons of magma were created by the friction. The continents began to buckle and thicken, and magma was thrust upward through the fissures created by the bending continents.

In very short order, the continuing volcanoes began to darken the skies again as the hydroplates ground to a halt. Temperatures plunged below freezing. The icy tendrils of death crept over the Earth like roots in soil. The polar ice caps began to relentlessly march southward as if intending to swallow the whole Earth in ice.

This second volley of volcanic activity was now pumping out millions of tons of tephra into the atmosphere. The skies began to darken for a second time. This time, the ash cloud no longer trap heat. Instead, it kept heat out by blocking the sunlight.

The winds began to blow again—bitter winds, cold winds. The howling winds began their mournful song, only this time they were filled with snow and ice. Blinding whiteout blizzards raced over the polar latitudes and froze even the oceans. The white winds raced unchecked around the world like huge hurricanes of snow. Snowdrifts became ice sheets, and the world was gripped once more in a titanic struggle to survive.

The fountains of the deep continued to gush forth. Volcanic ash still belched into the atmosphere from ensuing volcanoes. It would taper but not stop until the hydroplates slowed down enough to reduce the production of magma through the friction with the underlying basaltic rock.

For some time after, even after the fountains of the deep had long subsided, the belching volcanoes continued to thrust ash into the skies. The cleansing action of the now diminished rain took some time to completely eradicate all the dust that had been thrust into the atmosphere. The darkness may have lasted several months after they disembarked the ark.

Now the pendulum began to swing to the other extreme. Inside the ark, Noah's family shivered with cold—a cold they had never believed possible, a cold they had never experienced before. The tephra that continued to blacken the sky could have easily pushed the Earth to yet another total extinction scenario, until all the Earth became completely frozen. Scientists refer to this scenario as Snowball Earth.

For the second time, the shadow of death covered the planet in a veil of darkness as temperatures quickly plummeted to lethal extremes. This was the birth of the First Ice Age that marked the final death of the First Earth.

But even before Noah and his family disembarked, when the second darkness came and the bitter cold with it, the remnant of God's Chosen floating over the shoreless ocean must have wondered about the drastic temperature difference. Safe but cold inside the ark, they must have wondered, "Why has God caused this great cold to come when all living things have already been killed by fire and water?" They did not know that as water froze it made the oceans recede. The cold was necessary to bring forth the birth of the Second Earth. It was necessary to stabilize the meteorological system of the Earth. It was necessary to provide a temperate and habitable climate for the colonization of the Second Earth around its midsection.

The Sun shone red in the sky, a symbol of the blood that had been spilled by the violence of those who had terrorized the world. The red light reflected off the ice made all things a reddish hue. For a short time, we were no longer the blue and green planet. We were the blood-red planet. But in time, perhaps months after they disembarked, the skies would clear up once again, this time by the washing of periodical rain and snow. Our Second Earth now had a completely different meteorological cycle.

Light began to once again filter onto the surface of the Earth. It was the new dawning of our Second Earth. Our planet was born again, a symbol for all mankind to marvel at God's providence. Were it not for the rain and snow that cleared the skies of much of the tephra for the second time, the sky would have remained dark forever, and our planet would have become an uninhabitable and permanently frozen tundra over its entire surface.

Once the temperatures went beyond a critical point, runaway glaciations would have gone unchecked. Consequently, they would have covered the entire planet in a thick layer of ice. The frigid Earth would have become a Snowball Earth never again to thaw out. Any of these extremes could have effectively killed all the higher organisms on Earth, including Noah and his family in the ark.

But God was, is, and always will be in control. He sits as King over the Flood. He sits as King over the Earth forever. And even though the mountains melt and the islands fall into the sea and darkness once again veils our planet, we shall trust in God's providence and know that He always has a plan of deliverance for the meek and lowly of heart that belong to His fold.

When at last the Sun brightly dawned, free of the dust cloud that for some time permeated our atmosphere, it made such an impact on humanity that for a long time it remained deeply entrenched in the subconscious of the ancients. For that reason, the veneration of the Sun as the symbol of God became universal in all the ancient cultures that remembered the glorious dawning of the Second Earth.

THE DEATH OF THE FIRST EARTH

Two insurrections had marred our planet. The twin horns of Taurus brought forth fire from above and fire from below. They brought forth water from below and water from above. Twice the skies darkened. The first death covered the Earth with heat. The second death covered the Earth with water and ice. God will not be mocked. God sat as King over the Flood. He is King over all the Earth.

All the gods of the First Earth were defeated. Gabriel and the holy angels appropriately chained in the Great Abyss the Wicked Watchers who had instigated the Second Insurrection. All who mocked God and shed the blood of innocents perished.

CHAPTER 7
THE END OF THE FIRST EARTH – THE FIRST ICE AGE

Slowly the snowstorms in the polar regions and occasional rains in the equatorial regions began to wash the tephra from the skies. God had to thread the needle in a very small slot to counter one extreme with the other. Before the second death had run its course, ice had enveloped both poles of Earth and reached deep toward the equator. In some places, the ice sheets were 2 miles thick. Only a swath around the belt of the equator remained free of ice. The ark drifted in a giant river of water that went around the belt of the Earth with ice walls building ever higher and ever closer on both the north and south sides.

The following seven events in sequence led our planet into the First Ice Age.

1. The raging torrential rains and the mega-hurricanes spawned by the excess heat in both the ocean and the atmosphere expended energy and effectively cooled down our planet.
2. The second mechanism was the loss of the water vapor canopy. After precipitating the canopy, the temperatures on the planet would have no moderating force to keep it in the

meteorological homeostasis it had enjoyed prior to the Great Flood. The infrared radiation that was once trapped under the canopy and had acted like a blanket now escaped into space.
3. The third important mechanism was the downdrafts created by the jetting fountains of the deep. The returning water from the supersonic jets of the fountains of the deep fell to Earth from the top layers of our atmosphere as huge hailstones. The falling hail created downdrafts of super-cold air that began to flash-freeze animals in a matter of a few hours.
4. At first the darkening of the sky by the millions of tons of tephra that spewed into our atmosphere held the heat in check below them. However, once the storms and the fountains of the deep largely cleared the sky, the latent heat escaped into space unhindered. Temperatures began to plummet.
5. The fourth mechanism that led us to the Ice Age was the interruption of the ocean currents. The sliding hydroplates would have completely interfered with the oceanic currents. The disruption of these currents would have stopped its moderating influence as it brought warmer waters to the poles and cooler waters to the equator.
6. The second volley of volcanoes created by the grinding continents coming to a near halt once again filled our skies with ash. Now it prevented the sunrays from entering our atmosphere and warming the surface of the planet. The heat-generating volcanoes eventually were simply not enough to warm the atmosphere, and the global temperatures began to plummet, causing the almost immediate freezing of the deluge waters into the First Ice Age.
7. Those oceanic currents in the fractured new oceans would have taken some time to restart as the Sun began to warm the surface of the Earth. But that would need to wait until the air became cleared of volcanic ash. The now normal processes of snowstorms and rainstorms accomplished this much more

slowly than the mega-hurricanes that had ravaged for 40 days and 40 nights. The First Ice Age reached its maximum extent during that time frame.

Huge snowstorms, like giant hurricanes, swept throughout the planet as the heat dissipated and ice packs formed. The temperatures worldwide would have changed dramatically from the initial heat wave to a deep, sub-zero cold. Instead of hurricanes, monstrous blizzards would have ravaged the northern and southern latitudes as ice began to creep toward the center of the planet from the poles, reaching by some estimates to the 35th or 40th parallel latitudes. Eventually, the tephra would clear from the sky, and the Earth would begin to slowly warm up.

But from this point forward, the poles would ever remain frozen. The winters from that day forward became dangerously hostile to life. These giant ice sheets extending over two-thirds of the world would slowly melt and fill our oceans. But for some time after, the Sun was thinly veiled and darkened by the ash in the sky. It was the symbol of God's wrath on our world.

New Fire Festivals – A Memory of the Second Dawn

The emergence of the Sun, the Moon, and the stars from behind the haze created by the tephra was hailed as the New Dawn after the Great Flood. The ancients wrote of this. They developed elaborate rituals to commemorate it. The New Fire Festivals that give great fanfare to the rising Sun and the end of the winter cold are rooted in this memory. Archaeologists have dismissed these accounts as mythological, but the grain of truth found in these accounts is universally clearly discernible to those who understand the meteorological processes of the Great Flood.

Never before had the differences of the seasons been so pronounced. Every winter seemed to recount the long night of cold that followed the death of our First Earth. Every spring brought the hope that the New Dawn and the birthing of the Second Earth had given the survivors of the ark. God left an indelible reminder to mankind of how things would be if we once again chose to follow the bloody religion of the Serpent.

The First Earth had perished because of the violence that consumed our planet. The Great Deceiver had gained almost complete control over our Earth. God intervened and saved a remnant to begin anew. But even before the First Dawn was forgotten, Satan was busy wooing the hearts of mankind in order to once again establish his one-world kingdom. The Mayan texts speak of this time immediately before and after the Flood. They speak of an evil entity that gave glory to the Nephilim who drowned. Satan tried to once again embroil the people into the religion of the Serpent. Vacub-Caquix is none other than the Mayan name for Lucifer who sought to take the throne of heaven.

> It was cloudy and twilight then on the face of the earth. There was no sun yet. Nevertheless, there was a being called Vacub-Caquix who was very proud of himself.
>
> The sky and earth existed, but the faces of the sun and the moon were covered.
>
> And he [Vacub-Caquix] said: "Truly, they are clear examples of those people who were drowned, and their nature is that of supernatural beings.
>
> "I shall now be great above all the beings created and formed. I am the sun, the light, the moon," he exclaimed. "Great is my splendor. Because of me men shall walk and conquer. For my eyes are silver, bright, resplendent as precious stones, as emeralds; my teeth shine like perfect stones, like the face of the sky. My nose shines afar like the moon, my throne is of silver, and the face of the earth is lighted when I pass before my throne.
>
> "So then I am the sun, I am the moon, for all mankind. So shall it be, because I can see very far."

THE END OF THE FIRST EARTH – THE FIRST ICE AGE

> So Vacub-Caquix spoke. But he was not really the sun; he was only vainglorious of his feathers and his riches. And he could see only as far as the horizon, and he could not see over all the world.
>
> The face of the sun had not yet appeared, nor that of the moon, nor the stars, and it had not yet dawned. Therefore, Vacub-Cazuix became as vain as though he were the sun and the moon, because the light of the sun and the moon had not yet shown itself. His only ambition was to exalt himself and to dominate. And all this happened when the flood came (*Popol Vuh*, 93–94).

After some time, the skies cleared of the tephra. The Sun began to shine brightly, and the muddy postdiluvian world dried as the equatorial zones warmed up considerably. This is the Mayan memory of the New Dawn:

> The light of dawn fell upon all the tribes at the same time. Instantly the surface of the earth was dried by the sun. Like a man was the sun when it showed itself, and its face glowed when it dried the surface of the earth. *Before the sun rose, damp and muddy was the surface of the earth*, before the sun came up; but then the sun rose, and came up like a man (emphasis added) (*Popol Vuh*, 187).

Both the Mayas and the Aztec have provided in their mythology unprecedented proof of the fact that immediately following the Flood, our civilization began in darkness. Before the Flood, the inhabitants of the Earth had only seen the Sun through the filter of the water vapor canopy. The muddy world left behind by the Flood could not completely dry up until the dark skies were cleared and the heat of the shining Sun finally broke through. What a glorious day that was for Noah as God showed him the rainbow and made a promise to mankind that He would never again destroy the world with a flood.

THE DEATH OF THE FIRST EARTH

When the tephra finally cleared, the inhabitants were amazed at the intensity of the glowing Sun. This ancient memory is the reason Satan was so successful in fostering the worship of the Sun in all the ancient cultures. The Sun was the symbol of God to all ancient men. Only after Satan corrupted their religion did the symbol become the god. It is the reason so many cultures around the world were later obsessed with sacrificing to the Sun to make sure it would continue its path and never again hide its face from mankind.

We should not be surprised that ancient texts corroborate the story of the biblical narrative. It is the memory of the same ancient survivors of the same event. In fact, their "mythology" also corroborates the Holy Scriptures' account of the judgment of the Tower of Babel when the languages of man were confounded. From other passages in the *Popol Vuh*, we know that the inhabitants of the Earth spoke one language and lived together in the east.

> Then all the people arrived, those from Rabinal, the Cakchiquel, those from Tziquinahá, and the people who now are called the Yaqui. And there it was that the speech of the tribes changed; their tongues became different. They could no longer understand each other clearly after arriving at Tulán. There also they separated, there were some who had to go to the East, but many came here....
>
> Oh! We have given up our speech! What have we done? We are lost. How were we deceived? We had only one speech when we arrived there at Tulán; we were created and educated in the same way. It is not good what we have done (*Popol Vuh* Part III, 176–177).

Noah and his three sons became the progenitors of four tribes. It may be that these are known in the Mayan tongue as Rabinal, Cakchiquel, Tziquinahá, and Yaqui. The survivors of the Great Flood were initially located mainly in the area of Mesopotamia (the east).

THE END OF THE FIRST EARTH – THE FIRST ICE AGE

No doubt this Tulán was the area of the valley of Shinar where the Tower of Babel was built.

We also have the account of Friar Ordóñez. In 1773, the local Mayas took him from the Ciudad Real in the Chiapas region of the Yucatan to the abandoned ruins of Palenque. In his writing, he retold the story of its founding as related by the natives.

> He attempted to explain the ruins, which he called the great City of Serpents, in terms of local myths. He claimed that Palenque had been built by people who came from the Atlantic led by a man called Votan, whose symbol was the Serpent.
>
> This story of Votan had been contained in a Quiché Maya book burnt by the bishop of Chiapas, Nuñez de la Vega, in 1691. Fortunately the bishop had copied part of the book before committing it to the flames and it was from this copy that Friar Ordoñez had obtained his story. According to the book, Votan had arrived in the Americas with a retinue of followers dressed in long robes. The natives had been friendly and submitted to his rule, the strangers marrying their daughters. Though he had burnt the original book, Bishop Nuñez was sufficiently interested in the story to take seriously a report in it that Votan had placed a secret treasure in a dark, subterranean house. Searching his whole diocese for this treasure he eventually found what he presumed was it, ordering its guardians to surrender what turned out to be no more than a few lidded clay jars, some green stones (probably jade) and some manuscripts. These last he promptly burnt in the marketplace along with Votan's book.
>
> *According to the copy that came into the hands of friar Ordoñez, Votan made four trips backwards and forwards across the Atlantic to his old home called Valum Chivim.*

> *This the Friar identified as the City of Tripoli of Phoenicia. . . . According to the legend, on at least one of his voyages back home Votan visited a great city where a temple was under construction that would reach the heaven, though it would be doomed to lead to a confusion of languages.* Bishop Nuñez, writing in his own book *Constituciones Diocesianos de Chiapas*, was sure that the city Votan must have visited was Babylon with its famous tower, given that the real tower of Babel was a ziggurat and that Babylon was the greatest city on Earth at the time of the sea-faring Phoenicians, this was a tempting idea. The ziggurats of Mesopotamia were stepped pyramids with crowning temples, and were very similar in design to the pyramids in Palenque, so this was not as fanciful a suggestion as it sounds (emphasis added) (Gilbert and Cotterell, 1996, 18–19).

Sometime after the division of languages, a group migrated to the area we now call Central America and became the ancestors of the Mayas. Their memory of those living in the East is punctuated by the fact that their civilization began in darkness and that eventually they again strayed from the heart of heaven and began to worship the Serpent. It was at this point that the languages were confused.

They also multiplied there in the East.

> Many men were made and in the darkness they multiplied. Neither the sun nor the light had yet been made when they multiplied. All lived together, they existed in great number and walked there in the East.
>
> *Nevertheless they did not sustain nor maintain [their God]; they only raised their faces to the sky, and they did not know why they had come as far as they did.*

THE END OF THE FIRST EARTH – THE FIRST ICE AGE

> There they were then, in great number, the black men and the white men, men of many classes, men *of many tongues*, that it was wonderful to hear them (emphasis added) (*Popol Vuh*, 171–172).

Geneticists tell us that there are no genetic signs of the African people in the Indians of the New World. How then did they know of black men? The statues that display distinctly Negroid features are unexplainable unless their ancestors really did travel back and forth between the Old World and the New.

The Central American Indians are not alone in their memory of the great judgment of the Tower of Babel. In North America, the Acoma Indians, living at the northern border of New Mexico and Arizona, also speak of their God being angry with His people for continuously arguing. As a punishment, God divides the languages, causing them to emigrate.

> Some groups abandon the others and migrate to another location. Iatiku causes the people to speak different languages so it will not be as easy for them to quarrel (Gill and Sullivan 1992, 5).

Further east and north from the Acoma Indians, the Seneca, living just south of Lake Ontario, have a curious legend that also encompasses the story of the Tower of Babel.

> The woman chief who lived during the time when the earth was new and everyone spoke the same tongue and lived in peace. Godasiyo's village occupies both sides of a large river. Every night her people cross the river to attend dances and exchange goods with the people there. Eventually Chief Godasiyo's large white dog begins to cause trouble. Fearing a fight, the chief decides to remove her loyal followers to another residence upstream.

The people construct two birch bark canoes with a platform between them for Chief Godasiyo to ride on. The people make canoes for themselves and paddle upstream on either side of Chief Godasiyo's canoe. At the fork in the river the people begin to squabble about which way to go. The two men paddling Chief Godasiyo's canoe fight, causing her platform to split. Chief Godasiyo falls into the river and is transformed into a great fish. The people are *upset, but when they try to talk they find they no longer understand each other. Their* languages *are no longer the same and they become a divided people. This is the reason so many languages are spoken by the various tribes of the earth* (emphasis added) (Gill and Sullivan 1992, 103–104).

Here is what we the Scriptures and the Seneca have in common:

1. Everyone spoke one language when the Earth was new.
2. The civilization, which began in peaceful coexistence, turned violent.
3. A group is separated from the initial civilization by a boat.
4. The inhabitants of the boat are also now found fighting.
5. The languages are confounded, and humanity is divided into different races.

These are but a few examples of the historical evidence that is found throughout our world that corroborates the biblical story of the Great Flood and the Tower of Babel that was built soon after. We shall later deal more exhaustively with such examples. For now, the point I want to stress is that their accounts match the scriptural narrative not only in content but in sequence and descriptions of the mechanisms created by the Great Flood that our Judeo-Christian model proposes.

And so we see that the darkening of the sky after the Great Deluge and the freezing of the floodwaters may have caused the First Ice Age, but it was not the last ice age. As we shall see, the First Ice Age did not last long. It may surprise some readers that the Second Ice Age is clearly associated with the critical juncture in human history when the languages were divided at the Tower of Babel. Our Second Earth declined so quickly from its birth that in a few centuries it was once again threatened with another near extinction catastrophe. But that story will have to wait until we finish this account of the Death of the First Earth.

Thus far, we have given you a scenario that can explain the physical and natural processes that ended our First Earth in a global deluge. Now let us speak of the empirical evidence that supports this narrative.

The Formation of the Mid-Oceanic Ridges and Rifts

Volcanologists tell us that some volcanoes are formed when the cracks in the crust caused by earthquakes allow magma to travel up to the surface. But as previously stated, that would have initially been most acute at the impact sites and at the distal or opposite end of the points of impact where the pressure waves would have impinged at the other extreme of the Earth. Then the second wave would have come as the continents began to grind to a halt as the underground aquifers were depleted enough.

These seven asteroids created intense pressure waves that by their powerful impacts would have induced an initial outward bulge in the crust relative to the direction of the path of the meteors at the opposite end of the impact zone. The striking meteors in the Northern Hemisphere must have sent pressure waves that impinged upon the crust in the area of the Siberian Traps, causing an immense gash in the crust that sent forth millions of cubic tons of magma to the surface.

The three southern meteors would have done the same in the continental area we now know as India, which was at that time attached to eastern Africa. That bulge would have ruptured the crust of the Earth into many pieces as it literally splintered, forcing magma outward as rivers of molten rock. Enormous flows of magma would have belched out from underneath to spill over the surface of the planet in that area, creating what we now call the Deccan Traps.

The later collapse of that bulge would have caused another pressure wave to travel backward as it rebounded. Hence, the crust on the impact side would have also received several rebound thrusts from below as the pressure waves bounced back and forth to the opposite ends of the trajectory lines of the impacts. They would have traveled from the points of contact to the distal ends and back several times. We can picture this, for example, if we throw a brick into one side of a pool. Waves radiate outward from the point of impact, strike the opposite side, and then bounce back toward the site of impact several times until the energy dissipates. It was the bouncing and repeated pressure waves that created the curious step formations we find in these enormous igneous provinces.

The rebound action from returning pressure waves that traveled through the interior of the Earth and back also helped buckle the subterranean floor of the newly formed Atlantic Ocean upward over the impact sites. Having lost the enormous weight of the granitic continental rock above them, the basaltic floor rose up some 7 miles to form the Mid-Atlantic Ridge.

These fissures in the once single supercontinent made by the initial impacts in each of their individual areas of impact then began to widen by the action of the ejecting water along the Mid-Atlantic Ridge. As the fissure widened and material was sent skyward by the jetting fountains, the enormous weight of the granitic shelf that had previously existed was steadily reduced all along the giant fissures that formed the outlines of the new continents. It was as if a giant zipper had broken the single supercontinent into seven smaller continents.

Where once 10 miles deep of granite pushed down on the subfloor along the length of this "zipper," now there was only the weight of water that was jetting upward. That created a negative pressure on the basaltic subfloor. The basaltic understructure from below began to rise with the help of each successive returning wave to fill the void created by the eroding fountains. In that way, the basaltic rock rapidly bulged upward all along the cracked crust.

Once enough of the granitic structure above the basaltic layer was eroded and thrust skyward by the ejecting water from the underground aquifers, the subfloor rose dramatically. In other words, as that enormous weight was removed from

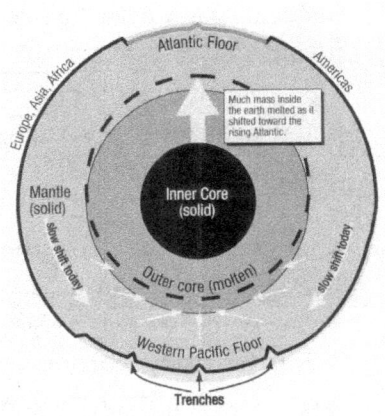

Subsidence of the Pacific floor created by the buckling subterranean bedrock in the Atlantic
(Courtesy of Walt Brown, *In the Beginning*)

the basaltic floor below, the basaltic floor began to push upward. The positive pressure of the rebounding waves coming back from the opposite side of the world added to the negative pressure by the eroding continents above. In that way, the Mid-Atlantic Ridge dramatically surged upward within a relatively short period of time.

Subsequently, the upward movement of matter from the interior of the Earth to fill the area of the uplifting subterranean bedrock on one side of the world would have caused the sea floor on the opposite end to subside or sink toward the interior of the planet. It is for that reason that the Pacific Ocean wrinkled in the form of deep trenches as matter below it was sucked down to fill up the rising floor on the other side of the planet. The rising of the Atlantic floor thus formed the deep underwater trenches of the Pacific Ocean on the other side of the planet.

> The gigantic pressure immediately under the floor *before* the rupture corresponded to the weight of almost 10 miles of rock. . . . Afterwards, with almost 10 miles of rock

suddenly gone; only the strength of the chamber floor and 10 miles of water on top of it resisted this upward pressure. Consequently, as the rupture widened, the Mid-Oceanic Ridge suddenly buckled upwards forming the now familiar mountainous ridge.

The continental drift phase began with hydroplates sliding "downhill" on the lifted slopes of the ridge. The continents slid on a layer of water away from the rising Mid-Atlantic Ridge. This removed more weight from the rising portion of the subterranean chamber floor, causing it to rise even faster and accelerate the hydroplates even more.

As that portion of the chamber floor rose to become the Atlantic floor, it stretched horizontally in all directions, just as a balloon stretches when its radius increases. This stretching produced cracks parallel and perpendicular to the Mid-Oceanic Ridge. Because this process began first in what is now the Atlantic, the Mid-Atlantic Ridge and its cracks are the most prominent of the Oceanic ridge system. Aided by the two enormous impacts that gouged that area, the crack down the middle of the Atlantic was the first to form.

Obviously the great confining pressures in the mantle and core did not allow deep voids to open up inside the volume of our planet as the Atlantic floor rose. Instead, what happened is that even deeper material was "sucked" upward. *Throughout the entire diameter of the inner earth,* material shifted toward the rising Atlantic, forming a broader, but shallower, depression on the opposite side of the earth-what is now the Pacific and Indian Oceans.

Just as the Atlantic floor stretched horizontally, as it rose, the western Pacific floor compressed horizontally as it subsided. Subsidence in the Pacific and Indian Ocean began a startling 20–25 minutes after the Atlantic floor began its rise, the time it takes for a seismic wave to pass through the earth. Both movements eventually contributed to the "downhill" slide of hydroplates.

Centered on the Pacific and Indian Oceans is the concentrated trench region of the western Pacific. As material of the western Pacific was sucked down, it buckled downward forming trenches. The Atlantic Ocean is centered near longitude 21.5 degrees west latitude 10 degrees south, while the concentrated trench region is centered near longitude 159 degrees east and latitude 10 degrees north, almost exactly opposite each other (Brown 2001, 123–124).

The plate tectonic theory cannot explain the fact that ridges are not in accord with the direction in which the plates are supposed to be sliding. The hydroplate theory, on the other hand, predicts that the stretching of the Atlantic floor upward would cause the suction of the Pacific floor downward at the opposite side of the planet to fill the void. That is clearly observed in the formation of the many deep oceanic trenches in the Pacific Basin.

The Plate Tectonic Theory and Deep Ocean Trenches

Just within the last decade of the second millennium, the use of a submersible robot sub called *Alvin* allowed man to explore for the first time an underwater region 4 miles below the surface of the Atlantic Ocean.

The little robot photographed the volcanic process in action as lava and superheated salt water seeped out into the ocean floor. *Alvin* brought back even more surprises than scientists had anticipated. They were amazed to find that life actually existed in this extremely hostile environment. Scientists watched in wonder as superheated water of 700 degrees Fahrenheit spewed out into the ocean, leached with minerals in hot springs called smokers.

They are the last remnants of the mighty fountains of the deep. There are still vast amounts of water below our continents that fuel these smokers. The new discovery of deep, underground aquifers that lie below the continents shows that they may contain twice the volume of water found in our surface oceans. No longer can the mighty fountains of the deep be challenged as scientifically impossible. The evolutionary objections have been proved wrong because of their ignorance of the true fact that God first created our world as a water planet.

> *In the beginning God created the heavens and the earth. The earth was formless and void, and darkness was over the surface of the deep, and the Spirit of God was moving over the surface of the waters. Then God said, "Let there be light"; and there was light. God saw that the light was good; and God separated the light from the darkness. God called the light day, and the darkness He called night. And there was evening and there was morning, one day.*
>
> *Then God said, "Let there be an expanse in the midst of the waters, and let it separate the waters from the waters. God made the expanse, and separated the waters which were below the [expanse from the waters which were above the expanse; and it was so. God called the expanse heaven. And there was evening and there was morning, a second day.*
>
> *Then God said, "Let the waters below the heavens be gathered into one place, and let the dry land appear"; and it was so. God called the dry land earth, and the gathering of the waters He called seas; and God saw that it was good.*
>
> —Gen. 1:1–10

These smokers are simply the remnants of the mighty fountains that burst open by the striking meteors that brought an end to our First Earth. Yet 4 miles below the surface of the ocean in the midst of this hostile acidic and completely dark environment filled with hydrogen sulfide is a wide variety of organisms that are still able to thrive. Tiny shrimp, clams, crabs, and 6-foot tubeworms thrive, deriving their energy from the process of chemosynthesis rather than photosynthesis. It is as though God's grace was poured out even on this mechanism of death.

Lava still pours out of the fractures between the continents. There is enough lava that spews out each year in this Mid-Atlantic Ridge that spans some 40,000 miles in length to bury the state of New York. The ridge sometimes reaches 5 miles in height, forming huge, underwater mountains. Some of this was formed as the result of the continuous volcanic process, but most of it was the result of the subterranean floor buckling during the Great Flood in a very short period of time.

The plate tectonic theory, however, stipulates that the growth of the mountain ridges has been taking place at the slow rates we observe today; that is, through the slow process of the eruption of magma at our present time. Gradualism permeates all evolutionary models, but the impacts of meteors do not result in gradual changes; they result in cataclysmic, rapid changes. Evolutionists who ignore the power of such impacts insist that the continents are being moved by the upwelling magma that then solidifies and pushes outward laterally.

Today, this process can be observed on the surface of the planet in Iceland where the ridge comes out of the ocean and often creates havoc as the superheated magma interacts with snow and ice. In 1996, an eruption in the Icelandic Ridge melted 336 feet of snow that was piled on it, causing a severe flood that raced unchecked, wiping out bridges and roads in its path to the ocean.

But the fact that this magma is seeping to the surface does not mean it is stressing the huge continents in a lateral movement. Logic stipulates that the soft, pliable magma will seek the route of least resistance and flow upward, creating higher ridges instead of moving the enormous plates sideways. It makes much more sense to say that because the plates are moving sideways, the magma comes out to fill the void, and not the other way around. The movement of the plates was instigated by the mechanism of the Great Flood and has now slowed down to a mere fraction of the speed it once had.

If the magma were pushing the plates outward, we would not expect the trenches between the two continents to be depressed as they are. In Iceland, we can walk down that trench several meters deep with one continent at one side and the other continent on the opposite side. That is evidence that the continents are sliding away from one another, and then the lava comes up from beneath to fill the vacated space.

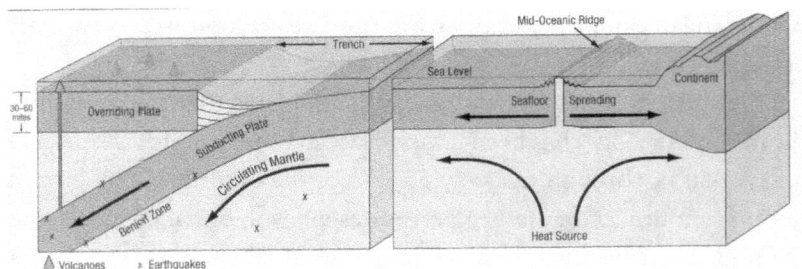

Tectonic plate theory
(Courtesy of Walt Brown, *In the Beginning*)

The plate tectonic theory tells us that today the continents are continuing to move away from each other as the lava coming up from the Mid-Atlantic Ridge cools in the deep Atlantic waters. As it solidifies, it pushes the plates laterally. At the opposite end of the plate is the subduction zone where the crust is crushed against the next plate with increasing force. One of the two plates moving against the other must go under as the other slides above it. The plate that goes under is called the subducting plate, and the other one is called the overriding plate. For example, in North America, the Pacific Plate is being subducted under the overriding North American plate. Scientists claim that this process forces the opposing Pacific Plate to be thrust downward into the interior of the planet.

THE END OF THE FIRST EARTH – THE FIRST ICE AGE

As the result of this subduction, the tectonic plate theory stipulates that not only the granitic plates are being driven to the interior of the Earth but ocean water is also being funneled into the interior. They therefore surmise that the internal heat of the core of the planet then superheats the ocean water. The rocks melt into magma, and the water turns to steam trapped by the floating, hardened crust above it. For that reason, they claim, when volcanoes erupt, along with magma and tephra, an enormous amount of water vapor is ejected into our atmosphere.

But that makes no sense. Two enormously dense, heavy plates grinding past one another could hardly be expected to allow even an infinitesimal amount of water between them. The pressures are just too great. It cannot enter from the surface. At those intense pressures, there are no porous materials. The deeper one goes below the surface, the more the pressure of the weight of the rocks limits the depth that water may seep from the surface. That limit is about 5 miles from the surface. It is inconceivable that these enormous pressures, not only from the weight of the two enormously heavy plates but also from the lateral forces slamming them into each other, could allow even a molecule of water between them.

At this depth, pressures are so extreme that even microscopic fissures are sealed tightly, and no flow can occur. The denser rock would simply shut the water out. Hence, any water that comes from depths below 5 miles has not been brought below from the surface. These underground aquifers were created during the creation of our planet. Nevertheless, deep drills have shown that salt water exists far below that level. The hydroplate theory can also explain the presence of water vapor in volcanic eruptions through the salt water that once existed in greater quantities in these subterranean chambers.

The hydroplate theory also opposes the tectonic plate theory in its explanation of the formation of the deep oceanic trenches. If the plate tectonic theory were correct, then the subducting plates should create an increase in mass as the subducting plate is forced under the opposite overriding plate. The crunching of these tectonic plates as they scrape by one another would create a much denser rock in the areas of subduction. But the physical evidence observed is exactly the opposite.

> The most striking phenomenon associated with the trenches is a deficiency in gravity. . . . Measurements of gravity near trenches show pronounced departures from expected values. These gravity anomalies are among the largest found on earth. It is clear that isostatic equilibrium does not exist near the trenches. The trench-producing forces must be acting . . . to pull the crust under the trenches downward (Fisher and Revelle 1972, 122).

The evidence seems to corroborate the idea that material under the trenches has been sucked down to compensate for the rising Atlantic floor and not that it is being pushed down from above. The fact that isostatic equilibrium does not exist near these trenches is also evidence that the event that caused this subsidence did not happen millions of years ago or the spinning Earth and the effects of angular momentum and gravity would have long ago corrected the anomaly. Those trenches are not millions of years old. They have been created by some recent catastrophic event that caused the Pacific floor to sink and become less dense as a result.

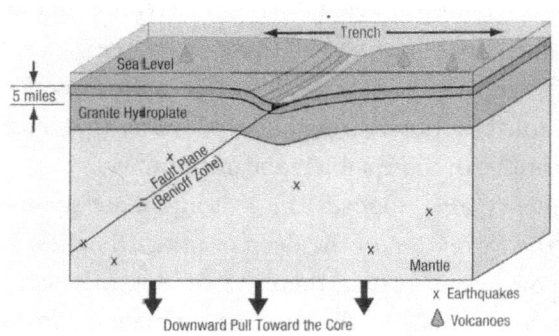

Hydroplate theory explanation for the formation of deep ocean trenches
(Courtesy of Walt Brown, *In the Beginning*)

The technique called *seismic tomography* measures the speed that seismic waves travel through our Earth. That allows us to determine the density and elasticity of rock materials they pass through. The P wave and S wave travel times depend on the properties of the rock they travel through.

Seismic waves travel faster through denser rock and therefore increase in speed with depth as pressure and density increase. The differences in travel time will therefore describe the differences in the density of the material. Earthquakes radiate seismic waves that travel through the Earth. By studying these waves and knowing the precise time of the earthquake and the time of arrival of the wave produced through a given path, we can determine the differences in rock properties over that particular path.

Through the study of seismic tomography, scientists were able to detect the major layers of the Earth before 1950, but the finer details were not delineated until the 1960s during the underground nuclear testing of the Cold War period. After thousands of readings from points all over the world and knowing the average velocity along these tens of thousands of different paths, computers can calculate the speed of the wave at every point inside the Earth and therefore determine its density.

For example, the density of the continental crust is on average 2.6–2.8 grams per centimeter cubed, and the P-wave velocity is 6 kilometers per second, while the mantle's density is 4.5–10 grams per centimeter cubed with a corresponding P-wave velocity of 8–12 kilometers per second. The solid inner core has a density of 13.5 grams per centimeter cubed, and the P-wave velocity is 11–12 kilometers per second.

The study of the seismic waves during earthquakes has therefore greatly increased our understanding of the geologic forces and makeup of our Earth's crust. Such studies support the idea that subduction is not taking place in the trenches because the earthquakes are almost always caused by horizontal tension and not by compressive tension as would be expected if subduction were taking place in those trenches as described in plate tectonics.

Almost 90% of all earthquake energy is released under trenches. Earthquakes often occur near sloping planes, called *Benioff zones* that intersect a trench. These earthquake zones enter the mantle at 35-degree to 60-degree angles below the horizontal, and extend to depths of about 420 miles.

During an earthquake, opposite sides of a fault unlock and rapid sliding begins along the fault. If the side of the fault nearest a distant seismometer moves toward the seismometer, a compression wave will be detected first. If the side moves away from the seismometer, a tension wave will be detected first. By looking at the first waves to reach many seismometers, one can deduce the orientation of the fault plane and whether the earthquake was triggered by compression or tension. *Earthquakes near trenches are almost always due to horizontal tension failures at right angles to the trench axis* (Brown 2001, 122).

The upper part of the crust is cold, hard, and brittle. Below the 5-mile mark, however, the increase in pressure and temperature makes the rock hot and pliable. Thus, the horizontal pressures exerted by the widening of the Atlantic Ocean caused the western Pacific floor to buckle and deform downward in arc- and cusp-shaped creases typical of a round surface. The depth of the Mariana Trench, for example, is 6.8 miles below sea level, while Mount Everest is only 5.5 miles high. The hydroplate theory therefore predicts that the rising ocean floor at the opposite side of the world created a vacuum under the Pacific floor when the fountains of the deep were opened and the Mid-Atlantic Ridge was formed. This has not only folded the basaltic floor inward but has also caused the sinking of the granitic block above it in the continents bordering the western Pacific Ocean.

Initially, this distal area to the point of impact would have bulged outward. The outward bulging of this area after receiving the initial shock wave of the meteors' impacts on the other side of the world would have precipitated enormous volcanic explosions and large outflows of magma. The release of this magma would have reduced the density in that region as the crust rebounded back toward the center of the Earth and collapsed into the form of trenches, which we now observe.

The heat generated by the sliding granite crust (hydroplates) over the basalt bedrock below also generated enormous amounts of magma that would have spilled out onto the surface through the cracks created by such dramatic contortions of the plates. For this reason, the ocean floor of the western Pacific is overlaid by huge amounts of molten basalt rock. We have already discussed the enormous lava flows that have evidenced these titanic forces.

It is significant to note that the hydroplate theory predicts that if one were to drill below that molten basalt floor, they would find the granite crust. The drills in the western Pacific have thus far been too shallow to probe below the surface of these giant lava flows generated by the shifting crust.

Evidence of this granitic composite block below the Pacific can be cited from the eruptive rocks west of the *andesite line*. Eruptive rocks west of this line that runs down the center of the Pacific Ocean are primarily andesite; that is, they are composed of such minerals as quartz, hornblende, and biotite, which are key components of granite (not basalt). The eruptive rocks east of the andesite line are primarily basaltic.

Moreover, if the plates were subducting below the overriding plate, as the plate tectonic theory stipulates, then we would expect to see the many layers of sediment being scraped off the top of the subducting plate by the harder rock of the overriding plate. The softer upper layers would be scraped into a rubble mound, or the layers would be compressed into folds. But trenches contain smooth, undistorted layers of sedimentation, which could not possibly be if it were being subducted. The subduction process would necessarily scrape these sediments into mounds or ridges as one plate scrapes over the top of the other. David William Scholl and his colleagues at the US Naval Electronics Laboratory Center have mapped these trenches and found that the sediment deposits are virtually undeformed.

> It would seem that the sediment sliding into the bottom of the trench should be folded into pronounced ridges and valleys. Yet virtually undeformed sediments have been mapped in trenches by David William Scholl and his colleagues at the U.S. Naval Electronics Laboratory Center. Furthermore, the enormous quantity of deep-ocean sediment that has presumably been swept up to the margins of trenches cannot be detected on sub-bottom profiling records (Menard 1969).

What is clear is that the event that caused these deep folds in our ocean floors cannot be attributed to lateral forces. The smooth layers of sedimentation and soft rock underneath it point to the downward buckling of the Pacific floor as predicted by the hydroplate theory.

As a matter of fact, it is doubtful that subduction zones exist at all. For one plate to subduct under another, it must depress at least 30 miles, which is the minimum thickness of these hypothetical tectonic plates as they have been crunched and thickened. But rock below 5 miles does not behave like solid rock. It is soft and pliable due to the enormous heat and pressure. Any lateral motion against it would simply displace the rock in a lateral motion and not in a downward motion since it behaves more like a liquid. The enormous pressure of the rock from below would not allow the subduction. The rock would simply swirl like an eddy in the flow of water.

THE END OF THE FIRST EARTH – THE FIRST ICE AGE

When two giant plates slam into one another, they do not gravitate downward against the pressure of the entire thickness of the Earth. Instead, they crumble upward against the much less dense air. They always choose the path of least resistance, which causes the plates to crunch and fold upward, thus thickening the plates and creating mountains rather than subducting them.

If subductions did exist, it would be expected that volcanoes would rise through the friction of one plate riding over the other. These volcanoes would then sprout from the side that is overriding above the descending plate because that is where the friction would be causing fissures and molten rock. But contrary to this, most volcanoes in the western Pacific lie on the opposite side of the trenches, on the supposedly descending side. It is more likely that the cracks caused by the downward buckling and the less dense rock produced by this downward suction are the real reasons these volcanoes are where they are.

The geology of the islands of New Zealand offers us another view into the mechanism that caused these enormous deep-water trenches. To begin, the very highest mountains are made of marine sedimentary rock that had to have been at least 80 meters under water for them to form. That is substantiated by the nature of the marine fossils found in these layers. It is certain that the highest peaks of the islands were all once under water. That, of course, is also evidence for the global nature of the Great Flood.

The mountain ridges have been driven upward by the buckling of the continent as it slides away from the impact area. But in spite of this buckling and thickening, the majority of that area has sunk under the rising seas and the depression of the basaltic floor due to the rise of the Mid-Atlantic Ridge on the opposite side of the planet. Surrounding these islands is an enormous, wide land shelf that comprises the former micro-continent of Zealandia. This continent is presently submerged some 5,000 feet under water. But during the First Earth, this entire continent used to be dry land. The present islands are merely the highest peaks of the mountains in this continent, which is 93 percent submerged.

> Scientists from New Zealand, New Caledonia, and Australia have published a new paper which claims that the southwestern Pacific Ocean harbours an almost entirely submerged continent—Zealandia. (*National Geographic*, 2017)

Zealandia covers an area of 1.35 million square miles, an area larger than Greenland or India. It was once connected to Australia, which was connected to Antarctica before the impact of the larger meteor shattered them into their present forms.

The underwater continent is made up of two almost parallel ridges that are separated by a deep rift. These ridges are made of granitic continental rock that was once above sea level. Since even at the lowest point sea levels were some 430 feet below our present levels, the land mass must have sunk more than 4,500 feet.

Why is it so deeply thrust underwater? The evolutionists say the continental crust there is thinner than usual and consequently does not float as well. But how did it get thinner?

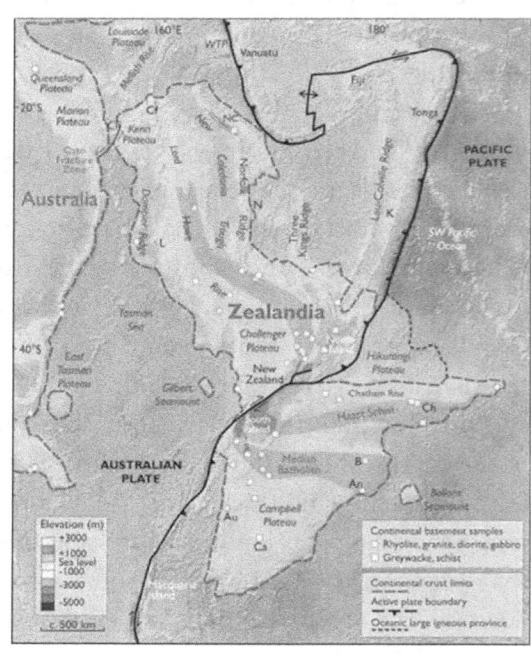

National Geographic, "Is Zealandia Really the 8th Continent?" https://web.archive.org/web/20191030221631/http:/www.nationalgeographic.com.au/nature/is-zealandia-really-the-8th-continent.aspx

THE END OF THE FIRST EARTH – THE FIRST ICE AGE

We know it was once out of the water, so it must have been thick enough to float.

That the continent was once above water is conclusively proved by petrified logs of fossilized forests found in Curio Bay that are closely related to Norfolk Pine. The giant gas deposits found in the submerged continent are also evidence of the total destruction of the thick fauna that existed in this area prior to the Great Flood.

It was obviously sucked under by the rising Mid-Atlantic Ridge at the other side of the globe that caused the material of the Earth in this area to sink toward the center of the Earth. No doubt the deep rift that separates the two long ridges was also created by this process and aided by the lateral motion of the continents, which now further causes it to buckle.

The evidence shows that our Earth has undergone enormous tectonic upheaval since the once pristine and stable First Earth died its watery death and was changed in a relatively short period of time. Much continues to change, albeit at a much slower pace. But the time will come again when large changes will occur in another short period of time.

As our Second Earth continues to move toward a global government, judgment will come upon us once again. Our planet will undergo drastic meteorological changes. The frequency and intensity of earthquakes shall signal the coming of the end of our Second Earth. Our Earth is a reflection of the decline of our human moral condition. The violence that brought forth the judgment of the First Earth ought to give us pause to consider our present course.

In short, the hydrological and geological processes of the Great Flood were not some tranquil, filling process such as the gradual filling of one's bathtub. The enormous forces of the hydraulics of rushing flood waters carrying timber, rock, mud, and all living beings and animals of every size and type in its path completely devastated the entire civilized world. Such destructive forces left us very little evidence of their cities and manmade buildings. The absolutely devastating power of the hydraulics involved crushed and splintered what was made by man.

More Evidence of a Global Hydrological Event

There are many reasons that point to a singular, catastrophic event and not a series of minor events separated by vast amounts of time. For example, the global geological evidence seems to show a global inundation as the only truly logical way to explain the formation of metamorphic rock in the level of abundance found on our planet.

Metamorphic rock is created from sedimentary rock at extreme temperatures and pressures. For example, marble is created from limestone (a sedimentary rock) when its temperature exceeds 1,600 degrees Fahrenheit with a combined pressure of the weight of a column of rock 23 miles high. The slow-moving tectonic plates envisioned by the evolutionists could not have generated the same pressure depicted by the hydroplate theory.

The combination of the water pressure from the Global Flood above it and the lateral pressure and temperature created by the sliding continents could easily explain the formation of metamorphic rock. It is much harder to explain how rock buried under 23 miles of rock could rise to the surface or one would have to speculate that mountains were in the past much higher than today. That runs contrary to physical evidence that shows that mountains are instead getting higher as time goes by and that in the past they were much lower.

The standard geologic model for the formation of metamorphic rock stipulates that the rock rose to the surface through the erosion of the rock above it throughout millions of years. But diamonds, for example, are formed from carbon under the enormous pressure of a column of rock some 75 miles high. Even for millions of years, the erosion of 75 miles of rock is a pretty steep order.

In addition, most metamorphic rock was formed in the presence of water, adding more evidence to the idea that it was created during the Global Deluge. The fact that our highest mountain is only 5½ miles high gives us good reason to suspect that these metamorphic rocks could not have been formed by the standard models geologists insist.

How could these rocks have formed in the presence of water 75 miles below the surface? It is more consistent with the physical data to conceive that the rocks were heated and pressurized by the enormous compression of the gliding continents during the continental drift phase of the Great Flood.

If our Judeo-Christian model is correct, then one would expect the archaeological evidence to predict that prediluvian buildings, works of art, or utensils would not be composed of metamorphic rock since most metamorphic rocks were created by the action of the Great Flood.

Furthermore, the very presence of the enormous deposits of limestone in the world (about 10–15 percent of sedimentary rock) is difficult to explain through our present slow, geological processes. The Earth contains much more limestone than it should, especially because most of it is without impurities that would inevitably drift in if they formed according to standard evolutionary, slow, gradual geological processes. That suggests that these vast deposits of limestone were rapidly precipitated from the water since the underground salt water from the aquifers was so highly pressurized that when it came to the surface, there was a mass precipitation event in the much lower pressure at the surface. These mass precipitation deposits were then subsequently and suddenly buried in a global inundation that did not allow time for living things to intrude. All of this can be best explained through the mechanism of a single catastrophic event such as the Global Deluge.

The evolutionary assumption that most of Earth's limestone deposits were formed by marine life is unsupported by the physical evidence. The limestone holds more calcium and carbon than today's atmosphere, oceans, coal, oil, and living matter combined. Moreover, if marine organisms had created the limestone, all the deposits would be laden with shells.

This is not the case for many of the major deposits around the world such as the White Cliffs of Dover in England. The fine, powdery, chalk cliffs were more likely formed through the precipitation of sediments from water, as would be predicted by the release of the subterranean aquifers during the Great Flood. The limestone held in suspension under the enormous pressures below the Earth would then precipitate after coming to the lower pressures on the surface of the Earth.

> Most of the recognizable materials composing the Chalk have not been proved to be of organic origin by those who have studied it, and [the few organic] portions are, moreover, distinctly subordinate in amount to the amorphous matrix and spheres, save for some local exceptions. The number of these exceptions are so few as to make the scarcity of organic remains a remarkable feature, for one would expect more of them.
>
> The lack of mechanical wear; the evidence absence of currents, as shown by massiveness and lack of stratification: the perfectly preserved minute spheres and cells: and the absolute lack of any evidence of an organic origin of the dense material, all favor the view that the Chalk was inorganic in origin (Tarr 1925, 259).

I live on a peninsula almost 300 miles long called the state of Florida, which is sitting entirely on a limestone base. Some of it has been created by marine life, but some of it has not. Limestone can naturally precipitate from water under certain conditions. When carbon dioxide dissolves in water, it forms a weak, acid solution called carbonic acid. It dissolves the limestone in the water, and when the excess carbon dioxide is consumed, it reaches a saturation level.

There is an underground river that runs below the entire length of the state of Florida, carving countless tunnels throughout the sedimentary rock. If the water evaporates, the process is reversed, and limestone precipitates. We can see this process in caves where stalagmites and stalactites form, but it has also been observed on beaches.

> Finally, limestone sometimes precipitates along coasts of some eastern Caribbean islands, making their normally clear coastal waters suddenly cloudy white. Studies of this phenomenon have shown that limestone precipitates when CO_2 suddenly escapes from carbonate-saturated groundwater near the beach (Hanor 1978, 241).

The presence of large salt domes throughout our planet also suggests that a Global Flood deposited them. Huge salt deposits bulge upward in the shape of domes, sometimes in layers covering 100,000 miles and in some places up to a mile thick. What geologic process could cause the formation of such enormous salt layers other than a Global Flood?

The huge salt mines in the interior of the United States, for example, are impressive in size and depth. The formation of the bulging domes can be explained by the pressure exerted on the salt

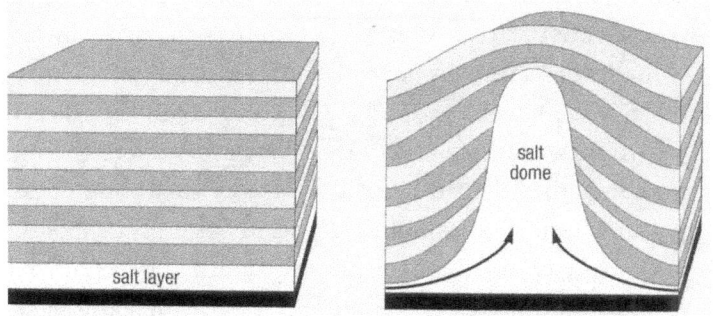

Salt domes created by the rapid deposit of sedimentation
(Courtesy of Walt Brown, *In the Beginning*)

layers from the denser sediments forming above them. When a small section of the salt layer rises, either due to a weakness in the layer above it or greater pressure from lateral sources, the pasty salt layer surrounding it flows horizontally to fill the void and subsequently pushes the dome ever higher.

If the sedimentary rock above it were pliable enough, as if it had been recently deposited, then the formation of these giant salt domes would be much more likely than if these sedimentary layers were deposited over millions of years and cemented hard through time. Salt domes would be difficult to explain through small increments and long periods of time once the rock was solidified.

The existence of vast stores of muck also poses an enigma for the evolutionists. Muck covers one-seventh of the Earth's surface, all surrounding the Arctic Ocean. It generally occupies treeless terrains on flat land not surrounded by mountains from which they could have eroded. Such formations could hardly be expected without the mechanism of a global deluge.

> Russian geologists have drilled through 4,000 feet of muck without hitting solid rock. Where did so much eroded material come from? What eroded it?
>
> Oil prospectors, drilling through Alaskan muck, "have brought up an 18-inch long chunk of tree trunk from about 1,000 feet below the surface. It wasn't petrified—just frozen." The nearest forests are hundreds of miles away. Williams describes similar discoveries in Alaska:
>
>> Though the ground is frozen for 1,900 feet down from the surface at Prudhoe Bay, everywhere the oil companies drilled around this area they discovered an ancient tropical forest. It was in frozen state, not in petrified state. It is between 1,100 and 1,700 feet down. There are palm trees, pine trees, and tropical foliage in great profusion. In fact, they found them lapped all

over each other, just as though they had fallen in that position.'

How were these trees buried under a thousand feet of hard frozen ground? (Brown 2001, 164).

Such vast evidence of giant forests being covered by a thousand feet of permafrost can only be adequately explained by the mechanism of a global flood. The evidence found 1,700 feet below the surface shows that vast forests of tropical plants were uprooted and mixed in the hydraulics of the Great Flood and then frozen before decomposing. What uniformitarian scenario can explain this in a gradualist timetable? How does tropical foliage become encased in ice?

The vast physical evidence shows that our First Ice Age came suddenly and reached out its icy tendrils to engulf what was before tropical land in one quick, catastrophic, hydraulic event. No uniformitarian gradual mechanism can explain such drastic changes in such large areas.

CHAPTER 8
THE SCIENTIFIC EVIDENCE FOR THE ANTEDILUVIAN WORLD

The Evidence Regarding a Uniform, Mild Climate
If our Judeo-Christian model is correct that the antediluvian world was shielded by a water vapor canopy that moderated temperatures throughout the planet by means of the greenhouse effect, we would expect the geological record to show that both flora and fauna of temperate creatures would have been able to live in these extreme remote areas of the poles that are presently under impossible frigid conditions that are incompatible with higher forms of life.

> With respect to climate, the fossils show that there was a uniformly mild climate in high and in low latitudes of both the northern and the southern hemispheres. That is, there was a perfectly uniform, non-zonal, mild, and springlike climate in every part of the globe. This does not mean that the climate was of necessity the same in all parts of the earth. There were differences, but not the present extremes. Sir Henry H. Howorth, a noted geologist and competent interpreter of these fossils says: "The flora and fauna are virtually the only thermometer with which we

can test the climate of any past period. Other evidence is always sophisticated by the fact that we may be attributing to climate what is due to other causes. But the biological evidence is unmistakable; cold blooded reptiles cannot live in icy water; subtropical plants, or plants whose habitat is the temperate zone, cannot ripen their seeds and sow themselves under arctic conditions."

Or another outstanding authority, Professor Alfred R. Wallace, says: "There is but one climate known to the ancient fossil world as revealed by the plants and animals entombed in the rocks, and the climate was a mantle of springlike loveliness which seems to have prevailed continuously over the whole globe. Just how the world could have thus been warmed all over may be a matter of conjecture; that it was so warmed effectively and continuously is a matter of fact." . . .

Or Professor George McCready Price writes: "It would be quite useless to go through the whole fossileferous series in order for there is not a single system which does not have coral limestone or other evidence of a mild climate way up north, most systems having such rock in the lands which skirt the very pole itself. The limestone and coal beds of the carboniferous period are the nearest known rocks to the North Pole. They crop out all around the polar basis; and from the dip of these beds, they must underlie the polar sea itself. But it is needless to go through the systems one after another, for *'they uniformly testify that a warm climate has in former times prevailed over the whole globe'*" (Rehwinkel 1951, 7–8).

Our world that was, our First Earth, enjoyed a long period of mild climate throughout the entire globe, and that cannot be disputed from the biological evidence found in the fossils. The overwhelming evidence in every part of the world is undeniable, even by the staunchest of evolutionary scientists. That our First Earth underwent a violent and extreme meteorological and geological upheaval that suddenly and catastrophically changed it forever, causing the majority of the flora and fauna to become extinct, is now accepted even by evolutionists.

The Chicxulub meteor strike scenario is now popularly held even by most of the staunchest evolutionists because they cannot refute the obvious and overwhelming evidence now cited even by evolutionary geologists. In spite of the torpedoes to the broadside of gradualism, old dogmas die hard. Evolutionists will not easily accede to the removal of the long ages necessary for evolution to have a fighting chance at being plausible. They well know that the odds become even more remote without the huge spans of time they need for small changes to accumulate into big changes. Their evidences for these long time periods are refuted in my book *The Descent of Man* (Book 4 in the series).

What creationists have been ridiculed for saying for many years has now become popularly accepted by the status quo of the scientific community. They have quietly sidelined their previous dogmatic and uncompromising anti-catastrophe uniformitarian dogmas in dissimilate embarrassment, but they refuse to abandon the ship of gradualism.

The evidence in the fossils undeniably shows that our magnificent world closely reflected the original intent of God for humanity. Our present world is genetically only a shadow of a shadow of the world that was. The fact is that everything in the antediluvian world grew larger and stronger and in much richer and wider varieties. Animals of huge dimensions were common for the simple reason that the flora aided by the almost perfect conditions of a controlled greenhouse grew immense and plentiful. The fossils show a far greater variety of genera and species than what we find today in the aftermath of the Flood.

It is an accepted fact that the fossils of that time represented a more robust and more perfect example of all the species. Moreover, every species exhibited a much wider variety of phenotypes or a wider character complex. That is in great contradiction to the general evolutionary process that claims we should be evolving upward. Evolution predicts that the variety of living creatures will grow exponentially with time, and yet the opposite is the irrefutable, empirical evidence.

The fossil evidence clearly reveals that the only evolution that is actually occurring is the devolution of all life as a result of the Fall. Our Second Earth is but a shadow, a bad photocopy, of the First Earth. It is estimated that only 5 percent of the species from our First Earth survived into our Second Earth.

If this catastrophe had occurred millions of years ago, as they claim, then one would expect that the species would have adapted and differentiated once more to produce the variety that once was. With the passage of time, the evolutionary process would predict a greater number of species. If evolution were true, then this mysterious and as yet conclusively undefined evolutionary mechanism would have, by necessity, instigated an even more pronounced effort to differentiate and adapt all living things to the new climactic conditions. This is elementary logic.

Instead, we find that the number of species continues to decline even today. More poignantly, no new species has ever been recorded by this mysterious evolutionary mechanism they dogmatically consider to be real. Instead, animals are becoming extinct as time goes by and not the other way around. That is an empirical reality that cannot be refuted. Our world is decaying, and the result of man's rebellion continues to wreak havoc on the Earth. What the true scientific facts clearly declare is that our Second Earth has devolved significantly from the spectacular grandeur and beauty of the First Earth.

THE SCIENTIFIC EVIDENCE FOR THE ANTEDILUVIAN WORLD

Evidence in the Ice

If this series of catastrophic events that brought about the Noahic Flood truly took place, we would expect to find evidence of tropical flora and fauna that lived on our prediluvian planet in presently frozen areas. They would have been captured in the frozen waters of the great inundation of our First Earth and kept in store for us in those remote areas of the ice cap of the First Ice Age that did not melt in the meteorological process that rapidly brought about the Second Ice Age.

And that is precisely what we find today. How else can one explain the findings of frozen mastodons through immense tracts of land stretching miles and miles in the Alaskan and Siberian Tundra? How can we explain that a Russian drilled through 4 miles of muck and found a tree trunk that was frozen instead of fossilized? American drillers also discovered that in Alaska.

> Oil prospectors, drilling through Alaskan muck, have "brought up an 18-inch-long chunk of tree trunk from almost 1,000 feet below the surface. It wasn't petrified—just frozen." The nearest forests are hundreds of miles away. Williams describes similar discoveries in Alaska:
>
> Though the ground is frozen for 1,900 feet down from the surface at Prudhoe Bay, everywhere the oil companies drilled around this area they discovered an ancient tropical forest. It was in frozen state, not in petrified state. It is between 1,100 and 1,700 feet down. There are palm trees, pine trees, and tropical foliage in great profusion. In fact, they found them lapped all over each other, just as though they had fallen in that position (Williams 1980, 54).

The empirical evidence suggests a flood sheet scenario that wiped out an ancient, tropical forest and then flash-froze it. What other than the Global Flood could explain such a scenario? The same applies to the mastodons, rhinoceros, horses, and other grazing tropical animals that were found quick-frozen. When thawed out today, these mastodons are found to have been quick-frozen with fresh vegetation still intact in their stomachs and sometimes even in their mouths.

The fossils in these areas, as well as the variety of pollen and samples of grasses found in their stomach contents, prove without doubt that these areas of present-day tundra climate were then fertile and temperate steppes.

It is important to note that the shifting continents cannot be attributed to the situation in Siberia. The Asiatic continent did not move north; it has instead moved laterally. The fossils there show that these tundra regions were teeming with horses, wooly bison, wooly rhinoceros, deer, and many other animals that could have only survived in a temperate climate. Their fossil evidence indicates that these regions were much warmer, which substantiates the Judeo-Christian model's claim that our planet was like a greenhouse due to the water vapor canopy over the First Earth.

Evolutionists, grasping at straws, might propose that local floods drowned these animals, but what are the chances that local floods occurred in Alaska, Siberia, and all other land regions that in our present day remain as frozen tundra? And how can they explain the fact that after they drowned they would have been quick-frozen? Animals falling in ice will still decompose internally. How, then, can vegetation be undigested in their stomachs? Moreover, if the climate was cold enough to freeze ice, then there could be no floods.

In the early 10th and 11th centuries, Arab traders penetrating deep into Russia began a lucrative trade in the ivory tusks of the wooly mammoth. The mammoth is a member of the elephant family that thrived, according to evolutionists, over the entire landmass of the Pangaean continent of the world that was. They have been found well into the Siberian tundra region of northern Russia.

Today, practically the only form of life that can survive the frigid climate of these extreme northern areas are certain bacteria, lichens, and a small variety of plant life. But before the Flood, this entire area enjoyed rather mild temperatures that allowed the growth of a variety of grasses and plant life in seemingly endless prairies. This was clearly a more-than-suitable environment for these giant ancestors of the modern elephant.

Standing approximately 13 feet high at the shoulders, their tusks protruded 9–10 feet in front of them, with particularly large tusks weighing as much as 180 to 200 pounds each. In comparison, the average elephant tusk today weighs a measly 40 to 50 pounds.

The modern Siberian inhabitants of the more moderate regions of this icy world have long exploited the remains of these frozen giants that from time to time have been exposed. The natives considered the gigantic remains to be giant moles living underground. They imagined that the giant creatures would die immediately if they came in contact with the sunlight. This superstition is understandable if we consider that the frozen remains had not yet decayed when they were found. The flesh of these creatures was intact, and it seemed logical to them that they could not have died that long ago.

Often they found the head and tusks sticking out of the ground on the bank or shoulder of a flooded river, perfectly preserved from the moment of their watery death some 6,000 years ago. To all appearances, it is as if they had just died moments before. Most were found almost lifelike, frozen fast in a standing position, not lying down as an old, sick elephant would do before death. Therefore, to these modern-day natives, it seemed that as soon as these creatures saw the light of day, they would die.

In the vast majority of cases, wild animals such as the wolf that inhabited these regions would scavenge the portions of the animal that had thawed out and were protruding from the frozen earth. Little did they know they were dining on meat several thousands of years old, animals that had been flash-frozen. Moreover, the fact that all these animals were not scavenged at the time of their death is evidence that the catastrophe that befell them was universal. There were no predators left to scavenge them because they also perished in the cataclysm.

In August 1799 a Russian hunter looking for mammoth tusks came across an oddly shaped block of ice on the shoreline of the Laptev Sea in north-central Siberia. The summer sun had melted some of the ice, exposing two projections that later turned out to be tusks.

Two years later, the hunter returned to the area during the summertime and found that one side of the animal had been exposed to view, while the rest of the body was still frozen. It was not until 1806 that Michael Adams, of the Imperial Academy of Science at St. Petersburg, reached the site. By this point, nearby villagers has hacked off some of the flesh and fed it to their dogs. Bears, wolves and foxes had eaten the rest, leaving only a skeleton. Now known as the Adams mammoth, the skeleton is on display in St. Petersburg Zoological Museum.

More recently, the Jarkov mammoth was discovered in 1997 by a family of that name who came across a tusk protruding from the frozen ground of the Tamyr peninsula in northernmost Siberia. A group of latter-day mammoth hunters arrived at the scene and speculated that an intact mammoth carcass could be lodged in the ice—an entire mammoth! In October 1999, a helicopter lifted a twenty-three-ton ice block with tusks protruding bizarrely from it up and out of the frozen tundra, and hauled it to an ice cave. There, as recorded by a Discovery Channel film crew, scientists began defrosting the remains with hair dryers.

The Jarkov mammoth turned out to be mostly bones, but even so, a bit of soft tissue remained. It looked like a strip of beef jerky.

Coincidentally a second defrosting mammoth (the Hook mammoth) happened to be located nearby, and some of the expedition's researchers travelled to the site. One of them, Alexei Tikhonov, cut off a piece of what appeared to be mammoth muscle. Jokingly, he offered it to those present all of whom refused the morsel. And so, braced by a few shots of vodka, he took a bite himself. "It was awful," he said. "It tasted like meat left too long in the freezer" (Mammoth meat is so common in Siberia that fox trappers use it as bait.) (Church and Regis 2012, 144–145).

In some places, the remains of these animals had been carried into heaps, creating enormous islands of fossil ivory. The mechanism for achieving such a thing could only be explained by the hydraulics of a flood. Nikolai Vereshchagin, chairman of the Russian Academy of Science's Committee for the Study of Mammoths, has estimated that along the 600-mile Arctic coast, there are more than half a million tons of buried mammoth tusks. Evolutionists do not argue this fact, but they fail to produce a credible gradualist mechanism that could account for the empirical evidence left behind.

So plentiful were these deposits that a lucrative trade in ivory was spawned by their discovery. Considering the weight of the typical tusk at 100 pounds, we can estimate that there must have been some 5 million mammoths that lived along the Arctic coast. But do not think that their habitat was limited to this area.

It seems that before the supercontinent of Arza was split into the present continents, these magnificent beasts roamed the whole Northern Hemisphere, uninhibited by the present Atlantic Ocean. From Alaska and throughout all of North America, Britain, Germany, and into Russia, these mammoths roamed freely in proliferate numbers. For a more detailed study of the mammoth and the Flood, I wholeheartedly recommend Henry Howorth's book *The Mammoth and the Flood*.

THE DEATH OF THE FIRST EARTH

The Berezovka mammoth found in 1901 was flash-frozen in a struggling position in a freshly eroded bank some 100 feet above Siberia's Berezovka River. It is presently displayed at the Zoological Museum in St. Petersburg, Russia, in the position it was found. Its trunk and part of its head were scavenged by modern predators but have been reconstructed. It took Russian scientists led by Dr. Otto F. Herz a month to excavate the remains of this marvelous beast from the icy ground. Ten pony-drawn sleds took this 50-year-old male mammoth more than 2,000 miles to the Trans-Siberian Railroad where it was shipped to the museum.

> Berezovka was upright, although his back was excessively humped and his straightened hind legs were rotated forward at the hips into an almost horizontal position. This strange, contorted position was further exaggerated by his raised and spread front legs. Several ribs, a shoulder blade, and pelvis were broken. Amazingly, the long bone in his right foreleg was crushed into about a dozen pieces, without noticeably damaging surrounding tissue. There had been considerable bleeding between the muscles and the fatty and connective tissues. His shaggy, wirelike hair, some of it 20 inches long, was largely intact. His erect penis was horizontally flattened. (This organ in an elephant is round, S-shaped, and never horizontal.) (Brown 2001, 164–165).

In order to reproduce the physical evidence found in this mammoth, we must conclude that the beast must have been quickly covered by ice that crushed his bones while still keeping them in place. Otherwise, the leg would have been severely mangled. The weight of the beast upon his penis then flattened it as the ice above him compressed him to the ground.

The following picture taken by Dr. Walter Brown shows the animal's penis in the erect and flattened condition it was found. As Dr.

Brown viewed the condition of the animal's reproductive organ, he realized that this explained the conditions that caused the demise of the beast. Slow suffocation of male elephants can produce penile erection. Because the body is amazingly designed to regulate internal functions, when oxygen was in short supply, the brain reduced the oxygen consumption of less critical systems, causing his penile erection.

The Berezovka mammoth in the St. Petersburg Zoological Museum, Russia. The flattened, erect sexual organ is shown in the middle-bottom of the picture. (Courtesy of Walt Brown, *In the Beginning*)

Suffocation is also implied with four other frozen giants. Vollosovitch . . . concluded that his second buried mammoth, found with a penile erection on Bolshoi Lyakhov Island, had suffocated. A third example is provided by Dima, whose "pulmonary alveoli suggested death by asphyxia" after "great exertion just before death." The Pallas rhinoceros also showed symptoms of asphyxiation.

> The blood-vessels and even the fine capillaries were seen to be filled with brown coagulated blood, which, in many places still preserved its red colour. This is exactly the kind of evidence we look for when we want to know whether an animal has been drowned or suffocated. Asphyxia is always accompanied by the gorging of the capillaries with blood.

Von Schrenck's rhinoceros was found with expanded nostrils and an open mouth. Investigators concluded, "that the animal died from suffocation, which it tried to avoid by keeping the nostrils wide asunder." In all, three mammoths and two rhinoceroses apparently suffocated. No other cause of death has been shown for the remaining frozen giants.

Sanderson describes another strange aspect of Berezovka.

> Much of the head, which was sticking out of the bank, had been eaten down to the bone by local wolves and other animals, but most of the rest was perfect. *Most important, however, was that the lips, the lining of the mouth and the tongue were preserved. Upon the last, as well as between the teeth, were portions of the animal's last meal, which for some almost incomprehensible reason it had not had time to swallow.* The meal proved to have been composed of delicate sedges and grasses. . . .

Another account states that the mammoth's "mouth was filled with grass, which had been cropped, but not chewed and swallowed." The grass froze so rapidly that it still had "the imprint of the animal's molars." Hapgood's translation of a Russian report mentions eight well-preserved bean pods, and five beans found in its mouth.

> *Twenty-four pounds of undigested vegetation were removed from Berezovka* and analyzed by Russian scientist V. N. Sukachev. He identified more than 40 different species of plants: herbs, grasses, mosses, shrubs, and tree leaves. Many no longer grow that far north; others grow both in Siberia and as far south as Mexico (emphasis added) (Brown 2001, 165).

Evolutionists have no known mechanism that could reproduce all the conditions found in the Berezovka mammoth. But the hydroplate theory can explain all of them. The jetting water from the fountains of the deep was thrust above the atmosphere where the effective temperature is several hundred degrees below zero Fahrenheit. The water quickly froze and eventually returned as hail, causing a downward draft of frigid air from the upper atmosphere to drop with the massive hailstorm from above. That effectively dropped the temperatures to about -150 degrees Fahrenheit, which was needed to flash-freeze these giants in a matter of hours and then subsequently buried them under tons of dirty hail. In that way, the animals suffocated, and their lungs were filled with the particulate matter contained in the hail.

The type of ice found around these frozen giants indicates that it formed under conditions of low atmospheric pressure and contained salt and rock, as well as dissolved carbon dioxide. These are all conditions that are predicted by the hydroplate theory. Normal hail is produced by evaporated water, which contains no salt. Only the supersonic jets of the fountains of the deep could energize salt water above the atmosphere to create this unusual form of Type-3 ice.

The wooly mammoth has been popularized by evolutionists as an animal that inhabited areas of extreme cold and inaccurately depicted by evolutionary-inspired artistic depictions of Neanderthals hunting them in the snow. It is popularly believed by many evolutionists that man hunted them to extinction. The fact that so many were found flash-frozen has led evolutionists to assume that the animal lived in cold climates during their presumed long ice age. But there is absolutely no evidence to support such an assumption. On the contrary, the anatomical evidence suggests that mammoths were no different than modern elephants. Their skins were similar in thickness and structure, lacking oil glands, making them susceptible to cold, damp climates.

Mammoths' hair lacked the erector muscles to fluff them up and create insulating pockets of air such as those found in arctic animals. The long hair on a mammoth's legs hung to its toes. Had it walked on snow, the ice would have caked on its hairy ankles and pulled the hair each step it took in the snow.

All hoofed animals living in the snow have fur instead of hair. The accumulation of snow on the greaseless hair of the mammoth would have worked against it by allowing more snow to touch its skin, increasing the heat transfer 10- to 100-fold. That would have required the animal to consume much more food in order to maintain metabolism during an extended ice epoch where food would have been scarce

As a matter of fact, the modern elephant, which differs from the mammoth only by four or five nucleotides, can be found today existing naturally and exclusively in warm or hot climates (Cherfas 1356). Moreover, the elephant gets a stomachache if the temperature comes close to the freezing point, and their newborns are susceptible to pneumonia. They must, therefore, be kept warm and dry in zoos that are located in colder climates. Such conditions in the wild would have kept them from surviving, much less thriving, in the numbers we find in these regions.

Had they truly lived in such cold climates as evolutionists naively assume, they would have had to eat snow to obtain the 30–60 gallons of water they need each day to survive. The metabolic heat needed to melt those amounts of snow would consume half the elephant's daily caloric intake in an environment that could not support such abundant grazing.

Today's elephants spend an average of 16 hours a day foraging for food in areas that are relatively lush both in summer and winter. It would be impossible to provide the large quantities of food necessary to sustain a mammoth in such cold environments. An average elephant today requires 330 pounds of food every day, and elephants are decidedly smaller than mammoths.

Contrary to these evolutionary artistic depictions, the environment of the mammoth was completely different. Fruits of trees some 90 feet tall and temperate species of grass have been found in their stomach contents, which prove that the area was indeed a temperate zone. In the Siberian islands, vast quantities of fossilized forests with leaves and fruits such as plums have been found. They could not have been transported to this area by rivers or the leaves and fruits would have been gone during their transport.

Such animals as the vole, which burrows, could not have dug through the thick permafrost that presently covers this entire arctic region. It would have been impossible for voles to have survived in this region during a prolonged ice age, as evolutionists imagine.

Buried in the frozen soil of the tundra encircling the entire North Pole are vast cemeteries of flash-frozen creatures of all kinds, not just the more celebrated mammoths. Remains of an untold number of creatures such as bison, horses, sheep, rhinoceros, giant oxen, tigers, reindeer, antelopes, camels, musk sheep, giant beavers, donkeys, badgers, lions, elk, giant wolves, ground squirrels, cave hyenas, and bear also thrived in this enormous ecosystem in great numbers. Some are completely preserved in ice, and the Arctic wolves and polar bears feed on them today when they become exposed and thaw out. The fact that often both carnivores and herbivores are found buried together suggests that their deaths are contributable to a singular catastrophe that killed them simultaneously.

How else would you explain the enigma that below the miles of ice in Antarctica, we have found the world's richest deposits of oil and coal? Both are products of decaying animal and plant life that could not have existed in the Arctic and Antarctic regions unless there was a more temperate climate in those areas at that time.

Unlike Siberia, Antarctica was not located as far south toward the pole during the First Earth as it is presently found. Through the movement of the plates, it has shifted farther south from its original position between South America and South Africa. Certainly, rivers once flowed in this incredibly pristine continent, for the sedimentary deposits on the ocean floors are proof that mighty rivers once flowed through the heart of that continent. It is, in fact, proof that our planet once had a mild and temperate climate throughout.

Had the movement of Antarctica taken the millions of years predicted by evolutionary tectonic theory, all the vegetation would have long ago decomposed before reaching the polar freezing temperatures. There would not have been any way the giant coal deposits could have formed without these giant mounds of washed-up vegetation being exposed to huge pressure.

The impact of the Land Wilkes meteor was so terrific that it caused a spider-like crack in the crust of the Earth. We can see one crack heading north as the Mid-Atlantic Ridge, one crack from the same spot heading west under South America, and a third crack heading east under Africa and then running north on the eastern side of Africa, which would have been the culprit that broke India from the African hydroplate. The rise of the basaltic floor where these cracks meet, along with the force of the 35-mile-long meteor traveling at 20 miles per second, is what shifted Antarctica directly south where it is now stable at the South Pole.

The speed of movement of the continental hydroplates and the rapid and intense fluctuations in temperatures also came in a time frame that was much more drastic than evolutionists realize or are willing to admit. The initial movement of Antarctica was undoubtedly instigated by the two relatively close meteor strikes in the Southern Hemisphere that fractured the supercontinent into five separate landmasses (South America, Africa, Antarctica, Australia, and India) and caused the subsequent rising Mid-Atlantic Rift as the weight of the moving continents was removed over that area of the basaltic floor. Antarctica's movement has since been minimal due to the angular momentum of the spinning Earth and its location at the exact pole.

Australia initially moved eastward but now, due to the centrifugal force of the spin of our Earth, is beginning to move northward but at a much reduced pace. The sliding hydroplate of India as it broke off from Africa moved in a northeastern trajectory, smashing into the Asiatic hydroplate and creating the Himalayan Mountains. These mountains did not exist prior to the Great Flood, and neither did the Andes Mountains in western South America or the Rocky Mountains in North America. They were created by the buckling continental hydroplates as they ground to a halt.

I suspect that the rapidly forming First Ice Age helped lock in continents and slow their drift by the enormous weight of the glacial sheets of ice that covered the entire north and south poles. Trapped under the enormous glacial weight of the First Ice Age, all plant life and animals were frozen *in situ*.

However, in the thick equatorial belt during the dawning of the Second Earth, the landscape was littered with uprooted vegetation and carcasses of animals that drowned. Here, where the temperatures were not below freezing, was a world of mud and death.

The enormous amount of decomposing matter in the aftermath would be quite difficult for us to imagine today. The closest we can come to viewing such a spectacle are the aftermaths of giant tsunamis such as the ones in Sri Lanka and Japan. Everywhere you look, everything is covered in mud. The bodies of all humans and animals become bloated and swarming with flies. The acrid smell of rotting flesh fills the air. The process of decomposition generates copious amounts of greenhouse gases. Within several months, the injection of these greenhouse gases would have begun to warm the Second Earth.

We can see these drastic changes created by temperature throughout the planet as we look back in time to the type of fauna that once existed in our equatorial regions that are now rapidly becoming more and more arid. Under the great Sahara Desert, modern satellites, equipped with cameras that can capture images in certain varying wave lengths, have shown that buried under tons of shifting sand is evidence of vast forests teeming with life. Once upon a time, this area had fertile valleys and many winding rivers. As our world has slowly lost its glaciers, the rising temperatures have created vast areas of deserts and wasteland where vegetation is scarce and life is highly untenable. In a 2017 article in *Smithsonian Magazine*, Lorraine Boissoneault wrote:

> When most people imagine an archetypal desert landscape—with its relentless sun, rippling sand and hidden oases—they often picture the Sahara. But 11,000 years ago, what we know today as the world's largest hot desert would've been unrecognizable. The now-desiccated northern strip of Africa was once green and alive, pocked with lakes, rivers, grasslands and even forests. So where did all that water go? (Boissoneault 2017).

In our present-day meteorological conditions, it would be quite impossible for the Arctic regions to have tropical forests without the equatorial regions being hot wastelands of flowing desert sands. The fact that during the First Earth there was a mild and moderate climate throughout the entire supercontinent of Arza cannot be explained without a thin water vapor canopy to moderate the temperatures. Some evolutionists might counter that this disparity is due to the movement of the continental plates. There are three huge problems for that explanation:

1. It does not explain the flash-freezing.
2. The continent of Asia moved eastward, not northward.
3. The movement of the continental plates in Antarctica does not explain how the Arctic Ocean floor contains the largest coal bed in the world. This area has not shifted in the same way that Antarctica migrated southward as a result of the hydroplate shifts precipitated by the meteor strike that caused the Great Flood.

These huge deposits must have been created by the vegetation debris of the Great Flood that washed over not only the North

American continent but also the Asian continent, including Siberia, and into the Arctic Sea.

The same continental-size, sheet-flooding process could have also added to the giant coal deposits of Antarctica. What slow, gradual, geologic process would bring to the polar regions the largest deposits of vegetation in the world and leave us with flash-frozen forests that have not fossilized in millions of years?

The uniformitarian bias of evolutionists impedes them from recognizing the rapid rate that meteorological processes are capable of changing. This myopic view may be disastrous for our future preparedness as we face the end of our age and the coming Third Ice Age.

If, as our Judeo-Christian model claims, the Global Flood of Noah is a historically accurate event, then we would expect to be able to make certain predictions regarding our genetic variability that, if substantiated by the hard facts or the empirical evidence, would lend scientific credence to the historicity of the great genetic bottleneck of the Global Flood.

The Genetic Evidence

If the biblical model of creation and the Great Flood is, in fact, historical, then we should be able to find evidence of this genetic funnel when man passed through a near-extinction phase through the study of the comparison of our mitochondrial DNA. The evidence garnered from the mitochondrial DNA that provided indisputable evidence for the first of the claims offered by the Judeo-Christian model is absolutely true. We all come from a singular set of parents.

The mitochondrial Eve and the Eve of the Scriptures are, as creationists have maintained, one and the same. But it is also the creationist's position that since Adam and Eve, we have funneled again through another single set of parents—Noah and his wife (our second Adam and Eve of the Second Earth).

And that is precisely what the developing genetic information is declaring. Recent population studies of the mitochondrial DNA and the rate of mutations have led Lynn Jorde and Henry Harpending to confirm the fact that the Earth at some point in our distant past went through the hourglass of a near extinction phase where only a few survived some cataclysmic event. This mitochondrial evidence soundly disproves the evolutionary illusion that mankind evolved separately from apes in several parts of the world.

> Patterns of gene differences among humans contain information about the demographic history of our species. Haploid loci like mitochondrial DNA and the nonrecombining part of the Y chromosome show a pattern indicating expansion from a population of only several thousand during the late middle or early upper Pleistocene. Nuclear short tandem repeat loci also show evidence of this expansion. Both mitochondrial DNA and the Y chromosome coalesce within the last several hundred thousand years, and they cannot provide information about the population before their coalescence. Several nuclear loci are informative about our ancestral population size during nearly the whole Pleistocene. They indicate a small effective size, on the order of 10,000 breeding individuals, throughout this time period. This genetic evidence denies any version of the multiregional model of modern human origins. It implies instead that our ancestors were effectively a separate species for most of the Pleistocene (Harpending et al. 1998).

Although the conclusion that this hourglass may represent 10,000 breeding individuals, I doubt seriously that this conclusion was not tainted by their evolutionary presupposition. But they are not alone. Stanley Ambrose, an anthropologist at the University of Illinois has come to the same conclusion.

In 1998, he suggested that Michael Rampino's work might explain this phenomenon as found through the study of the mitochondrial

DNA. Ambrose believes that the Toba super-volcano may have been the cataclysm that brought humanity to near extinction, creating this bottleneck in our ancestry.

However, that is grasping at straws. No single super-volcano can accomplish such a cataclysm. Well, they are getting there. The previous diversity in DNA prevalent in the antediluvian civilization was reduced to a mere trickle through a handful of survivors. This massive reduction within the genetic pool of the human race reaffirms why all humanity today is almost identical in our mitochondrial DNA.

The reader might find that odd considering the seemingly wide variation of phenotypes in the human family. But these outward differences are so minute as to be almost insignificant. Our genetic composition is near homogeneous and unexplainable from an evolutionary standpoint that insists on enormous spans of time for changes to evolve. Had these millions of years really existed and had evolution been true, then one would expect a huge variation in our genetic makeup. It's just not there.

Mankind has existed for thousands of years, not millions. It is also obvious that there was a genetic bottleneck in history. Today, the genetic evidence is forcing them to admit that. Now scientists are beginning to believe that humanity escaped extinction by the skin of its teeth. Really?

It is here where the Scriptures truly enlighten us. They warn us that modern man would be "always learning and never able to come to the knowledge of the truth" (2 Tim. 3:7). They just cannot admit, no matter what the evidence says, that this bottleneck that almost caused the extinction of the human race is the same as the time of the Great Noahic Flood when only a few survivors lived to repopulate the Second Earth.

It matters not to them that all our ancient ancestors wrote of this as a historical reality. Their elitism and intellectual arrogance render all others as having an inferior mind and lacking a scientific understanding of reality. Perhaps they should consider the fact that Darwinism is not science but rather a worldview that interprets the scientific facts through an atheistic grid. It is a naturalistic religion that does not explain the scientific facts but instead subjectively colors them to rationalize their worldview.

As a result of the loss of Earth's protective canopy that would have effectively filtered the harmful cosmic rays, there has since been a marked increase in the mutation ratio for all creatures living in the diminished Second Earth. We now have an ever-increasing chance of genetic differentiation.

If evolution were true, one would predict that the variety of species would increase if, in fact, mutations were the mechanism for evolution. The diminishing protection of our deteriorating magnetic field, coupled with the thinning ozone layer and the deterioration of the Van Allen belt, ensures us of an ever-increasing amount of harmful radiation that will bombard the inhabitants of our dying planet. Yet there is no corresponding increase in the differentiation of the species. Where is this evolution they so adamantly pontificate? If anything, we are witnessing an increase in cancer and other negative effects of greater cosmic radiation.

In the aftermath of the Flood, the distribution of these once gigantic organisms became drastically quarantined to limited areas that under the new zonal climactic conditions could provide the sustenance necessary for survival according to the intrinsic habitat needs of the species. The reduction in the total area of land capable of sustaining the lush tropical vegetation that thrived globally before the Flood proved to be the end of the giant creatures that originally inhabited our antediluvian planet.

The First Earth was replete with an unimaginable variety of animals. That almost seems unbelievable to us, much like a fairy-tale. For example, there were flying birds that stood 10 feet high, a full 2 feet higher than the modern ostrich. There were lobsters or crustaceans 6 feet in length of that same family that roamed the ocean floors. Just one of these rascals would be more to eat than you could catch in an entire lobster season today; that is, if you could avoid being eaten.

There were dragonflies with a wingspan of 2½ feet. There were bats the size of sheep with heads that resembled crocodiles and a wingspan of 15 feet. I don't know about you, but I certainly would not have been anxious to meet one of those silent, flying creatures of the night. No doubt it is the memory of these gruesome bats that played so heavily in the minds of the Mayas, for they made the bat an evil god.

Amphibians belonging to the frog family grew as long as 10 feet. And there was a much wider differentiation among the apes. These numerous extinct varieties are the ones exploited by evolutionists today in order to prop up the dismally inadequate theory to be artificially inserted in their imagined human evolutionary ancestry.

No doubt, the magnificent variety that is in existence today is still marvelous to behold. But it is rather insignificant and miniscule in light of the world that was. The meteorological changes after the Flood that now govern our planet were radically different, and so was the resulting landscape. The Earth was no more a lush paradise. The freezing of the poles and the subsequent catastrophic reduction in foliage left a considerably smaller area that could sustain tropical forests.

Mountain ranges now soared high toward the sky as the moving hydroplates crunched the continents as they ground to a halt. Humanity experienced cold as never before. Huge areas were covered in ice and snow. Other areas were so arid that almost all vegetation failed to survive in these newly forming deserts. These enormous changes affected the survivability of both animals and plants.

Insects that once had a wingspan of 2 feet were now living in areas so drastically reduced in foliage that they simply became easy prey. Reptiles, some as long as 150 feet, that roamed the land in herds of hundreds were now destitute of the rich foliage of the world and simply starved to death.

Obviously, the predators that depended on these large animals were also destined for extinction. The drastic fluctuation in temperature brought on by the more drastic seasons became the death knoll for the cold-blooded creatures that regulated their internal temperature by their external environment. And so the stable environment that allowed the huge reptiles to thrive in the First Earth gave way to a more volatile and hostile environment. The age of reptiles was over.

Consequently, the mammals that internally regulated their temperature with their internal metabolism were better suited for survival in this new and inferior world of fluctuating temperatures. The only reptiles that managed to survive were those who were more compact and could consequently be adequately sustained by the diminished food supply. Their territories, which once spanned almost the whole planet, were now greatly reduced to the relatively narrow corridor of the equatorial temperate zones.

Here is the interesting thing about this whole matter. Although evolutionists have finally conceded that there was a catastrophic event that, as they say, reduced the species of the world by about 95 percent and that there was an equal bottleneck in our human history where only a few survived, they still can't bring themselves to admit that a worldwide flood caused it. That, of course, would have too many theological implications that they are, as of yet, unwilling to face. The geological, genetic, and paleontological evidence is, however, condemnatory of their myopic view.

Evidence in the Fossils

What would be the geologic landscape left behind and the location of the fossilized remains of animals drowned by the onrushing hydraulics of such a worldwide flood such as the Bible proposes? One would expect to find in many areas large numbers of different animals, both predator and prey, grouped in areas of runoffs caused by the Flood. And that is precisely what archaeologists have unearthed. In examining the evidence, they have documented numerous giant burial grounds of these gargantuan prediluvian animals throughout the entire Earth.

In North America, the Red Deer River Valley in Alberta, Canada, stands out as one of these curious and common massive sites of fossil remains. Thousands of dinosaurs have been entombed and fossilized there, staggering the imagination. Remember that for an animal to become fossilized, it must be encased in mud at or soon after death. In other words, the creature must be fully encased in mud in a relatively short period of time before the body decomposes and is turned to dust. Thus the body must be covered almost immediately or there will be no bones left to leave an imprint.

The scenario naively proposed by the evolutionists just doesn't cut it. A few dinosaurs might have, by coincidence, died in a mud hole and become fossilized in time. But these common mass graveyards that contain a wide variety of land-dwelling species that did not forage in lakes are found intertwined with those that did, as well as with marine animals of a completely different biohabitat. That speaks rather of a large-scale sheet flooding that took everything in its path and deposited the carcasses in specific runoff areas. The carcasses of these animals that became encased in the turbulent, mud-laden waters of the Flood in due time became fossilized.

There is no way to explain these mass fossil deposits without an enormous, hydraulic mechanism to cause them. The problem for evolutionists is that this seems to be the rule and not the exception. It is a universally attested truth that these mass graveyards are represented throughout the entire planet.

In a few isolated incidents, we find that mud holes or tar pits became a snare for animals that were caught in them, and there is evidence of carnivores attempting to scavenge the unfortunate creatures caught in this lethal trap. But the mass graveyards do not paint such a picture. These creatures are all entombed whole without any evidence of predation evident in the massive number of fossils that resulted.

I strongly recommend Alfred Rehwinkel's book *The Flood* for those who would like to research this topic more thoroughly.

> What is true of North America, Europe, and Asia also appears true in South America. According to Howorth, the dilluvial deposits containing the fossileferous remains of animals of various kinds are found in Bolivia, on the Plateau, on the Great Pampas west of the great mountain range in Peru and Chile, from Caracas to the North to Patagonia in the South. In Argentina they are found close to the sea level, while in Bolivia they are found 12,000 feet above the Ocean. Prominent among the fossils found are those of the Mastodons a giant armadillo, the horse, the Megatherium, Glyptodont and other species. And as in North America, so in South America the Mastodon appears to have had a geographical range over nearly the whole continent. And not only are fossils of this animal found in every part of that great body of land, but the conditions in which they are found are similar or the same as those in North America, Europe, Asia or elsewhere.
>
> Bones are found in great heaps or individually; they are found on slopes or on plains; they are found near rivers; or they are found far removed from any body of water or swamp, without signs of gnawing or rotting. In fact, the remains that are found indicate that parts of South America, at least at one time, were inhabited by a rich mammalian fauna of which many genera have disappeared entirely.
>
> As to the cause of death of these myriads of animals, the great naturalist Darwin has the following to say:

> It is impossible to reflect on the changed state of the American continent without the deepest astonishment. Formerly it must have swarmed with great monsters; now we find mere pygmies compared to with the antecedent allied races. The greater number if not all of these extinct quadrupeds lived at a period and were contemporaries of the existing seashells. Since they lived, no very great changes in the form of the land could have taken place. What then has exterminated so many species and whole genera? The mind at first is irresistibly hurried into the belief of some great catastrophe; but, thus to destroy animals, both large and small, in Southern Patagonia, Brazil, on the Cordillera of Peru, in North America, and up to the Bering Strait, we must shake the entire framework of the globe.

Darwin though hesitating to accept a theory of a great catastrophe, has no satisfactory solutions. But, his distinguished successor d'Orbigny has the courage to draw the inescapable conclusion when he writes:

> I argue that the destruction was caused by an invasion of the continent by water, a view which is completely in rapport with the facts presented by the great Pampian deposit, which was clearly laid down by water. How otherwise can we account for this complete destruction and the homogeneousness of the Pampas deposit containing bones? I find an evident proof of this in the immense number of bones and of entire animals whose numbers are greatest at the outlets of the valley, as Mr. Darwin shows. . . . This proves that the animals were floated and hence were chiefly carried to the coast (Rehwinkel 1951, 213–215).

First and foremost, even Darwin admits that the fossil records indicate that some catastrophe affected all species since so many, both small and great, were annihilated, leaving us a much reduced sample of living things in our present time. Thus, the mechanism that caused this unprecedented reduction in species and the enormous varieties within the species was of a total and complete catastrophic nature that affected all living things throughout the planet. Hence, for the catastrophe to affect all species on the planet, the cataclysm must have been a catastrophe of a global nature.

Modern evolutionists envision not one but many catastrophic events that struck at different times and restarted the evolutionary clock in the surviving organisms. Some claim disease and epidemics as the culprit that wiped out many species. Others claim striking meteors, and yet others point to volcanic activity. The timing and the methods of extinction may vary among evolutionists, but all of them now agree that massive extinction events have occurred in our past.

The other area they all agree on is the rejection of the biblical notion of a Global Flood. The reason for their objection no longer comes from a rejection of the potential for global catastrophes as it once was when Darwinism was first presented. During those early years, catastrophism was flatly rejected as unscientific because evolutionists had wholeheartedly embraced the gradualist uniformitarian hypothesis and the naturalist worldview that rejects any possibility of divine action.

Today, they can no longer claim that global catastrophes cannot occur. Thus, the rejection of the divine judgment of God remains the primary foundational presupposition of the naturalist, atheistic religion that causes them to reject the possibility of a global deluge.

But what does the geologic, empirical data found in our world say? The geologic evidence of enormous sedimentation deposits around the entire breadth of our planet supports a global, hydraulic event. Mountains must have at one time been under water since even at 12,000 feet in Bolivia and at the other side of the world some

29,000 feet above sea level in the Himalayan Ridge, we still find the sedimentary deposits of this Flood. That indicates conclusively that the Flood was of a worldwide nature.

The remains of the animals that were killed and fossilized in enormous runoffs were not gnawed upon by other animals. That clearly signifies two important points: (1) the nature of the catastrophe was such that no animals were left to prey upon the carcasses before they were either encased in mud and entombed or flash-frozen in the polar latitudes; and (2) the cause of the catastrophe that fossilized them was hydraulic in nature. The means of the death of these animals must have clearly been drowning since the remains are found most numerous in the areas where the waters would have floated them into runoffs.

No objective analysis of the empirical evidence can point to any other cause than what must have been an enormous global flood since we find this pattern throughout the entire planet. I am not asking you to believe in unsubstantiated mythology. I am asking you to consider the cold, hard facts and give me an alternative explanation that can better explain these facts, if you can.

Mass burials are not exclusive to the frozen areas of our planet. Throughout the entire breadth of our planet, geologists have uncovered mass burial deposits of dinosaur fossils that clearly evidence a sudden and catastrophic death that can only be explained if they were caused by a gigantic inundation. One example is found in the Dinosaur National Monument in Utah in the United States. It was there that Earl Douglass found the much-celebrated fossils of the brontosaurus in 1909, which is presently displayed in Pittsburgh's Carnegie Museum.

In the 1970s, after unearthing many more fossils of this giant sauropod, scientists came to the conclusion that this animal did not actually live in swampland as was once believed. This idea had been formulated because these giant sauropods had been encased in mud in order to become fossilized. The evolutionary predisposition of the scientists caused them to be antipathetic toward the notion of the death of these animals through the mechanism of a flood.

The idea that their massive weight had to be buoyed by water and that they were slow, lumbering beasts eventually gave way to a revised view that perhaps these were even warm-blooded and not cold-blooded animals. Furthermore, scientists now realize that the burial site was not necessarily the home park or range where they lived. Their watery death did not come as a result of gradual, natural attrition but of a giant hydraulic event.

The Dinosaur National Park is, in fact, a small section of the Morrison Foundation, a sedimentary deposit that stretches from New Mexico in the southern half of the United States to Canada. The evidence in the fossils found through the Morrison Foundation clearly depicts the fact that these animals were buried alive. Some of them came to rest after being transported by the Flood in the typical stiff, *rigor mortis* positions.

The clay formation in many of these deposits is composed of volcanic ash, which provides further evidence of the enormous volcanic upheaval that precipitated the Great Flood. The evolutionary notion that these fossils were deposited along the shores of rivers has now been discredited.

The empirical evidence shows that the largest concentration of fossils has been found at the bottom and not the sides of these giant runoffs, caused by an enormous inundation. Had these animals been killed individually and washed up by rivers, their bones would be concentrated on the sides or shores of those rivers.

> The notion taught for decades at the Quarry Visitor Center by DNM rangers, that dinosaurs were washed up on a point bar along the bank of a meandering river, is now discredited. Bones are especially concentrated in the bottoms, not the sides, of the scour channels. The sand grains and pebbles in the sandstone are dominantly composed not of

quartz, the typical river sediment, but of altered tuff and chert fragments of probable volcanic origin. The lowest of the three levels, where dinosaur bones are most abundant, contains isolated larger pebbles dispersed in a sandy matrix, a texture unlike that of normal rivers. The texture and composition of the lower interval suggests deposition from a muddy suspension, not normal bedload transport in a river. Mudflows associated with catastrophic floods during the recent eruptions at Mount St. Helens volcano produced fluidized sediment slurries in wide river valleys and deposited similar textures (Hoesch and Austin 2004, v).

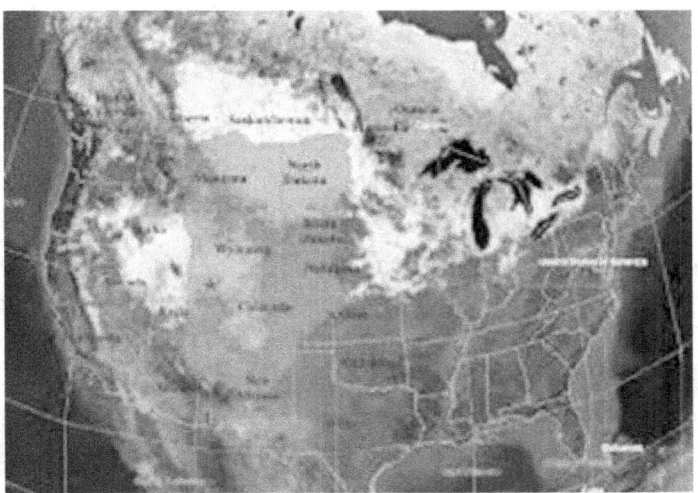

Map showing the extent of the Morrison Formation from New Mexico, USA to Canada (https://www.slideserve.com/toni/michael-p-taylor-and-mathew-j-wedel-powerpoint-ppt-presentation))

Along with these giant sauropods are other fossilized invertebrates such as unionid clams and gill-breathing snails that require watery habitats of low turbidity, and that suggests that the mechanism of burial that brought these to rest together was a catastrophic flood and not the normal deposits of their native habitat.

Quarry invertebrates include not only the unionid clams, but also two genera of gill-breathing snails from the prosobranch family. Modern snails from this family, that are nearly identical to these fossil forms, require in their life-cycle waters that are (1) perennial, (2) well-oxygenated, and (3) low in turbidity. Such conditions could hardly have been met during deposition of the Quarry sandstone bed, much less the overall Brushy Basin Member. This enigma has been called "the Morrison gastropod problem." The snails must also be regarded as part of the death assemblage (Hoesch and Austin 2004, v).

What possible explanation other than the Great Flood can the evolutionists propose to account for a wholesale slaughter of millions of animals that would flash-freeze them in the northern regions and encase them in mud in the more equatorial regions? What event could possibly inundate the entire Northern Hemisphere as evidenced by the fact that animals were flash-frozen throughout the entire North Pole, from North America to Siberia, that would not cause the lower areas of the world to be equally flooded? And when we examine the Southern Hemisphere, we find these same huge, sedimentary deposits that killed off animals of all biohabitats in one catastrophic event. The preposterous assertion that these events happened independent of one another belies the subjectivity and utter self-deception involved in their evolutionary illusions.

What could cause the entire American continent to be flooded and not affect the rest of the world? When we see the evidence cited earlier regarding South America and see the evidence regarding North America, how can we develop an evolutionary mechanism that can account for continental-size inundations and not link them together as one event? There is no other way to divide the pie. The entire planet was deluged, period. The evidence is overwhelmingly clear.

These animals were simply engulfed by a watery chaos that froze in the northern and southern polar regions once the greenhouse effect was removed by the precipitation of the water vapor canopy. It is further obvious that this process also embedded the remains of these drowned beasts in mud in the more moderate zones, causing them to become fossilized so today we have no excuse and cannot deny that God did judge the world.

Today, some 6,000 years or so later, we can study the still fresh samples of the stomach content of these frozen animals and determine the flora that once existed in the tropical antediluvian world around the arctic regions. Prior to the Great Flood, tropical plants flourished in these presently extremely hostile arctic zones that today exceed 65 degrees below zero Fahrenheit. What other mechanism can cause the climate of entire vast territories stretching from North America to Siberia to drop from tropical temperatures to 150 degrees below zero Fahrenheit, which is what would be required to flash-freeze mastodons?

Vast areas of fertile grasslands and luscious forests teeming with herbivores and carnivores were piled into heaps by the rushing waters of the Flood, which in time formed the vast oil and coal deposits that dominate the poles. The Alaskan pipeline is famed for its ability to provide the United States with an enormous reservoir of oil. The entire Arctic Sea is lined completely by the largest reservoir of carboniferous rock on our planet. How else can all this be explained?

What is obviously apparent is that this Global Deluge has radically changed the topography of our planet, and our Second Earth bears little resemblance to our original home as we continue our trajectory through time, journeying around the Sun as our galaxy zips through the vastness of space.

Not only did our topography change, but our oceans also changed dramatically. As the Global Deluge overran the land, it absorbed enormous quantities of minerals in the water. Moreover, the fact that the unusually salty waters in the subterranean chambers provided about half of our present volume of water in the oceans of our planet has resulted in quite significant changes to our ecosystems.

The once pristine and pure waters of the oceans were dramatically changed, giving them the salinity they now exhibit. Our beautiful planet was thrown headlong into a vastly inferior and decaying shadow of the world that was. In this way, our magnificent First Earth perished.

Gradual versus Catastrophic Sedimentary Depositions

How can we differentiate between slow and gradual uniformitarian deposition and sudden cataclysmic deposition? There are five elements of the geologic evidence that need to be considered in order to determine if they are gradual depositions or catastrophic depositions.

1. The first telltale sign of catastrophic sedimentary depositions is the wide breadth of scope of the sedimentary layers. All around the world we find continental-size sedimentary layers.
2. The second telltale sign is the homogeneous continuity of the individual layers. It must be noted that oftentimes these homogeneous layers are so large that they are literally continental in breadth.

    Gradual uniformitarian depositions, according to evolutionists, are created by the passage of millions of years of slow deposition. If this is correct, these layers could not possibly exhibit homogeneous characteristics in thickness and composition for such enormous spans of geographical areas due to the variability of local erosion patterns that would have applied unequal forces to such large areas.

    Gradualism would predict uneven erosion patterns that would prohibit such large, regular deposition layers. The layers would be subject to localized erosion forces that vary greatly from one area to another. It would also predict a more heterogeneous composition of the sedimentary layers due to the natural variation of different forces that large spans of time would have necessarily impacted by the nature of changing local conditions.

3. The third telltale sign is the enormous distance the source of the deposits traveled before sedimentation, which evidences the immense global hydraulic forces that were involved in the transport of the actual foreign material to that area rather than a localized event.

4. The fourth telltale sign is the pristine nature of the sedimentation without showing widespread signs of perturbation by burrowing creatures as would be expected by the slow, gradual evolutionary process. If these multiple layers formed millions of years apart as evolutionists insist, they would contain widespread signs of perturbation. What this lack of perturbation signifies is a large-scale catastrophic annihilation of these burrowing creatures during the actual cataclysmic sedimentation process.

5. The fifth telltale sign is the incontrovertible evidence that massive volumes of rapid sedimentation occurred globally, which was responsible for killing marine creatures as well as freshwater creatures, together with terrestrial and even flying creatures in massive fossil gravesites. These enormous compilations of such varied and naturally separated biohabitats particular to these fossilized creatures can only be explained by catastrophic, large-sheet flooding scenarios that impacted all ecosystems simultaneously.

The fact that such massive gravesites, ones that included creatures from many ecosystems killed together, are found so frequently all around the world is simply more rationally explained by the mechanism of a global catastrophic flood than repeated and independent large-sheet flooding scenarios throughout millions of years. The gradualist would have to explain each of the multiple independent mechanisms that caused these large-scale flooding scenarios that created the many fossil graveyards around our entire planet that affected such diverse biodomes simultaneously.

Taking into consideration these five points, let us now consider some of the empirical evidence in the geologic data that substantiates a global catastrophic origin of the strata.

> The detailed discussion of the Grand Canyon strata demonstrates in a conclusive manner that the evidence associated with these limestone, sandstone, and shale strata strongly favors their catastrophic deposition by water on a grand scale over a widespread area, contrary to the oft-repeated claims that these strata were deposited during long ages of slow-and-gradual deposition. Indeed, for such rapid sedimentation to have occurred on a widespread scale, the evidence points to the ocean having been over the continent, the sediments being transported very long distances after erosion in great quantities from source areas. The sum total of evidence in these strata is thus very compelling for their flood deposition. However, it also needs to be recognized that many of these same features found in this strata that are consistent with catastrophic flood deposition are also found in similar and other types of strata in many other parts of the world (Snelling 2009, 519).

Andrew Snelling is a geologist and research scientist who earned his PhD from the University of Sydney, Australia, in 1982. Unfortunately, the technical nature of his two-volume series is not appreciated by the majority of readers in our present culture who have limited concentration and prefer to communicate through short sentences on social media.

Let us look at some of these giant deposition zones around the world. In Utah we find the Shinarump Conglomerate that has an average thickness of 15 meters, or almost 49 feet, of a single sedimentation layer that spans more than 260,000 square kilometers in Utah and several of its neighboring states.

The composition of this layer is sand and rounded pebbles, typical in streambeds or river deposits, but the area covered is so vast, continuous, and uniform that it is quite impossible that it could have been created by any meandering stream or river. Its uniform consistency implies a single event of massive hydraulic forces such as sheet-flooding in a relatively short period of time and not a slow, gradual process created by meandering rivers over millions of years.

> However, the Shinarump Conglomerate does not match any modern depositional environment, and especially does not compare to the modern analog of a braided stream system. Specifically, where is there any place in the world today where streams are depositing sand and conglomerate of such massive uniform thickness like this over such a vast area of 260,000 square kilometers, or even close to that? There is simply not one known. Streams make deposits that meander through a valley, but they don't create uniform deposits over tens of thousands of square kilometers. Thus, it is far more realistic to explain this conglomerate formation as deposited by a massive sheet of rapidly flowing water *en masse*, in what therefore had to be a catastrophic event over such a vast area in a very short time. Such conditions are totally consistent with Flood deposition (Snelling 2009, 519–520).

This phenomenon we observe in North America is not a local phenomenon. Going all the way to the other side of our planet in central Australia, we also find two massive conglomerates, the

Uluru arkose and the Mt. Currie Conglomerate, that also evidence catastrophic depositions by massive hydraulic forces in conjunction with repeated earthquakes in a single catastrophic event.

Technically known as an inselberg, Uluru is an isolated rock-mass or monolith that rises steeply on all sides to a height of about 340 meters above the surrounding desert plain of Central Australia. It is, in effect, an enormous outcrop of beds of arkose, a coarse sandstone consisting of poorly sorted, jagged grains of other rock types, and feldspar. The arkose occurs in multiple layers that together form a cohesive massive rock unit, and these beds dip at 80-85º. The cumulative thickness of the arkose through the entire length of Uluru is at least 2.5 kilometers, but from drilling below the surrounding desert sands, the total thickness of this arkose has been determined at almost 6,000 meters. Its full lateral extent is poorly known, due to paucity of other outcrops, but the Uluru Arkose is very conservatively estimated at covering an area of at least 30 square kilometers.

Thirty kilometers west of Uluru is Kata Tjuta, a series of huge, rounded, rocky domes, the highest being Mt. Olga about 600 meters above the desert floor. These spectacular domed rock-masses cover an area of about 40 square kilometers (8 km x 5 km), and consist of layers of conglomerate dipping at 10–18º to the southwest, with a total cumulative thickness of 6,000 meters. This massive conglomerate unit, known as the Mt. Currie Conglomerate, extends under the desert sands to other outcrops over an area of more than 600 square kilometers. The conglomerate is poorly sorted and contains boulders up to 1.5 meters in diameter, as well as cobbles and pebbles, held together by a matrix of finer fragments and cemented sand, silt, and/ or mud. The pebbles, cobbles, and boulders are generally rounded and consist mainly of granite and basalt, but also some sandstone, rhyolite, and several kinds of metamorphic rocks.

Though the outcrops of the Uluru Arkose and the Mt. Currie Conglomerate are isolated from one another, the available evidence clearly suggests that both rock units were formed at the same time and in the same way. . . .

While large alluvial fans are known on the earth's surface today, none are forming over such vast areas with such massive thicknesses, or with the scale of intensity of the sheet flooding that would have been required to transport such enormous quantities of conglomerate and sand such long distances with a ferocity capable of carrying boulders up to 1.5 meters across. Furthermore, if deposition had been episodic over millions of years, there ought to be evidence of erosion (such as channels) and weathering surfaces between the layers within both the conglomerate and the arkose, while some compositional and fabric variations would be expected between successive layers. However, in the exposure at Uluru and Kata Tjuta, the arkose and conglomerate compositions, respectively, and their fabrics, are uniformly similar throughout the 2.5-kilometer thickness at Uluru and the 1.8-kilometer thickness exposed at Kata Tjuta, and the layering is extremely regular and parallel. . . .

Furthermore, the ubiquitous fresh feldspar crystals in the Uluru arkose would never have survived the claimed millions of years of deposition, as feldspar deposited in sheets of sand only centimeters thick spread over many tens of square kilometers and exposed to the sun's heat, water, and air over countless years would decompose relatively quickly to clays. . . .

The implication of all this evidence is that the deposition of the arkose and the conglomerate concurrently as lateral equivalents required an amount and force of water sufficient to erode, transport, and deposit at least 4,000 cubic kilometers of boulders, pebbles, cobbles, and sand distances of at least tens of kilometers in successive continuous pulses, so as to stack the resultant layers to a thickness of 6,000 meters over at least 600 square kilometers, all probably in a matter of hours or days at the very most! This description is consistent with what we know of turbidity currents and submarine debris flows. However the scale, intensity, and rapid repetition would not only have required cataclysmic flooding, but repetitive fault movements and earthquakes to trigger the currents and flows responsible for the rapid successive pulses of erosion, transport, and deposition (Snelling 2009, 520–522).

What is abundantly clear in the strata is that a global cataclysm of unprecedented and almost unimaginable power affected our entire planet and left for us the incontrovertible empirical evidence that cannot be explained by the gradualist evolutionary model. The Genesis record is not a mythological lore. It is a spacetime, historical record of the events that brought forth the death of the First Earth.

Uluru or Ayer's Rock in central Australia
(https://www.australiankoshertours.com/p/uluru-ayers-rock.html)

CHAPTER 9
THE ARK—THE WOMB OF THE NEW EARTH

We have thus far answered the first three arguments levied against the historicity of the biblical Flood. We have provided physical evidence and a rational mechanism to account for the historical narrative of Scripture that this cataclysm was global in nature and not the embellishment of local flood lore. We have shown that natural phenomena could have provided the rational physical mechanisms for the water levels necessary to flood the entire Earth and cover the low, primitive mountains of our First Earth.

We have further accounted for the mechanism necessary for the waters to recede through the freezing of the polar ice caps and the thickening of the continental hydroplates that would have brought them higher than their relative position to the ocean level of the First Earth.

We have also provided a mechanism to power the dispersion that caused the diversification of humanity into the separate nations speaking different languages through the Second Ice Age that concurred with the judgment of the Tower of Babel.

Now we come to the last of evolutionists' arguments regarding the size of the ark and its capacity to fulfill the purpose of saving eight people and two of every kind of living creature, as declared in Genesis.

Argument 6 – No wooden boat could have the measurements described in Scripture.

There are some today who scoff at the idea that one boat could carry two of every animal and Noah's family for the duration of the flood as the Scriptures claim. They boldly and unabashedly assert that no wooden ship could be that large or it would fall apart. Our naturalistic spectacles blind us from seeing that our ancients had the technology necessary to build such a ship. Modern archaeology has now found that the ancients were indeed capable of building wooden ships more than 400 feet long. Moreover, we shall see that the ship Noah built was more than ample to carry all the animals plus the food necessary for their voyage.

Critics scoff at the notion that a boat could actually carry two of every animal on Earth and consequently immediately categorize this claim as mythological. We shall provide the empirical evidence that this is just not so. But let us begin with the historical evidence.

The hard fact is that this specific detail of the Flood story is held in common with the memory of numerous and varied cultures all around the world, and evolutionists simply summarily ignore it. For example, in the Babylonian account, God told their Noah to "(cause) to go into the ship the seeds of all living creatures" (*Gilgamesh*, Tablet XI, line 27).

We find this commonality in many varied accounts of the Flood in continents far and wide from the Middle East. For example, in Southern Africa, the Zulu had this story:

> The African story of this constellation tells of a great flood, similar to the biblical tale of Noah and his Ark and the Greek myth of Deucalion and Pyrrha. *The gods warned*

Grandfather Teye that a flood was coming that would overwhelm the world, and that he should build a raft and *put all the humans and animals on it* (clearly he had to build an enormous raft) (emphasis added) (McDonald 2000, 55).

In the next chapter, we will cover many of the historical accounts that support the biblical narrative, but for now, my point is that this feature is internal evidence that the Flood was global in nature. Due to their biased evolutionary presupposition, evolutionists dismiss these commonalities as simply coincidental and classify these ancient memories as mythological. The historicity of this global account is therefore completely disregarded as unscientific for three main reasons that contradict their evolutionary presupposition. Anything that contradicts the evolutionary presuppositions must therefore be regarded as mythological.

Let us now deal with their contention that a wooden ship this large is impossible to make.

1. Primarily, they contend that a sophisticated boat construction of the dimensions recorded in Scripture could not be technologically possible at the evolutionary stage man was in during that age. Humanity, in their minds, simply had not advanced enough in technology to construct a wooden boat of those enormous dimensions. Some have even arrogantly claimed that wooden boats of this size could not stand the strains and would shatter into pieces.
2. Secondarily, they insist that no boat could carry two of every kind of animal in the world.
3. Finally, post-modern man scoffs at the idea that Noah could have gathered two of every kind of animal. They certainly do not accept the notion that the animals came and entered two by two. Such animal behavior is, in their minds, simply mythological.

As we shall see, all these evolutionary assumptions are flawed. Let us deal with each contention one at a time.

1. Ancient Man Could Not Build a Wooden Ship That Large

To begin, let us consider the size of the ark. In Genesis 6:15–16, God's command to Noah is recorded in regard to the building of the ark. God specifically instructed Noah to construct an ark of gopher wood that was to be 300 cubits long and 50 cubits wide with a height of 30 cubits.

> *This is how you shall make it: the length of the ark three hundred cubits, its breadth fifty cubits, and its height thirty cubits. You shall make a window for the ark, and finish it to a cubit from the top; and set the door of the ark in the side of it; you shall make it with lower, second, and third decks.*
> —Gen. 6:15–16

Obviously, the Lord gave Noah specific instructions on how to build the ship. Those intricate orders are not recorded in Scripture because they are superfluous to the task or purpose of the narrative. But we can safely assume that Noah did not fly blindly in this endeavor. In fact, the Lord's intimate involvement is highlighted by the fact that it was He who closed the door of the ark before the waters of the Flood came.

> *Those that entered, male and female of all flesh, entered as God had commanded him; and the* LORD *closed it behind him.*
> —Gen. 7:16

So what are the dimensions in our measurements? How long is a cubit? It is roughly the measurement from the elbow to the tip of the fingers for an average man. But as you might have guessed, this differed from one civilization to the other. There are three measurements for the size of a cubit. The Egyptians have a royal cubit with a length of 20.65 inches and a smaller cubit of 17.6 inches; the Babylonians had a royal cubit of about 19.8 inches; and the Hebrews had a long cubit of 20.4 inches and a short cubit of 17.5 inches.

Remember that Noah was not a Hebrew. Abraham had not yet been born. All the descendants of Noah carried over the use of the cubit from the previous prediluvian civilization. It is therefore quite difficult to defend one size over another as the standard that Noah used.

If we were to use the Egyptian royal cubit, that would mean the ark was a staggering 516.25 feet long, 86.04 feet wide, and 51.62 feet high. In order to imagine the incredible size of this ship, let me compare it to a measurement that might be more tangible to the modern person. That means the length of the ark was more than a football field and a half in length, five stories high, and eight stories wide. That was a huge ship.

It is very possible that the ship could have been built on the measurements of the royal cubit. That would, of course, create a much larger payload to accommodate the many animals Noah was ordered to carry. But for the sake of argument, let us consider the size as though it were predicated on the very smallest of the cubits. If the cubit chosen was the 17.5-inch, short cubit, then the length of the ark would still be a whopping 437.5 feet long, 72.92 feet wide, and 43.75 feet high. That would make the ark longer than a football field by 40 yards, almost 1½ times the length of a football field.

The size of the ark is so impressive that modern Western man did not exceed that size until 1884. It was not until the advent of steel ocean liners that the *Etruria*, a Cunard liner, actually exceeded the size of the ark (using the short cubit). The engineering of giant ocean liners is no doubt a great achievement for modern man, but there are many human achievements of this nature that had long ago been achieved and then later forgotten by mankind.

In our modern arrogance, we often fail to see that ancient man was not the brutish, inferior, half-apes that evolutionists are prone to claim. Arrogance has indeed been the hallmark of evolutionary theory. In fact, most evolutionary dogma has traditionally been built on a Eurocentric, historical perspective. It was this intellectual arrogance that as a natural consequence led Europe to the elitist Nazi worldview.

In reality, however, a study of ancient Chinese history shows that many of the inventions credited to Western man had already been invented by the Chinese, sometimes many years prior. Yet Western academia looked upon the Chinese and Japanese cultures as well as the African cultures as savage and inferior races during the heady days of the evolutionary revolution in science.

This elitist mentality has carried through all the way to our present time, albeit perhaps better disguised in our modern age. From the time of Darwin until the end of World War II, this type of thinking was the rule rather than the exception in Western academic circles. This applied to all of Europe, not just Germany.

For example, men such as Boule, a prominent French anthropologist and ardent evolutionist, regularly referred to Blacks and Japanese as "men of the lower races," or sometimes the "savage or inferior races," thinking that the European whites were the most evolutionary advanced humans on the planet. Evolutionists readily accepted the idea that some races were intellectually superior to others, and that, of course, also translated to our ancient ancestors who they deemed less evolved.

> In the Mousterian period it represented a belated type existing side by side with the direct ancestors of *Homo Sapiens*; its relation to the latter was similar to that which exists at the present day between the races we call inferior and superior races. Perhaps one might go so far as to say that it was a degenerate species (Boule 1957, 144).

Arrogance is ignorance. Those who look down on people from another race or time do so on a false, narcissistic premise. It stems from an evolutionary illusion that they are intellectually superior to others. Those who lift their pinky while drinking tea and think they are more civilized than those who don't are nothing more than fools blinded by illusions of grandeur.

The mitochondrial DNA study in Berkeley has proved without a doubt that all races stem from a single matriarch. In fact the differences among our species are less variable than in most other species of animals around the world.

The capacity of the human mind has not changed one iota since Adam. Man was as capable then of doing great things as he is today. If anything, those capabilities have declined since our brains are certainly smaller than Cro Magnon man who was simply the Adamic race prior to the Great Flood.

Our ancient forefathers were not brutish, ape-like men. Neither did we ascend from men-like apes. It is this false evolutionary presupposition that leads some to the false conclusion that modern men are more evolved than ancient men. It is this narcissistic arrogance that leads them to believe that men at the time of Noah did not have the intellectual capacity to engineer a boat of such grandeur.

The plain truth is that man can engineer pretty much whatever he sets his mind to. Necessity, after all, is the mother of invention. Prior to Noah, there was no need for a boat that size. There were no other continents to explore. Our First Earth had a continuous, single landmass that could be explored via land or small boats to navigate rivers, streams, and lakes. It was not until the breaking of the supercontinent of Arza and the time it took for our population to reach a certain density level that man once again had the resources to accomplish such feats. It was after the Tower of Babel that the need arose to navigate great stretches of water to reach lands that were now separated by seven seas.

Contrary to the evolutionary assumption, if we look at Chinese history, it may surprise you to find out that they were master builders of huge wooden ships long before the West. Our Oriental brothers were not the savage races that the Eurocentric evolutionists falsely imagined. To begin with, they, like all other human beings around the world, are, after all, our brothers in every sense of the word. They descended from Noah as we did.

We have already discussed the scientific evidence that disproves the evolutionary idea that races evolved in separate lineages from apes (see Volume 4 of this series, *The Descent of Man*). We will not delve further into this beyond saying that all mankind shares the mitochondrial DNA evidence that without any reservation proves we have the same ancestry as Adam and Eve. It substantiates the biblical narrative that stipulates without equivocation that our Black brothers and our Oriental brothers are literally our brothers from at least 10 common ancestral parents from Adam through Noah.

In fact, the very language of the Chinese gives evidence of Noah's ark. The unique system of writing developed by the ancient Chinese people was in some sense similar to hieroglyphics; that is, they used symbols called pictograms to represent certain things. These ancient pictograms eventually developed into the more complex ideograms of the present Chinese language that are, in fact, quite ancient in and of themselves.

In these ancient pictograms and ideograms developed thousands of years before the first Christian missionaries visited China, we find evidence of the true religion existing at the very inception of their Chinese culture. For example, the Chinese ideogram for a ship is the symbol of the ark of Fa-He (the Chinese Noah) in which the eight sole survivors of the Great Flood repopulated the Second Earth. It is composed of three other ideograms that describe eight people in a boat.

Hence, the ideogram for a large ship is a composite of three other ideograms—the ideogram for a boat, the ideogram for the number eight, and the ideogram for people, represented by an open mouth. And so we see that the ancient Chinese people seem to have developed ideograms that represent the first of a thing as the symbol for the same things thereafter.

Since Noah's ark was the first large ship in their memory, it has then been used to represent all ships thereafter.

Boat   **Eight**   **Mouth**   **Ship**

The arrogance of modern scholars has been made evident by their insistence that ancient men did not have the technology to make huge ships. But as archaeology advances, these claims are proving to be quite incorrect. They have largely underestimated ancient man's technological ability.

For example, in the Ming Dynasty, the Chinese sent out an enormous armada of ships to India under the eunuch admiral Zheng He. Not only was ancient man capable of building these ships, but in fact, they mass produced them.

> Incredibly, the largest ships in the fleet (called "*baoshan*," or "treasure ships") were likely between 440 and 538 feet long by 210 feet wide. The 4-decked baoshan had an estimated displacement of 20-30,000 tons, roughly 1/3 to 1/2 the displacement of modern American aircraft carriers. Each had nine masts on its deck, rigged with square sails that could be adjusted in series to maximize efficiency in different wind conditions.
>
> The Yongle Emperor ordered the construction of an amazing 62 or 63 such ships for Zheng He's first voyage,

in 1405. Extant records show that another 48 were ordered in 1408, plus 41 more in 1419, along with 185 smaller ships throughout that time (Szczepanski 2019).

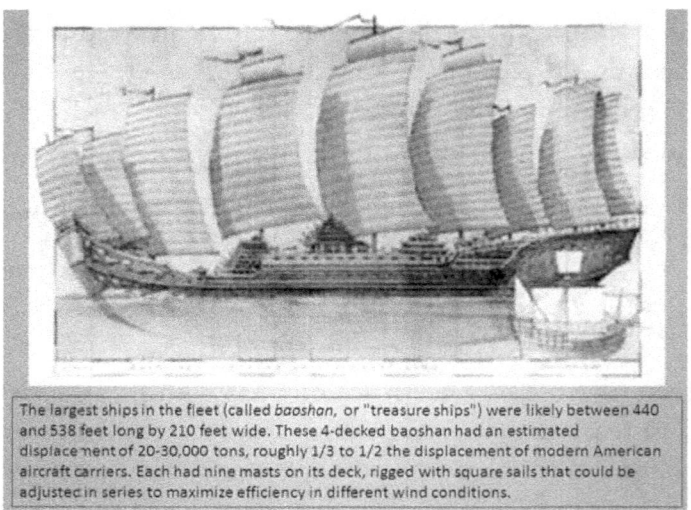

The largest ships in the fleet (called *baoshan*, or "treasure ships") were likely between 440 and 538 feet long by 210 feet wide. These 4-decked baoshan had an estimated displacement of 20-30,000 tons, roughly 1/3 to 1/2 the displacement of modern American aircraft carriers. Each had nine masts on its deck, rigged with square sails that could be adjusted in series to maximize efficiency in different wind conditions.

(https://www.timetoast.com/timelines/1400-1900-china)

Clearly, the arrogant claim that a wooden ship of this size would break apart is nothing more than evolutionary spin at its worst. In fact, the Romans also built enormous wooden ships. Modern scholars long ridiculed the ancient accounts of huge grain ships built by the Romans. They ignorantly claimed that the Romans could not have possibly attained the ship technology necessary to build such enormous ships; that is, until the Italians discovered in a small circular volcanic lake (Lago di Nemi) the remains of two huge ships.

The two ships built by Caligula in the first century AD showed that Roman technology far exceeded what evolutionists had erroneously allocated to them through their myopic evolutionary spectacles. In fact, we now know that by using ships of this enormous size, Caligula was able to bring from Egypt the gigantic stone obelisk that now stands in front of the Vatican cathedral.

The first ship discovered in Lago di Nemi is known as *Prima Nave*. It was constructed with a length of 70 meters (230 feet) and a beam of 20 meters (66 feet). The second ship, called *Seconda Nave*,

Caligula's ship found in Lago di Nemi

was even larger at 73 meters (240 feet) in length and a beam of 24 meters, or 79 feet.

But long before Caligula, the Greeks were also building giant ships. Plutarch and Athenaeus both mentioned a ship built by Ptolemy Philopator that had 40 banks of oars. The ship had a length of 280 cubits and a height to the top of the stern of 48 cubits. Using the small cubit, the ship would be more than 410 feet long and 70 feet from top to stern. If we were to use the large cubit, the ship would be 481 feet long and 82 feet from top to stern.

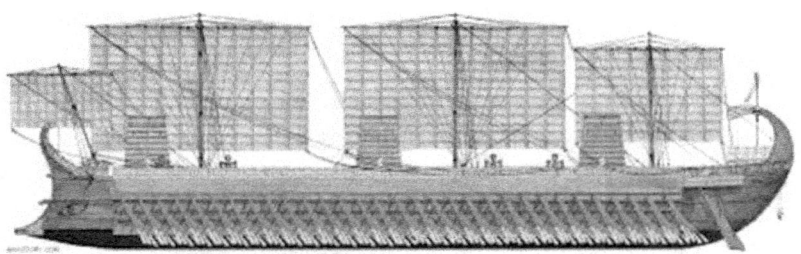

Hellenistic war galley with a massive Polyreme with a crew of 4,000. (Weapons and Warfare, https://weaponsandwarfare.com/2015/07/14/the-successors-and-naval-competition-2/)

The 40 banks of oars were manned by no fewer than 4,000 rowers. Beyond that, the ship had 400 sailors who manned the riggings and other logistic necessities. As if that were not impressive enough, the ship had on deck the further capacity to carry 3,000 armed warriors who were ready for battle. It was an impressive, gargantuan wooden ship whose intent was clearly to demoralize any opponent by its sheer immensity.

Every one of these gigantic, wooden ships was engineered as military ships for propulsion through water. Noah's ark had no need for propulsion. It was not a complicated warship with fancy rigging and places for oars. It was not designed to plow through the sea but simply to float as a barge. It was designed to warehouse seeds of life for a new beginning. It was designed to be the womb of the Second Earth. It was designed to harbor life safely through the storm of all storms that ended our First Earth. In fact, its ratio in size (6:1) has been shown to be the maximum in efficiency and stability used by modern shipbuilders. So how did Noah know that?

> Modern-day mathematical studies have shown that the ark must have been a remarkably stable ship. Experienced designers will recognize that the ratio of length to width of 6 to 1 is considered to be the optimum design for stability, and is used in construction of many different types of ships, from warships to racing sailboats.
>
> The length of the ark, 450 feet or so (using an 18-inch cubit), would tend to provide insurance that the ark would not be subjected to any wave of equal magnitude acting throughout its entire length. The ark's chances of capsizing were therefore, lessened.
>
> The cross section of 75 feet by 45 feet (18-inch cubit) is also significant. The center of gravity for such a section can be calculated as well as the buoyant forces of the water for any given degree of tilt, and conclusions drawn. It can be shown that for any degree of tilt up to 90 degrees, the ark would tend to right itself. Noah's Ark was indeed optimally designed to perform under adverse conditions (La Haye 1976, 250).

If, in fact, the technology of shipbuilding is an evolutionary art, how did Moses, writing 1,300 years before the birth of Christ, know these sophisticated engineering calculations displayed by the ratios of the ark he described in Genesis? More to the point, how did Noah, 4,000 years before Christ, know about it? The answer is simple. The Scriptures tell us that God gave him the instructions.

2. The Load Capacity of the Ark

Perhaps the most common critique against the historicity of Noah's ark comes from the argument that it could not possibly have sheltered all the animals necessary to regenerate the Second Earth. The calculations to examine this question have two components:

1. What is the load capacity of the ark?
2. What is the load capacity required for the animals it must house? That must be calculated by first determining how many animals must be sheltered in the ark.

The reader might be surprised to find that the ark's load capacity brings it in magnitude to the level of tonnage that is comparable with today's modern steel ships. The grand total of the volume it contained was a whopping 1.396 million cubic feet if we are using the short cubit of measurement. Since the Scriptures tell us that it had three decks, then it had a total deck area of approximately 95,700 square feet.

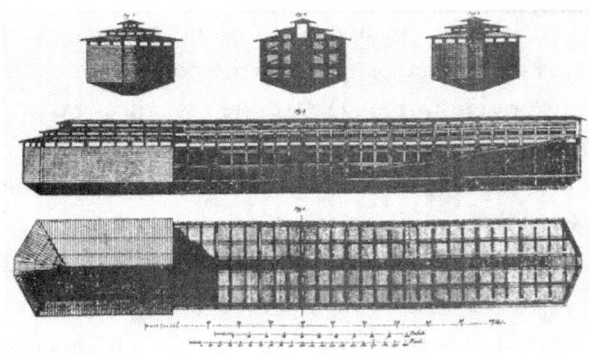

The biblical dimensions and shape of Noah's ark (Used by permission from Tim La Haye and John Morris, *The Ark on Ararat*)

In order to bring it to a tangible form for the modern reader, this is the equivalent of the carrying capacity of 522 standard stock railroad cars (as computed by Henry M. Morris and John C. Whitcomb in *The Genesis Flood*). Imagine standing at a railroad crossing while a train with 522 stock cars goes by. Then you will get a feeling for the carrying capacity of the ark (assuming the short cubit was used in its construction).

In order for the ark to fulfill its purpose of regenerating the Second Earth with the variety of animals that presently inhabit our Earth, it only had to provide space for the progenitors of each species. The variability within the species may be carried within the DNA of their ancestral progenitor. Now let us assume that all the present species that are presently exhibiting a wide variety of subgroups were reduced to their singular ancestral stock.

For example, today we have a wide variety of dogs ranging in size from the Chihuahua to the Great Dane and including the wolf, the fox, and other animals that modern taxonomy regards as a different species but are, in fact, included in the biblical concept of the "kind" because they come from the same progenitor. All of them came from a singular ancestral stock. That is a point that modern evolutionists do not dispute. The genetic components of the ancestral dog carried with it the potential phenotypes of all the present and varied forms displayed on our planet today.

Since 1700 when the sweet pea was developed and the science of genetics was birthed, we have genetically separated some 500 varieties from the singular ancestral genetic stock. But the potential for this enormous variety was present in the DNA of the first ancestral pea from the very beginning. Hence, Noah did not need to have every kind of dog in his boat. He only had to have one that contained the ancestral DNA of all our present dogs, wolves, foxes, and so on.

But not all the animal species found in our world today needed to go in the ark. Some like fish, mollusks, and other marine creatures could survive in the ocean. Insects could likewise survive in floating debris. Only a small minority needed to go into the ark. The number of the ancestral stock that were present in the ark can be deduced through the science of taxonomy. Whitcomb and Morris, writing on this subject, said:

> Ernst Mayr, probably the leading American systematic taxonomist lists the following number of animal species according to the best estimates of modern taxonomy.
>
> | MAMMALS | 3,500 |
> |---|---|
> | BIRDS | 8,600 |
> | REPTILES and AMPHIBIANS | 5,500 |
> | FISHES | 18,000 |
> | TUNICATES | 1,700 |
> | ECHINODERMS | 4,700 |
> | ARTHROPODS | 815,000 |
> | MOLLUSKS | 88,000 |
> | WORMS, etc. | 25,000 |
> | COELENTERATES etc. | 10,000 |
> | SPONGES | 5,000 |
> | PROTOZOANS | 15,000 |
> | TOTAL ANIMALS = 1,000,000 | |

When we consider that of this total there was no need for Noah to make any provisions for fish (18,000), tunicates (marine chordates such as squids) (1,700), echinoderms (marine creatures such as star fish and sea urchins) (4,700), mollusks (mussels, clams, oysters, etc.) (88,000), coelenterates (corals, sea anemones, jelly fish, hydroids) (10,000), sponges (5,000), or protozoan (microscopic single-celled creatures, mostly marine) (15,000).

That eliminates 142,000 species of marine creatures. In addition, some mammals are aquatic (whales, seals, porpoises, etc.), and the amphibians need not be included; a large number of the arthropods (815,000 species) such as lobsters, shrimps, crabs, water fleas, and barnacles are marine creatures. The insect species, arthropods, are very small, and many of the 25,000 species of worms as well as the insects could have survived on floating debris outside the ark.

For all practical purposes, one could say that at the outside there was need for no more than 35,000 individual vertebrate animals on the ark. The total number of so-called species of mammals, birds, reptiles, and amphibians listed by Mayr is 17,600, but undoubtedly the number of original "kinds" was less than this.

We can assume that the average size of these animals was about the size of sheep. Furthermore, Noah was not required to take the largest or even adult specimens. There are only a few very large animals, and even those could have been represented on the ark by young ones. The following computations will give an idea of the accommodations available:

> The number of animals per car varies greatly, depending on the size and age of the animals. . . . Reports of stock cars and railroads show that the average number of meat animals to the carload is for cattle about 25, hogs in single deck cars about 75, and sheep about 120 per deck.
>
> This means that about 240 animals of the size of sheep could be accommodated in a standard two-deck stock car. *Two trains hauling 73 such cars each would thus be ample to carry the 35,000 animals. We have already seen that the Ark had the carrying capacity equivalent to that of 522 stock cars of this size!* (emphasis added) (1971, 68–69).

This means that almost twice as many stock cars are left empty. Obviously, there is more than enough room for all the animals, especially if you consider that we are using the short cubit, which almost assuredly was not the case. The use of the royal cubit would result in a 15 percent larger payload capacity in the ark, or another 78 carloads. By themselves, those carloads had the capacity to take half the total number of animals required for our Earth to contain the number of present variations in the total number of species that survived the Great Flood.

That leaves more than ample room for the storage of food for the animals and for Noah's family—plus a billiard room, a gym with a treadmill, a racquetball court, a small basketball court, a bowling alley, and a smoking lounge in case one of Noah's' children smoked Cuban cigars.

3. Gathering and Caring for the Animals

All kidding aside, there is yet another consideration that I think is of the utmost importance in understanding the task of maintaining and feeding these animals for the duration of their voyage. The Lord could have kept the animals that were not being used for food (e.g., chickens for eggs and goats or cows for milk) in a state of hibernation, reducing the need to feed and care for them.

We are all familiar with the phenomenon of hibernation and are intrigued by this suspended state of animation that allows animals to go without food for months. I am well aware that most animals do not hibernate, but it also didn't rain until the world became completely engulfed in a watery chaos. In other words, if God can cause a worldwide flood, surely the rest is a piece of cake.

In addition, we are also enthralled by the almost miraculous ability some animals have in their migratory patterns to pick up and leave an area and head to another area they have never been to as if there were a tiny computerized homing device inside their brains. Some travel thousands of miles, either swimming upstream to spawn or flying through previously unknown territories, either to mate or escape the harsh winter, and all of that is performed with uncanny accuracy year after year and generation after generation.

Is it not possible for God to have used this migratory instinct to bring to the ark the representatives of the species He wanted to carry over to the New World, the postdiluvian Second Earth? The denial of the evolutionist is predicated on their false assumption that God does not exist and therefore He cannot intervene in nature.

I am not speaking about an unknown mechanism that has not been observed such as what is proposed by the punctuated equilibrium theory. Both hibernation and migration are phenomena that can be observed and verified by us today. Since the seven oceans of our present world did not separate the antediluvian supercontinent of Arza, this migratory call to the ark could have easily brought two of each kind to the ark as the Scriptures testify. Hence, all three of evolutionists' arguments against the historicity of the ark are baseless and cannot be substantiated by any empirical data.

Another consideration we must consider is that God may not have wanted all the animals that lived in the First Earth to survive into the Second Earth. There is no reason to believe that God had to save every kind. If in the new limited environment some species would not be able to survive, it would be nonsensical to bring them on the ship.

In fact, there seems to be a deliberate change in the meteorological conditions of the Second Earth that is purposefully unfavorable for the giant reptiles, especially the large carnivores. Perhaps the giant, terrible lizards that roamed the First Earth were not animals God intended to inhabit our world. I strongly suspect that these were the result of demonically inspired genetic interference designed to eradicate the seed of Eve and interrupt the lineage that would bring forth the Messiah to fulfill the prophecy of the Dragon Doom voiced by God in Genesis 3:15.

The demonic realm cannot create life, but like men, they can alter existing beings and change them radically through gene manipulations. It is my contention that the Great Flood was designed to eradicate the Neanderthals as well as the dinosaurs that had terrorized the sons of Adam. Had God not stepped in, we would not be alive today.

Here, the reader must understand that this is not an opinion based on the revelation of Scripture but rather on my own personal deductions. It is important to note the difference. Too often, Christians make no distinction between their opinions and the biblical narrative. But it does not make sense to me that God would have made the lion eat grass like the ox at the beginning of the First Earth and at the same time create giant carnivores like the Tyrannosaurus rex.

If the events regarding the Global Flood described in the Scriptures were, in fact, historical events, we would expect the historical chronicles left by the memory of ancient man to correlate with the geological evidence. As we read the accounts of the worldwide deluge emanating from all the major cultures of the world, it is striking that they all insist that the Flood was of a global nature, that it was precipitated by God because of the violence or wickedness rampant in man, that it saved only a few, that it saved the animals, that it killed all remaining life, that the event was brought on by the fountains of the deep bursting open, that it was a horrendous storm filled with high winds as well as thunderous sounds and lightning, that the Earth shook, that fires raged, that the world became dark and cold, that they landed on a mountain, and that all men first spoke one language that was later confounded into many.

And yet most evolutionists summarily disavow any of the ancient Flood accounts by subjectively declaring them the memory of local floods. However, that claim is quite contradictory to the common claim pervasive in these accounts; namely, that the Flood was literally worldwide and that only a few were saved by the providence of God. It is also contradicted by the empirical evidence of the continental-size sedimentary deposits that are found in the strata throughout the planet.

What is more, most of these ancient chronicles outright declare that it was a judgment of God upon the people of their world for their violence. Let us explore some of these accounts that, according to evolutionists, have independently developed worldwide. Second to the Global Deluge is the commonality of the judgment of the Tower of Babel that confounded the languages and separated mankind into nations.

CHAPTER 10

THE TOWER OF BABEL AND THE SECOND ICE AGE

The Second Insurrection during the First Earth brought terrorism to a level never before known to mankind. The line of the Messiah was at risk of being destroyed, and God intervened out of His grace for mankind. He fenced in evil so goodness could survive. Judgment came swiftly on the heels of fire, water, and ice, cloaked in darkness. Enoch had earlier confirmed Adam's prophecy, and it came to pass that our First Earth drowned.

When the Sun dawned red on the horizon, Noah's family stepped out into the Second Earth and beheld a new and very different world. Nothing would ever be the same. As far as the eye could see, from horizon to horizon, all things were devastated. Rotting corpses filled the air with the stench of death. Mud blanketed our planet. The lush green forests were no more. Rotting vegetation floated on the water in endless, bobbing islands covered with mud. Our world had once again diminished in grandeur. From that point forward, life expectancy and longevity diminished radically. Little did the sons of Noah know that it would diminish again radically after the judgment of the Tower of Babel just several hundred years into their future. Our rebellion has ever brought us steadily into a more hostile environment.

THE DEATH OF THE FIRST EARTH

Our universe is also dying. Stars and galaxies are turning into super-massive black holes. Our Earth's magnetic field is decaying. Our oceans are becoming polluted. Our forests are being cut down. Our atmosphere is being filled with toxins. We have not cared for the planet as God commanded Adam.

Each time we followed the Enemy of Man in his insurrections, the curse of death came more quickly. We are but a shadow of what we were intended to be so far has the race of man fallen from its sublime state when Adam walked with God in the Garden.

But it seems that mankind never learns from the past. When prosperity comes, we forget God. We gravitate toward the lust of our flesh and turn our backs on the Creator. Selfishness rears its ugly head, and mankind blindly turns to the religion of the Serpent that offers mankind wealth, power, and the immediate gratification of our sensual greed. Like Jacob's firstborn, Esau, we myopically reach for the pot of porridge and the immediate gratification of our senses and relinquish our eternal inheritance. Like Adam and Eve's firstborn, Cain, we seek to replace the grace of God with our own arrogance and pride through the paltry works of our own hands. We reject the Great Redeemer and choose instead to become our own gods.

That in a nutshell is the history of humanity in every age since Adam. The United States is no exception. Within 200 years after our glorious American Revolution, our nation has become another bloated tyrannical bureaucracy whose federal government has slowly centralized all power. The day of the mom-and-pop banker is gone. Giant monopolies rule the banking industry and the petroleum industry. Lobbyists have more power in Washington, DC than the voice of We the People. Individual freedoms have been whittled to the bone. Tyrants seeking to gain popularity have snared our people in a web of dependence through lavish federal entitlements that rob from those who work to give to those who take. Our educational institutions have become indoctrinal institutions that rabidly teach atheism.

We are rapidly moving toward a welfare state. Why should anyone work if the government meets their basic needs? Never mind that our national debt will soon end in bankruptcy and all will suffer terribly for it. We do not look beyond today. It was no different at the beginning of our Second Earth. Mankind spoke one language. They were one people living in the Land of Shinar. This was the ancient Sumerian civilization founded by Noah, but by the third generation from Noah, mankind had no other thought than to seek pleasure. Tyrants rose to power through the age-old addiction created by those who wish to climb to power by making their supporters dependent on them rather than God. That was the genius and the folly of Nimrod.

Arrogance and Pride – Nimrod's Folly

> *Now the whole earth used the same language and the same words. It came to about as they journeyed east, that they found a plain in the land of Shinar and settled there.*
> —Gen. 11:1–2

Within three generations after the Great Flood, the seeds of discontent were already sprouting rebellion in the grandchildren of Noah. God's blessings had been upon them, and they not only thrived but they prospered, as evident from the archaeological data of the Sumerian civilization. The population flourished.

The idea that all mankind were one people and one language is not particular to the Hebrew Scriptures. It is found in most ancient civilizations. For example, the Mayan people in Central America, separated by the Atlantic Ocean from the Old World, wrote about this in their sacred book *Popol Vuh*.

> Then all the people arrived, those from Rabinal, the Cakchiquel, those from Tziquinahá, and the people who now are called the Yaqui. And there it was that

the speech of the tribes changed; their tongues became different. They could no longer understand each other clearly after arriving at Tulán. There also they separated, there were some who had to go to the East, but many came here. . . .

Oh! We have given up our speech! What have we done? We are lost. How were we deceived? We had only one speech when we arrived there at Tulán; we were created and educated in the same way. It is not good what we have done (*Popol Vuh*, 176, 177).

According to Flavius Josephus, Hebrew tradition says that God repeatedly sent messages through His prophets for the people to disperse and colonize the entire Earth. But mankind refused to obey, choosing instead the comforts of the cities and the benefits offered by the centralization of power. At that time, a mighty hunter and powerful man named Nimrod rose to power. Filled with arrogance due to his extreme physical abilities, he led the people to rebel against God.

Now the plain in which they first dwelt was called Shinar. God also commanded them to send colonies abroad, for the thorough peopling of the earth, that they might not raise seditions among themselves, but might cultivate a great part of the earth, and enjoy its fruits after a plentiful manner. But they were so ill instructed that they did not obey God; for which reason they fell into calamities, and were made sensible, by experience, of what sin they had been guilty; for when they flourished with a numerous youth, God admonished them again to send out colonies, but they, imagining that the prosperity they enjoyed was not derived from the favor of God, but supposing that their own power was the proper cause of their plentiful condition they were in, did not obey him. Nay, they added to this their disobedience to the Divine will, the suspicion that they were therefore ordered to send out separate colonies, that, being divided asunder, they might the more easily be Oppressed.

Now it was Nimrod who excited them to such an affront and contempt of God. He was the grandson of Ham, the son of Noah, a bold man, and of great strength of hand. He persuaded them not to ascribe it to God, as if it was through his means they were happy, but to believe that it was their own courage which procured that happiness. He also gradually changed the government into tyranny, seeing no other way of turning men from the fear of God, but to bring them into a constant dependence upon his power. He also said he would be revenged on God, if he should have a mind to drown the world again; for that he would build a tower too high for the waters to be able to reach! And that he would avenge himself on God for destroying their forefathers.

Now the multitude were very ready to follow the determination of Nimrod, and to esteem it a piece of cowardice to submit to God; and they built a tower (Josephus 1960, 30).

Once more, the demonic arrogance took hold in people's hearts, and their pride blinded them. Prosperity made them believe it was the work of their hands that brought them riches and happiness. Through tyrannical control of the government, Nimrod promoted an entitlement culture and a welfare state "to bring them into a constant dependence upon his power."

Within 300 years, mankind had abandoned God in favor of the bloody religion of the Serpent. How quickly they forgot the injustices that ruled mankind with an iron fist by the terrorists of the First Earth. How quickly they forgot the violence of the occult when it was in full flower. The dark angel's seditious lies won over many to be enticed with sorcery, lust, and power. The religion of the Serpent once again began to rule the hearts of men. But let us not judge too hastily. Our nation is in its third century, and look how far we have strayed from the United States Constitution. The House of Representatives that our Founding Fathers instituted to control our money and be the voice of the people has now been given to a private banking cartel known as the Federal Reserve. We are going down the same road unless we wake up and change it.

It was in the sixth generation from Adam that the Second Insurrection brought forth the death of the First Earth. It was also in the sixth generation from Noah that the Third Insurrection took place that brought forth the judgment of the Tower of Babel. It was in the days of Peleg, six generations from Noah, that the people were divided by the judgment of the Tower of Babel (Gen. 10:25). And thus we see the providence of God that although man has a free will to choose his own way, God still controls the affairs of mankind.

Iraq museum المتحف العراقي

Borsippa was an important ancient city of Sumer built on both sides of a lake about 17.7 kilometers (11.0 miles) southwest of Babylon on the east bank of the Euphrates. The site of Borsippa is in Babylon Province, Iraq, and is now called Birs Nimrud, identifying the site with Nimrod. The ziggurat, the Tongue Tower, one of the most vividly identifiable surviving ziggurats today, is identified in the Talmud and in Arab culture with the Tower of Babel.

From Adam to Noah there were 10 generations, and God's grace brought forth a new covenant with mankind—the Rainbow Covenant (Gen. 9:1–16). From Noah to Abraham there were also 10 generations, and God established a new covenant with mankind—the Abrahamic Covenant (Gen. 15:1–18). And from Abraham to David there were 14 generations, and God established a new covenant with mankind—the Davidic Covenant (2 Sam. 7:8–16). In that day, God promised that through David would come the Seed of Eve to sit upon the throne of Israel. The first Temple of God was built in Jerusalem.

But Israel once again turned to the worship of the Mother Goddesses. The temples and groves dedicated to Ishtar dotted the land, and God judged the nation. Jeremiah and Isaiah warned Israel, but their ears were closed and their hearts were hardened. The children of David abandoned the Lord, and in the 14th generation from David, in the days of Jeconiah, the Temple was destroyed on the 9th of Av, and God led Israel captive into Babylon.

But God kept his promise to David. Seventy years later, as prophesied by Jeremiah (Jer. 29:10), Israel returned to the land, and the Second Temple was built. But Israel once again abandoned God. They sought to find righteousness, not by God's grace but by the works of their hands, like Cain. They began to heap on human traditions and made them equal to the Word of God.

> *The Pharisees and the scribes asked Him, "Why do Your disciples not walk according to the tradition of the elders, but eat their bread with impure hands?" And He said to them, "Rightly did Isaiah prophesy of you hypocrites, as it is written:*
>
> *THIS PEOPLE HONORS ME WITH THEIR LIPS,*
> *BUT THEIR HEART IS FAR AWAY FROM ME.*
> *"BUT IN VAIN DO THEY WORSHIP ME,*
> *TEACHING AS DOCTRINES THE PRECEPTS OF MEN."*

THE DEATH OF THE FIRST EARTH

Neglecting the commandment of God, you hold to the tradition of men.

—Mark 7:5–8

And so, 14 generations from Jeconiah, Jesus was born, the son of Adam, the son of Noah, the son of Abraham, the son of David, the Seed of Eve, the Messiah.

But Israel did not recognize their day of visitation. They struck the Shepherd, and the sheep were scattered. Zechariah warned of this day.

> "Awake, O sword, against My Shepherd,
> And against the man, My Associate,"
> Declares the LORD of hosts.
> "Strike the Shepherd that the sheep may be scattered;
> And I will turn My hand against the little ones"
> (emphasis added).

—Zech. 13:7

Isaiah saw this:

> *Who has believed our message?*
> *And to whom has the arm of the Lord been revealed?*
> *For He grew up before Him like a tender [a]shoot,*
> *And like a root out of parched ground;*
> *He has no stately form or majesty*
> *That we should look upon Him,*
> *Nor appearance that we should be attracted to Him.*
> *He was despised and forsaken of men,*
> *A man of sorrows and acquainted with grief;*
> *And like one from whom men hide their face*
> *He was despised, and we did not esteem Him.*
> *Surely our griefs He Himself bore,*
> *And our sorrows He carried;*

> *Yet we ourselves esteemed Him stricken,*
> *Smitten of God, and afflicted.*
> *But He was pierced through for our transgressions,*
> *He was crushed for our iniquities;*
> *The chastening for our well-being fell upon Him,*
> *And by His scourging we are healed.*
> *All of us like sheep have gone astray,*
> *Each of us has turned to his own way;*
> *But the* LORD *has caused the iniquity of us all*
> *To fall on Him.*
>
> —Isa. 53:1–6

And when the Shepherd who came to bear their sins was rejected by the ruling class of Israel who were puppets of the Romans, the Second Temple also was destroyed on the 9th of Av, the exact day that Solomon's Temple was destroyed by Babylon, so that all men could know that it was God who made it come to pass.

What Satan meant for evil God turned for good that all men would know that He is sovereign over all things in the universe for He rose from the dead the third day. And upon the cross, the Seed of Eve dealt the first of two mortal wounds to Lucifer's head. There upon the cross He became the Lamb that was sacrificed for the redemption of all mankind. When Satan thought he had gained his ultimate victory—killing the Seed of Eve—our sins were washed away, and salvation came to all mankind.

And so we see that man's entire history has been one of repeated rebellion toward God and contempt for His grace. It was so in the very beginning of the First Earth when the First Insurrection deceived Adam and Eve. It was so in the sixth generation from Adam when the line of Cain and eventually the children of Seth were deceived by the Second Insurrection. It was so in the very beginning of the Second Earth when the Third Insurrection in Babylon deceived the descendants of Noah. It shall be so again at the end of the Second

Earth when mankind shall take the seal of the Antichrist in the Fourth Insurrection. Each insurrection brought forth a judgment. The Fourth Insurrection shall bring forth the destruction of the Second Earth.

Lucifer in his attempt to usurp the throne of God has always sought to centralize power. There were one people, one language, and one culture when the Second Earth began. This was the Sumerian civilization. God sent forth His prophets to encourage the people to disperse and colonize the Earth, but Nimrod tried to be the supreme leader of all mankind. The centralization of power was feeding the greed of man and robbing the people of their individual freedoms. The dream of establishing Lucifer's global kingdom over mankind was at the brink of fulfillment yet again. Our world was in peril of being ruled by the death grip of the dark angels. The great suffering of the innocents was buried and forgotten as man myopically rationalized their greed to satisfy their baser instincts. Those who remained faithful to God were now a small remnant.

Mankind was again desiring to usurp the place of God, and they built a tower they thought could reach to the heavens. The fundamental doctrine of the occult, the desire for godhood, became the accepted norm of most of the descendants of Noah. They sought esoteric knowledge—the knowledge of wickedness, the knowledge of sorcery offered by the demons. One would think that God would have evaporated all mankind once and for all.

But our God is a God of grace and mercy. Because of His grace, He intervened again. Once more, He caused the oceans to rise. The First Ice Age began to rapidly melt due to the excess of greenhouse gases from the aftermath of the Great Flood. The rising seas inundated the Valley of Shinar and forced the progenitors of our Second Earth, centered in Babylon, to abandon the land and disperse. In that way, the languages were divided, and the nations were born. Power was decentralized. The Gentile nations began with the monotheistic religion of Adam and then Noah. This was the judgment of the Tower of Babel.

> *They said to one another, "Come, let us make bricks and burn them thoroughly." And they used brick for stone, and they used tar for mortar. They said, "Come, let us build for ourselves a city, and a tower whose top will reach into heaven, and let us make for ourselves a name, otherwise we will be scattered abroad over the face of the whole earth."*
>
> —Gen. 11:3–4

God was not pleased. The centralization of power led to the rapid deterioration of morals. Man turned again to the religion of the Serpent that seeks equality with God. They sought to reach heaven by the works of their hands. Once again, man followed the way of Cain. Once again, they turned to the Mother Goddess Ninhursag. The worship of the crescent moon gods, the horned gods, brought forth the terror of human sacrifice again to stain the land red as it had in the time of the Neanderthals. This was the Third Insurrection, and God through His grace intervened once more.

The haughty Nimrod thought he had built a tower that could foil God if He tried to drown mankind again with another flood. He covered it in pitch to make it waterproof. But it was all a show of bravado from a megalomaniac with visions of grandeur.

Nimrod knew God had promised Noah that He would never again drown mankind. It was the Rainbow Covenant that Shem, Ham, and Japheth witnessed along with their father, Noah. Everyone knew this. Perhaps this false sense of security made them irresponsible toward God. Nimrod exploited this. He was a master of propaganda to inflate his power and ego. Tyrants have ever been the same. So he covered his burnt, strong bricks with tar and claimed boastfully that he was impermeable to God's judgment. "It was built of burnt brick, cemented together with mortar, made of bitumen, that it might not be liable to admit water" (Josephus 1960, 30).

By this time, the polar Ice caps were melting rapidly, and the ocean levels began to rise. The Land of Shinar began to slowly flood and suffered terribly from saltwater intrusion. A great storm made the sky dark, and Nimrod most assuredly began to wonder if God had gone against His promise. There is no doubt in my mind that Nimrod erroneously thought that after he weathered the storm he could blame God for lying to the people.

But it was not God's intent to drown humanity again. He would not go back on His word. Although mankind did not keep its side of the covenant, God's word is irrevocable. Instead, a mighty east wind brought forth a terrible storm. Thunderous booms reverberated in the heavens, and the crack of a lightning bolt struck the giant tower and caused the tar to explode. The work of man's hands crumbled, burned to the ground, and was no more. It was a foreshadowing of the death of the Second Earth.

The arrogance of Nimrod was made bare. Many were brought to their knees before God, and their languages were confounded. The faithful went out to colonize the world as God had commanded. In that day the Gentile nations were born, and God began a new way.

> *So the* LORD *scattered them abroad from there over the face of the whole earth; and they stopped building the city.*
>
> *Therefore its name was called Babel, because there the* LORD *confused the language of the whole earth; and from there the* LORD *scattered them abroad over the face of the whole earth.*
>
> —Gen. 11:8–9

God established the separate nations and decentralized power to keep Satan from gaining the global throne. Ever since, Satan's minions have been hard at work to undo the curse of the Tower of Babel. To this day, the globalist agenda of the followers of the Great Usurper spin their wicked web to net all nations under one crown.

That has been the demonic dream of conquerors and empire builders since that day. It is the goal of the esoteric network in the elite global financiers of the Western world. And it is the same global aspirations of the Islamic conquerors and ruthless colonizers from the East, fanned by the wings of demons. Both sides work against the middle. Satan does not care which side wins. Either way, he puts his man on the throne of Earth.

That day will one day come. But Satan shall not stand. The Champion, the Seed of Eve, shall return to make things new again. That day, He will establish the Everlasting Covenant with Israel. In that day, the Gentile nations shall be destroyed in the battle of Armageddon, and the Third Earth shall be ruled from Jerusalem by the Prince of Peace.

> *God comes from Teman,*
> *And the Holy One from Mount Paran. Selah.*
> *His splendor covers the heavens,*
> *And the earth is full of His praise.*
> *His radiance is like the sunlight;*
> *He has rays flashing from His hand,*
> *And there is the hiding of His power.*
> *Before Him goes pestilence,*
> *And plague comes after Him.*
> *He stood and surveyed the earth;*
> *He looked and startled the nations.*
> *Yes, the perpetual mountains were shattered,*
> *The ancient hills collapsed.*
> *His ways are everlasting.*
>
> —Hab. 3:3–6

To seek a global government is to seek to undo the judgment of the Tower of Babel. Their end will be the same as the Sumerian civilization. In this way, the Sumerian language, the language of our forefathers beyond the Flood, thus became a dead language. No other language has ever evolved from it. Unlike all other languages in the world, it has no philological developmental history before or after. It appeared from seemingly nowhere after the Great Flood, and it died suddenly by the judgment of God.

But fortunately for us, some Babylonian priests kept the old language alive in hidden scribal circles in Babylon. Those records give us a clue to this ancient language, but it is a sparse and much diminished view. The dark veil of time obscures the history of our failure as a people to follow the way of God.

It was at this precise time when Satan had once again established dominion over most of mankind in Babylon that the runaway deglaciation reached the highest sea levels, and the thermohaline conveyor belt in the Atlantic Ocean was quite likely interrupted by the melting waters of the glaciers. The ice caps and giant glaciers created during the First Ice Age had largely melted. The rising waters forced many to abandon the Land of Shinar, and the Tower of Babel was destroyed by the Lightning Bearer. God's divine intervention brought mankind back from the brink and caused the children of Noah to go out in obedience to God to populate the entire Earth.

Rapid Deglaciation and the Second Rise of the Ocean Levels

"But how," you might ask, "could the polar ice caps melt in such a short interval?" The clues are found in the Flood story itself. If, in fact, a Global Deluge took place, we would expect that in the aftermath, the surface of the planet would be riddled with the rotting corpses of the animals that perished, as well as enormous heaps of decomposing vegetation that were uprooted by the massive, unleashed, hydrological forces. In the areas that were not frozen, the decomposition of both vegetation and animals would have emitted enormous amounts of greenhouse gases into our atmosphere.

Even more significant are the large amounts of carbon dioxide and sulfur dioxide released from suspension in the subterranean waters of the underground aquifers that would have added further fuel to the runaway deglaciation. That would have generated a continuing spike in the amount of carbon-12 (a greenhouse gas) found in the atmosphere. As the glaciers melted, exposing other corpses, it allowed the freshly thawed carcasses to decompose and further accelerate the process with more greenhouse gases.

Additionally, as the oceans warmed, the trapped carbon dioxide and methane gas would escape. That would have been catastrophic, especially because the deforestation of the First Earth during the Great Flood would have left the Second Earth incapacitated to absorb the excess carbon dioxide emitted. The great forests, the lungs of the Earth, turn carbon dioxide into oxygen through photosynthesis.

As the deglaciation process progressed, more decomposing matter was exposed, creating a steady infusion of methane and carbon dioxide into the atmosphere of the early Second Earth. It was a perfect storm. This rapid infusion of greenhouse gases invariably spiked the global temperatures and caused an accelerated deglaciation, which once again made the ocean levels rise dramatically in a relatively short period of time.

The rise in ocean levels was certainly not in the same dramatic fashion as when the crust of the Earth was cracked by the two horns of Taurus. There were no jetting fountains of the deep generating high winds and rain. There were few volcanic eruptions. The major cataclysmic movements of the now seven continents were nearly over. But nonetheless, year by year, the oceans gradually swallowed more land, and the inhabitants understood well that judgment was being pronounced for their wickedness. The Sumerian civilization crumbled and imploded as the tribes separated and fled the Valley of Shinar.

It was not God's intent to drown mankind but rather to scatter them abroad. The inundation was eventually arrested through the shutdown of the newly formed thermohaline ocean conveyor belt of the Second Earth in the Atlantic Ocean. The planet was sent into another Ice Age. Our Second Earth was gripped with bitter cold as the people trekked toward their new lands. The Mayan memory of this cold has been kept intact in the *Popol Vuh* so modern man can wonder at God's power. The awesome power of God was again made evident in the hearts of men. And so began the rule of the Gentile nations throughout the planet.

What is the thermohaline ocean conveyor belt?

The New Temperature Regulator – Thermohaline Ocean Conveyor Belt

Ironically, the fear of global warming has brought new research and insights to our meteorological global processes. As a result, even evolutionary scientists now no longer dispute the idea that sudden catastrophic climactic changes can occur in a relatively short period of time. Through a 10-year World Ocean Circulation Experiment that began in 1990, scientists have discovered that ocean currents help maintain meteorological global homeostasis. The climate of our Second Earth is literally stabilized by bringing warmer water to northern regions through a continuous flow of ocean currents such as the Gulf Stream. Conversely, there are also cold deep-water currents that travel to warmer regions through the same thermohaline (thermo = heat, haline = salt) process.

This thermohaline process is what allows England to have a relatively mild climate at the same latitude that Canada and Alaska have polar bears. The warmer water in these ocean currents contains more salt compared to fresh water and is therefore denser than the northern waters. As a result, when the warm ocean currents reach the northern latitudes and cool down, becoming even denser, the water sinks and is subsequently returned through deeper, cooler currents.

The greater density of the water due to the salinity and cooling process gives it the momentum necessary to sink and literally power the flow of the currents. That provides an indispensible cyclical system that moderates and stabilizes the global climate.

This system in the Atlantic is called the Atlantic Conveyor. But it is not peculiar just to the Atlantic Ocean, for similar currents accomplish the same stabilizing effect throughout our entire planet. There are three major thermohaline loops that transfer both warm-water currents and cold-water currents around our world. The second loop regulates the Indian Ocean, and the third loop regulates the Pacific Ocean.

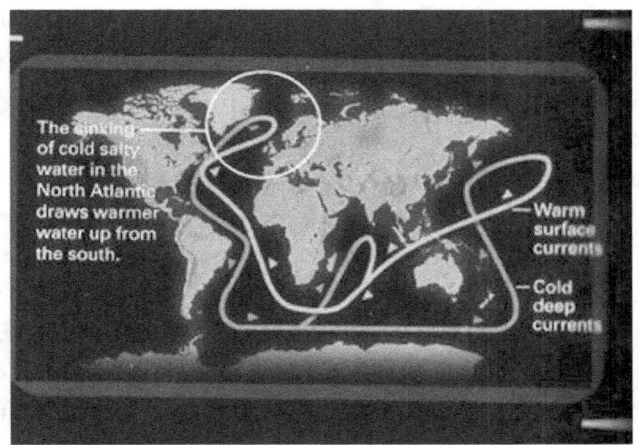

The ocean currents (conveyor belt) that stabilize our climate through the thermohaline process

The alarming news is that scientists have discovered that this process may be at risk of completely collapsing, perhaps even in our generation. Today's polar ice caps have been maintained by the accumulation of years of precipitating snow and are basically composed of freshwater ice. The melting, giant glaciers continuously feed the relatively saltless water of the North Sea. As the ice sheets melt and continue to mix with seawater, it reduces the salinity levels of the ocean and threatens the ability of the current to sink with enough force to continue the currents.

Scientists believe that the interference of this melting fresh water into the currents may stop the carefully balanced thermohaline system that causes these currents to flow, which maintains our global climate in homeostasis. If the salinity in the seawater is below a critical point, it will not be dense enough to drop the required depth of at least 100 meters to power the currents. In other words, the dilution of these saltwater ocean currents can shut off the conveyor and eliminate the present global meteorological balance that creates a stable environment and moderates global temperatures.

I suspect that it already happened once before during the judgment of the Tower of Babel. Our thermohaline conveyor belt came to a screeching halt probably just a few hundred years after the Great Flood. The rapid deglaciation was instigated by an enormous amount of greenhouse gases that brought about an exponentially accelerating warming trend.

Unfortunately, except for the extreme polar regions, this melting process would have exposed much of the evidence of the cataclysm that ended our First Earth that was previously preserved in ice. Had these animals been kept frozen under the glacial ice cap, it could have further substantiated the historicity of this global hydraulic event with rich evidence of the Great Flood. But much of the ice melted, and the bodies of the animals and people that perished decomposed.

Only the carcasses in the tundra regions where the ice did not melt or where those creatures were interred in the permafrost sedimentary layer escaped total disintegration through decomposition. These are the only remainders of the specimens that died in the Great Flood and that are accessible to modern man today.

But their numbers are still staggering. Many have been turned into fossils. And for this reason, the mechanism of the Great Flood thus better accounts for these giant fossil beds that, under the uniformitarian bias, are quite difficult to explain.

Once the conveyor belt was interrupted, the poles began to freeze again in a relatively short period of time. That Second Ice Age was birthed at the time of the Tower of Babel. In other words, within several hundred years of the birth of the Second Earth, the ice pack of the First Ice Age largely melted, and the oceans rose within a few dozen meters of the maximum ocean level of the Great Flood.

In less than 300–400 years after the Great Deluge, the ocean levels once again threatened large areas of the world. However, due to the crunching of the continents as they ground to a near halt, land was thickened and thrust upward.

Initially, the continents moved laterally under the lubrication of the deep saltwater aquifers. Once the aquifers evacuated most of their water, the granitic continents began to sag at the tips and grind against the basaltic subfloor below. This friction caused the continents to buckle and thicken, thus elevating them higher. In turn, that allowed for the second rise in the ocean levels and a much more moderate incursion into the land. God's providence is once again illustrated here for those who have eyes to see and ears to hear.

The newly developed ocean conveyor belt currents that formed after the Great Flood shut down completely with this rapid infusion of fresh water from the process of runaway deglaciation. The density reduction of the seawater due to a lower salinity level, along with the rise in global ocean temperatures that also causes a density reduction of the seawater due to thermal expansion, stopped the ocean circulation that moderated global temperatures.

Evolutionary scientists have documented the fact that a second such process did occur; they refer to it as the Younger Dryas. They theorize that the combination of the infusion of fresh water and the rise in the mean ocean temperatures would have caused the conveyor belt to fail when seawater lost the density necessary to sink with enough force to drive the currents. The net effect of that would have shut down the ocean currents that keep our global temperatures in balance in our Second Earth.

During the early stages of deglaciation of the First Ice Age, much of the meltwater from the Laurentide Ice Sheet that covered North America would have emptied primarily into the Gulf of Mexico. As the deglaciation process continued, eventually the ice margin retreated sufficiently northward to open up the drainage eastward into the St. Lawrence Seaway near modern-day Newfoundland. At that point, the deglaciation process would have accelerated, gaining speed almost exponentially.

Ice sheets reflect much of the sunlight that strikes its surface. On the other hand, the darker, recently exposed Earth would absorb much of the radiant heat, causing the warming process to gain momentum with mounting speed. Thus, the more the darker surface of the planet was exposed, the more heat was absorbed and the faster the process of deglaciation accelerated.

We are witnessing the very same phenomenon in our rapidly shrinking glaciers today. The evidence that contradicts the uniformitarian dogma is before our very eyes. Geological and meteorological processes can change with great rapidity, causing enormous consequences.

The drainage from the St. Lawrence Seaway would have drastically changed the salinity level of the subpolar North Atlantic Ocean. Low salinity and the volume expansion due to the warming ocean would cause the seawater to not be dense enough to sink through the pycnocline level (the salinity density gradient that is about 100 meters in depth).

By effectively shutting down the overturn, the thermohaline process would be stopped all together, and the ocean conveyor belt that distributes heat throughout our planet would cease to exist. Hence, the Northern Hemisphere would cease to be injected with the warm water from the Gulf Stream to moderate its temperatures. The poles would begin to freeze over again within a relatively short period of time. The rapidly warming trend that followed the First Ice Age caused the glaciers to melt and the ocean levels to rise again, perhaps some 20 to 30 meters above our present level.

The rising ocean levels that inundated the Valley of Shinar would have created great pressure to migrate from that area. The quickly rising sea simply flooded much of that low-lying area all the way to the city of Babylon. We find this peak recorded in the event scientists refer to as the Flandrian Transgression that overtook much of the Middle East around the time of the Tower of Babel.

As the sea levels rose several meters above even our present level, the water engulfed much of the area where most of the initial survivors of the Great Deluge had settled. That is the land of Shinar referred to in Scriptures located around the valley of the Tigris and Euphrates Rivers.

This second warming trend caused by the combined greenhouse gases could have easily shut down the ocean conveyor belt at a given critical point. Within a relatively short period of time, our Second Earth experienced the Second Ice Age that caused the waters to subsequently recede again.

Today, much of the area they may have inhabited may be found under the waters of the Persian Gulf since our ice caps have almost melted for the second time. That critical point is not far off.

Evolutionists have no mechanism that could create such vast amounts of carbon-12 that would affect this dramatic temperature change since they believe these events took place over long periods of time. It is a mystery to them. Our Judeo-Christian model, on the other hand, sees this as evidence that a Global Flood did occur, injecting vast amounts of carbon dioxide in suspension in the pressurized salt waters of the underground aquifers that burst open and flooded our planet, leaving large amounts of decomposing vegetation and animal carcasses in its wake.

The greenhouse gases released in the normal process of decomposition would have greatly helped significantly raise our global temperatures. It stands to reason that it could have caused the thermohaline process to fail. By shutting down these regulatory currents, the world was once again thrust into a Second Ice Age. This second glacial extension did not have the same intensity as the first, but it came close to it.

Although this second process was more tranquil than the previous, it still had a kick to it. The rapid melting of glaciers created enormous shifts in weight over the continents that destabilized them. This shift in weight as the ice melted could have also triggered the firing of several super-volcanoes. By the time Nimrod led mankind's third rebellion, the movements of the hydroplates may have built up enough potential energy in stress to slip as the colossal weight of the ice above them, causing dramatic isostatic changes. The Earth may have experienced another series of large earthquakes and volcanic eruptions.

In other words, the rapid removal of the 2-mile-thick sheets of ice over the continents would have undoubtedly created enormous shifts in weight that would have caused the continents to slip once more. Certainly, the caldera over Yellowstone had reduced the weight over the thin-walled crust above the magma chamber just by the loss of the ice pack above it. But the grinding over the surface created by the retreating ice may have also carved the crust above the dome a bit thin. The triggering of earthquakes below would have agitated the trapped gases within the magma chamber and caused it to explode through violent outgassing. I suspect that the third blast from Yellowstone may have come at that particular time.

Once more, ash belched out into our atmosphere, and the sunlight was occluded. Another long winter covered the face of our planet as our ancestors dispersed throughout the Earth and the shadow of death loomed over mankind.

The Second Ice Age

This time, the gently rising oceans had not drowned the whole Earth, but the darkness and rising waters reminded the new colonizers of the cataclysm of the Great Deluge that had ended their previous world. It caused most of mankind to turn back to God and abandon their rebellion.

This time, it was the disruption of the ocean currents and perhaps even the subsequent eruption of super-volcanoes that caused the Earth to enter the Second Ice Age. Those who were not convinced by the rising waters had grounds to think differently as darkness and then ice once again covered most of our Earth. The heat wave was arrested, and cold—incredible cold, bitter cold, and darkness—returned to our world.

According to modern research, the North Atlantic polar front readvanced to approximately 45 degrees north. That is roughly 5–10 degrees from the first maximum glacial extent of the First Ice Age. Thus, the second glacial extent almost reached the same extent of the previous Ice Age. Of course, evolutionists do not believe these two events occurred in the time frame I am suggesting. Their timelines are vastly different and in accord with their failed uniformitarian hypothesis.

It is a fact that during the Great Flood the ocean levels rose more than 430 feet above their previous normal level. This dramatic change in sea level has been clearly substantiated, even by evolutionary scientists. Our ocean levels are not static. As the Second Earth warmed rapidly, the oceans rose rapidly, but they never again reached the apex achieved during the Great Flood. This time, they stopped just short of the point where life would have once again been extinguished. It was a divine wake-up call.

As the waters froze once again, reforming the ice caps for the second time, the oceans in turn receded dramatically. That aided in the dispersion of the nations that sailed across the Atlantic Ocean to the Americas. Many islands that are now completely under water would have provided a stepping stone for travelers to cross the Atlantic.

Nevertheless, the sea level at its lowest point still remained higher than the previous prediluvian level. This change in volume is due to the shifting of the saltwater reservoir to the surface of the Earth's crust, which, prior to the Great Flood, was stored in the subterranean chambers. In effect, the continents also sank as the subterranean aquifers were depleted. Fortunately, the thickening more than counterbalanced this and lifted our continents higher.

These new glaciers of the Second Ice Age probably developed a bit more slowly than during the First Ice Age. Super-cold air was not thrust downward by the downdrafts of high altitude air created by the jetting fountains of the deep. This time, there was no ejecta from a striking meteor. The tephra from the volcanic activity during this phase was much reduced compared to the immense eruptions created by the impacts of the seven giant meteors.

Nevertheless, winter storms of great intensity and fury blanketed the polar regions, and the ice and snow eventually crawled toward the equator, bringing upon us the Second Ice Age. The colder water once again trapped much of the greenhouse gases, and our meteorological processes were tamed for the second time.

The new glaciers would now melt at a much slower pace than those of the First Ice Age. Huge snowstorms would have once again raged throughout the frozen ice caps, scrubbing much of the greenhouse gases. The depletion of further infusion of new greenhouse gases from rotting corpses and vegetation previously experienced would have added a more pronounced stability to this second glacial extent. Most visible traces of that global kill-off that were above ground would have by now disintegrated.

The migration of the nations was limited at first to this narrow band around the equator. These new colonies later ventured toward the poles as the ice caps slowly receded.

The accumulation of snow and the process of precipitation then further stabilized this Second Ice Age. The deglaciation of the Second Ice Age has proceeded at a much slower pace, bringing us to our present day. But beware. We have almost reached the end of this process once again.

The Second Maximum Glacial Extent

The forward advancement of these glaciers, given the complete shutdown of the ocean conveyor belt currents and a darkened sky, could have proceeded much faster than what most evolutionists wearing their myopic uniformitarian spectacles would suppose. From the shutdown of the conveyor belt in the Atlantic Ocean to the second glacial maximum extent, the entire process may have happened within a matter of months. No one knows for sure.

After the Second Ice Age reached the second maximum glacial extent, it had considerably reduced the ocean levels again. The meteorological processes of the Second Earth also stabilized considerably without the destabilizing infusion of the decomposition gases that had created the instability that led to rapid warming and rapid deglaciation immediately following the Great Flood.

Moreover, the growing forests that sprouted in the interval would have grown in size to more adequately remove the carbon dioxide from the atmosphere. That would have helped stabilize the meteorological processes. We are nevertheless in an inferiorly oxygenated environment with only about 21 percent oxygen in our air compared to 35–37 percent oxygen prior to the Great Flood due to the infusion of many greenhouse gases involved in the Great Flood catastrophe.

The oceans have since been rising slowly but steadily as our planet continues to warm. Today, our ocean levels are about 120 meters above the prediluvian level and only a few meters away from the highest point reached just prior to the Second Ice Age when our conveyor belt last failed. But we must take careful note of the fact that our planet is once again rapidly warming due to a variety of reasons, including but not primarily the impact of manmade industrial greenhouse gases so politicized in our nation. We are quickly nearing the climate cycle that began with the Second Ice Age during the judgment of the Tower of Babel. No doubt this will likely coincide with the demonic plan to undo the division of the nations and bring forth a global government.

We are seeing today the events that are leading to that climactic end of this age. The greatest present danger we face in our modern world is not posed by the emission of greenhouse gases created by the burning of fossil fuels as some have erroneously presupposed. Serious as that threat is to our planet, it is dwarfed by the ominous danger lurking silently below our oceans.

Even today we find large reservoirs of frozen methane gas under the oceans that were created by the rotting flora and fauna destroyed in the Great Deluge. They were kept in deep storage by the Second Ice Age. As long as the oceans are cool enough to keep these gases in their frozen state, they remain trapped as they have been since the Second Ice Age. If the ocean temperature is cold enough, then there is no problem keeping these greenhouse gases frozen in their deep ocean floors.

But if the ocean temperatures reach a critical point, these gases will be released into our atmosphere. It would create another global catastrophe. Should the temperatures of the deep oceans rise enough to release their gases into our atmosphere, our Second Earth will face the Third Ice Age. Such a massive release of greenhouse gases would once again precipitate a drastic rise in temperatures that would cause the conveyor belt to cease, plunging us into a Third Ice Age.

The world as we know it would greatly change in a rather short period of time. All we need to do is look at what our world would have looked like during the First Maximum Glacial Extent (FMGE) in order to understand the true gravity of the situation that may soon overtake us.

> Areas that are densely populated today, Chicago, New York, Manchester, Amsterdam, Hamburg, Berlin, Moscow—in fact most of North America and Northern Europe–were absolutely uninhabitable due to the fact that they were covered by ice-caps several kilometers thick. Conversely, many areas that are uninhabitable today—on account of being on the bottom of the sea, or in the middle of hostile deserts such as the Sahara (which bloomed for about 4000 years at the end of the last Ice Age)—were once (and

relatively recently) desirable places to live that were capable of supporting dense populations.

Geologists calculate that nearly 5 per cent of the earth's surface—an area of around 25 million square kilometers or 10 million square miles—has been swallowed by rising sea-levels since the end of the Ice Age. That is roughly the equivalent to the combined areas of the United States and the whole of South America (Hancock 2002, 53).

After the floodwaters of the Great Deluge became frozen in the First Ice Age, the mean ocean level would have been at its lowest point in the entire history of the Second Earth. And conversely, the giant glaciers would have been at their maximum extent (First Maximum Glacial Extent). The freezing of the poles formed immense ice caps at both poles of our planet. That would have reduced the sea level and dramatically extended the coastline of our present continents. It would have meant that much of the continental shores would have been considerably wider than presently observed. Indeed, it would have been hard to recognize the outlines of our modern-day continents.

Although they would have been covered in ice, the British Isles would have been connected to Europe by a land bridge that is presently inundated under the English Channel. Malta would have been joined to Sicily, and Sicily would have been joined to Italy. All the islands would have been much larger. In the Caribbean, the Florida peninsula would have been much wider, and the Bahamian island would have been joined together. Cuba would have been a much larger island joined to Haiti and the Dominican Republic. Many of the present-day Caribbean islands would have been united into larger tracts of lands.

Taiwan and Japan would have been joined to Mainland China whose territory would have been immensely greater. Stretching from the island of Taiwan for some 1,000 kilometers north and east, the area that is now called the Yellow Sea would have been dry land. The islands of Japan would have created a crescent-shaped land bridge that could have been crossed from Mainland China through the northern tip all the way down to the southern tip and back to Mainland China.

Prior to the Great Flood, Malaysia, Indonesia, and the Philippines would have been joined to the mainland of Southeast Asia. That would have formed a huge tract of land measuring some 3 million square kilometers that are presently as deep as 100 meters under water. After the First Ice Age, that area may have sunk so deeply due to the formation of the Mid-Atlantic Ridge that perhaps not as much land would have been above water as the First Maximum Glacial Extent. Australia, Tasmania, and New Guinea would have been one landmass. But prior to the meteor strike, this area of Arza (the single continent of the First Earth) would have been a lush and vast forest teeming with life.

The Black Sea could have been a fertile valley, and perhaps even the Mediterranean Sea was not a sea before the Great Flood. Perhaps it was a valley or even a freshwater lake. At a given point, the Atlantic burst through the Strait of Gibraltar between Africa and Spain, inundating the Mediterranean Sea. As the ocean level continued to rise, the Mediterranean Sea would have eventually burst past the Bosporus Strait, causing a colossal incursion into previously fertile dry land and creating what we now call the Black Sea.

The Persian Gulf as far as the Strait of Hormuz would have been dry land and a veritable paradise with the Tigris and Euphrates Rivers providing plenty of water for farming in that area. No doubt the earliest survivors of the Great Flood who recolonized the Second Earth were drawn to this lush Fertile Crescent where the climate was perfect until the glaciers retreated and the seas rose again.

Here they first established a postdiluvian civilization when all of humanity spoke one language and were one people. It was during the Flandrian Transgression, created by the runaway greenhouse gases of the decomposing debris from the Great Flood, that this area became inundated again, forcing the inhabitants to scatter. As the waters rose, the inhabitants of the Sumerian civilization slowly migrated north into the area we know as Turkey and northern Iraq. It stands to reason that it reached its highest crest during the time of the Tower of Babel spoken of in the Scriptures.

Immediately after the Great Flood, Sri Lanka would have been joined to India. At its southern tip, India would have extended more than 150 kilometers farther into the Indian Ocean. The coastline of India would have far exceeded its present form. And that is particularly so in the northwest area near the site of the original Indus-Sarasvati civilization who had originally colonized northern India after the Tower of Babel.

They migrated into northern India after the dispersion of the nations from the Land of Shinar when the Second Ice Age brought the ocean levels back down near where they had been after the First Ice Age. Great tracts of land all along this northwestern coast would have been above water. All in all, more than 1 million square kilometers of India that are presently under water would have then been dry land. The Maldives islands just south and west of the tip of India would have been one large, long, singular island extending several hundred miles from north to south with only a few narrow channels to cross in between.

Estimates place more than 25 million kilometers of the Earth's surface that are presently under water as land that would have been dry during the First and Second Maximum Glacial Extents. That is particularly important since very little marine archaeology has been conducted in these areas, and that might provide vast storehouses of information about our ancient ancestors who would have quite likely settled in these coastal areas that are now totally inundated.

Travel between the continents would have been easier since they were a bit closer than today. The relatively closer positions of the fractured plates in this early period, as well as the greater landmass due to the lower sea levels, would have facilitated the migration of our ancestors after the Tower of Babel.

As time goes by, the ice caps continue to melt, and the oceans inevitably rise accordingly. In the meantime, the continents continue to drift farther apart, causing the plates to continue to wrinkle and build higher mountains. Many of the early cities from the initial inhabitants of the Second Earth that might have sprung up in these coastlines would now be completely submerged under the rising oceans.

Underwater exploration of our continental coastal regions is at its very earliest stages. Scuba (self-contained underwater breathing apparatus) gear was not invented until 1943 by the late Jean Jacques Cousteau and Émile Gagnan. The technology necessary to do underwater archaeological research is practically brand new. And we have just begun to scratch the surface of marine archaeology. I suspect that in the not-too-distant future we will discover many advanced cities that date back to this early period in our Second Earth, cities that are completely submerged under the oceans.

This process may have deep implications to our civilization in the future. Low-lying nations such as the Netherlands and Bangladesh stand to be completely submerged if the oceans rise high enough.

But we must not be deceived by the evolutionary bias that the antediluvian civilization or the early civilizations of the Second Earth were primitive and unsophisticated. The idea that the civilization of the First Earth was indeed a high civilization is contained in the history of all the major ancient civilizations. If, in fact, we find cities submerged under water, it will show that they had a high degree of technology. If mankind undertakes the challenge of exploring these underwater cities, the evolutionary idea that human civilization is rather recent will be disproved, and the biblical model will be exonerated

Do not for one moment think that our present civilization is not intimately connected to the events that shaped our past. The global impact of the events that brought forth the death of the First Earth is still being felt today. In fact, it will direct the events that will end our Second Earth.

It is highly probable that the rise in the frequency and strength of earthquakes we are presently experiencing is connected to the shift in weight between the plates as the polar ice caps continue to melt into the oceans. As the Earth spins, the weight of its landmasses is seeking to find equilibrium.

As the polar caps melt, massive and rapid shifts in weight from the poles elsewhere can precipitate the motion of the plates that will result in an increase in earthquakes. If our ocean levels reach the same point that the thermohaline conveyor belt was arrested the last time, we will certainly be doomed to suffer the same consequences. The question is not if but when.

CHAPTER 11
THE THREAT OF A FUTURE ICE AGE

Scientists influenced by the uniformitarian dogma have traditionally thought that meteorological changes come slowly through vast eons of time. But lately, these scientists are beginning to understand that this is not always so. As a matter of fact, it has been the recalcitrant insistence on the uniformitarian model that until recently has persistently kept the scientific community from detecting and heading off the disastrous effects of global warming. Sadly, this issue has been so highly politicized that I am afraid now it may be too little too late.

Global Warming Is Real

The undisputed scientific evidence amassed in the last three decades points to a volatile and rapidly changing planet as the process of global warming is accelerating at a pace heretofore not dreamed of by the uniformitarian horse blinders of evolutionary scientists. The 10 hottest days in recorded history have all occurred since 1987, according to a 2005 *Time* magazine article.

Since 1970, mean ocean surface temperatures have risen about 1° F. Those numbers have moved in lockstep with global air temperatures, which have also inched up a degree. The warmest year ever recorded was 1998 with 2002, 2003 and 2004 close behind it (Kluger 2005).

According to the National Oceanic and Atmospheric Administration (NOAA), the top 10 years are 2010, 2005, 1998, 2003, 2002, three years—2006, 2009, and 2007—tied for sixth place, 2004, and 2012. The global annual temperature has increased at an average rate of 0.28 degrees Fahrenheit since 1970.

> The December 2014 average combined global land and ocean surface temperature was record high in the 135-year period of record, at 0.77°C (1.39°F) above the 20th century average of 12.2°C (54.0°F).
>
> The December 2014 globally-averaged land surface temperature was the third highest on record, at 1.36°C (2.45°F) above average. The globally-averaged ocean surface temperature was also third highest for December on record, at 0.55°C (0.99°F) above average.
>
> The average combined global land and ocean surface temperature for January–December 2014 was the highest on record among all years in the 135-year period of record, at 0.69°C (1.24°F) above the 20th century average ("Global Climate Report – December 2014").

Global warming goes through cycles where one year might be colder than the previous, but what we must look at is the long view and specifically the glacial extents. I will now show you the global temperature reports posted by the NOAA for the last few years, from 2014 through 2017, and let you come to your own conclusions.

The combined average temperature over global land and ocean surfaces for November 2015 was the highest for November in the 136-year period of record, at 0.97°C (1.75°F) above the 20th century average of 12.9°C (55.2°F), breaking the previous record of 2013 by 0.15°C (0.27°F). This marks the seventh consecutive month that a monthly global temperature record has been broken. The temperature departure from average for November is also the second highest among all months in the 136-year period of record. The highest departure of 0.99°C (1.79°F) occurred last month.

The average global temperature across land surfaces was 1.31°C (2.36°F) above the 20th century average of 5.9°C (42.6°F), the fifth highest November temperature on record. Most of Earth's land surfaces were warmer than average or much warmer than average, according to the Land & Ocean Temperature Percentiles map above, with record warmth notable across most of equatorial and northeastern South America and parts of southeastern Asia. Parts of the western United States, southern Greenland, portions of northern Asia, and parts of southern South America were near to cooler than average. No regions were record cold in November ("Global Climate Report – November 2015").

The combined average temperature over global land and ocean surfaces for May 2016 was the highest for May in the 137-year period of record, at 0.87°C (1.57°F) above the 20th century average of 14.8°C (58.6°F), besting the previous record set in 2015 by 0.02°C (0.04°F). May 2016 marks the 13th consecutive month a monthly global temperature record has been broken—the longest such streak since global temperature records began in 1880.

The May 2016 global land and ocean surface temperature departure from average was also the lowest monthly temperature departure from average since August 2015 and, unlike the past five consecutive months (December 2015 through April 2016), did not surpass 1.0°C (1.8°F). May 2016 tied with June 2015 and August 2015 as the 12th highest monthly temperature departure among all months (1,637) on record. Overall, 13 of the 15 highest monthly temperature departures in the record have all occurred since February 2015, with February 1998 and January 2007 among the 15 highest temperature departures.

The average global temperature across land surfaces was 1.17°C (2.11°F) above the 20th century average of 11.1°C (52.0°F)—the third highest May temperature on record, behind 2012 (+1.26°C / +2.27°F) and 2015 (+1.21°C / +2.18°F). This was also the lowest land monthly temperature departure from average since September 2015, which had a temperature departure of 1.14°C (2.05°F) above average.

May 2016 was characterized by warmer to much warmer than average conditions across Alaska, Canada, Mexico, Central America, northern South America, northern Europe, Africa, Oceania, and parts of southern and eastern Asia, according to the Land & Ocean Temperature Percentiles map above. Areas with record warmth included much of Southeast Asia and parts of northern South America, Central America, the Caribbean, the Middle East, and northern and eastern Australia. Near- to cooler-than-average conditions were present across much of the contiguous U.S., central and southern South America, and much of central Asia. No land areas experienced record cold temperatures during May 2016. According to NCEI's Global Regional analysis, five of the six continents had at least a top nine warm May, with Oceania observing a record high average temperature for May since continental records began in 1910 ("Global Climate Report – May 2016").

The combined global average temperature over the land and ocean surfaces for November 2017 was 0.75°C (1.35°F) above the 20th century average of 12.9°C (55.2°F). This value tied with 2016 as the fifth highest for November since global temperature records began in 1880. November 2017 marks the 41st consecutive November and the 395th consecutive month with temperatures at least nominally above the 20th century average. The 10 warmest Novembers have occurred during the 21st century. The global land and ocean temperature during November has increased at an average rate of +0.07°C (+0.13°F) per decade since 1880; however, the average rate of increase is twice as great since 1980. The global land surface temperature was the ninth highest on record at 1.10°C (1.98°F) above the 20th century average of 5.9°C (42.6°F) ("Global Climate Report – November 2017").

It is absolutely essential that Christians become aware of this issue that has unfortunately become politicized in America. Do not allow the political pundits to blind you to the enormous danger of this climactic problem. We who understand the mandate given to us by God to care for our planet must not allow the interests of the industrialists to blind us and cause us to neglect our serious responsibility to our planet. What we cannot allow is the globalist movement to use this as a pretext to take away the sovereignty of nations in the name of saving the world. There is not one single thing man can do to change the cyclical meteorological trajectory that our Second Earth is on. It is nearing its death.

Nevertheless, conservation should be an issue that is strongly supported by conservative Jews and Christians. To do anything less is to concede our responsibility given to us by the Creator as caretakers of His realm (Gen. 2:15) to those who do not even believe in Him. Although there is great debate as to the influence of carbon emissions as the reason for this climactic change—and that has not convinced me—the fact is that climactic change is taking place nonetheless. We cannot ignore it.

The end of our Second Earth shall bring great climactic and geological changes to our planet, which we must become aware of. The events that took place at the end of our First Earth can bring enlightenment to the events afoot in our world. For this reason, I feel the need to discuss these coming changes so we can also better understand the drastic measures that took place in our past.

The interruption of the thermohaline conveyor belt may not be too far in the future. This will, in effect, plunge us into a Third Ice Age, perhaps within a few years or maybe even a few months from its collapse. This is no fairy-tale. It is hard, scientific fact. The Greenland ice sheet that is some 100 miles wide and 400 miles long with a thickness of 2 miles at the center is disappearing or melting at a rate of 30 cubic miles per year.

The old uniformitarian concepts have begun to give way to a more realistic understanding of meteorological forces that can act with global consequences relatively quickly. The scientific resistance to catastrophism is beginning to wane. Scientists no longer ridicule these potential catastrophic mechanisms such as the one that brought about the Global Flood. And yet incredibly, they manage to keep their evolutionary horse blinders on when it comes to the issue of the Global Flood.

Global warming is a real threat to our planet. What is not true is that our industrial exhausts are the cause of it. It is simply the cyclical meteorological process that through time inexorably marches no matter what man tries to do to stop it. According to the September 2004 issue of *National Geographic* magazine, in the northern city of Barrow, Alaska, the average temperature has risen 4.16 degrees Fahrenheit in only 30 years. In Juneau, the average temperature has risen 3.54 degrees Fahrenheit. In Anchorage, Alaska's most populous city, it has warmed up 2.26 degrees Fahrenheit. At the planet's opposite pole, the average temperature in Antarctica has risen 9 degrees Fahrenheit in the last 50 years.

Based on data taken from satellites from 1979 to 2003, the ice sheet of the Arctic that used to span from shore to shore between Canada and Siberia has shrunk 9 percent per decade. Some scientists are predicting that by the end of this century, the ice will completely disappear during the summertime, that is if the present rates do not accelerate. There is evidence to substantiate that it may be accelerating.

For the past few years, record-breaking heat waves have consumed almost the entire United States for weeks on end. By July 19, 2011, 22 people died that year in America due to heat-related causes. In East Africa, the heat has produced droughts of unprecedented nature. Crops have failed, and famine has resulted as thousands of the young and elderly drop like flies.

Sonar readings by submarines have documented a startling 40 percent thinning of the Arctic ice in the last 30 years. The beautiful and famous snow-capped peak of Mount Kilimanjaro in Africa has diminished its snowcap by 80 percent since 1912. The Unteraar Glacier of Switzerland's majestic Alps has retreated more than 1 mile since the 1800s.

Peru's Quelccaya Ice Cap is retreating at a rate of 600 feet per year, and scientists predict that it will be completely gone by the year 2100. Thousands in that area who depend on this source of drinking water will be left destitute of the liquid of life. This grave problem is worldwide. The globalists have deftly adopted the position that this problem is manmade in order to attempt to execute power over the industrial capacities of individual nations. Their plan is to execute global control over the air and waterways through the United Nations and in that way begin their process of centralizing power over national rights in our world.

We must not allow them to use this excuse to erode our national sovereignties. If we fail to separate these two positions by denying that global warming is real, we shall eventually be walking into their trap. When the world begins to see the truth of global warming, those who champion our national sovereignties will be discredited, and the globalists will accomplish their goal. We must acknowledge that global warming is real and prevent the globalists from using it as a battering ram to erode our national sovereignties.

In China, the glaciers on the Qinghai-Tibet Plateau that feed the Yellow River are also melting at a rate of 7 percent per year. The Gangotri Glacier, the principal glacier that feeds the Ganges River in India, is melting at such an accelerated rate that it will disappear entirely within a few decades. The mighty Ganges will then be reduced to a seasonal river that flows only during the time of the monsoon.

These two glaciers alone feed the Indus River, the Ganges River, the Mekong River, the Yangtze River, and the Yellow River in Asia. The dire repercussions to the Chinese people, the Indian people, and the people of Southeast Asia who rely on them for drinking water and irrigation will be catastrophic. If the glaciers continue to melt at this pace, by the middle of the 21st century, famine will rule Asia with an iron grip.

> Glaciers in the Garhwal Himalaya in India are retreating so fast that researchers believe that most central and eastern Himalaya glaciers could virtually disappear by 2035. Arctic sea ice has thinned significantly over the past half century, and its extent has declined by 10 percent in the past 30 years. NASA's repeated laser altimeter readings show the edges of Greenland's ice sheet shrinking. Spring freshwater ice breakup in the Northern Hemisphere now occurs nine days earlier than it did 150 years ago, and autumn freeze up to 10 days later. Thawing permafrost

has caused the ground to subside more than 15 feet (4.6 meters) in parts of Alaska. From the Arctic to Peru, from Switzerland to the equatorial glaciers of Man Jaya in Indonesia, massive ice fields, monstrous glaciers, and sea ice are disappearing fast ("Signs from Earth" 2004, 14).

In March 2002, a twin satellite system called GRACE (Gravity Recovery and Climate Experiment) was placed in a polar orbit. There is about 137 miles between the two satellites in the same orbit. They orbit about 310 miles above the surface of the Earth and are able to detect minute gravitational shifts on the surface of the planet.

Last March, geophysicists Isabella Velicogna and John Wahr at the University of Colorado at Boulder published a paper in the *Science Express* that used GRACE data to show that the *ice sheet covering Antarctica has shrunk by an average of 36 cubic miles of ice per year*—surprising, given that many climate models predict a thickening of the ice as higher global temperatures lead to more evaporation and precipitation. "It's very difficult for models to reproduce the physics of glaciers, and this shows that the models aren't as good as we'd like them to be," Velicogna says.

Velicogna and *her colleagues also measured a dramatic loss of Greenland ice, as much as 38 cubic miles per year between 2002 and 2005*—even more troubling, given that an influx of fresh melt water into the salty North Atlantic could in theory shut off the system of ocean currents that keep Europe relatively warm. (A separate group at the University of Texas published figures extrapolated *from GRACE data showing that Greenland lost as much as 57 cubic miles of ice each year between 2002 and 2005*; NASA shortly plans to publish data reconciling the two studies.) *"It's a wake-up call," says Velicogna, "because there is a lot of water that can go from the ice sheets into the ocean. Both ice sheets are significantly losing mass, and that affects sea level. If sea level is going to rise, that will affect a lot of coastal areas."*

This past December an entire session of the American Geophysical Union's fall meeting was devoted to movement of water in and out of giant watersheds all over the world. Speakers presented eight papers, on topic ranging from the hydrologic impact of the Three Gorges Dam in China to the impact of climate change on Siberian river systems. All the new findings were based entirely on data from GRACE. Notable results *included a report from researchers at MIT that Alaska lost an average of 10 and a half cubic miles of ice each year from 2003 to 2005* (emphasis added) (Flamsteed 2007, 48).

Perhaps the reason their models of glacier formation and depletion are not accurate is because their uniformitarian assumption requiring enormous ages for significant changes is completely out to lunch. The rapid and volatile nature of such huge climactic changes in a relatively short period of time does not fit well with their long-term evolutionary ideology.

In September 1979, the Arctic Sea ice extended 2.78 million square miles. By 2005, it had shrunk 21 percent. Scientists predicted then that the ice cap may not exist by the end of the 21st century. In September 2007, the Arctic Sea ice only reached 1.65 million square miles, a whopping decrease of 23 percent in only two years. In other words, it took seven years to shrink 21 percent and then only two years to shrink 23 percent.

Once impenetrable as shipping lanes except for ice-breakers, the Arctic has shrunk so much that ships are now able to navigate on the east side as well as the west side of the Arctic ice to completely circumnavigate it. The long-sought-after and elusive Northwest Passage is no longer a myth.

Scientists are now predicting that the ice will cease to exist year round by 2030. However, some computer models have predicted that it will disappear even earlier. The rise in ocean levels and the flooding of coastal regions may be much faster than uniformitarian scientists are able to imagine. The truth is that within the larger cycles of weather are smaller cycles so no one really knows when that critical point will come, but we must be cognizant of this radical reality of catastrophic proportions that could have global implications.

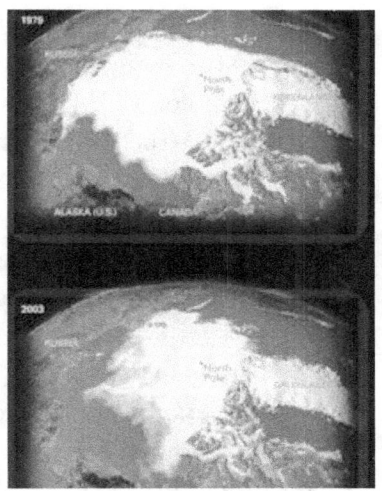

A comparison between satellite data from 1979 to 2003 shows the radical retreat of Arctic ice due to global warming. Some computer models predict the ice will be completely gone during the summer months of 2013. (http://www.jennyelainegoldstein.com/rooting-for-fruit/2009/07/13/wanted-caretaker-for-arctic-sea-ice)

Robert Corell, chairman of the Arctic Climate Impact Assessment, reported, "We have seen a massive acceleration of the speed with which these glaciers are moving into the sea. The ice is moving at 2 metres an hour on a front 5km [3 miles] long and 1,500 metres deep" (Brown 2007, 8).

According to Corell's observations flying over the Ilulissat Glacier, giant moulins (holes created by swirls of melting water) are allowing swirls of melted water to the base of the glacier. The melt water then lubricates the base of the glacier and allows it to slide over the surface of the land at an unprecedented rate, exactly how the continental hydroplates glided when they were broken apart.

The pieces of ice falling into the sea are so large that it is triggering minor earthquakes in Greenland. The speed the ice is melting is outpacing any previous predictions. However, the melting of the Arctic ice cap will not produce any appreciable rise in sea levels because it is already floating on the sea.

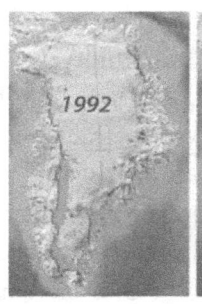

A comparison of the Greenland ice sheet from 1992 to 2002 (https://math.ucr.edu/home/baez/zoom/zoom.pdf))

Nevertheless, the melting of the polar ice cap will precipitate the speed of flow of the Greenland ice sheets since the lack of Arctic ice would offer no resistance to the path of the glaciers. If the Greenland ice sheets melt, then sea levels are predicted to rise 7 meters (23 feet).

However, rising temperatures in ocean water worldwide also cause thermal expansion and help raise ocean levels. I have lived in South Florida since 1961 and worked almost 30 years as a firefighter in Miami Beach. Never before have I seen the ocean level at high tide rise to the point that during certain moon cycles the ocean water covered Collins Avenue under several inches of water as it spilled over the walls. The sea is rising.

Our problems are not just at our northern pole. The Antarctic also provides great risk to our ocean levels if warming continues unabated. If the West Antarctic ice sheet breaks up and falls into the sea, it will add another 5 meters to the sea level for a total of 39 feet all together. Unfortunately, many scientists believe that the Antarctic ice sheet will fall before Greenland. It may well be that we have already crossed the natural threshold to prevent this catastrophic situation.

The rise of 39 feet in sea levels would bring us back to the maximum height of the sea prior to the Second Ice Age and to approximately the same point when the Atlantic conveyor belt was interrupted during the time of the Tower of Babel. That would bring us to the Third Ice Age in short order and destroy civilization in all but the equatorial regions of our planet.

Once again, giant glaciers will form, extending from both polar caps toward the equator. Life as we know it will enter a radical change with mass migrations toward the center of our planet. I suspect that this will be happening at the end of the seven-year tribulation period prophesied in Scripture to end our Second Earth. I do not have a crystal ball, nor do I claim to be a prophet. But the First Earth ended with the First Ice Age, and the Tower of Babel judgment ended with the Second Ice Age, so it thus seems to me quite like God to end the Second Earth with a Third Ice Age.

The Intensity of Hurricanes and Tornadoes – A Sign of the End of Our Age

I certainly do not relish being the bearer of bad news. In fact, I hate it. But I have no choice but to speak the truth as God has shown me. The end of the Second Earth is coming. But before this cataclysmic point, the impact of the warming trend will be felt throughout the planet as changing rainfall patterns wreak havoc.

Areas where precipitation once created fertile, arable land may receive too much rain and cause floods, which will wash away the topsoil. Meanwhile, other areas will receive too little rain and change into arid or desert land that is unsuitable for farming. We are seeing all the deserts around the world expand outward, already swallowing arable land at a steady, constant rate.

The rise in heat will power huge thunderstorms and trigger powerful Category 5 (Fujita scale) tornadoes that will negatively impact our cities and industries. Rivers will flood large sections of arable farmlands and destroy crops and homes like modern man has never experienced. Hurricanes of unbelievable intensity will rip through towns and bring further havoc to the economy.

According to James Elsner, a geographer at Florida State University, the warmer seawater has boosted the average wind speeds of powerful hurricanes from 140 miles per hour to 157 miles per hour. The catastrophic effect of that cannot be appreciated unless we account for the destructive power it represents. The power of a hurricane is doubled every 5 miles per hour that the wind increases. That means an increase of 17 miles per hour has increased the destructive power of hurricanes by exponentially doubling it more than three times from the previous average.

> The intensity of North Atlantic hurricanes and the number of Category 4 and 5 hurricanes have increased since the 1980s. These increases are due in part to warmer sea surface temperatures in the areas where Atlantic hurricanes form and pass through (Bradford).

In April 2011, we saw a marked rise in F-5 tornadoes, punctuated by a wave of destruction not equaled in the past. The Tuscaloosa, Alabama, tornado of April 27, 2011, had a funnel that was 1 mile wide, packing winds of 265 miles per hour. The monster trekked across Alabama and Georgia for a record-breaking 300 miles. The previous record was a tornado in 1925 that traveled 219 miles from Missouri through Illinois and finally broke up in Indiana, killing 747 people. In just the month of April 2011, there were more F-5 tornadoes in the United States than the yearly average, and the season was not over.

Heavy super-cell thunderstorms have produced unprecedented swarms of tornadoes numbering in the hundreds for a single event. Anyone who has listened to the weather channel can tell you that the number and intensity of cataclysmic weather-related events are rapidly increasing.

In the spring of 2011, the Mississippi and Missouri Rivers flooded like never before, causing widespread destruction of farmlands and homes. In mid-July that year, the floodwaters that devastated the Midwest had not yet retreated. Record floods were also reported in Australia and China and many other parts of the world. Our world is rapidly changing right before our eyes.

In those areas where no rain falls, the opposite effect will bring devastation to our economies. The evaporation rates will increase as a result of higher temperatures, thus reducing lakes and rivers even more. The world's freshwater supply for drinking and irrigation will become severely impacted by this trend. Water restrictions will become more commonplace until they become permanent and mandatory requirements.

Tinder-like conditions will spark wildfires that will ravage arid areas. In July 2011, Texas found itself in the most severe drought condition in recorded history. The temperatures during the first half of July hovered at more than 100 degrees for days on end. Non-irrigated crops were simply abandoned. Irrigated crops fared better but remained in danger for some time. The really big problem looming on the horizon is that the nonrenewable aquifer that provides water for that area is being drawn down to dangerous levels.

A 2013 article in the *Washington Post* discussed this phenomenon.

> Volatile weather patterns marked by shortened winters, stifling heat waves and prolonged droughts....
>
> That dangerous combination of factors helps explain the increasingly voracious wildfires that have ripped through the western United States in recent years, say scientists, lawmakers and historians.
>
> While the deaths of 19 firefighters Sunday in Arizona marked the most lethal firefighting incident in generations, the 8,400-acre blaze that led to the tragedy has become more the norm than the exception....
>
> The trend seems unlikely to change anytime soon. The Quadrennial Fire Review, a wildfire crystal ball of sorts that comes out every four years, predicted in 2009 that the effects of climate change would lead to "greater probability of longer and bigger fire seasons, in more

regions in the nation" – in particular, shorter, wetter winters coupled with warmer, drier summers (Brady and Kim 2013).

In mid-August of 2013, multiple large wildfires burned in nine states between Montana and Arizona, blanketing the entire Western Unites States. The prospects in our near future do not seem very good to prevent such catastrophic forest fires.

> By 2041, there will likely be 35 percent more of these large, catastrophic fires per decade, according to Cochrane. "That translates to four extreme fire events for every three that occur now."
>
> However, that risk is not spread evenly, Cochrane explained. Forests in the western United States, southeastern Australia, Europe and the eastern Mediterranean region that extends from Greece to Lebanon and Syria are among those areas at highest risk (South Dakota State University 2017).

Droughts and famines are in the near horizon for planet Earth before the end of this century. The rising seas will add insult to injury as many of the coastal cities will be completely inundated, causing mass migration to higher land even before the catastrophic interruption of the ocean conveyor belt sends us into the Third Ice Age.

We can already see the rapid growth of the Sahara Desert building speed as the ocean temperatures rise and the rainfall patterns change in Africa. South of the Sahara, the region that borders the forests below and span the entire breadth of Africa, is called the Sahel. In the northern region of the Sahel, the average yearly rainfall is a paltry 6 inches. Sometimes the rain falls but never hits the sand since it evaporates in the hot air before reaching the ground. On the other hand, in the southern region, the yearly rainfall may be as much as 35 inches.

Each year the rains fall farther and farther south, and the Sahel is shifting southward as the Sahara, like a growing cancer tumor, continues to engulf more and more of Africa. In the northern Sahel, desert dunes no longer anchored by vegetation are swallowing villages whole. Precipitation continues to become spottier, and the precariousness of human lives in these areas is becoming a serious future problem. Curiously, it seems as though the areas conquered by the Muslims are the ones becoming engulfed by deserts.

The world, hypnotized by the evolutionary gradualist paradigm, does not seem to grasp the urgency of the cataclysm that looms in the near horizon. If we do not take our uniformitarian blinders off, we will not be able to see that famine is coming, and it is coming in a big way in Africa within the next few decades.

The Fourth Insurrection

Every demonic insurrection in the past has resulted in God's judgment. The First Insurrection in the Garden at Eden caused us to be barred from the tree of life so wickedness could not become eternal. Our expulsion from the Garden left us in a diminished Earth. This First Earth ended with the judgment for the Second Insurrection. The Great Deluge washed away our world and resulted in the First Ice Age. The Third Insurrection brought forth the judgment of the Tower of Babel, and the people were dispersed and the languages confused. It left us in the Second Ice Age.

The Fourth Insurrection shall cause us to lose the Second Earth since it will be destroyed by a global earthquake of unprecedented proportions and catastrophic tectonic movements that will change the contours of our continents once again. I suspect the continents will come together at the coming of the true ruler of our Earth, the Prince of Peace. It will leave us in the Third Ice Age.

The prophet Daniel foretold this Fourth Insurrection. A prince from the north shall make a peace covenant for seven years, but in the middle of those seven years, he shall come to destroy God's people and declare himself the god of this world. He will step into the Holy of Holies, the inner sanctum of the Temple of God in Jerusalem, and usurp the throne of the Messiah.

> *And he will make a firm covenant with the many for one week, but in the middle of the week he will put a stop to sacrifice and grain offering; and on the wing of abominations will come one who makes desolate, even until a complete destruction, one that is decreed, is poured out on the one who makes desolate.*
> —Dan. 9:27

Just prior to that, Lucifer will release from the Great Abyss the demons chained for their part in the Second Insurrection so they may join his minions in attacking the throne of God in heaven.

> *Then the fifth angel sounded, and I saw a star from heaven which had fallen to the earth; and the key of the bottomless pit was given to him. He opened the bottomless pit, and smoke went up out of the pit, like the smoke of a great furnace; and the sun and the air were darkened by the smoke of the pit. Then out of the smoke came locusts upon the earth, and power was given them, as the scorpions of the earth have power. They were told not to hurt the grass of the earth, nor any green thing, nor any tree, but only the men who do not have the seal of God on their foreheads. And they were not permitted to kill anyone, but to torment for five months; and their torment was like the torment of the scorpion when it stings a man....*
> *They have tails like scorpions, and stings; and in their tail is their power to hurt men for five months. They have as king over them, the angel of the abyss; his name in Hebrew is Abaddon, and in the Greek he has the name Apollyon.*
> —Rev. 9:1–5, 10–11

This release of the angels who had been judged for their crimes in the Second Insurrection shall come just prior to the middle of that week of years. Their leader is called Abaddon (Hebrew) or Apollyon (Greek), which means the Destroyer. That demon will most likely be Azazel, the war god who taught man the art of war, or perhaps Shemihaza, the dark watcher who taught man the art of sorcery.

Lucifer, having regained full power of his fallen angels, will attack the temple of God in heaven. The great red dragon who deceived the angels and instigated the rebellion that led a third of the hosts of heaven to side with him will make his final move to gain the throne of God. But the Great Usurper shall fail.

> *Then another sign appeared in heaven: and behold, a great red dragon having seven heads and ten horns, and on his heads were seven diadems. And his tail swept away a third of the stars of heaven and threw them to the earth. . . .*
>
> *And there was war in heaven, Michael and his angels waging war with the dragon. The dragon and his angels waged war, and they were not strong enough, and there was no longer a place found for them in heaven. And the great dragon was thrown down, the serpent of old who is called the devil and Satan, who deceives the whole world; he was thrown down to the earth, and his angels were thrown down with him.*
>
> —Rev. 12:3, 4, 7–9

The occult motto "as above as it is below" will carry deep significance. It is at this exact time that the Antichrist will attack the Temple of God in Jerusalem and step into the Holy of Holies to claim that he is the god of this world. But from that moment forward, he will have only three and a half years (42 months) to reign, for at the end of the week of years, the Messiah shall return to end the wrong. For the next three and a half years, the Earth shall suffer the seven vials of judgment that shall end in the complete atonement of our Second Earth.

> *There was given to him a mouth speaking arrogant words and blasphemies, and authority to act for forty-two months was given him. And he opened his mouth in blasphemies against God, to blaspheme His name and His tabernacle, that is, those who dwell in heaven.*
>
> *It was also given to him to make war with the saints and to overcome them, and authority over every tribe and people and tongue and nation was given to him. All who dwell on the earth will worship him, everyone whose name has not been written from the foundation of the world in the book of life of the Lamb who has been slain.*
>
> —Rev. 13:5–8

That is the Fourth Insurrection. It shall bring forth another intervention by our Holy God. This is the time of the seventh trumpet of judgment that contains seven bowls of wrath. For the next three and a half years, God's wrath will be poured upon the Earth to atone for the sins of mankind. The final judgment, the seventh bowl, shall end the Indignation on the 42nd month of the date of the abomination that caused desolation. It is the time of Yom Kippur. The seventh bowl shall signal the end of the Second Earth.

> *Then the seventh angel poured out his bowl upon the air, and a loud voice came out of the temple from the throne, saying, "It is done." And there were flashes of lightning and sounds and peals of thunder; and there was a great earthquake, such as there had not been since man came to be upon the earth, so great an earthquake was it, and so mighty. The great city was split into three parts, and the cities of the nations fell. Babylon the great was remembered before God, to give her the cup of the wine of His fierce wrath. And every island fled away, and the mountains were not found. And huge hailstones, about one hundred*

> *pounds each, came down from heaven upon men; and men blasphemed God because of the plague of the hail, because the plague was extremely severe.*
>
> —Rev. 16:17–21

In that day, mankind shall gather their armies together at a place called Armageddon to make war with the Prince of Peace. There the end shall come for the rebellion. There the Indignation shall be judged. There shall the dragon be chained and sent into the Great Abyss by Michael the archangel. The end of the Second Earth shall come with a global earthquake so powerful that every building in every city of the world will be reduced to rubble. The islands will disappear under the seas. The mountains shall crumble to the ground. The valleys shall be raised. And Jerusalem shall be lifted up literally through isostatic motion.

The devastation shall be utterly horrific. All the continental plates shall shift violently at the roar of the Lion of Judah. There shall the Second Earth die underneath a global hailstorm of such fury that the destruction of the works of man shall be utterly complete. David saw this day and wrote of it in Psalm 18. Although some of that prophetic message had to do with David's deliverance from Saul, some of it was meant for the future situation in which Israel shall find herself in the same dilemma with the Antichrist surrounding her while she is safe beneath the Eagle's wings.

> *In my distress I called to the* Lord;
>   *I cried to my God for help.*
> *From his temple he heard my voice;*
>   *my cry came before him, into his ears.*
> *The earth trembled and quaked,*
>   *and the foundations of the mountains shook;*
>   *they trembled because he was angry.*
> *Smoke rose from his nostrils;*

> *consuming fire came from his mouth,*
> *burning coals blazed out of it.*
> *He parted the heavens and came down;*
> *dark clouds were under his feet.*
> *He mounted the cherubim and flew;*
> *he soared on the wings of the wind.*
> *He made darkness his covering, his canopy around him—*
> *the dark rain clouds of the sky.*
> *Out of the brightness of his presence clouds advanced,*
> *with hailstones and bolts of lightning.*
> *The LORD thundered from heaven;*
> *the voice of the Most High resounded.*
> *He shot his arrows and scattered the enemy,*
> *with great bolts of lightning he routed them.*
> *The valleys of the sea were exposed*
> *and the foundations of the earth laid bare*
> *at your rebuke, LORD,*
> *at the blast of breath from your nostrils.*
>
> He reached down from on high and took hold of me;
> he drew me out of deep waters.
> He rescued me from my powerful enemy,
> from my foes, who were too strong for me (emphasis added).
> —Ps. 18:6–17 NIV

In that day, David's prophecy shall come true, and those hiding beneath the Eagle's wings shall be protected miraculously from the Enemy of Man.

> *My soul is satisfied as with marrow and fatness,*
> *And my mouth offers praises with joyful lips.*
>
> *When I remember You on my bed,*
> *I meditate on You in the night watches,*

> *For You have been my help,*
> *And in the shadow of Your wings I sing for joy.*
> *My soul clings to You;*
> *Your right hand upholds me* (emphasis added).
> —Ps. 63:5–8

The sections of these psalms that are emphasized are prophetic of the return of the Messiah and the destruction of the Gentile nations. They are a description of global tectonic upheaval and the complete destruction of our Second Earth. But God's chosen shall be kept safe underneath the Eagle's wings. He shall rescue them from the ark of the Second Earth to begin the Third Earth. Zechariah speaks of this isostatic elevation of Jerusalem into a wide and high plain where the climate shall no longer be a desert wilderness and where she will never have to fear for her safety.

> *And the* LORD *will be king over all the earth; in that day the* LORD *will be* the only one, *and His name* the only one.
> *All the land will be changed into a plain from Geba to Rimmon south of Jerusalem; but Jerusalem will rise and remain on its site from Benjamin's Gate as far as the place of the First Gate to the Corner Gate, and from the Tower of Hananel to the king's wine presses. People will live in it, and there will no longer be a curse, for Jerusalem will dwell in security.*
> —Zech. 14:9–11

I believe that at this point, the movement of the continents shall end the thermohaline conveyor belt, and the Third Ice Age will begin with a global hailstorm of unimaginable power. Imagine hailstones weighing 100 pounds each. Cars will be crushed. No roof will be able to deflect such monstrous missiles from on high. That will signify the beginning of the Third Ice Age and the death of the Second Earth. Our Earth will change with such speed that most of us will be utterly amazed. It has already happened in the past. It will happen once again.

CHAPTER 12

THE HISTORICAL EVIDENCE — A COMPARISON OF THE GREAT FLOOD ACCOUNTS, THE CREATION STORIES, AND THE DIVISION OF LANGUAGES WORLDWIDE

The voice of the LORD is over the waters;
  the God of glory thunders,
The LORD thunders over the mighty waters.
The voice of the LORD is powerful;
  the voice of the LORD is majestic.
The voice of the LORD breaks the cedars ...
The LORD sits enthroned over the flood;
  the LORD is enthroned as King forever.
—Ps. 29:3–5, 10

Argument 7 – The ancient chronicles regarding a global flood are nothing more than embellished local flood accounts

The naturalist claims that the story of a global flood is simply an embellished mythology of local floods. We have already provided the empirical geological data that evidences a Global Flood, but now we will also document the universal themes found in all the ancient traditions that claim it was, in fact, a global catastrophe.

We have in our human history many examples of ancient stories of local floods. They were not embellished to claim that the flood was global. Why, then, do we insist that ancient man universally decided to lie and change the story of a local flood into a global flood? For what purpose? For what gain? Would any man caught in a local flood seek to also save all the animals in his region? Why, then, include this almost incredulous feature in an embellished form of a local flood? How can this story be a universal tradition expressed by every major culture? How can the specifics be so similar if they were independently derived from the minds of various cultures separated by mountains, oceans, and deserts?

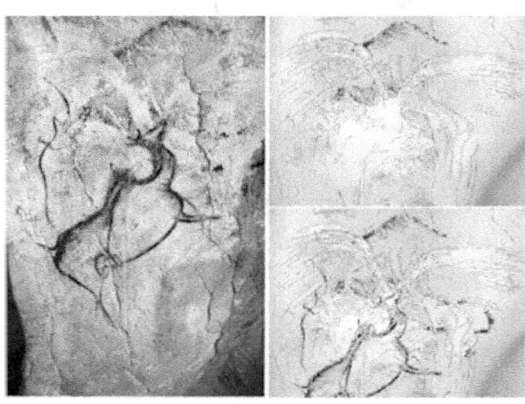

Neolithic cave paintings in Chauvet may depict the breaking of the fountains of the deep. These cave painters had red pigment available to them and used it often. Why are these eruptions not painted red if they were, in fact, volcanic? If you look at the cracks on either side of both fountain paintings, it seems rather to show a cracking of the Earth and a release of a fountain of water. The deer's horns are painted as if the deer were coming from the sky and rupturing the crust of the Earth with its horns, which causes the fountains of the deep to spring forth water.

If it had been a volcano, red ochre would have lit up the spray in red. Instead, what we find in Chauvet are several paintings depicting something almost like a meteor shower striking at the same time, and the funnels of the ejection do not spring from mountaintops but from flat ground.

One would expect a volcanic eruption to be pictured from the cone of the volcano. Yet we see multiple white mushroom clouds like a multiple meteor strike would create instead of a wind-driven plume like a volcano that would swerve toward the direction of the prevailing wind. Of course, evolutionary-biased individuals would not in a million years consider that this may be the recording of the tragedy that brought forth the Global Flood.

The answers will become obvious to the reader since a comparison of the accounts shows such universal consistency that it cannot be summarily dismissed as sheer coincidence. In fact, there is a curious cave painting by the inhabitants of the First Earth, which archaeologists call the Neolithic Age, that may depict the breaking of the fountains of the deep.

It is important to note that Neolithic artists used red ochre as a tint. These spouting fountains are not volcanic eruptions colored in red but eruptions colored in white that may be depicting the breaking of the fountains of the deep and the drowning of the animals.

A Comparison of the Great Flood Accounts

Obviously, an exhaustive list of the worldwide flood accounts would fill an entire encyclopedia. But for the purposes of this work, I will recount a smattering of the Global Flood mythologies throughout the major cultures of the world and leave the readers to come to their own conclusions as to the historicity of the biblical claim.

The reader should consider these ancient descriptions of the global cataclysm in light of the volcanic and tectonic forces that were at play after the meteors struck our planet. The evidence found in these ancient accounts brings credibility to the historicity of this multifaceted cataclysm involving earthquakes, fires, volcanic eruptions, tsunamis, and major hurricanes. The arrogance of evolutionists to think of our ancestors as dimwitted idiots lacking in intellectual prowess to accurately record historical events is beyond measure. Their descriptions may be phrased in terminology they can understand due to the sophistication in technology and scientific understanding of our universe, but their accounts are no less accurate if we take these things into account.

For example, the Greek account clearly shows that the oceans were completely perturbed. It also shows that there were volcanic upheavals and terrible earthquakes during this flood.

> Harshly then he thundered, and heavily and terribly the earth re-echoed around; and the broad heaven above, and the sea and streams of ocean, and the abysses of earth. But beneath his immortal feet *vast Olympus trembled*, as the king uprose and earth groaned beneath. And the *heat from both caught the dark-colored sea*, both of the thunder and the lightning, and *fire from the monster*, the heat arising from the thunder-storms, *winds*, and burning lightning. And all earth, and heaven, and sea, were boiling (Hesiod).

In the eighth century BC, Hesiod, a Greek poet, wrote of a legend where a serpent-like creature that is able to fly causes complete havoc upon the Earth. If we understand the symbolism of the flying serpent as it is uniformly interpreted in all cultures, then we can understand what is responsible for this catastrophe.

Comets have a luminous tail that to ancient man would seem like a flying serpent of fire. Asteroids also create a vapor trail as they enter our atmosphere that can be seen as the tail of a serpent in the eyes of ancient men. The ancient writings universally described asteroids and comets in such terms. The Egyptians speak of flying serpents of fire. That is also attested by the Australian aborigines. The cosmic serpent Yurlunggur, which curiously is also associated with the rainbow, is held responsible for the deluge as we shall later see in their Flood account. How else could ancient man describe such wonders?

The catastrophe that a striking comet or asteroid could bring upon our planet would be described in much the same way as the Greeks described the cause of the Great Flood. The word used for *disaster* comes from two words, "dis," which means evil, and "aster," which means star. For this reason, comets and asteroids have universally been portents of evil stars throughout human history. It is part of the ancient memory passed down by the survivors of the death of the First Earth.

Hesiod's account of this legend depicts a volcanic upheaval of enormous magnitude and a flood whose ocean waters were heated and extremely agitated. It speaks of thunders that echo throughout the Earth. Could these be the sonic booms created by the ejecta and the meteor strikes? He speaks of the Earth groaning. This no doubt is an allusion to earthquakes. Hesiod speaks of streams in the ocean in the abyss of the Earth, and that is exactly how a wall of water rising from the abyss of the Earth would be described.

Hesiod speaks of the oceans being dark. That is what we would expect with the hydraulics of the Global Flood stirring the sediments below and eroding the sides of the continents through the jetting fountains of the deep as well as the ejecta from the meteor strikes and the volcanic ash. He speaks of fire, lightning, and thunderstorms with horrendous hot winds. He speaks of the boiling oceans. This is no doubt speaking of the action of volcanoes in the watery expanse of the Great Flood and perhaps even the agitation created by the very fountains of the deep when exiting the subterranean chambers.

The fiery, flying serpent who struck the Earth brought disaster to our planet, and all mankind perished but Deucalion (Noah) and his wife, Pyrrha, the red-haired daughter of Pandora, earlier known as Eve. I will speak later about this as I cover the Flood accounts in Europe.

Let us begin with the ancient accounts from the Middle East. They would be the most accurate since they were the closest civilization geographically and chronographically to the actual disembarking of Noah's family on Mount Ararat in Turkey.

1. The Sumerian, Babylonian, and Assyrian Accounts of the Great Flood

a. The Sumerian Account of the Flood

Perhaps the oldest civilization of the Second Earth is the Sumerian civilization. The Sumerian language is the only language not related to any other language in the world. It was known as Emku, which means "the language of the people." Evolutionary historians are perplexed to find a culture that developed without any interconnection with another, as if it had landed from outer space. The language not only had no precursor but it also had no succeeding language that evolved from it. It stands alone as an island language in the history of mankind.

> The Sumerian people themselves remain something of a mystery. Their own name for themselves was "the Black-Headed People." Their language was unrelated to any other known language, so their origins will probably never be known (Haywood 2012, 15).

The mystery is no mystery. The Sumerians were the survivors of the Great Flood and began the recolonization of our Second Earth in the Valley of Shinar. The earliest extant documents are mostly administrative or economical in nature and date back to the third millennium BC. An analysis of these signs that form their language shows clearly that they are mostly abstract. That means they had by that time lost their original pictographic form.

It can be thus concluded that they do not represent the original writing form and that there had been a long history of development of the language prior to that time. Hebrew tradition tells us that it was Enoch, the seventh generation from Adam in the First Earth, who became the first scribe. Writing, therefore, probably existed for many years prior to the Sumerian colonization of the Second Earth after the Great Flood.

Because there is not a single language that evolved from Sumerian, it is my opinion that it was the language of the First Earth that later changed during the judgment of the Tower of Babel into the varied dialects that broke up the people into nations. Therefore, it is almost certain that the Sumerian civilization was the initial civilization founded by the survivors of the Great Flood. For this reason, I am inclined to think that Ziusudra may have been Noah's real name in the language of the First Earth, the language of Adam, Seth, and Enoch.

Although the oldest record of written language currently comes from Egypt, it is clear that the Sumerian written language existed long before the writing of the tablets we have been fortunate to find. Sumer in Akkadian (Assyrian and Babylonian) is called Shumeru. It is from this word that we get the English word Sumer. But in Sumerian, it is known as Kienger.

When Noah disembarked with his children, they settled in the land of the Valley of Shinar. The ice caps at that time were at their maximum glacial extent. The land of Shinar was a far, green country filled with trees and pasturelands and had moderate temperatures. Several cities sprang up quickly as they prospered in the far green land. The city of Uruk with a population of tens of thousands became the world's largest city in the Second Earth. It was there that the worship of An represented by the symbol of the Sun (Uru) began to be corrupted into the Religion of the Serpent.

By the latter part of the Sumerian decline, the Sumerians were worshiping Inanna, a Mother Goddess. Humanity had once again slipped into the occult. The rapid deglaciation dramatically raised global temperatures. The area now had little rainfall and was becoming a desert wasteland except for the sections irrigated by the Tigris and Euphrates Rivers. The seas had risen, and at the end of that meteorological cycle between the end of the First Ice Age and the beginning of the Second Ice Age, practically all of Shinar was under salt water from the incursion of the rising seas. It was at this point that the judgment on the Tower of Babel was pronounced and the languages were divided, leaving Sumerian as a fossil language. It was miraculously kept alive by some Babylonian Semitic scribes who wanted to preserve for posterity the memory of the decline and judgment of mankind.

Fortunately for us, we found some of their written records on clay tablets. The Sumerian account of the Noahic Deluge was found in Nippur. In that account, five cities of the First Earth are named. This was the order in which they were established: Eridu, Bad-Tibira, Larak, Sippar, and Shuruppak. Zi-ud-sura (Noah) was a man from Shuruppak of the First Earth, a city founded by his father. It was from this city that Flavius Josephus tells us Noah fled for fear that his family would be killed by the corrupted Nephilim who now controlled the city.

For that reason, after the establishment of the new colony in the Second Earth, some cities were named after those who had disappeared under the Deluge. The city of Shuruppak in ancient Babylonia is therefore not the same as the city mentioned in the Sumerian account that existed prior to the Great Flood.

What is extremely important is that in the first Sumerian account, we find all the major elements that are in common with the Hebrew and Babylonian accounts. However, the reader must understand that by the time this account was written, several thousand years had passed from the time of the Great Flood, and the nations had once again become embroiled in polytheism and the occult. Hence, the Deluge accounts were, in effect, marred by esoteric and occult interpositions made by later scribes. Only the Hebrew account is free from such interpositions because it was divinely inspired.

> While the tablet itself dates only to about the time of Hammurabi, the story it relates is unquestionably older.
>
> This tablet contains six columns of writing. . . . The preserved portions of the first two columns contain a brief account of the creation and of the founding of five prediluvian cities of Babylonia. The remainder of the composition deals with the story of the deluge, to which the first two episodes are probably introductory (Heidel 1963, 102).

Hence, the Noah in the Sumerian account is named Zi-ud-sura, which means "found long life." That name was renowned in the entire ancient world. It is found in many other works of ancient literature, including "The Death of Gilgamesh," "The Poem of Early Rulers," and "The Instructions of Shuruppak." It is obvious that ancient men from many nations knew Zi-ud-sura as an actual person and not some mythological character in lore. Gilgamesh apparently was involved with the dispersion of settlements as had been instructed by God after the Global Flood. It reads in part:

> ...... having travelled all the roads that there are, having fetched ...... from its ......, having killed ......, you set up ...... for future days .... Having founded ......, you reached .... Having brought down the old ...... forgotten forever and ......, he (?) carried out correctly .... the flood ...... the settlements of the Land (*Gilgamesh* Part D, lines 1–11).

We can see in "The Poem of Early Rulers" perhaps a mention of the Nephilim who had been overthrown, as well as a mention of veneration for Zi-ud-sura (their Noah). *The antiquity of this tablet is testified by several comparisons of this composition that were found at later dates, including from Emar and Ugarit dating to about the 13th century BC.*

> ......is not made .... those men were overthrown. ....
> the king? He reigned 36,000 years! .... the king, the one
> who ascended to heaven? ...... he who, like Zi-ud-sura, tried
> to find life? ("The Poem of Early Rulers" lines 1–16).

Obviously, nobody reigned 36,000 years, but our knowledge of Sumerian language is quite fractured, and I doubt this was the number intended by the writer. But the point being made here is that the writer understood who their Noah was, and more importantly that his goal in life was to preserve life to begin the Second Earth. "The Instructions of Shuruppak" may have preserved for us the Sumerian names of some of the patriarchs named in the Tanakh.

> In those days, in those far remote days, in those nights, in those faraway nights, in those years, in those far remote years, at that time the wise one who knew how to speak in elaborate words lived in the Land; Curuppag, the wise one, who knew how to speak with elaborate words lived in the Land. Curuppag gave instructions to his son; Curuppag, the son of Ubara-Tutu gave instructions to his son Zi-ud-sura: My son, let me give you instructions: you should pay attention! Zi-ud-sura, let me speak a word to you: you should pay attention! Do not neglect my instructions! Do not transgress the words I speak! The instructions of an old man are precious; you should comply with them! ("The Instructions of Shuruppak" lines 1–13).

The one called "the wise one, who knew how to speak with elaborate words" was the father of Zi-ud-sura (Noah). Therefore, the father of Noah who is called in Sumerian Curuppag is Lamech, the son of Ubara-Tutu, who in the Hebrew language is known as Methuselah. These are no mythological stories. These are records of actual human beings, and the names of their family members written in the ancient Sumerian language of the First Earth are evidence of the historicity of the Genesis record. It is almost certain that the ancient city of Shruppak was named after Noah's father, whose name in Sumerian is Curuppag.

The similarities among the Sumerian accounts of the Great Deluge and the Hebrew account are quite striking and show that this was undisputed and common knowledge to ancient man. Only the arrogance of modern man could suggest that these accounts were fabrications of man's fantasy or the embellishment of a river flood.

It is imperative that we pay attention to the Sumerian descriptions of the forces of the windstorm as well as the hydraulics involved in this cataclysm. The ark did not gently float in a sedentary sea as some might have mistakenly surmised or as it would have been stated if this were a mythological lore not based on a true event.

The forces at work in a catastrophic upheaval, as we have proposed from the striking meteors, are of such a nature that mega-hurricanes, tidal waves, tsunamis, and earthquakes would by necessity be associated with it. Hurricane-force winds and rushing walls of water devastating all in its path would have obliterated the cities and most manmade structures, leaving little behind that would be recognizable. The Sumerian narrative is true to form and displays the nature of the catastrophe that fell upon the First Earth, as stipulated in our Judeo-Christian model.

It is exactly such a catastrophic global storm that is described by the ancient Sumerians. They describe not one windstorm but all the mighty windstorms on the Earth coming together.

> All the mighty windstorms blew together;
> at the same time the rainflood swept over the ...
> When for seven days (and) seven nights
> The rainflood had swept over the land
> (And) the windstorm had driven the giant boat about on
> the mighty waters (*Gilgamesh* Column V, lines 1–5).

Worthy of mentioning is the fact that another fragment found in Nippur corroborates the biblical account in that it mentions the fountains of the deep as well as the rain from above as the two main sources for the global inundation. It also mentions that the rain stopped before the fountains of the deep, as declared in the biblical account. These commonalities can hardly be considered accidental by rational minds. They accurately describe the very mechanisms we have proposed as the physical causes that triggered the Global Flood.

> Above Adad made scarce his rain
> Below (the fountains) were stopped so that the flood could not rise at the source (*Gilgamesh* Fragment IV, lines 29–30).

The Sumerian account, which is arguably the oldest account, contains the fact that the Flood did not begin to subside until the fountains of the deep were stopped. That is no mere coincidence. They were stopped on the 17th day of the month of Nisan, exactly five months after they had been uncorked. So the world would know that judgment came from God, it came on the fifth month because five is the number of Satan, and in this record, God showed His sovereignty over the demonic hierarchy.

Also, in the Sumerian account after Zi-ud-sura disembarks, he offers a sacrifice to God who smells the sweet savor of the sacrifice and blesses him for his faithfulness. That is also reflected both in the Babylonian account and the Hebrew account. It is further recorded in the Sumerian tablets that Zi-ud-sura is granted eternal life and sent to Dilmun. The Hebrew name for Eden is Tilmun. In essence, what the tablets reveal is that when Zi-ud-sura died, he went to paradise in what the New Testament refers to as Abraham's bosom.

In the Sumerian culture, An was the Great Creator and ruler of the universe. He was sometimes called En-Ki, which means Lord of the planet, or Earth. The name of our firstfather in Sumerian is Adamu, or sometimes Adapa. It is interesting that they also had a deity named Nin-ti, which means the "lady of the rib." Sound familiar? As in all cultures, the various names for the one true God eventually devolved into polytheism.

We find in the later Akkadian (Assyrian, Babylonian) and Persian accounts a very similar story that contains all the same major elements of the Hebrew account in Genesis. In the Assyrian account, the Noah figure is called Atrahasis, which means "extremely wise." God also warned Atrahasis that a flood will come to wipe out humanity and gave explicit instructions on how to build the ark. Again, all the major elements of the story are included in these accounts.

Some evolutionists have insinuated that this is an embellishment of a river flood, but the text mentions Apsu the ocean, and Atrahasis is required to roof the ark as a ship that needs to contend with an angry ocean and to cover it with pitch to waterproof it. A local river flood would hardly have required a completely enclosed ark. "Roof it like the Apsu" (*Atrahasis* Table III, line 29). The same line is repeated word for word in *The Epic of Gilgamesh* (*Gilgamesh* Tablet XI, line 31). It is hard to reconcile the saving of animals and the total destruction of all mankind with a river flood.

The darkness created by the ash and storm clouds was so complete that the epic claims one person could not see another (*Atrahasis* Tablet III, line 13). That exact wording is used in *The Epic of Gilgamesh* (Tablet XI, line 111). Such a description could not have been invented by the imagination of sheer storytellers independent of one another. In fact, the reason for the Flood was declared as the destruction of the occult centers that had led mankind away from God. "By our... a flood [will sweep] over the cult-centers; To destroy the seed of mankind..." "All the windstorms, exceedingly powerful, attacked as one, At the same time, the flood sweeps over the cult-centers" (*The Eridu Genesis*).

Obviously, God was wroth with mankind for following the religion of the Serpent and the Mother Goddesses of the Nephilim and destroyed the First Earth. We see here a parallel with God's word that he would wipe out all of mankind. No local river flood could accomplish that. No local river flood would require a ship built in such a fashion. And no river flood would require either the saving of the animals or the black rain associated with the Great Flood.

The Sumerian knew God as An. In Akkadian, He is known as Ea. In Hebrew, He is known as El. The pronunciation for the name of Noah and God may be different because the languages were divided, but the description of the one true God is always the same.

It was the Sumerian civilization who turned back to the religion of the Serpent and built the Tower of Babel. Some historians have blamed the downfall of the Sumerian culture on the loss of fertility in their soil due to salt deposits. Their explanation for that is only partially true.

> There was a price to pay for Sumeria's precocious development, however. Salts left behind in the poorly drained soils when irrigation water evaporated under the hot sun gradually damaged their fertility, reducing crop yields and sending the Sumerian cities into decline (Haywood 2012, iv).

The author is correct to point out that salt incursion sent their civilization into decline. But it had nothing to do with canals from the Euphrates River. It was the rising seas that engulfed the Valley of Shinar that did the real damage of bringing salt into their land. The melting polar caps precipitated the rising oceans and then the Second Ice Age, which subsequently helped disperse the nations when God confounded their languages.

b. The Babylonian Account of the Flood

In the *Epic of Gilgamesh* that we touched on earlier, Utnapishtim (Noah) retells the story and describes the events that transpired just prior to the first rain. The name Utnapishtim means "the Far Away." This may be speaking of the fact that Noah apparently moved far away from his sons, perhaps even to China as the Chinese contend, or that when he died he went to the faraway land of Paradise.

According to the Babylonian account, the skies darkened to such an extent that there was almost no light during the day. Visibility was greatly reduced to the point where one could not see another person next to them. That is also peculiarly what happens when the ejecta of meteors is thrust into the atmosphere and the ejected material eroding from the sides of the continents by the ferocious fountains of the deep are also thrust into the stratosphere or when volcanism has created enormous clouds of tephra.

Huge amounts of sediment as well as latent moisture are shot into the upper atmosphere and held aloft by the wind cycles generated by the rapidly rising waters of the gushing fountains. We can see the effect of large amounts of moisture in the darkness of cumulus nimbus clouds. But even more graphic is the darkness created by volcanic eruptions that spew volcanic ash into the sky in perhaps thousands of billowing columns. The combination of these things would have brought upon our world a deep darkness in the noon of day. No common river flood can account for any of these facts recorded by our ancestors. For evolutionists to dogmatically claim that this is describing a local river flood is ridiculous, to say the least.

This effect is especially magnified by the ejections of super-volcanoes. It was the mechanism of the Great Flood that created the super-volcanoes we have today. Due to the friction of the sliding hydroplates, the melting rock formed under the great pressure of the continents grinding over the basaltic floor would rise through fissures and sometimes create lava domes in stretched and weakened areas of the surface of the continents that might have been stretched too thin by their initial lateral movement. When these domes bulged too far—that is, when their internal pressure became too great—they burst through the thin crust above them as super-volcanoes.

The Yellowstone Caldera alone burst three times as the North American continent trekked westward. Each of these erupting super-volcanoes is a powerful force that can produce global consequences of unimaginable force. The gargantuan tons of tephra thrust into the atmosphere by the 21 super-volcanoes we presently have on our Earth have the potential to block all light completely and cause a runaway snowball Earth by blocking all the sunlight from its surface.

Our Sun's rays would have been completely shut out from the surface of the Earth by the opaque clouds of particulate matter that these super-volcanoes thrust into the atmosphere. Even in the more subdued, singular eruptions of normal volcanoes such as we have experienced in our modern day, the aftermath can cause it to be pitch dark at midday in local areas. But during the Great Flood, the darkness was global as recorded by civilizations all over the planet.

This phenomenon was observed just recently on the island of Montserrat and also at Mount St. Helens in Seattle, Washington, as news crews recorded people driving with their headlights on in the dark at midday. To little avail, drivers desperately used their cars' windshield wipers to clear the accumulating tephra from their windshield as the ash reached depths of 3 feet even in nearby states.

The historical evidence from ancient records for the breaking of the crust of the Earth into seven continents during the cataclysm of the Great Flood is quite persuasive. There is a phrase used in the description of the event recorded in the Babylonian tablets that corroborates the breaking up of the crust of the Earth at that particular junction in time with incredible exactitude. "The land he broke like a pot" (*Gilgamesh* Tablet XI, line 107).

I would dare any evolutionist to explain how water from a river flood could break the land like a pot. The use of this terminology seems quite suggestive that the ancients knew that the crust of the Earth had been fractured "like a pot" into shards. The single supercontinent they knew in the First Earth broke up into seven shards, or seven continents. This is the observed reality in their eyes. The analogy of a broken pot is therefore quite descriptive and uncannily accurate.

In the following verses of Tablet XI of *The Epic of Gilgamesh*, it is also clear that the land had become completely darkened and that all men were covered with clay. The clay may well be the combination of ejecta, tephra, and the mud produced by the swirling waters of the Flood. Such a description lends credence to the historicity of this global event.

It is further documented here that the Babylonians believed this Great Flood destroyed "all mankind." This was not a local flood as the naturalists slyly try to imply. It was not a local river flood but rather an oceanic global flood.

> The raging of Adad reached unto heaven
> *[and] turned into darkness all that was light.*
> *The land he broke like a pot*
> No man could see his fellow.
> The people could not be recognized from heaven.
> In truth, the olden time has turned to clay.
> And *all mankind* had turned to clay (emphasis added).
> (*Gilgamesh* Tablet XI, lines 105–107, 111–12, 118, 133).

According to the ancient Babylonians, this cataclysm was a distinct break in the history for all humanity. "In truth, the olden time has turned to clay. And *all mankind* had turned to clay." The sight of the countless corpses covered with mud and volcanic ash floating in the water must have been horrific. That description is a historical description of the aftermath of the Global Deluge.

This same memory is probably the origin of the Mayan myth that the creation of man was of clay and wood. Anyone who has witnessed the aftermath of a flood can attest to this claim. It seems like all that is left as the flood subsides are mud and broken pieces of wood. Trees are uprooted, and huge trunks are snapped like twigs from the sheer force of the swirling hydraulics. Huge boulders are pushed along, crushing everything in their path. Everything is covered in a layer of mud.

The Babylonian flood account has survived in several tablets. Some are considered 5,000 years old. All of them have the same recognizable story with the Noah figure known variously in the Babylonian, Assyrian, and Persian accounts as Utnapishtim, Zi-ud-sura, Xisuthros, or Atrahasis in their particular dialect. Here are the common points:

1. In each case, an angered God warns the Noah figure that a worldwide flood would occur to judge the rebellious inhabitants of the world.
2. He is instructed to build a ship to save himself and his family, as well as a pair of all the animals.
3. The flood then destroys all mankind.
4. The aftermath is filled with mud and darkness.
5. The Noah figure sends out birds to determine if the land has dried.
6. The Noah figure lands on a mountain and disembarks.
7. He then makes a sacrifice to God, which God found pleasing, and is blessed by Him for his faithfulness.

The Babylonian *Epic of Gilgamesh* was found in the ancient city of Nineveh in the ruins of the Temple Library of Nabu (the biblical Nebo). It was actually found in the palace library of the old Assyrian King Ashurbanipal (seventh century BC).

> The date of the composition of the Gilgamesh Epic can therefore be fixed at about 2,000 B.C. But the material combined on the tablets is undoubtedly much older, as we can infer from the mere fact that the epic consists of numerous originally independent episodes, which, of course did not spring into existence at the time of the

composition of our poem but must have been current long before they were compiled and woven together to form our epic (Heidel 1963, 15).

Apparently, this Gilgamesh, who is the central figure of the poem, was a verifiable person listed in the Sumerian list as a king who ruled in the First Dynasty of Uruk. Roman author Claudius Aelianus who lived during the second century AD corroborates the very existence of Gilgamesh some 1,600 years before the tablets were discovered in Ashurbanipal's library. This is no mythical invention of human minds. These are real people who lived in our Second Earth and carried with them the memory of Noah's Flood.

Undoubtedly, there is a great deal of exaggeration involved in the retelling of the story through the passage of time. Many of the exploits have obviously been embellished, but nevertheless, there is within the story an actual historical basis from which it sprang.

It is the same historical basis from which the Sumerian, Assyrian, and Persian accounts were derived. One might argue that these civilizations were centered in the Middle East and would have therefore been subject to influence from one another. But what about all the other cultures in the world that were not in contact with the Sumerian civilization?

There is without a doubt an actual historical event that is verifiable simply because it is recorded in the history of all the other major cultures of the world that were independent of and far removed from Mesopotamia. If we assume that the Great Deluge took place in about 4000 BC, then by the time *The Epic of Gilgamesh* was compiled and recorded in the clay tablets found in Ashurbanipal's library, the story of the Flood would have already been 2,000 years old.

It is absolutely incredible that considering the enormous spans of time, the account remained astonishingly parallel to the biblical account, which has been divinely kept from such embellishments.

Consider the following similarities found in the Babylonian and biblical accounts:

A Comparison of the Babylonian and Hebrew Flood Accounts

NOAH'S ACCOUNT (GENESIS 6–8) THE BIBLE	UTNAPISHTIM'S ACCOUNT TABLET XI – THE EPIC OF GILGAMESH
1. The Flood was the result of judgment from God because of the violence of humanity. "Now the earth was corrupt in the sight of God, and the earth was filled with violence . . . I am about to destroy them" (Gen. 6:11, 13).	1. The Flood was a judgment as a result of the evil in the hearts of humanity. "Shuruppak – a city which thou knowest, . . . that city was (already) old . . . (Now) their heart prompted the great gods (to) bring a deluge" (*Gilgamesh* Tablet XI, lines 11, 13–14).
2. Noah was commanded by God to build an ark. "Make yourself an ark" (Gen. 6:14).	2. Utnapishtim was commanded by the gods to build an ark. "Tear down thy house; build a ship!" (*Gilgamesh* Tablet XI, line 24).
3. Noah was commanded to bring into the ark two of every animal in the world. "Every living thing of all flesh, you shall bring two of every kind into the ark, to keep *them* alive with you; they shall be male and female" (Gen. 6:19).	3. Utnapishtim was commanded to carry with him the seed of all living creatures. "(Cause) to go into the ship the seed of all living creatures" (*Gilgamesh* Tablet XI, line 27).
4. The number seven is crucial in the development of the Flood. In the biblical account, the duration is 40 days, but it is recorded that the Flood began to rise on the seventh day. "It came about after the seven days, that the water of the flood came upon the earth" (Gen. 7:10).	4. The number seven is crucial in the development of the Flood. "When the seventh day arrived, the tempest, the flood, Which had fought like an army, subsided in its onslaught" (*Gilgamesh* Tablet XI, lines 129–130).
5. The Flood covered all the land (not a local flood). "The water prevailed more and more upon the earth, so that all the high mountains everywhere under the heavens were covered . . . and the mountains were covered" (Gen. 7:19, 20).	5. The Flood covered all the land (not a local flood). "The wind blew, the downpour, the tempest, (and) the flo(od) overwhelmed the land" (*Gilgamesh* Tablet XI, line 128).

6. In the Genesis account, the dove and the raven were used by Noah to determine if the Flood had receded enough to find dry land. "Noah opened the window of the ark which he had made; and he sent out a raven" (Gen. 8:6). "Then he sent out a dove from him . . . but the dove found no resting place . . . for the water was on the surface of all the earth" (Gen. 8:8–9).	6. In *The Epic of Gilgamesh*, Utnapishtim used the dove, the raven, and the swallow for the same reason as Noah. "(Then) I sent forth a raven and let (her) go. The raven went away, and when she saw that the waters had abated . . . she . . . did not return" (*Gilgamesh* Tablet XI, lines 152-154). "When the seventh day arrived, I sent forth a dove and let (her) go" (*Gilgamesh* Tablet XI, lines 145-146).
7. "Then Noah built an altar to the LORD, and took of every clean animal and of every clean bird and offered burnt offerings on the altar" (Gen. 8:20).	7. After Utnapishtim disembarked, he made a sacrifice to God who smelled the savor of the sweet sacrifice and blessed him.

If the Babylonian account of the flood were the only other story of the deluge in history, we could conclude that the biblical narrative could have been "borrowed" from theirs. But that is not the case. The flood story as well as the creation story and the story of the dividing of the languages at the Tower of Babel are all found in the history of practically every major culture in the world.

2. The Accounts of the Flood in Europe

a. The Scandinavians

The ancient Indo-European tribe began in the area we now call Iran. Some traveled south into northern India and others north into the Russian steppes. One group from the Russian steppes went east through China, and the other went west through all of Europe. In Europe they eventually became known as the Celtic tribes, extending as far north as the Scandinavian countries and as far south as Spain. The Nordic people left a legend in *The Poetic Edda*, a work of great and unknown antiquity that speaks of the Global Flood cataclysm.

Mountains dash together
Giant maids are frightened,
Heroes go the way of Hell,
And heaven is rent in twain. . . .
The sun grows dark,
The earth sinks into the sea,
The bright stars
From heaven vanish;
Fire rages,
Heat blazes,
And high flames play
'Gainst heaven itself.

"Mountains dash together" – This no doubt is describing a tectonic upheaval that causes mountains to dash against one another. It matches perfectly with our Judeo-Christian model and shows this to be a global phenomenon and not some local tale. No river flooding can cause mountains to dash together.

"Heaven is rent in twain" – It would certainly seem to a bystander that the sky had been separated in two by an impassible column of gushing water that reached to the heavens. Could this be speaking of the fountains of the deep thrusting into heaven like a curtain of jetting water dividing the heavens? Or could this be speaking of the meteors streaking through the sky and separating the heavens by their ejecta?

"The sun grows dark" – Here again is an allusion to the darkness that covered the entire Earth due to (1) the ejecta from the seven meteors, (2) the eroding action of the fountains of the deep, and (3) the tephra and the latent moisture that built into enormous dark storm clouds that brought down the black rain.

"The earth sinks into the sea" – Certainly from their perspective the land is sinking into the water. Does that sound to you like a local flood? The Earth did not sink into a river. It sank into the sea.

"The bright stars from heaven vanish" – Again, the combination of the ejecta and tephra and the monster storm clouds darkened the skies so the night stars were no longer visible. That same phenomenon will once again visit us at the end of the Second Earth.

"Fire rages" – How does a blazing fire come from a flood in a local river flood scenario?

"Heat blazes" – How does a flood produce heat? That indicates either the heat generated by striking meteors or massive volcanic activity. Hardly could a local river flood have caused such thermal global consequences.

"And high flames play 'gainst heaven itself'" – This is either a description of super-volcanic eruptions that burst into the heavens or the very ejecta of the striking meteors. No local river flood can cause such cataclysmic descriptions.

This ancient account describes in detail a flood accompanied by a cataclysmic upheaval that released enormous fire and heated the planet in an unprecedented magnitude. It is in no way descriptive of some passive, minor local flood by a swollen river. To insist on this local flood scenario is to absolutely disregard any of the internal evidence enumerated by all the ancients.

Fire raging, mountains dashing together in massive earthquakes, the sun darkening, the land sinking under the ocean water, the stars disappearing into the black sky, fire shooting up to the heavens, and an unprecedented heat are all aspects of the scenario that the biblical model of the Flood suggests as a global cataclysm. That anyone could interpret this as a local river flood is beyond reason.

b. The Greeks' Account of the Flood

We have already briefly mentioned the Flood story preserved for us by Hesiod. The uncanny commonalities observed in these ancient stories cannot be ignored. In each of these cases, the Flood is not simply a tale of gently rising water. In each of them we find mighty waves and angry oceans, fire and flames shooting into the sky, strong storm winds, black rain, thunderous noises, and darkened skies so the stars or Sun can no longer be seen. How can we correlate these events with a small local flood?

The ancient Greeks called their Noah Deucalion. The story is told that Zeus, angry at humanity, caused a great rain to fall and flood the entire Earth. Deucalion built a strong, wooden box and filled it with supplies. He then climbed into it with Pyrrha, the red-blonde daughter of Epimetheus and Pandora. After the Flood receded, the box landed on a mountaintop. There on Mount Parnassus, the two disembarked and proceeded to make sacrifices to the gods.

It should be first noted that the Greek pantheon is a heavily corrupted version of the biblical narrative. If you look carefully here and there, you can find pieces of the story of creation, the Great Flood of Noah, and the Messiah as the Son of God coming to atone for our sins. Unlike the evolutionary imagination that the worship of God has evolved in the mind of man as he ascended from the apes, the scriptural position is that the worship of the one true God began with the very first man who breathed air and inexorably devolved with time. The corruption of the truth led by the rebellious angels has ever since profaned the truth into countless counterfeits. Zeus was the title of the original one true God in Greece before the corruption of polytheism created the Greek polytheistic pantheon.

Permit me for a moment to take a side tour in order to give the reader a little background to support my previous statement. Archaeology is not the only area in science that substantiates the biblical narrative. The science of philology or the history of the development of languages also proves to us that the biblical record is, in fact, accurate. The scriptural narrative tells us that Noah alighted on Mount Ararat, and afterward most of humanity dwelt in the plain of Shinar. From there the languages were confounded, and the nations of the world became segregated by the languages. The science of philology proves to us that this central area of the world was, in fact, the cradle of all known languages. "No other region of the globe presents a similar union of extreme human types distributed amongst a common center" (*The Human Species*, 176).

> Philology, also, points to this same conclusion. . . . On the East are the monosyllabic languages, on the North the polysyllabic or agglutinative languages, and on the West and South the inflectional or Aryan languages, of which the Sanskrit is an example, being closely allied to nearly all the languages of Europe. . . . Moreover, it is to this center that we trace the origin of nearly all our domesticated plants and animals. . . . Naturally, therefore, the same high authority writes, "There we are inclined to say the first human beings appeared and multiplied till the populations overflowed as from a bowl and spread themselves in waves every direction (*The International Standard Bible Encyclopedia, Volume 3* 1997, 406).

It was after the dispersion created by the judgment of the Tower of Babel that the Ur people moved to the area of ancient Persia. The inflectional language spoken by the first of these Ur people is classified by philologists as the Indo-European language and is sometimes referred to as the Old European Language. Another term used for this proto, or original language, is the Ur language. It is characterized as the original or proto language from which all the Indo-European languages evolved. The Celtic name for the constellation Taurus is Uruz. The name Tau-uruz means the last and the first. It is the same as the Alpha and the Omega of the New Testament written in Greek or the Hebrew Aleph and Tau of the Old Testament. It is a title of the timeless and eternal one true God.

However, the Indo-European language is not the original language of mankind but rather that of the Aryan civilization that was a splinter of the Hamitic lineage who inhabited the area we now know as Iran. These migrated both toward the south into India and north into the Russian steppes around 2000 BC, probably due to the meteorological changes in that area becoming more arid. From these Russian steppes, they migrated east into China, reaching the Pacific Ocean, and also west through Europe, reaching the Atlantic Ocean.

Evidence of the Indo-European wide span of conquest is found in the derivative languages of the areas they occupied. The area they conquered is vast. From Norway down to the British Isles, down to Ireland and Spain, eastward through Central Europe past the Baltic area into the Lower Volga where the white Russians reside, then a thin swath cutting China down the middle all the way to the Pacific and from the Russian steppes down to Iran, and finally east to India, all the respective languages of these countries owe their origin to the Indo-European people who began in Iran.

It may come as some surprise that the inhabitants of India being of darker complexion also have Aryan inhabitants of ancient Persia as part of their ancestry. But philologists have proved conclusively that Sanskrit, the ancient language spoken in the Indus Valley in the northern part of India is, in fact, a derivative of this Indo-European language that was also ancestral to the languages developed from the blue-eyed, blonde, and light-skinned Celtic people who conquered most of Europe. That is why the people of northern India are lighter skinned and have a different language than the original inhabitants of India who still reside in the south and whose language is Tamil, closely associated with the language of Madagascar.

> Scholars now know that no less than eleven basic idioms are related in the same way as Latin and Sanskrit. Among them are Tocharic (spoken by an extinct Russian steppe-people), Indo-Iranian, Hittite, Armenian, Slavic, Baltic, Greek, Illyrian, Italic, Germanic and Celtic. From these almost fifty modern languages have developed, from Russian to Serbo-Croat and Norwegian. Their root, the *Ur*-language, has been similarly reconstructed by scholars,

though they cannot tell if it was ever actually spoken. . . . Indeed contemporary scholars have reached virtually along parallel lines of thought, the conclusion that there must have been a people speaking Indo-European, whose members must therefore count as the ancestors of the Celts, as of the Indians, Armenians and Romans (Herm 1993, 72, 75).

At the end of the 19th century, Frederick Max Müller, a formidable German scholar involved in studying the science of language and early Indian religion at Oxford, established some important, undeniable, philological links between the names of Greek gods and Hindu gods spoken in Sanskrit from the Vedic literature. He then discovered that this philological link also applied to many of the names of the deities in the ancient European tradition.

The science of philology has since scientifically established that the vast array of gods in the European pantheon that Caesar was confronted with in his time actually devolved from a common origin shared with the Hindus that began in Iran.

The ancient "sky god" of the Hindus in the Vedic tradition was known as Dyaus Pita. This is one and the same as the Indo-European God of the Ur people in Iran known as Dyeus pater, or Sky Father. The Greeks know Dyeus as Zeus. He is known in Latin as Deus or Deo, in Spanish as Dios, in ancient Irish as Dia, and in Persian as Deva. All these were derived from the same common name known to the Ur people immediately after the Great Flood who descended from Ham as Dyeus Pater, or Heavenly Father.

The ancient progenitors of the Celts had been worshiping Dyeus for some 2,000 years after the Great Flood before they ventured south and eastward to India and north and westward to Europe. By Caesar's time, some 4,000 years after the Flood, this same God was still recognized as Dis Pater, the Sky Father of all, from whom the Celts still claimed they originated.

Of course, polytheism had by this time firmly established the worship of countless gods, and the worship of Dyeus Pater was grossly neglected. He was relegated to the position of just another god instead of the only one true God.

> Caesar, who instinctively but not unjustifiably compared the gods of the Gauls with those of the Romans, mentions a father of the gods, a *dis pater, whom "the Celts reckon to be father of their tribe.* They say they have learned this from the Druids." There is no reason to doubt his assertion. This celestial patriarch may have been a Chronos who was replaced, as in other religions, by a trinity – to begin with at least (emphasis added) (Herm 1993, 156).

Chronos may have been the name for the one true God known by the original inhabitants of Greece who descended from Noah's son Japeth. The lineage of Japeth was known for their seafaring accomplishments. They colonized Greece, Italy, most the Mediterranean islands, Carthage, Spain, Ireland, and England long before the Celtic invasion that later brought the name Zeus to Macedonia in the northern part of Greece. The Celts were, in fact, descendants of Ham. Nevertheless, the point is that all the ancients believed in a supreme God who lived in the heavens. Because of this God's universal popularity, archaeologists have given Him the peculiar title of Sky God.

Many of the later names in the Celtic pantheon that we take to mean other gods were just derivations from this original God. For instance, the god Tyr in Britain is one and the same as Teiwaz in the Scandinavian countries and is also linguistically derived from Dyeus. "Philologists, for instance, derived Tyr's name from a word for god represented by Latin *deus*, Iranian *deva*, and Old Irish *dia*" (Davidson 1993, 147).

In like manner, the Nordic god Thor was then a devolved version from Tyr, having many of the same character qualities such as the hammer and the lightning bolt. In addition, titles describing God's many qualities were given to him, who later became known as a separate god. For instance, the very ancient god known as Dagda, which means the Good God, was simply a title that described his attribute of goodness. I am convinced that this was simply a descriptive title of Dyeus the Dagda. It is no different than the endearing name Abba, meaning Daddy, which the Hebrews used for Yahweh.

Similarly, the Celtic god Belenos, which meant the Bright and Shining One, is the same title given to Shang Ti by the ancient Chinese who also knew Him as the Creator. These titles were in all cultures inevitably later construed as names of separate gods. But again, as with the Egyptians, they initially represented different aspects of the singular deity. Shang-Ti of the Chinese, Ptah Atum Ra of the Egyptians, and Belenos of the Celtics all alluded to the shining Sun as the symbol of the supreme God of the heavens who created the universe.

> The true derivation is from dagos, "good," and deivos, "god," ... Dagda is also called Cera, a word perhaps derived from *kar* and connected with the Lat. *cerus*, "creator" and other names of his are *Ruad-rofhessa*, "lord of great knowledge," and *Eochaid Ollathair*, "great father," "for a great father to the Tuatha Dé Danann was he." ... Dagda is called "the god of the earth" "because of the greatness of his power" (MacCulloch 1992, 77–78).

It is clear that the Celts considered Dyeus their father. To then recognize Dagda as also their father seems to be a clear indication that in the past they were connected as one and the same person. Similarly, the attributes accorded to both Dagda and Dyeus of creator and all knowledgeable are implied by the titles Ruad-rofhessa and Eochaid Ollathair.

As we survey the vast array of gods found in every culture of the world, there are distinct qualities that clearly earmark the one true

God taught by Noah to his descendants. Anthropologists throughout the world have had to admit the peculiar similarity of these gods worldwide and have categorized them with a distinct title, the Sky Gods.

This "heaven dweller god" may be described by various cultures with different names. His dwelling may also be referred to by different names since the languages have become separate and distinct. Someone may call this heaven Elysium (Britain); another may call it Annwn (Welsh); the Irish call it Tir na n-Og (the Land of Youth); the Greek call it Olympus; the Egyptians, Duat; the Nordic people call it Asgard; the Chinese call it T'ien. But in all cases, this Sky God is considered the Supreme God, Father, and Creator of the universe who dwells in heaven.

So we may say that the confounding of the languages may have caused the Egyptians, the Mayas, the Chinese, and every other culture to call God by a different name than the Ur people, but the sameness of the descriptions of this God is proof of the sameness of His identity.

The Egyptian name for the Creator is Ptah. But it is the same as Dyeus Pater, the God of the Indo-European progenitors of the Celts. And He is the same God referred to by the Santal people in India as Thakur Jiu. He is also the same God of the Ohlmec and the Mayas, the Heart of Heaven (Zamna and Tonatiuh, respectively). The Chinese recognized Him as Shang-Ti and the Ethiopians as Magano. The Koreans worshiped Him as Hananim, the Babylonians as El, and the Sumerians as An. Each and every one of them is the same as the One we recognize today as the God of Abraham, Isaac, and Jacob— Jehovah. He has made Himself known to all the people of the Earth so that we are without excuse.

At the other end of the spectrum from the Sky God are the horned gods of darkness such as Cromm Cruaich and Cernunnos who required human sacrifices. These are the names of the gods who initially represented the enemy of the real God of the universe,

Jehovah, known as the heavenly Father. They are always associated with horns, serpents, or trickery.

In antithesis to the usurpers, the Sky Gods are modeled after the constellation Orion and are pictured as holding a club or hammer and sometimes a lightning bolt in their right arm. These, of course, are symbols of the Great Deluge and the destruction of our First Earth.

The gods of the hammer represent a benevolent Supreme Being. The hammer represents the meteors that struck the Earth and broke the crust. The lightning bolt represents the storms that broke out afterward and brought the flooding rains. It is the memory of the judgment of God that brought the death of the First Earth. And invariably where the gods of the hammer are found, the images of the horned god Cernunnos are not found. And the inverse is also true. The hammer held on the right arm is a symbol of the power of the right arm of God to destroy His enemy. That is the title given to the Messiah by the Hebrew Scriptures. The Messiah is always the right hand of God. We shall see the right arm of God at the end of the Second Earth. Isaiah foresaw it.

> *Transgressing and denying the* LORD,
> *And turning away from our God,*
> *Speaking oppression and revolt,*
> *Conceiving in and uttering from the heart lying words.*
> *Justice turned back,*
> *And righteousness stands far away;*
> *For truth has stumbled in the street,*
> *And uprightness cannot enter.*
> *Yes, truth is lacking'*
> *And he who turns aside from evil makes himself a prey.*
> *Now the* LORD *saw.*
> *And it was displeasing in His sight that there was no justice.*
> *And He saw that there was no man,*

THE DEATH OF THE FIRST EARTH

And was astonished that there was no one to intercede;
Then His own arm brought salvation to Him,
And His righteousness upheld Him.
He put on righteousness like a breastplate,
And a helmet of salvation on His head;
And He put on garments of vengeance for clothing
And wrapped Himself with zeal as a mantle.
According to their deeds, so He will repay,
Wrath to His adversaries recompense to His enemies;
"A Redeemer will come to Zion,
Arise, shine; for your light has come,
And the glory of the L<small>ORD</small> *has risen upon you.*
For behold, darkness will cover the earth,
And deep darkness the peoples;
But the L<small>ORD</small> *will rise upon you*
And His glory will appear upon you.
"Nations will come to your light,
And kings to the brightness of your rising.

And they will call you the city of the L<small>ORD</small>,
The Zion of the Holy One of Israel.

"Whereas you have been forsaken and hated
With no one passing through,
I will make you an everlasting pride,
A joy from generation to generation.
You will also suck the milk of nations
And will suck the breast of kings;
Then you will know that I, the L<small>ORD</small>, *am your Savior*
And your Redeemer, the Mighty One of Jacob."
—Isa. 59:13–18, 20, 60:1–3, 14–16

THE HISTORICAL EVIDENCE

> *The LORD has bared His holy arm*
> *In the sight of all the nations,*
> *That all the ends of the earth may see*
> *The salvation of our God.*
>
> —Isa. 52:10

The god Taranis is perhaps the most widely acclaimed in this category and is often equated with Jupiter in Italy and Thor in Scandinavia. It is quite evident that this is the god Caesar referred to as Dispater and from whom they believed they had descended, making him one and the same as Dyeus Pater (Ju Piter in Latin).

> Caesar says that the Celtic Jupiter governed heaven. A god who carries a wheel, probably a sun-god, and another, a god of thunder, called *Taranis, seems to have been equated with Jupiter. . . . In some cases the god with the wheel carries also a thunderbolt,* and on some altars, dedicated to Jupiter, both a wheel and a thunderbolt are figured (emphasis added) (MacCulloch 1992, 29).

The wheel symbol is the symbol of power over the Earth and is also recognized as the symbol of the Sun. Thus, the lightning bolts that ended the First Earth and the hammer that shattered the crust of the Earth are the One who rules the dawning of the Sun and is the ruler of all Earth. It is the account of the darkening sky in the Great Flood that brought forth the Second Earth when the Sun dawned anew and Noah repopulated our planet. But Isaiah foresaw that this same darkness will come at the end of the Second Earth.

> *For behold, darkness will cover the earth,*
> *And deep darkness the peoples;*
> *But the LORD will rise upon you*
> *And His glory will appear upon you.*
>
> —Isa. 60:2

It should not surprise us that in the corrupted religion of the Serpent man would consider himself as having descended from the gods. That was literally the case during the First Earth when the Neanderthals ruled our planet. It is a profaned version of our real origins. God fashioned Adam with his own hand and breathed life into him, therefore we are literally God's children. We descended from heaven. And although we are the children of light, we are not gods.

What we find universally is that God is in every sense the Dispater of all humanity. That is attested by the Egyptians of old as well as the Incas of Peru, the Mikados of Japan, the kings of Uganda in Africa, and so on. It is a common thread found in every continent.

By the time Caesar was writing about the Celts, they had been in existence more than 2,000 years, and the concept of Dyeus had long been corrupted. Unfortunately for Caesar, he did not have at his disposal the vast scholastic work we can draw from presently to establish the interconnection of these gods.

As we survey the Celtic pantheon, there are particular traits we can point to in order to differentiate the gods who are derivatives of Dyeus. In contrast, we can also discern those who depict the Great Usurper, Satan.

In ancient times, the symbol of the Sun as the preeminent body in the sky was a picture or symbol of the one true God. It is my suspicion that the gods who are pictured with a wheel (representing the Sun) or a lightning bolt (misunderstood by the ancient Celts as a ray from the Sun) are divinities who owe their origins to names that describe Dyeus. That is not only born out of philology but by the ancient tradition of the Zodiac.

Invariably, those divinities who wield a lightning bolt, a hammer, or a club such as the one wielded by the constellation Orion defeating the false lion and Hercules defeating the many-headed snake, are uniformly the enemy of the Serpent and as such are depicting the role of the Messiah. It is therefore no coincidence that the Mayan counterpart of Dyeus Pater, called the Heart of Heaven or Huracan, is also represented in a form where he wields the lightning bolt. "In the sky above is Heart of Heaven who, by His other name of Huracan, appears as three forms of lightning" (Taube 1993, 54).

In His lightning form, He is known as Kauil. It is also significant that the name *Huracan* means "hurricane." To the survivors of the Great Flood, a hurricane and a lightning bolt would surely be descriptive of the awesome power of God that was released in judgment of the world during that cataclysm that ended our First Earth.

It is therefore also no coincidence that the Celts would depict God in the same form. It is safe to say that probably this form developed after the Flood, while the hammer or club preceded it since it was derived from the Zodiac and then reinforced by the cataclysm that ended the First Earth. The hammer that fractured our Earth into seven continents is none other than God. Therefore, the original Inca God, Viracocha, is also depicted as wielding the lightning bolt and thunder. It is a universal motif carried in the memory of the ancients derived from the children of Noah.

Like Thor, the ancient Celtic God Taranis is considered a sky god who controls both lightning and thunder. Our word for thunder is clearly a derivative of this god (as well as the Spanish word for thunder, *trueno*). Taranis, like Jupiter, Zeus, and Thor, wields a lightning bolt and is often pictured carrying a hammer.

The fact that the ancients considered them as one is attested by the choice of names given to the specific day of the week associated with this God. Thor's day became Thursday, and in Spanish the same day is called Jueves, derived from Jupiter. He was considered a good God and the protector of the people, and the thunder of His power shall extinguish our enemy.

The thunderous roar of the striking meteors, the exploding fountains of the deep, the thunderous volcanic eruptions, and the thunder and lightning that followed during the hurricanes created a deep impression in the minds of the inhabitants of the ark. It is this ancient memory that links those attributed to the God of the heavens. It should therefore not surprise us if we find this to be the character of Jehovah in the Hebrew Scriptures.

> *Now when the Philistines heard that the sons of Israel had gathered to Mizpah, the lords of the Philistines went up against Israel. And when the sons of Israel heard it, they were afraid of the Philistines. Then the sons of Israel said to Samuel, "Do not cease to cry to the Lord our God for us, that He may save us from the hand of the Philistines." Samuel took a suckling lamb and offered it for a whole burnt offering to the Lord; and Samuel cried to the Lord for Israel and the Lord answered him. Now Samuel was offering up the burnt offering, and the Philistines drew near to battle against Israel. But the Lord thundered with a great thunder on that day against the Philistines and confused them, so that they were routed before Israel* (emphasis added).
>
> 1 Sam. 7:7–10

Job speaks of the power of the thunder of God who pierced the fleeing serpent called Rahab. The name *Rahab* in the Hebrew means literally "storm" or "arrogance," and it is most likely alluding to the storm of the Great Deluge caused by the arrogance and pride of Satan and his demons when they filled the antediluvian world with their violence and wickedness. The sin of the Second Insurrection brought Rahab the harlot to join the demons in the creation of the Nephilim. Great darkness and a storm of violence were brought upon our planet, but God pierced the flying serpent with His hammer and lightning and ended their violence and bloodshed.

As the meteors pierced our Earth, so God pierced the rule of the religion of the Serpent with the destruction brought forth by the impact of the meteors. God in His providential care overcame the total destruction that would have ended all life on our planet through the Flood. God's Flood returned the world to the seed of Eve and by His breath then cleared the heavens from the ash, darkness, and sin that consumed the First Earth.

> *He quieted the sea with His power,*
> *And by His understanding He shattered Rahab.*
> *By His breath the heavens are cleared;*
> *His hand has pierced the fleeing serpent.*
> *Behold, these are the fringes of His ways;*
> *And how faint a word we hear from Him!*
> But His mighty thunder, who can understand?
> (emphasis added).
>
> —Job 26:12–14

The name Rahab is used in parallel with tannin, "the dragon," and is sometimes used in Scripture to refer to nations such as Egypt and Babylon that have followed after Satan, accepting the corrupted religion of the dragon (Ps. 87:4, 89:10). The insinuation is that these nations have become prostitutes for Satan as the women of the First Earth did with the religion of the Mother Goddesses.

The biblical story of the prostitute Rahab aiding Joshua to conquer Jericho is a symbol of the Gentile church that, having turned initially away from God, will in the end help Israel during the return of Christ on the day He destroys the Second Earth at the seventh trumpet. Jericho is a symbol of the realm of the Antichrist and his pact with the Gentile nations at the end of our Second Earth that shall be vanquished after the seventh trumpet judgment in Revelation as it was vanquished by Joshua (a symbol of Yeshua) on the seventh day after the seventh trumpet was blown. Having previously been instructed to remain quiet during the six previous blasts of the horn, the nation of Israel was instructed to roar on the seventh trumpet. This is the roar of the Lion of Judah. The walls of Jericho crumbled at the seventh trumpet as the walls of every city in our Second Earth shall crumble at the roar of the returning Lion of Judah during the judgment of the seventh trumpet in the book of Revelation.

There are several gods depicted as wielding a hammer of justice. They are in most cases local names for the same god. Such, I believe, is the case with Sucellus and Smertullos, who are simply local forms of Thor. "On a Paris altar and on certain steles a god *attacks a serpent with a club*. The serpent is a chthonian animal, and the god, called *Smertullos, may be a Dispater*" (emphasis added) (MacCulloch 1991, 35).

The story of the battle of good against evil is depicted throughout the world as a divine hero who, in the end, finally defeats the Serpent. Whether this is portrayed by the early Quetzalcoatl of the Olmecs, by Horus of the Egyptians, by Hercules of the Greeks against Medusa, or by Smertullos against Yormungand, the serpent of the Celts, the story emanates from the prophecy of the constellations in the Zodiac such as Orion, Ophiuchus, and Hercules that were known since the First Earth.

The image portrayed in the Zodiac is Orion bashing the head of the impostor lion with a club, or Hercules bashing the multi-serpent head of Medusa, or Ophiuchus keeping the serpent from reaching the Corona Borealis (representing global rule), or Hercules stepping on the head of the Serpent constellation. It is a depiction of the culmination of the ageless cosmic battle when the Messiah figure will strike the deadly blow to the head of the Serpent and once and for all defeat the enemy of humanity for all time. It was known during the First Earth by the prophecies of the Zodiac, and it is known in our Second Earth through the divine instrument of the Holy Scriptures.

The Celts were no different than anyone else in the world. They regarded the Serpent as the personification of evil. The Egyptians called this serpent Apep, who is associated with Set, the enemy of Horus, their Messiah figure. The Celts called it Yormungand or Iormungand. In the Zodiac, he is also known as Hydra the water serpent. The names may differ, but they are one and the same—Satan.

The Greeks depicted him as Typhon, a serpent that ruled the seas and causes storms, or a three-headed serpent called Medusa who turns people to stone. This, of course, is an allusion to the judgment of the Great Flood. And of course, the vanquisher of Medusa and Draco (Python, the dragon) in the stars is Hercules (the son of Zeus).

The Aztecs called him Kukulcan, the flying serpent responsible for the Great Flood, who usurped the throne from Quetzalcoatl, the Messiah figure of the Mayas. In Chile, the Mapuche associate a serpent figure with their story of the Great Flood.

In Australia, the aborigines call him Wollunqua who is associated with Yara-ma-yha-who, a small, red man sporting an enormous head, with no teeth and octopus-like fingers that sucked the blood out of men. He was depicted as a vampire swooping down from a tree, as he did with the first victim in the Garden. Each time he kills a man, the victim is miraculously revived but returns in a much smaller form and with redder skin until he eventually turns into Yara-ma-yha-who. He is called the Rainbow Serpent because the rainbow was first seen after the Great Flood.

In the Hindu tradition, he is called Nagarajan and associated with Vishnu, the enemy of Krishna, their Messiah figure. The Kundalini depicted in yoga is, in fact, a representation of Nagas, or serpent gods. Kundalini is a Sanskrit word meaning "coiled up one."

In the Chinese, he is Shen Lung, or the god dragon. He is also known as Fohi, represented by the head of a man and the torso of a serpent. Both the serpent and the dragon are deeply rooted in the occult religion of Taoism.

The Sumerians knew him as Ningizzida, the Babylonians as Tiamat. The people of Fiji knew him as Ratumaibulu. The Koreans knew him as Eobshin. The people of West Africa knew him as Aidophedo. In the Vodou of Benin, he is known as Dan. The Gnostics call him Ourobouros. Everywhere around the world the Serpent is known as the god who gives wealth, sex, and power; he symbolizes Satan, the Enemy of the Sky God, the Creator of the heavens and the Earth.

The idea of the evil eye personified in Medusa is also clearly depicted in all the major cultures as a characteristic of those gods representing Satan. In the Celtic pantheon, it is clearly depicted by Balor whose evil eye destroyed all those who looked upon it. Throughout the world, Neolithic cultures worshiped the religion of the Mother Goddess instigated by the Neanderthals. These are often depicted with masks having large almond eyes. The eyes are occult symbols of illumination into the esoteric knowledge of the demonic hierarchy.

Returning now to the Greek Noah named Deucalion and his red-blonde wife named Pyrrha, according to Greek tradition, she is the daughter of Pandora. The famous story of Pandora is that she opened a forbidden jar that was supposed to be food. When she opened the lid, instead of food she released sickness, misery, and death into our world. The only good thing left at the bottom of the jar was hope. What do you think that story represents?

It is the story of Eve in the Garden at Eden. It is the story of the Fall of Man when Eve ate the forbidden fruit from the tree of the knowledge of good and evil. They already knew good from walking in the Garden with the Creator. It was the knowledge of evil with which the Serpent deceived Adam and Eve. But we are not as those who have no hope, for our hope lies in God and in His Redeemer who will come to bring peace back to our fallen Second Earth. That day shall birth the Third Earth. The hope for Eve on that fateful day came from the voice of God when He promised that through her seed the Deliverer would come to rescue mankind and return our world to the way it was. The Hebrew prophets previsioned that day.

> *For a child will be born to us, a son will be given to us;*
> *And the government will rest on His shoulders;*
> *And His name will be called Wonderful Counselor,*
> *Mighty God,*
> *Eternal Father, Prince of Peace.*

> *There will be no end to the increase of His government or of peace,*
> *On the throne of David and over his kingdom,*
> *To establish it and to uphold it with justice and righteousness*
> *From then on and forevermore.*
> *The zeal of the LORD of hosts will accomplish this* (emphasis added).
>
> —Isa. 9:6–7

This is the story of the true Aquarius, the replenisher of water, who will come at the end of the Second Earth to establish the Third Earth under His reign. That Earth will not be exactly as it was in the Garden, but the Fourth and Final Earth shall be. In that day, the universe shall be renewed. He comes to make all things new. In the Omega Point, sin will be remembered no more, and the curse shall be no more forever.

And so it is that Noah's wife was the last legitimate daughter of Eve who did not profane her blood lineage through the travesty of the Second Insurrection. She was the hope for the Second Earth, the womb that birthed every race that walks and talks in our present world. She was my mother as well as yours. She was the ark whose womb carried the seed of Eve to bring forth at the appointed time the Messiah who would bring an end to the transgression. That fiery redhead, perhaps even with freckles, was the second Eve of all mankind. She probably had a feisty personality and a hell of a temper. You can rest assured that Shem, Ham, and Japheth were kept on course with their duties to help their father build the ark.

The similarities in the stories do not end there. Not only the Greek Deucalion but also the Sumerian and Babylonian accounts parallel the biblical narrative and record that their respective Noah sacrificed to God after disembarking on Mount Ararat.

3. The Account of the Flood in the Pacific

a. The Samoans

The Samoan aborigines in the Samoan islands of the South Pacific have their own account of the worldwide flood.

> Then arose smell...
> the smell became smoke, which again became clouds...
> The sea too arose, and in a stupendous catastrophe of nature the land sank into the sea..
> The new earth (the Samoan Islands) arose out of the womb of the old earth. (Williamson 1933, 8)

Note that the catastrophe was preceded by smoke that billowed into the clouds, again the mechanisms that brought forth fire such as reentering ejecta and volcanoes. The idea that the old Earth sank into the ocean and the new Earth arose from the ocean is also consistent with the biblical account of the Flood.

This is not the description of a localized flood but of a global cataclysm that birthed a new Earth from the womb of the old Earth. It was on the first day of the 10th month, 73 days after the fountains of the deep stopped, that the first mountain peaks were seen protruding from the global ocean. It was seven months and 13 days after the fountains of the deep were uncorked. So we see the number seven of God coming to the rescue of the ark.

On that day, the 17th of Nisan, the ark rested on Mount Ararat. On that same day of the month, Moses would cross the Red Sea and Jesus rise from the dead. The watery womb of the First Earth contained the ark of God that brought forth new life and the resurrection of the Second Earth.

b. Australia

The island continent of Australia must surely be one of the most unique places in our world. Species of animals have survived there, cut off from the rest of the world and not surviving anywhere else.

One would therefore expect that the aborigines of Australia would be completely free from any influence of the Hebrew and Babylonian accounts of the Great Deluge and would thus be considered a reliable witness in regard to the authenticity of this event should they also possess a deluge myth.

And they do.

> Several aboriginal Australian peoples, especially those whose traditional homelands are along the tropical northern coast, ascribe their origins to a great flood which swept away the previous landscape and society. Meanwhile, in the origin myths of a number of other tribes, the cosmic serpent Yurlunggur (associated with the rainbow) is held responsible for the deluge (Hancock 1995, 194).

I find it noteworthy that the reference to the cosmic serpent, Yurlunggur, equally affirms the universality of Satan as the embodiment of evil. I find it even more fascinating how the Australian name for the Serpent is so similar in pronunciation to that of the Celts, Iormungand or Yormungand.

In their myths, the idea of a Rainbow Serpent is associated with a shooting star that struck the Earth and, according to the aborigines, brought the ocean from the sky. That took place in the distant past, a time they call "the dream time." Once again, we have further direct confirmation that the Great Flood was precipitated by a meteor strike.

The special significance of this ancient time is attested by all ancient cultures. The Egyptians fondly called it the Zep Tepi, "the First Times." The Mayas called it the Land of the Mist. No doubt the special meteorological features of the First Earth made the Second Earth look like a nightmare. The fact that the rainbow was seen after the rain is no small coincidence. It had never rained before.

The fact that the ocean was seen as dropping from the sky is also no coincidence. There is no doubt in my mind that a wall of geysers shooting into the sky and filling the Atlantic Ocean as well as flooding the land must have left a deep impression on the minds of men and would lead them to think that the ocean fell from the sky. Or, as the Hebrew account says, "The fountains of the great deep burst open" (Gen. 7:11).

Other Mauri myths speak of fires coming from the sky. That is no doubt a reference to the ejecta that would have pummeled the Earth and brought forth great conflagrations before being doused by the rising waters of the Great Flood. The volcanic upheaval created by the meteor strike would have been catastrophic.

Evolutionists must face the fact that these myths, though some through time have been embellished in varying degrees, are, in fact, speaking of the same historical event in terms that could be related to the familiar things known to the people who observed them, who could not explain it any other way. But the undeniable fact is that fire, wind, and water destroyed the First Earth, which is corroborated by a barrage of evidence spanning all seven continents.

4. The Account of the Flood in Asia

a. China

Moving north to the region of China, we come to our Oriental brothers and sisters. Chinese tradition states that Noah migrated toward China after the Flood and with his wife repopulated that region. The Oriental people of the world claim to be the direct descendants of Noah and his wife. In the Chinese language, Noah was Fa-He.

A formidable ridge of mountains that separates the land of China from the civilizations that settled in the Middle East served them well as a natural barrier, which gave the Chinese an independence from the influence of other cultures.

But that mountain barrier did not exist in the First Earth before it was cracked. I suspect it did not exist as it does in the present condition at the beginning of the Second Earth. This enormous ridge of mountains grew to its present formidable size subsequent to the arrival of the Chinese people since the plate containing India has continuously pushed upward toward the Asiatic plate.

During the early part of the period following the Great Flood, the passage toward China would probably not have been as difficult since the mountains were considerably smaller. As the resistance between the plates increased, the pressure between them also increased, and as it sought the area of least resistance, the jutting mountains pushed upward and sealed for a long time the Proto-Chinese people from the rest of the world.

That served to protect them from invasion and ensured a continuous chronicle of their undisturbed genetics. Like the African Bushmen who were isolated by the Kalahari Desert in the southern cul-de-sac of Africa, the Chinese were largely undisturbed by invasions. Is it a coincidence that the Chinese also carried in their memory the rebellion of mankind that led to the Global Deluge?

> Early Jesuit scholars who were among the first Europeans to visit China had the opportunity in the Imperial Library to study a vast work consisting of 4320 volumes, said to have been handed down from ancient times and to contain "all knowledge". This great book included a number of traditions which told of the consequences that followed "when mankind rebelled against the high gods and the system of the universe fell into disorder" : "'The planets altered their courses. The sky sank lower towards the north. The sun, moon and stars changed their motions. The earth fell to pieces and the waters in its bosom rushed upwards with violence and overflowed the earth" (Hancock 1995, 193–194).

There is good reason to believe that the seven meteors in various sizes could have affected the angle of the Earth's orbit, causing the appearance of a shift in the motion of the planets. We have already documented that our Earth's orbit around the Sun is pushed out 5 million miles at one end. It is quite likely that the elliptical orbit of the Earth was caused by the meteor strikes, changing it from a more circular orbit as exhibited by our neighbors Venus and Mercury. It may have also turned us from our initial axis to our present tilt, which aggravates the intensity of the seasons by keeping one hemisphere away from the direct rays of the Sun. It is the tilting of the axis that caused the stars to sink toward the north.

If the orbit of the First Earth were circular, there would have been less dramatic climactic changes in the seasons. Earth's elliptical orbit of the Sun and the tilt of its axis aggravate the seasons considerably toward extremes in our diminished Second Earth. That may have caused our year to increase slightly, causing the lunar calendar to go off synchrony from the solar calendar.

Thus the Chinese memory—"The planets altered their courses. The sky sank lower towards the north. The sun, moon and stars changed their motions" (Hancock 1995, 194)—seems to provide clear observational proof of this change in our axis and our orbit.

And once again, we have the familiar story of the severity of the Flood coming from the bosom of the Earth, not some sedate mythological rendering of a local flood but rather a violent, cataclysmic upheaval that brought the floodwater from the depths of the Earth and altered the entire planet by breaking the supercontinent. "The earth fell to pieces and the waters in its bosom rushed upwards with violence and overflowed the earth" (Hancock 1995, 194). No clearer explanation of the bursting fountains of the deep and the shattering of the continents can be found that corroborates our Judeo-Christian model.

Again, we have another reference that refers to the shattering of the Earth's crust that caused the waters in the subterranean aquifers to "rush upwards" into the sky "with violence." This is an exact depiction and the exact order of events that describes the jetting saltwater reservoir found in the subterranean chambers as the hydraulic plate theory describes. Is this also a coincidence? How many facts have to match the ancient chronicles before evolutionists stop calling them coincidences?

The water contained in the bosom of the Earth cannot be denied. Steam is one of the major components volcanoes give off. Even the analysis of volcanic ash shows the evidence of water inside the magma. In fact, the greater the degree of water, the more explosive the magma eruptions are. The water turns to vapor and expands 1,700 times in volume as it is released from the pressures below the ground. That causes it to spew forth the lava in explosive displays as it exits the volcanic cones. We have already documented that below the crust more salt water exists today than in all our oceans. When will evolutionists begin to believe the ancient chronicles?

b. India

In India, Noah was known as Manu. The story is told that Manu, while making ablutions, found in the hollow of his hand a small fish. The tiny little fish begged Manu to spare his life and take pity on him; Manu proceeded to place him in a jar. The story that unfolds reminds me of a children's book I once read to my children. The following morning, the fish had miraculously outgrown the jar and asked Manu to please throw him into a lake. Soon after, the fish (actually a manifestation of Vishnu) grew too large for the lake and asked Manu to throw him into the sea.

Manu complied, and as a reward, the great fish, that now had golden scales and a singular large horn protruding out of its head, warned Manu that a great flood would come to destroy the inhabitants of the Earth. He then sent Manu a large ship and ordered him to fill it with a male and female of every living species and the seeds of every plant.

After fulfilling his assigned task, Manu fastened a rope from the great ark to the horn of the fish. The flood immediately covered the entire Earth. The great fish swam, pulling the ark to "the Mountain of the North." It is assumed that this mountain is in the Himalayan Ridge, but I propose that this is, in fact, a more recent adaptation and that the initial inhabitants of the Second Earth lived to the south of Mount Ararat in the Valley of Shinar. The memory of this event would therefore include the mountain to the north for those who later ventured into the Hindus Valley after the confusion of the languages.

It is important to understand that in almost every case throughout the ancient world, descriptions of gods with horns are always symbols of the Impostor who we recognize as Satan. The Hindu account is, therefore, a highly perverted account from the very enemy of God. And yet the story contains the main elements of the true historical account.

Here again, the Noah figure was instructed to save both male and female of every kind as a worldwide flood annihilated the entire population of the world. And the boat came to rest on the mountaintop. Here is a question I have for the evolutionists: How does a local river flood send a boat onto a mountaintop?

5. The Account of the Creation and Flood in Africa

a. Egypt

In the northern part of the African continent, the ancient Egyptians held that the god Thoth became angry with the inhabitants of the Earth for their wickedness. In a funerary text that was discovered in the tomb of the Egyptian Pharaoh Seti I, we have this recorded conversation accredited to Thoth:

> They have fought fights, they have upheld strifes, they have done evil, they have created hostilities, they have made slaughter, they have caused trouble and oppression. . . . [Therefore] I am going to blot out everything which I have made. This earth shall enter into the watery abyss by means of a raging flood, and will become even as it was in primeval time (*Egyptian Book of the Dead*, Chapter CLXXV).

Again, we find corroborated in the mythology of the different nations the familiar story of man rebelling against God. Man's violence was such that God needed to intervene, and therefore He saw fit to judge mankind by a worldwide flood that annihilated the entire previous civilization. "I will blot out man whom I have created from the face of the land, from man to animals to creeping things and to birds of the sky; for I am sorry that I have made them" (Gen. 6:7). The flood is again pictured as a raging flood that killed globally and not some local event.

The Egyptian account and the Babylonian account further corroborate the biblical narrative in Genesis that says that prior to the land appearing, the Earth was covered with water. Our primal planet was a water-world before God brought forth the land.

b. Bantu Tribe in Central Africa

The story of the worldwide Flood is not the only element that is corroborated by various cultures. The creation story and the confounding of the languages are equally recorded throughout the cultures of the world. The Boshongo people who belong to the Bantu Tribe in Central Africa record in their creation account the same story narrated in Genesis when God walked in the cool of the day with Adam prior to the Fall:

> According to the Boshongo, a Bantu Tribe in Central Africa, the Universal Creator Bumba walked among mankind, saying unto them, "Behold [the] wonders [of the Earth], They belong to you" (Barrow and Tipler 1996, 94).

c. The Zulu Tribe in Southern Africa

The Zulu account of the Great Flood is associated with the constellation Leo in the Zodiac.

The African story of this constellation tells of a Great Flood, similar to the biblical tale of Noah and his ark and the Greek myth of Deucalion and Pyrrha. *The gods warned grandfather Teye that a flood was coming that would overwhelm the world*, and that he should build a raft and put all the humans and animals on it (clearly he had to build an enormous raft). Grandfather Teye was most persuasive and everyone came except a stubborn old lion called Mbube. Mbube said that he wanted Grandfather Teye to come and tell him only after the rains had started, since he himself had grave doubts about any flood coming at all. The flood came, and the raft floated away, leaving Mbube to drown. Mbube was sorry and his pitiful cries and apologies were heard by the Sun God, who took pity on him and turned him into a constellation called, "The Lion Left Behind" (emphasis added) (McDonald 2000, 55).

In this ancient Zulu tradition we find the same parallels that are common to all the Great Flood accounts. The Zulu, Noah (Teye), was warned by God of an impending flood that would overwhelm the entire world. He was instructed to build a raft that would save humanity and all the animals. The account does not speak of a local flood but of a global cataclysm. No local flood would require the saving of the animal species. The internal evidence in all these accounts contradicts the naturalist's presupposition.

d. The Dogon People of West Africa, the Tiv People of Northern Nigeria

The creation story recorded in Genesis is a historical account that was known to all peoples that descended from Noah. We can find the elements of this story in Central America, with the story of Zamna (Olmec), Tonatiuh (Mayan) creating the world with His spoken word. In India, we find this in the Brahman story of the great ohm. In Egypt, we find that Ptah created the universe by speaking it into being from His thoughts. After the Egyptian religion deteriorated, Ptah was relegated to the god of the craftsmen. We can find these same common elements in many other parts of the world.

> Before the universe came into being it already existed as a thought in the mind of Amma (God), the supreme creator divinity, say the Dogon people of West Africa. They attribute the appearance of all things to the deliberate intention of God, and there is a similar implication in the Hindu myth of Brahma imagining the universe in meditation, his divine thoughts then taking material form.
>
> The idea of God as supreme artist occurs throughout the Africa continent. For example, the Tiv people of Northern Nigeria, who are well known for their woodwork, think of God as the Carpenter, who carved the world in accordance with his vision of a perfect place (Willis 1993, 18).

Perhaps the fact that Jesus as well as his stepfather, Joseph, were carpenters is not accidental.

6. The Account of the Flood in South America

a. The Amazon Indians

Deep in the western jungle of the Brazilian Amazon lives a tribe of Indians known as the Cashinaua. There, in the remotest part of the world, hidden from civilization until just recently, this tribe has passed on to their young, generation after generation, the story handed down to the elders since their earliest fathers.

> There was a time when the lightnings flashed and the thunders roared terribly and all were afraid. Then the Heaven burst and the fragments fell down and killed

> everything and everybody. Heaven and earth changed places at the same time and nothing that had life was left upon the Earth (Mitrovic).

What possible catastrophic event could have caused these Indians to remember in their folklore such an ominous tale? "Fragments fell down and killed everything and everybody." Could that be speaking of the falling ejecta from the meteors? Or perhaps it is speaking of falling debris from volcanic explosions. "Lightnings flashed and the thunders roared terribly." Surely no one can deny that these stories all carry the elements of sonic booms, falling rocks from the sky, and volcanic upheaval unparalleled in human history so that "nothing that had life was left upon the Earth." Noteworthy is the fact that the thunderous booms and lightning flashes, which are telltale signs of meteors entering our atmosphere, preceded the bursting of the heavens and the coming flood.

The memory of the thunderous noises made by the striking meteors and the cracking of the Earth's crust to unleash the fountains of the deep would have made an indelible impression that was not soon forgotten on the minds of the ancients. Again, this is not a local flood but rather a global catastrophe. And yet human nature is such that in time, man has chosen to forget in order to ignore the God who sits on the throne of heaven.

b. Tierra del Fuego

At the southernmost tip of the South American continent is a land sarcastically known as Tierra del Fuego (Land of Fire). Perhaps it was named this because without a fire, it would be difficult to survive there since it is bitterly cold. Here, at the tip of Argentina close to the continent of Antarctica, live a people known as the Pehuenche.

> Another Tierra del Fuegan tribe, the Pehuenche, associate the flood with a prolonged period of darkness: "The sun and the moon fell from the sky and the world stayed that way, without

light, until finally two giant condors carried both the sun and the moon back up to the sky" (Bierhorst 1988, 165–166).

The prolonged period of darkness associated with the Flood is once again evidence of both the volcanic upheaval spewing millions of tons of tephra and the giant mushroom cloud that resulted from the force of the impacting meteors. It suggests that this must have completely blanketed the Earth in darkness and thrown it into the First Ice Age. That same fate also awaits us at the end of the Second Earth when darkness triumphs once more, only to be extinguished by the dawning light of the returning Prince of Peace.

During the Great Tribulation period, God shall judge our Second Earth for the Third and Fourth Insurrections. When the fourth angel sounds his trumpet right before the middle of the seven years, a third of the stars and a third of the Moon and a third of the Sun will be darkened. But by the time we come to the fifth bowl of wrath toward the end of the seven-year period, the entire kingdom of the Antichrist will be completely darkened.

> *The fourth* angel *sounded, and a third of the sun and a third of the moon and a third of the stars were struck, so that a third of them might be darkened and the day would not shine for a third of it, and the night in the same way.*
>
> *Then the fifth* angel *poured out his bowl on the throne of the beast, and his kingdom became darkened; and they gnawed their tongues because of pain, and they blasphemed the God of heaven because of their pains and their sores; and they did not repent of their deeds.*
>
> —Rev. 8:12, 16:10–11

c. Andean People

In the Andean culture of South America, we also find the story of God sending a Great Flood that destroyed the Earth and then saving a couple to recolonize the new world.

In the Andean culture of South America, the sun god, after sending a devastating flood to the earth, causes his son Manco Capac and his daughter Mama Ocllo to teach the arts of civilization to the survivors (Willis 1993, 26).

7. The Account of the Flood, the Creation Story, and the Confounding of the Languages According to the North American Indians

a. The Wijot Tribe

In the northern part of California, the Wijot tribe has the following account:

> The Creator (Gudatri-Gakwitl) decides to destroy the world through a flood. Gudatri-Gakwitl (Above Old Man) was discontent with his creation; "the people who are furry and cannot speak clearly are more like animals than humans. The hero Condor, knowing that Above Old Man plans to destroy the world by a flood hides with his sister in a basket. When the waters finally recede, Condor finds only birds and a raccoon. He marries his sister and they have a human child, beginning a lineage of people who can talk and are not furry" (Gill and Sullivan 1992, 4).

There is in this one story a mixture of several biblical stories. First, of course, is the statement that God was going to judge the entire Earth because of the sin of humanity. What was that sin? Curiously, the Wijot Indians point to a description of some men who were "furry" and were "more like animals than humans." I think that may be an allusion to the Nephilim the Bible speaks of in Genesis 6. Perhaps the Neanderthals were a very hairy species.

It does not say that humans behaved like animals; it says they are more like animals than humans. It indicates that the description of the Nephilim hybrids engendered for the sole purpose of eliminating the seed of Eve and preventing the birth of the One who would bruise his head and fulfill the prophecy of the Dragon Doom.

The part about not speaking an understandable language may also be referring to the dispersion in the Tower of Babel sometime after the Flood. The two stories that occurred in such a distant past could have merged together, as is the case in many mythological accounts.

Noteworthy is also the reference to the hero being the Condor. The Eagle and the Condor are symbols of the Messiah, universally used by almost all cultures. The mixing of the creation story with the Flood and the Tower of Babel is a common occurrence in Indian mythology. That is no doubt due to the fact that when the tribal elders verbally communicated these stories, they were lumped together in one telling as the most important of their ancient memories.

b. The Acoma Indians

The Acoma Indians in northern New Mexico Arizona speak of their God being angry with His people for continuously arguing. As a punishment, He divides the languages, causing them to emigrate and cease their squabbling. "Some groups abandon the others and migrate to another location. Iatku causes the people to speak different languages so it will not be as easy for them to quarrel" (Gill and Sullivan 1992, 5). And so we find that the story of creation, the Great Flood, and the division of the languages at the Tower of Babel are common motifs found in the ancient folklore of all people.

c. Earth Diver Stories of Emergence

It is Interesting that American Indians have developed what anthropologists term "earth diver stories." That is, their stories begin with animals attempting to dive deeply into the primordial sea to bring back a bit of mud from which to create the present Earth. It is rather reminiscent of the Egyptian primordial mound rising out of the sea and the biblical statement, "Let the waters below the heavens be gathered into one place, and let the dry land appear" (Gen. 1:9).

This may also be the intertwining of the memory of the deluged Earth being totally covered with water while Noah attempts to send out birds to bring back evidence that there is dry land somewhere. The initial attempts failed until, of course, the dove brought back an olive branch, a symbol of peace and of Israel for all humanity. From that point on, the olive branch became a symbol of peace and a new start. But it is important to also note that it is the symbol of God's people. Israel is the natural branch, while the Gentiles are the wild olive branches grafted onto the natural branch of the olive tree. So we see that the olive tree is a symbol of those who believe in the one true God.

It is only natural that to those floating on the water, the ground seemed to rise out of the sea when in reality it was the sea that was abating. When the waters rushed over land, it was chaotic and cataclysmic, but the recession of the seas was quiet and sedate. It simply seemed that the land was slowly rising from the depths of the sea. Man could not imagine how the waters could have receded once they had overwhelmed the land.

Where could the water drain? How could the water level lower? They had never seen polar caps before. They knew nothing of snow, sleet, and glaciers. They had absolutely no inkling of how dry land could appear from the depths of an ocean.

> Earth diver is a type of creation tale found widely throughout North America. *In the beginning the entire world is covered with water. The earth diver, portrayed as Beaver, Duck, Mink, Muskrat, Turtle, or Loon, dives to the bottom of the water and brings up a small bit of soil that the creator transfers into land. . . .* In the Iroquois origin story, Turtle succeeds after various other animals try unsuccessfully to bring up soil to support Woman

Who Fell from the Sky (emphasis added) (Gill and Sullivan 1992, 78).

The Chiricahua and Mescalero Apaches currently live just south of the Acoma Indians in the New Mexico and Arizona areas. Their creation story is also intertwined with the Flood story. Thus, their emergence begins with the Flood. It is only natural that the emergence of land in the Second Earth would be confused with the creation story of the First Earth.

d. The Navajo

The Navajo believe that in the beginning, the world was a featureless expanse of dried mud. In this world of mud, the First Man and the First Woman built a sweat lodge in which they envisioned and planned a New World.

Of course, a more fitting description of the landscape following the ravages of the worldwide deluge is not possible. I can envision Noah and his wife locked up in the ark waiting for the waters to subside. The heat from the volcanic activity must have initially elevated the world's temperature, creating a veritable sweat box inside the ark. Noah and his wife waited patiently, wondering what the future of the Second Earth would be like once the forces that were unleashed subsided.

As the ferocious hurricane-force winds and the explosive volcanic activity subsided, the poles began to freeze, and the temperature plummeted in the less temperate regions. The skies might have remained darkened by the tephra for some time, causing the temperature to plummet further before finally stabilizing. Our world had changed forever, never to be the same again.

e. The Arapaho, the Pima, and the Pawnee

The God Creator of the Arapahos is called Nesham. The Creator of the Pima tribe is Tcu-unnyikita. The Creator of the Pawnee Tribe is called Tirawahat. According to all three of their mythologies, the Creator destroyed the world to destroy giants who were living on Earth at that time.

That is a direct reference to the Nephilim, the race of giants who led the antediluvian world into sorcery and witchcraft. The entire population had turned to violence, and for that reason, God destroyed the world with the Flood. It is not a coincidence that these giants are recorded in the many histories of the varied cultures worldwide. The Greeks called them Cyclops, the Celts called them giants, the Egyptians called them the gods of the Zep Tepi, and the Hebrews called them Nephilim, or Tyrants. Modern man calls them Neanderthals.

f. The Seneca

The Seneca, just south of Lake Ontario, have a curious legend that encompasses the story of the Tower of Babel.

> The woman chief who lived during the time when the earth was new and everyone spoke the same tongue and lived in peace. Godasiyo's village occupies both sides of a large river. Every night her people cross the river to attend dances and exchange goods with the people there. Eventually Chief Godasiyo's large white dog begins to cause trouble. Fearing a fight, the chief decides to remove her loyal followers to another residence upstream.
>
> The people construct two birchbark canoes with a platform between them for Chief Godasiyo to ride on. The people make canoes for themselves and paddle upstream on either side of Chief Godasiyo's canoe. At the fork in the river the people begin to squabble about which way to go. The two men paddling Chief Godasiyo's canoe fight, causing her platform to split. Chief Godasiyo falls into the river and is transformed into a great fish. *The people*

are upset, but when they try to talk they find they no longer understand each other. Their languages are no longer the same and they become a divided people. This is the reason so many languages are spoken by the various tribes of earth (emphasis added) (Gill and Sullivan 1992, 103-104).

There is as much evidence for the biblical claim that we were all one nation with one language prior to the Tower of Babel as there is for the Flood and the creation story of innocence in the Garden of Eden.

From an evolutionary point of view, humanity should have evolved simultaneously throughout the Earth from our supposed ancestral apes and would have therefore developed languages and legends independently of each other. The notion of one global language contradicts the evolutionary model and is therefore generally repulsed by them. Yet the evidence throughout all cultures for a common language and people is as prominent as the story of the Flood, the creation story by the voice of God, the creation of man from clay, and the existence of angels and demons as well as heaven, hell, and a Messiah figure.

Naturalists simply refuse to believe it and subjectively choose to ignore it because it does not fit in their evolutionary framework. Thus, they simply relegate it to the category of fantastic mythologies not based on an actual event.

But how can all the cultures carry these same stories worldwide if we evolved independently of one another? Does not logic force us to face the obvious fact that there must have been some historical cataclysmic event in the distant past that was common to all these people and at the root of all these mythologies?

g. The Zuni and the Jicarilla Apache

The Zuni, who live just west of the Acoma people in western New Mexico by the Arizona border, believe that God caused the

Flood as a punishment for the sins of the people and specifically for the sin of incest.

The Jicarilla Apache speak of a time when all humans were equal. Then one day the sky appeared to be on fire, after which all people became different from each other. The sky on fire might be an allusion to the meteor streaking above the heavens before impacting our Earth or the shooting of a plume of ejecta that would have sent thousands of reentering rocks through the atmosphere glowing like stars. The ferocious impacts would have instigated cataclysmic volcanic activity that pummeled our First Earth during the first stages of the Flood.

> After the world has been made as it now appears, the hactcin *all live together in one huge lodge. At this time all people look alike. One day the sky appears to be burning.* The hactcin go to the sky to extinguish the fire. Before they leave, they make each person different from everyone else in appearance, intelligence, and character. The hactcin then depart, never to return to the earth (emphasis added) (Gill and Sullivan 1992, 109).

The Hactun may be the demons who engineered the Nephilim who were chained in the abyss by God's angels and shall remain there until the end of our Second Earth. The differentiation of individuals might be a condensed version of the developments of our different races of peoples created by the dividing of languages after the Flood.

Another possibility may be that the Hactun were the sorcerer Nephilim who seemed to disappear after the Great Flood. They were purposefully extinguished from the Earth by God's judgment.

h. The Iroquois

The Iroquois believed that the Sky God created man out of red clay and that the world was given to him for his domain. Again, the reference to clay may be the memory of the effects of the Great Flood as recorded in the book of Genesis. Or it may refer to the actual creation of Adam as recorded in Genesis when God fashioned him out of clay. Interestingly, the name *Adam* means "reddish." God is referred to as the Sky God by many ancient people such as the Celtic people of Europe, the Africans, the Chinese, the Koreans, the Hindu, the Australians, the Pacific Island people, the Aryans, the Sumerians, the Babylonians, the Egyptians, the South American Indians, the Central American Indians, and the North American Indians. It is also worth mentioning that in this account, the Sky God gave all creation to man in order for him to care for the Earth and the animals it contained.

> In the Iroquois origin myth the Earth was created primarily for the benefit of mankind by the people of the Sky World. The sky god Sapling created the first man out of red clay, and then made a compact between the Earth people and the Sky World:
> I have made you master over the Earth and over all that it contains. It will continue to give comfort to my mind. I have planted human beings on the Earth for the purpose that they shall continue my work of creation by beautifying the Earth, by cultivating it and making it more pleasing for the habitation of man (Barrow and Tipler 1996, 94).

i. The Eskimos of Alaska

In the northernmost region of the North American continent live the hardy Inuit people known as Eskimos. These Indians are no exception to the rule; they also bear witness to the Global Deluge and the accompanying earthquake that overtook the entire Earth, which would have been caused by the striking meteor.

> In Alaska there existed the tradition of a terrible flood accompanied by an earthquake, which swept so rapidly

over the country that only a few people managed to escape in their canoes, or took refuge on the tops of the highest mountains, consumed with terror (Guirand 1968, 426).

We have here the common motif evidenced in the Great Flood accounts where a few people were saved from a terrible flood that was precipitated by great tectonic activity. They escaped a Global Flood in a boat, raft, or canoe and eventually landed on a mountain.

8. The Flood, the Creation Stories, and the Confounding of the Languages According to the Meso-American Indian

a. The Mayan Account

It seems that in the *Popol Vuh*, the initial creation of man was considered an inferior creation. The Mayas remember the antediluvian civilization with contempt because they disregarded the Lord their Creator and were rebellious. Their memory is that man was originally made of wood without a soul. Moreover, they believed that as a result of mankind's disobedience, they were turned to monkeys. The *Popol Vuh* declares that because the inhabitants of the Earth forsook the Creator, the Heart of Heaven sent a Global Deluge that consequently annihilated them.

As an interesting side note, it is humorous that the Mayas turned the tables on the evolutionists and proposed that it was the monkey that devolved from man. Personally, I think the monkeys might be offended, considering the great destruction man has brought upon our world. "And it is said that their descendants are now the monkeys which now live in the forests" (*Popol Vuh* Part 1, Chapter 3).

The reference to monkeys may be a corrupted allusion to the Nephilim and the fact that in the eyes of God they were acting as animals. I believe their hearts being hardened into wood symbolically alludes to the fact that they had no spiritual interconnection with the Creator.

And instantly the figures were made of wood. They looked like men, talked like men, and populated the surface of the earth.

They existed and multiplied; they had daughters, they had sons, these wooden figures; but they did not have souls, nor minds, *they did not remember their Creator, their Maker.* . . .

They no longer remembered the Heart of Heaven and therefore they fell out of favor. . . .

Therefore they no longer thought of their Creator nor their Maker. . . .

These were the first men who existed in great numbers on the face of the earth.

Immediately the wooden figures were annihilated, destroyed, broken up, and killed.

A flood was brought about by the Heart of Heaven; a great flood was formed which fell on the heads of the wooden creatures. . . .

But those that they had made, that they had created, did not think, did not speak with their Creator, their Maker. And for this reason they were killed, they were deluged. *A heavy resin fell from the sky.* . . .

This was to punish them because they had not thought of their mother, nor their father, the Heart of Heaven, called Huracán. And for this reason the face of the earth was darkened and a black rain began to fall, by day and by night (emphasis added) (*Popol Vuh*, 89–90).

Again, we see man's rebellion against the Heart of Heaven. We see a time of great darkness, black rain, and a Global Deluge. According to the *Popol Vuh* (the ancient Maya Quiche scriptures), the Maya had migrated to Central America from somewhere across the Atlantic in the East. Their native history corroborates the biblical claim that immediately after the Flood, there was a time when all men spoke one language and worshiped God. Noah and his children followed after God. "*The speech of all was the same.* They did not invoke wood nor stone, and they remembered the word of the Creator and the Maker, the Heart of Heaven, the Heart of Earth" (emphasis added) (*Popol Vuh*, 172).

Within several hundred years after the Earth was repopulated, the people began to invoke wood and stone idols once again, turning from their Creator. It was at that time that they sought to build a tower to reach the heavens. They sought to build a temple to the demons who claimed to be gods.

Once more the Enemy of Man was at the threshold of global domination. Once more the religion of the Serpent was exacting a heavy toll on human blood. God stepped in to disperse man into nations, and the languages were consequently confounded. That is another area where the *Popol Vuh* supports the biblical narrative. It corroborates the story of the judgment at the Tower of Babel.

It is likely that the inhabitants of Meso America migrated to their present habitat from the East sometime after the Flood or perhaps after the Second Ice Age when the seas again retreated. The curious thing is that they describe that time following the Flood as a time when the world was dark and incredibly cold, thus corroborating the Ice Age that was responsible for lowering the oceans after the Great Flood.

> Now, the fire of the peoples [of Vucamag] had also gone out and they were dying of cold. . . . They could no longer bear the cold nor the ice; they were shivering and their teeth were chattering; they were numb; their legs and hands shook and they could not hold anything in them, when they came. . . .
>
> But the tribes did not perish when they came, although they were dying of cold. There was much hail, black rain and mist, and indescribable cold (*Popol Vuh*, 177, 178).

The description of the entire face of the Earth being darkened and the Deluge being created by black rain is also in complete accord with the Babylonian account and evidence of the Judeo-Christian model we previously proposed as the mechanism of the catastrophe that ended our First Earth. It is a far cry from the localized territorial floods that evolutionary-minded anthropologists try to promote in order to escape the implications of corroborating the biblical account. No local flood causes black rain and freezing weather.

The splitting of the supercontinent that geologists now refer to as Pangaea by the seven meteor strikes would have triggered worldwide volcanic eruptions that spewed millions of tons of tephra into the atmosphere. Some would return to the Earth in the form of black rain, but a good deal of it would remain in the stratosphere for some time after, creating a darkening that would have brought upon the survivors an "indescribable cold" as the *Popol Vuh* declares.

It is also possible and perhaps even more likely that this account of the Mayas is referring to the Second Ice Age that came with the judgment at the Tower of Babel. It was then that the nations of the world set out in different directions as the rise in sea level and the confounding of the languages short-circuited Satan's attempt to rule the world. Either a series of super-volcanoes or the shutting down of the ocean currents by the interference of the Atlantic thermohaline conveyor belt may have precipitated this Second Ice Age. In either case, the Second Ice Age once again caused the oceans to retreat.

The third possibility is that it could be a conflation of the two events. But nevertheless, the result of this global cataclysm described by the Mayas is, of course, akin to a nuclear winter scenario as it was during the aftermath of the First Ice Age following the Great Flood. The temperature worldwide would have changed dramatically, at first becoming very cold. Eventually, the tephra would clear from the sky, and the Earth would begin to warm up, but the poles would from now on remain frozen, melting now much more slowly. This global warming process continues to escalate even in our time.

THE DEATH OF THE FIRST EARTH

After the First Ice Age receded the waters of the Great Flood, the world was literally encased in mud. In the equatorial areas that were not frozen, it took some time for the mud to dry. It was not until the darkened skies cleared that the sun had the power to dry the mud. When the dawn of the Second Earth broke through the sky, it made a deep impact on humanity. No longer would they take the warmth of the Sun for granted. All this is corroborated by the Mayan flood account.

> The light of dawn fell upon all the tribes at the same time.
> Instantly the surface of the earth was dried by the sun. Like a man was the sun when it showed itself, and its faced glowed when it dried the surface of the earth.
> *Before the sun rose, damp and muddy was the surface of the earth*, before the sun came up; but the sun rose (emphasis added) (*Popol Vuh*, 187–188).

Before the Flood, the inhabitants of the Earth had only seen the Sun through the filter of the water vapor canopy. Thus when the tephra finally cleared, the inhabitants were amazed at the intensity of the glowing Sun. The muddy world left behind by the Flood could not completely dry up until the dark skies were cleared and the heat of the shining Sun finally broke through.

This ancient memory was the reason Satan was so successful in fostering the worship of the Sun. It is the reason so many cultures around the world were later obsessed with sacrificing to the Sun to make sure it would continue in its path and never again hide its face from mankind. Sadly, man was once again deceived to worship the creation rather than the Creator.

In their mythology, both the Mayas and the Aztecs have provided us with unprecedented proof of the fact that immediately following the Flood the inhabitants of the Earth spoke one language. The survivors initially were located mainly in the area of Mesopotamia (the East). Sometime after the division of languages, a group migrated to the area we now call Central America and became the ancestors of the Mayas. The memory of their relatives living in the East is that after the Great Flood they strayed from the Heart of Heaven and began to worship the Serpent. It was at this point that the languages were confused.

> Many men were made and in the darkness they multiplied. Neither the sun nor the light had yet been made when they multiplied. All lived together, they existed in great number and walked there in the East.
>
> *Nevertheless, they did not sustain nor maintain [their God]; they only raised their faces to the sky, and they did not know why they had come so far as they did.*
>
> There they were then, in great number, the black men and the white men, men of many classes, men *of many tongues*, that it was wonderful to hear them (emphasis added) (*Popol Vuh*, 172).

More of the Mayan history will be discussed in the chapter devoted to their civilization in *The Secret of the Lost Knowledge*. For now, we are concerned only with the aspect of their history that deals with the Flood and, coincidentally, the Tower of Babel. The bottom line of the denial of the Global Deluge by the evolutionists is the fact that they would have to concede the miraculous nature of the event and the fact that it was predicated on the judgment of a personal God with absolute morals and standards. It is the internal antipathy toward the notion that a God exists and that He holds us morally accountable that looms high in their subjective analysis of the chronological data.

b. The Aztec Account

The Aztecs, who later conquered the Mayas, also had a memory of a worldwide catastrophic flood that closely parallels the biblical narrative. Their Noah story begins with an unbridled torrential rain of such proportion that it created a worldwide flood so deep that all the mountains disappeared under the water, and men were transformed into fish. According to their memory of the Deluge, only two humans survived.

Their Noah is called Coxcoxtli, and his wife was Xochiquetzal. Their Noah counterparts had also been warned by the Creator of the impending doom and consequently instructed to build a huge boat.

As their story unfolds, we see the boat grounding on a mountain peak when finally the waters subsided. There they descended and rebuilt their civilization, but a curious thing occurred; their many children all of a sudden became dumb and were unable to speak until a dove on top of a tree gave them the gift of languages. The only problem then was the fact that all the languages ended up being different, and they could not understand each other (for a more exhaustive study, I suggest reading Sir James G. Frazer's *Folklore in the Old Testament: Studies in Comparative Religion, Legend, and Law*).

Again we see the story of the Deluge as well as the Tower of Babel intertwined in the mythology of these ancient people. It is only logical that these two events provided major turning points for humanity, and for that reason they are remembered by all cultures around the world. The idea that these memories could have sprung independently in all the nations is an irrational proposition. The statistical odds are simply too great for that to be a plausible consideration.

The story of the Tower of Babel, by inference, indicates that the technological knowledge that was carried over was of such an advanced nature that man in a relatively short period of time once again began to worship the naturalistic sciences and denied their Creator. They abandoned the Creator and turned to worship the creation instead.

It seems to me that we have now reached that same point in the history of humanity. We may not worship idols of wood, metal, and stone, but we have made ourselves into gods. Man is the arbiter of truth and morals. Our lust for absolute autonomy has made us into idols whose religion is scientism.

THE HISTORICAL EVIDENCE

Confounding the languages had as a consequence the side effect that scientific and technological advancements ground to a crawl. Communication is the key catalyst to scientific progress. In our previous century, man was able to bridge the communication gap through the use of radio and satellites. As a result, technology has once again skyrocketed, and man in his arrogant pride has again begun to worship his own creation rather than the Creator.

The movement toward a global government is again churning at full speed. We can see that from two separate sides. In the West, we see a movement toward a socialist, globalist form of government. In the East, we see the Islamic bid for a globalist, colonialist, autocratic tyranny. Either side brings Lucifer his global throne. Lucifer's bid for the global throne is gaining traction as never before in our generation.

The last time our world was at this crossroads, God confounded the languages, and a great deal of the antediluvian science was forgotten. Some groups were able to retain more of their ancient technological knowledge than others, and the resulting civilizations from these scattered remnants reflected to one degree or another the amount of knowledge they were able to retain.

Those who managed to record or memorize some of this antediluvian knowledge held a distinct advantage to their contemporaries. That is why we see civilizations such as the Egyptians rise out of the Great Flood and, without little traceable evolutionary history, build the greatest pyramids from the very earliest onset. The technology of this remarkable engineering feat is to this day not completely known. There is no gradual rise in technology. At once and abruptly, they are at the zenith of their civilization, and it only deteriorates after that.

Not only do all the civilizations of the world carry in their memory the Great Flood, but their archaeological evidence also points to the fact that a great civilization once thrived and was destroyed by this Flood. The faint memory, which can be seen in the mammoth works of the ancient people of Egypt, Mesopotamia, Meso America, Europe, Africa, China, and India, gives us an imperfect glimpse at the world that was.

c. The Hopi Account

In the accounts of the ancients, we find mixed in their stories elements of truth that corroborate our Judeo-Christian model that considers the Genesis record as a historically true account of our human history.

The Hopi people of Meso America even corroborate our position that the very axis of our planet was changed by the cataclysm created by the meteor impacts.

> Another version of this myth told by the Hopi people says that the first world was destroyed, as punishment for human misdemeanors, by an all-consuming fire that came from above and from below. The second world ended when the terrestrial globe toppled from its axis and everything was covered with ice. The third world ended in a universal flood (Willis 1993, 26).

In the Hopi version, we see that it was the wickedness of mankind that triggered this judgment. We also see that fire came first from above and then from below. That is quite in line with the meteor strike scenario that would be seen first as a ball of fire coming from heaven inciting tremendous volcanism, which then brought fire from below. The fact that the axis of the world became tilted is the main reason for the global flood to turn to ice. Had that not happened, the Flood would never have receded. Although the order may have changed by the continual retelling by their elders, they corroborate that there was, in fact, a global flood they considered universal and not a local river-flooding scenario as the evolutionists imagine.

There is no possible way to logically or scientifically conclude from a statistical standpoint that the numerous accounts of the

Global Flood found throughout the length and breadth of our planet developed independently of each other. What would be the statistical chance that all the major cultures of the world would have chronicled the events of a local flood in their respective areas and that each of these accounts would have described it as a global deluge where only a few survived a judgment of God because of the wickedness of humanity? The changing of the axis of the Earth, the change in the rotation of the Earth and Moon, the subsequent Ice Age, the darkened sky, fire coming from the sky and then from below, the water coming from the bosom of the Earth, and the dark rain—all these form the very elements that substantiate our Judeo-Christian model of a literal reading of the Genesis narrative.

Any rational mind that compares all these accounts would have to conclude that the similarities are too acute for them not to be referring to the same historical events experienced by our ancestors that are rooted in one common past. The coincidences are just too great. The mathematical probability of this Global Flood account, the creation stories, and the judgment of the confusion of languages occurring by random chance throughout the entire world independently of one another is simply an impossible conjecture. It is a fact that the evolutionists are the real people of faith—blind faith.

The common regard by all ancient cultures for the Serpent as the supreme evil entity, the memory of the worldwide Flood, the confounding of languages, the creation story, the belief in angels and demons, the belief in heaven and hell, the hope of a Messiah, the Zodiac, even the names of the days of the week all point to a single common origination point from which all civilizations gradually diverged. They point to the religion of Adam, Noah, and Abraham. They point to the one true God described in Genesis.

EPILOGUE
THE CHOICE BEFORE US

The future of humanity is determined by the collective impact of the individual choices that each of us makes. Without the knowledge that enables us to make the right choices, our future will be grim. The ability of Jews and Christians to impact their cultures with truth will be determined by the effort they make to understand our culture and to intelligently reveal the cloak of darkness imposed by the deceptive lies of the Enemy of Man.

If we fail to educate our children and ourselves, we shall surrender our progeny to the darkness that will envelop our world. Upon our shoulders is the responsibility to equip the saints to do the work of the ministry. If we fail to oppose the deception of the Great Usurper with intelligence, humility, love, and perseverance, our children shall suffer for it. We must not shirk the call to stand for truth in our generation no matter the cost. Anything else is cowardice.

Our postmodern culture has chosen to live in a divided field of knowledge as we earlier explained in the first book of this series that deals with existentialism. Truth has been divided into two unconnected spheres. Some have categorized religion or metaphysical reality in the upper story as relativistic, unverifiable, subjective, and irrational concepts that man can choose to believe. Science, on the other hand, is relegated to the lower story as verifiable, empirical, absolute, and rational fact. Between them is a great divide that cannot be traversed, an unbridgeable chasm imposed by their dualistic framework of reality.

This dualistic, divided field of knowledge is a subjectively accepted norm that has no rational foundation. It is an accepted provision that automatically disqualifies any metaphysical consideration from being true truth. It automatically allows only scientific data to be considered as absolute truth. Reason in this platonic dualism exists only in the lower story. Faith resides in the subjective upper story, and there is no interconnection of faith and reason.

By imposing this dichotomy, they automatically disqualify the metaphysical realm from any rational inquiry. But it is reason that shows the searching mind that this dualistic framework is irrational. If our universe is birthed in chaos and if, as the postmodern naturalists contend, all events are ordered through random and undirected processes, then there is no natural philosophical basis to legitimize reason. How does a random and undirected process develop an ordered and directed process of analysis called reason?

It is an irrational leap of faith to believe that our universe was randomly conceived and yet somehow the laws of science evolved by chance into absolute and universal axioms. How does random ordering create universal physical laws? How does random ordering create the supersymmetry observed in the macroworld as well as the microworld? How does random ordering provide a basis for even knowing if our thoughts are in any tangible way connected to the physical reality about us?

The subjective dualism imposed by the postmodern culture is, in effect, a metaphysical worldview that irrationally concludes that randomness evolved into a highly structured and complex order. There can be no absolutes if all was birthed in relativistic randomness. If absolutes exist, then truth is unified. The arbitrary division between faith and science is an artificial divide. True truth is universal. The unity of truth is a foundational Judeo-Christian worldview because God is the creator of truth. We cannot create truth; we can only accept it or reject it.

I must interject here with the strongest voice possible that the biblical narrative regarding the Great Flood is not just a matter of faith but rather a matter that must be decided by the scientific evidence at our disposal. And the evidence clearly substantiates that not only these rapid climactic changes can take place but also that they did take place in the past.

Those of us who have accepted the Judeo-Christian model as the real spacetime, historical, and actual process used by God to create the universe, our planet, life, and man have maintained from the very beginning that our faith is born out of true science. There is no division between true science and true faith.

True science cannot contradict true truth. And if the Holy Scriptures contain the truth revealed by God to humanity, then its claims are, in fact, historical and can be corroborated by true science. Therefore, our faith is not based on blind faith but rather on scientifically verifiable, empirical data. And I challenge the reader to objectively consider the facts to determine which model correctly adheres to reality.

It is for this reason that creationists have maintained that the creation of our universe was instigated by the Almighty and the record of the Holy Scriptures is historical and true. Although evolutionists may charge me with subjective thinking, as a direct result of my faith, I with equal force charge them with the very same conviction. Their worldview is tainted by their naturalistic presupposition that automatically disqualifies the metaphysical world as real. And whether they realize it or not, the many assumptions made to prop evolution are, in fact, the doctrines of their metaphysical worldview.

I dare say without equivocation that the driving force behind most who accept the evolutionary model is the underlying desire to do away with God and avoid any moral restraints inherent in the biblical view. For this reason, the evolutionary model is in direct contradiction to the biblical claim. And such claims as the Great Flood of Noah are therefore maligned and treated as mere mythological fairy-tales.

Their religion is atheistic evolution. It is a religion in the very real sense of the word, whether they like it or not. It is a comprehensive worldview from which they draw a set of morals and ethics. The sad thing is that they have an intolerant religion. They do not want anyone else to compete with them in the educational system. They want exclusive rights over the realm of the minds of our youth. That is not education; it is indoctrination. Education presents all sides of a subject and allows the student the freedom to choose.

But true science is not in contradiction with the truth revealed by the God of truth. And although I believe in the historicity of the Holy Scriptures, my reason for believing is that it is, from an objective viewpoint, the one that most closely correlates to the true scientific facts available to all thinking persons. The challenge I propose to the reader is to objectively analyze the empirical data and formulate your conclusions accordingly.

The Creator is the Alpha and the Omega, and His narrative stands the test of scrutiny. The end has been declared before the beginning so that all who wish to know the truth can receive it without compromising their rational capabilities. God said this:

> *"Come now, and let us reason together,"*
> *Says the* L*ORD*,
> *"Though your sins are as scarlet,*
> *They will be as white as snow;*
> *Though they are red like crimson,*
> *They will be like wool."*
>
> —Isa. 1:18

The biblical narrative is the story of the Fall of Man and the redemption offered by His amazing grace to all who will by faith simply turn to Him. For that reason, He came in the form of man to die on the cross. He took upon Himself the debt of sin we owed. To those who accept Jesus as their Savior, He freely offers righteousness with no strings attached. We cannot earn our salvation, nor can we steal it or buy it. It is the free gift of God to all who come to Him by faith.

> *For by grace you have been saved through faith; and that not of yourselves,* it is *the gift of God; not as a result of works, so that no one may boast.*
> —Eph. 2:8–9

> *He saved us, not on the basis of deeds which we have done in righteousness, but according to His mercy, by the washing of regeneration and renewing by the Holy Spirit.*
> —Titus 3:5

None of us are righteous enough to enter into heaven. We are fallen creatures riddled by sin. For that reason, God sent the seed of Eve to redeem us from the penalty of our sins. He alone is the Savior. All we can do is receive Him to be our Savior. When we do, He makes our sin as white as snow through the blood He shed on the cross.

The ark of God is a symbol of God's grace and the salvation that He provides for mankind in the midst of terrible judgment for wickedness. He is our ark to bring us into eternal life. Without Him we would perish.

All of this I have shared with you in order that you might come to the rational conclusion that the Creator of this universe loves us and sent His Son to buy us back from the slavery of sin. If we receive Him, in that very moment every sin we have done, are doing, and will do before we die is paid for by His sacrifice. He makes us perfect.

> *By this will* we have been sanctified through the offering of the body of Jesus Christ once for all.
>
> *And every priest stands daily ministering and offering time after time the same sacrifices, which can never take away sins; but He, having offered one sacrifice for sins for all time, SAT DOWN AT THE RIGHT HAND OF GOD, waiting from that time onward UNTIL HIS ENEMIES BE MADE A FOOTSTOOL FOR HIS FEET. For by one offering He has perfected for all time those who are sanctified* (emphasis added).
>
> —Heb. 10:10–14

How perfect is perfect? How forever is forever? If you are perfected forever, can you lose your salvation? The obvious answer is no.

I do not hope I will be going to heaven; I *know* I will be going to heaven—not because I am any better than anyone else but because He has made me perfect through the washing of my sins by His sacrifice on the cross. I simply placed my trust in Him as my Savior, and He made me clean—as white as snow.

Like the Apostle John said at the end of one of his letters, I say now unto you:

> *These things I have written to you who believe in the name of the Son of God, so that you may* know that you have eternal life (emphasis added).
>
> —1 John 5:13

God cannot force you into the ark. He simply asks that you step in by faith. The choice is yours. What will you do with His invitation?

The Future of the Second Earth

Not only do the Scriptures tell us of the end of the First Earth, they also warn us of the end of the Second Earth and the Third Earth. The Fourth Earth shall be eternal. It will be in a new universe, and we shall dwell in the presence of God. Sin shall be remembered no more, and the curse shall be no more. Our first step in the downward spiral of decay was taken when humanity was expulsed from the Garden at Eden as a result of rebellion toward God. It was there that the curse was birthed and death entered our planet. Our second step in the downward spiral became our loss of the world that was through the Flood, again as a result of our rebellion toward God. Our third downward step was in the Tower of Babel that resulted in the changing of languages and the establishment of the Gentile nations.

One would think that after these three drastic and cataclysmic events we would have learned our lesson. But the Bible says that twice more the world will be subject to the deleterious effect of our rebellion toward God. Violence will once again bring judgment upon our planet. Our topography and climate will once again be drastically changed.

The fourth time will be when Satan again attempts to gain political control of the entire world through an apostate religio-political system. But his future takeover shall not come to fruition without human help. He will attempt to gain the global throne because, aided by his sorcerer, the majority of humanity will once again choose to follow him instead of God.

The war gods, the Mahuzzim of the ancients, shall once again attempt to rule our planet. They shall empower the War King from the North and his sorcerer, or False Prophet, and they will oppose the Prince of princes. But as always, God will preserve a remnant of those who follow Him. And the destruction of that War King and his sorcerer will come by the right arm of God at the appointed time. Like Moses and Israel on the shore of Sinai, we shall stand by and watch our God fight for us.

> *When the transgressors have run their course,*
> *A king will arise,*
> *Insolent and skilled in intrigue.*
> *His power will be mighty, but not by his own power,*

THE DEATH OF THE FIRST EARTH

And he will destroy to an extraordinary degree
And prosper and perform his will;
He will destroy mighty men and the holy people.
And through his shrewdness
He will cause deceit to succeed by his influence;
And he will magnify himself in his heart,
And he will destroy many while they are at ease.
He will even oppose the Prince of princes.
But he will be broken without human agency.
—Dan. 8:23–25

This is the dreaded time of the Great Tribulation when the Fourth Insurrection of the dark angels shall mark the final period of the indignation. During those seven years, most of life as we know it on our Earth will die of disease, the ravages of war, famines, and polluting poisons (Rev. 6:1–8). The Second Earth will end with a series of devastating earthquakes of an unprecedented and global nature that will radically alter our planet in the same drastic manner that the death of the First Earth changed our planet.

Two global earthquakes will ravage Earth. The first will come when the Antichrist attacks the city of Jerusalem and enters into the Temple to declare that he is god. That is the abomination that causes desolation spoken of by Daniel and Jesus Christ (Dan. 9:26–27, Matt. 24:15).

The second earthquake will happen three and a half years later at the time of the Battle of Armageddon (Rev. 16:18–21). The second one will destroy all the cities of the world, reducing them to a heap of rubble. It shall level the large mountain ranges that have been built up by the tectonic forces since the Great Flood and shall create drastic isostatic changes on every continent. In that day, the entire topography and climate of the Second Earth shall once again drastically change. Then the Third Earth will begin.

In the very same way the previous judgment of the Great Flood disintegrated all the works of man and ended the First Earth, this enormous global earthquake will shake the world to its very foundation, leveling even the mountains. The islands will disappear under the waters of the rising oceans. They are merely mountains in the sea, and every mountain shall crumble in the wake of this enormous earthquake. It shall happen when the War King and his sorcerer come to make war with the Prince of princes.

> *And they gathered them together to the place which in the Hebrew is called Har-Magedon.*
>
> *Then the seventh angel poured out his bowl upon the air, and a loud voice came out of the temple from the throne, saying, "it is done." And there were flashes of lightning and sounds and peals of thunder;* and there was a great earthquake, such as there had not been since man came to be upon the earth, so great an earthquake was it, and so mighty. The great city [Jerusalem] was split into three parts, and the cities of the nations fell. *Babylon the great was remembered before God, to give her the cup of the wine of His fierce wrath.* And every island fled away, and the mountains were not found (emphasis added).
>
> —Rev. 16:16–20

As we come close to that time, the fragile world that was left behind after the Great Flood, our Second Earth, will become even more decayed than the world we live in today. Before the Second Earth has run its course, violence and terrorism shall rule our planet once again. The once pristine freshwater oceans of the antediluvian world will then be so polluted that they will hardly be able to support marine life.

Even today through pollution and overfishing, our oceans are being depleted at an alarming rate. Our ocean temperatures are rising, and soon, if this trend is not reversed, there will be a wholesale extinction of the coral reefs that provide the bottom rung of the food chain for our marine life.

The rising heat of the oceans will spawn numerous mega-hurricanes that will ravage our planet. The frequency of intense tornadoes will bring death and destruction as we have never seen before. Wars shall increase, and the frequency and intensity of earthquakes shall begin to announce the beginning of the end. When you see these signs, know that we are nearing the end of our Second Earth. Do not fail to see the signs of His coming, for earthquakes shall begin to shake our world with a violence and frequency we have never experienced before in the Second Earth.

The future will be filled with massive tsunamis in some places and droughts in others. Fires shall ravage the forests and savannahs of our wilting planet. Our freshwater supplies will dry up. Wars shall increase as the time of lawlessness terrorizes the planet. Food production shall be strained, and famine will soon begin to claim the lives of millions. This is the direct result of man's rebellion against God.

The violence of counterfeit religions spawned by the Serpent will bring terror to all humanity. A global religion shall rise that will bring terror to the hearts of every human who walks the Earth. Their globalist, colonialist agenda shall be championed by the demonic hierarchy to undo the curse of the Tower of Babel. The globalist agenda of the demonic hierarchy has not changed since the First Insurrection. But when they think they have succeeded, our Second Earth shall not be spared from judgment. Babylon shall fall. Jericho shall fall. The Pharaoh shall be defeated. The chosen of God shall be protected by the Living Ark as He protects His remnant of believers beneath the Eagle's wings.

The time will come when the forces of darkness shall supernaturally fuel the desire for sordid gain, and the greed and unchecked avarice of man shall reign supreme. The hearts of men will grow cold and hard. Peace and mercy shall flee from the land as the dark fires of Babylon spread abominable sorcery throughout all mankind. In the name of peace, they shall bring the crescent sword to bear upon the necks of the innocents. Violence shall once again rule supreme upon our planet. The blood of the innocents shall rise from the soil where it was spilt and beckon God as the voice of Abel for justice. "How long, O Lord, holy and true, will You refrain from judging and avenging our blood on those who dwell on the earth?" (Rev. 6:10).

Be patient, my brothers and sisters. Until every last soul who will cross into the light does so, God shall wait. But in the appointed time, your Champion shall come with the east wind. Remember the words of our Lord: "All those who take up the sword shall perish by the sword" (Matt. 26:52).

Wickedness has set her throne in the Land of Shinar. "And on her forehead a name was written, a mystery, "BABYLON THE GREAT, THE MOTHER OF HARLOTS AND OF THE ABOMINATIONS OF THE EARTH" (Rev. 17:5). Every nation shall succumb to the enchantment of her sorcery, the enticement of her riches, and the intoxication of her sensualities. They shall join themselves unto the harlot in all her splendor and glory. Then all that was great and good in the world shall be hidden, and those with a heart shall then wonder in darkness and despair at the arrogance and power of her sorcery. Who can stand against her? "And I saw the woman drunk with the blood of the saints, and with the blood of the witnesses of Jesus." (Rev. 17:6).

But to those who endure, it is given to them to become the rulers of the Third Earth, for the meek shall inherit the earth. Then judgments shall be levied upon those who have worshiped the Dragon in rebellion toward God. And for this reason, the judgments come in both forms of seven (representing God the Father) and three (representing God the Son).

So no one will mistake the Lamb whose number is three, who is pronouncing judgment on the Impostor and Usurper, each of the judgments will come in the same measure in which the sixth seal came previously and darkened the Sun. The darkness experienced at the death of the First Earth shall return. The shadow shall bring the coming night. In that day, the judgments shall come in one-third increments, resulting in the exact number of casualties. Man will not be able to claim coincidence.

In that day, the one-third judgments shall gather their portion. The strong arm of the King of the North shall not be able to stop the right arm of God. None shall be able to claim this as mere chance. Those in power shall attempt to blame these calamities on unfortuitous circumstances and freak events caused by "Mother Nature." They shall seek to deceive the world of its true origin. But none shall be without excuse, for the exact nature of the consequences shall point to the divine design they have so long refused to see as they remained entrenched in their naturalistic worldview. "The fool has said in his heart, 'There is no God'" (Ps. 14:1). But God shall require His just due.

When the one-third judgments begin, know that we have entered into the death spasms of the Second Earth. In order to show this pattern, I have linked the judgments of the first four trumpets together in the following excerpt.

> A third *of the earth was burned up, and a* third *of the trees were burned up, and all the green grass was burned up.* . . . *a* third *of the sea became blood, and a* third *of the creatures which were in the sea and had life, died; and a* third *of the ships were destroyed.* . . . *a* third *of the rivers and on the springs of water* . . . *became wormwood, and many men died from the waters, because they were made bitter* . . . *and a* third *of the sun and a* third *of the moon and a* third *of the stars were struck, so that a* third *of them would be darkened and the day would not shine for a* third *of it, and the night in the same way* (emphasis added).
> —Rev. 8:7–12

It may be that the Third Ice Age will come as the polar ice caps melt and pour forth their fresh water into our oceans. It may cause the ocean in that region to have a much-diminished concentration of salt. When the oceans reach a certain critical point and the water is not heavy or dense enough to drop with the force necessary to continue the ocean currents, then the ocean conveyor belt will grind to a halt. If this warming trend continues, soon the thermohaline conveyor belt may fail again.

Or it may be that the shifting continents will abruptly stop the ocean currents as God unites them again into a supercontinent with Jerusalem at the center of the world. Only God knows, but in that day, the Third Ice Age will begin and mark the death of our Second Earth.

Fear not, my brothers and sisters. God will restore the oceans in the Third Earth. Flowing eastward from the Temple of the Lord in Jerusalem, a river of life will empty into the sea. And the oceans will once again become fresh water and be filled with life. It is for this reason that the Messiah is known as Aquarius in the story of the Zodiac.

> *These waters go out toward the eastern region and go down into the Arabah; then they go toward the sea,* being made to flow into the sea, and the waters of the sea become fresh (emphasis added).
> —Ezek. 47:8

The Second Earth will die, but God will reserve for Him a remnant as He did in the First Earth with Noah. God is our protection. He is our ark who shall transport us safely through the wicked storm rising in the dark horizon. This story, however, is not the story of this book. It is the story in the next book of this series, *The coming Prince of Peace*.

Nevertheless, I have chosen to mention this here so the reader might understand that the record of the death of the First Earth in Genesis is not an allegorical tale but a very real, historical event. Failure to heed this warning will result in our inability to heed the warnings of the coming night that fast approaches us at the end of this age.

APPENDIX A

SUMMARY OF EVENTS REGARDING THE GREAT FLOOD AND THE TOWER OF BABEL

The story of Noah's ark is not a fairy-tale of unrealistic and extravagant mythological claims. The story of Noah's ark is, in fact, history, and it is scientifically verifiable as to its claims. The geological, anthropological, and meteorological evidence is overwhelming for the serious and objective student. The following points summarize our Judeo-Christian model.

1. The meteorological and geological conditions of our planet prior to the Great Flood were as follows:
   a. The Earth had only one supercontinent (Arza).
   b. The Earth's crust, or outer cap, was unbroken.
   c. There was a thin water vapor canopy surrounding the entire planet such as the one that exists on planet Venus, except much thinner.
   d. There was as a result of the water vapor canopy a greenhouse effect throughout the planet that maintained an ideal global temperature.

e. There was no rain; the Earth was covered by heavy dew each morning.
f. The high humidity and moderate temperature created a favorable condition for a lush flora, and consequently, an enormous variety of thriving fauna was throughout the entire planet.
g. The abundant flora created a super-rich oxygen environment of 35–37 percent of the total volume of our atmosphere. That, along with the abundance of food, provided for a much wider variety in the character complex of each kind and much larger specimens of all living things.
h. As a result of the weight of the small water vapor canopy, our atmosphere was slightly denser. Hence, a single breath of air provided much more oxygen than our less dense atmosphere of the Second Earth.
i. There were no polar ice caps.
j. The pristine, antediluvian ocean contained a minimal level of salinity.
k. The single ocean of the First Earth was much shallower than our present oceans and contained many areas of warmer waters that supported an enormous variety of fish and other marine animals.
l. A layer of supersaturated salt water with dissolved limestone and carbon dioxide existed 10–16 miles or so below the surface of the planet in interconnected subterranean chambers below the granitic composite superstructure of the upper crust and the basaltic layer that lay below it.
m. The surface terrain was probably fertile plains and undulating hills with mountains that were significantly lower than those that presently grace our planet. I suspect that God would most probably not have created mountains higher than what we presently call the tree line since in

that altitude the survival of life becomes precarious. The conditions of the prediluvian world were ideal for life.
- n. Because there was no rain, there were no thunderstorms with lightning.
- o. There were no hailstorms.
- p. There were no hurricanes.
- q. There were no tornadoes.
- r. There were no earthquakes.
- s. There were no tsunamis.
- t. There were no or few deserts.

2. The possible collision of seven large meteors could have been the cause of the unfolding events leading to the Flood. Collisions of this magnitude would most certainly have the force necessary to fracture the crust of the Earth. The following sequence is a condensed version of the events we propose transpired during the cataclysm that destroyed our First Earth.
    a. In the 600th year of Noah, in the second month, the month of Heshvan, on the 17th day of the month, all the fountains of the deep burst open, and the floodgates of heaven were opened (Gen. 7:11-13). The crust of the Earth was shattered into seven major tectonic plates by the force of the impacts of seven meteors.
    b. The ocean floor on the opposite side of the planet would have been raised by the force of the pressure waves created by the meteor strikes. The enormous pressure waves of energy traveling through Earth's core from the points of impact would most certainly have caused the crust on the opposite side of Earth to bulge out, first raising the ocean floor and causing the waters to spill over onto the land. The dramatic motion in the crust of such magnitude would have also produced large fissures that generated enormous

amounts of lava that were subsequently pushed to the surface from the magma layer and aided by these repeated waves traveling back and forth from one side of the Earth to the other.

c. In this way, the Siberian Traps and the Deccan Traps were formed by the pressure waves of the striking meteors as the bulging crust opposite the strike points poured millions of tons of lava to the surface, covering enormous areas that were sometimes 2 miles deep in huge lava provinces with the distinctive steps featured as each wave returned.

d. This multiple meteor collision would have shot upward enormous mushroom clouds of dust and rock into the stratosphere. They would have darkened the skies globally. Some of the larger material would have fallen back as burning ejecta and caused major conflagrations as well as a dramatic rise in global temperatures.

e. Earthquake swarms of enormous magnitude would have shaken the planet to its very foundation as the crust of the Earth ripped like a giant zipper between the strike zones.

f. Tsunamis of enormous size would have surely devastated the coastal regions.

g. Volcanic eruptions emanating from the cracks in the tectonic hydroplates would have spewed enormous amounts of water vapor and volcanic ash (called tephra) into the water vapor canopy. These particles, along with the ejected debris from the strikes, became the cloud nuclei that allowed the water vapor to precipitate as rain (black rain).

h. The supercontinent of Arza was shattered into the present seven continents. The axis of the Earth was tilted by the force of the impacts, and the rotation around the Sun was increased at one end by 5 million miles, causing it to be elliptical at that end.

i. Firestorms probably raged initially in the areas immediate to the volcanoes and at the impact points where the ejecta landed until the heavy rains began.
j. The enormous, combined energy of the seven meteor strikes cracked the granitic composite structure of the upper crust and weakened its integrity, allowing the uncorking of the subterranean saltwater chambers.
k. The seismic waves agitated the pressurized salt water that was saturated with carbon dioxide, sulfur dioxide, limestone, and olivine in these subterranean aquifers. The crack created by the meteors provided an escape route for the pressurized saltwater aquifer and a sudden outgassing to explode upward in violent form.
l. Enormous volumes of supersaturated and hot salt water escaped through the cracks formed by the various strike zones and began to shoot into the sky with violent force. This process continued throughout the ripping crust. All the fountains of the deep burst open within a single day, creating a wall of water that reached the stratosphere around the borders of the new seven continents.
m. The oxygen level (percentage of the overall volume) of our atmosphere decreased significantly in the course of this violent outgassing of CO_2. Our planet went from 35–37 percent oxygen to our present 21 percent oxygen.
n. Enormous chunks of rock and gravel along with salt water were shot into space. Some became comets, and others became asteroids; most of it fell back to Earth.
o. The crust of the Earth ripped on the line of less resistance along the Mid-Oceanic Ridge, traveling all around the planet like a giant zipper. This also caused the area we now call the Ring of Fire in the Pacific. It forms the border of all seven major continental hydroplates.
p. This raging curtain of pressurized water shot up at super-

sonic speeds as an enormous wall of geysers reached the stratosphere all around the ripped crust. The weight of 10–16 miles of granitic rock above the underground aquifers became the force that powered the fountains of the deep.

q. These powerful geysers eroded the cracked continents on both sides. As the 10–16 miles of rock above the level of the aquifers eroded and catapulted away from the shooting curtain of water, the cracks widened. The flowing wall of salt water continually eroded the sides of the continents on either side of the geyser. Once the opening was wide enough, the loss of that weight in rock caused the basaltic subterranean floor beneath the aquifers to rise some 7 miles from its previous location, creating the bulge we recognize as the Mid-Oceanic Ridges.

r. The newly formed continents slid down the sides of the bulge of the Mid-Atlantic Ridge laterally, gliding on the water in the aquifers below it. These continents are therefore more accurately termed hydroplates since they glided on the water below them the same way glaciers are now gliding over meltwater.

s. The Atlantic Ocean was formed as the continents separated. In fact, the singular ocean anciently known as Apsu was now divided into our present seven oceans—the North Pacific Ocean, the South Pacific Ocean, the North Atlantic Ocean, the South Atlantic Ocean, the Arctic Ocean, the Antarctic Ocean, and the Indian Ocean.

t. As the water exited the subterranean chambers and eroded the tips of the continents, the continents bowed downward at the tips, causing further cracks in the surface of the granitic superstructure. These cracks were from the surface downward as opposed to the cracks created by the sliding hydroplates from the bottom upward when they grinded to a halt.

APPENDIX A

u. The exiting water eroded the tips of the continents, causing the familiar V shape of continental slopes and shelves.

v. As the continents shifted, they compressed to form mountains, thickening as they contracted during the grinding process with the basaltic layer below. The Continental Drift also caused the landmasses to be pushed upward as the pressure mounted, thus creating the high mountain ranges we presently have. The drift was initially much faster. As the subterranean chambers emptied, the drift slowed down as friction increased between the granitic continental blocks and the basaltic layer below.

w. That friction caused massive melting of rock, especially pronounced at the distal points of the continental blocks where the continents ground to a crawl.

x. The grinding continents caused cracks that emanated from below. The melted rock spewed out through these cracks in the granitic superstructure as volcanoes and super-volcanoes, causing a second round of volcanic upheaval.

y. The deep ocean trenches in the Western Pacific formed as matter below it sunk to replace the matter that had risen at the opposite side of the planet when the basaltic floor of the Atlantic Ocean rose some 7 miles above its previous level.

z. Hail returning from space created downdrafts of frigid air from the upper atmosphere that flash-froze many animals and buried them in ice.

aa. As the water vapor canopy was exhausted, the temperature in the polar areas dropped dramatically. The greenhouse effect was nullified. In addition, since the skies darkened, light from the Sun was kept from warming the surface of the Earth. The drop in temperature was worldwide and dramatic, aided by the tilt in the axis created from the meteor strikes.

THE DEATH OF THE FIRST EARTH

bb. The flooded Earth then began to freeze at the poles, causing the waters to recede. Vast areas of fertile tropical forests that had been completely deforested by continentally wide sheet-flooding then became encased under ice. For this reason, the Arctic sea floor contains one of the largest deposits of coal in the world.

cc. The settling of the suspended sediments in the floodwaters caused the strata to form, encasing many animals. Those with the densest bodies sank first. The many earthquakes that followed caused the interred bodies to become stratified by their relative density.

dd. The rains stopped on the 40th day. On the 27th day of the third month, the month of Chislev, three days before the end of the month on the first day of the new moon, the darkened new moon, the water vapor canopy was exhausted, and darkness shadowed the planet. Tephra from the volcanic upheavals shadowed our dying planet. The Atlantic Ocean had widened to such an extent at this time that the pressure of the fountains was diminished, although water continued to be expelled from the fountains of the deep.

ee. For five months, the waters prevailed as the aquifers continued venting. On the 150th day, the fountains of the deep stopped, and the ocean reached its maximum level. On the 17th day of the seventh month (17th day of Nisan), which is now the first month, as God commanded Moses, the ark grounded on Mount Ararat. Today, all we have left of the fountains of the deep are the relatively small smokers that still pump superheated salt water leached with many minerals from the mid-oceanic rifts. The friction of the moving granitic hydroplates has superheated the water in the now almost depleted aquifers over the basaltic rock floor below.

ff. On that day, the Second Earth was redeemed when the ark landed on Mount Ararat on the 17th day of Nisan. The redemption of our Earth and Noah and his family was complete. The angel of death had passed over, and God's remnant was delivered by His grace (Gen. 8:1–4). That is exactly the same day Moses crossed the Red Sea when Israel was redeemed from slavery to Egypt. On that day, the armies of the Pharaoh drowned, but the remnant of God's people were brought across the Red Sea on dry land and freed from slavery. It is the Feast of Unleavened Bread, Hag ha Matzoth, the Feast of Firstfruits. On that same date, Jesus resurrected, bringing from the ark of Abraham's bosom God's remnant into our celestial abode. The spiritual salvation of mankind was complete. All those who would by faith accept the gift of salvation would henceforth be redeemed by the Lamb of God who was slaughtered on the cross. It is the firstfruits of the redeemed after the Passover Festival. It is the Feast of Firstfruits. It is the celebration after the Day of Redemption. It is the spring equinox. It is the day of resurrection.

gg. But darkness was over the face of the Earth. Tephra spewing into the air by the many volcanoes still erupting blanketed our atmosphere. Without the radiant energy of the Sun penetrating to the surface, the planet began to freeze at the poles, and the waters began to recede.

hh. On the first day of the 10th month, the month of Tammuz, which is now the fourth month, the tops of the mountains became visible (Gen. 8:5). Like small island peaks dotting a global ocean, the land began to reappear in a world of deep shadows. It is the summer solstice, but the day is still darkened, and the shadow still covers our Earth. Nevertheless, the darkness is thinning, and light is overcoming darkness.

ii. Three months later, Noah removed the covering over the ark, on the first day of the first month, the month of Tishri, the same day the First Earth was created (Gen. 8:13). It is Rosh Hashanah, the New Year. The Second Earth was birthed. It is the autumn equinox. Rosh Hashanah is also known as Yom Hazikaron, the Day of Remembrance. It is a designated time for us to remember that God created the universe, and the Aleph will cause the Tau to be carried out. It is a time to remember the creation of man in the Garden at Eden and lament the consequence of the Fall that alienated us from God. It is a time to remember the way God intended for mankind. It is a time to return to our proper place as originally intended, in alignment or intimate fellowship with our heavenly Father.

jj. Hebrew tradition holds that it was on the first day of Tishri that Adam and Eve were created (Sanhedrin 38b), beginning the First Earth. The *Gemara* explains that Rosh Hashanah is the day on which the Hebrew rabbis reckon their yearly cycles, or the four *tequfot*—the *tequfah* of Tishri, the autumn equinox; the *tequfah* of Tebet, the winter solstice; the *tequfah* of Nisan, the spring or vernal equinox; and the *tequfah* of Tammuz, the summer solstice. It is no coincidence that the two patriarchs Abraham and Jacob were born in Tishri and died in Tishri. However, the miraculous birth of Isaac from the dead womb of Sara was symbolic of the One who would be born of a virgin from Bethlehem Ephrathah. Isaac, the third patriarch, was therefore born on Passover, the same time Jesus was born and died, according to the earliest Christian traditions. The commonly celebrated nativity date adopted by the Catholic Church is a corrupted account. December 25 is an occult date that remembers the birth of Nimrod. The *natalis invicti solis*, or birthday of the invincible Sun, was a celebration of the Mithraic mystery religion that was unfortunately adopted by the Catholic Church as the birthday of Jesus who was born and died during Passover in the spring equinox. The idea that God created the world during the month of Tishri (autumn equinox) is a Hebrew tradition of great antiquity.

Among the rabbis who held this opinion, Rabbi Eleazer is quoted saying, "In Tishri the world was created; in Tishri the patriarchs [Abraham and Jacob] were born; in Tishri the patriarchs died; on passover Isaac was born; on New Year [Tishri 1] Sarah, Rachel and Hannah were visited [i.e. remembered on high]; on New Year Joseph went forth from prison; on New Year the bondage of our ancestors in Egypt ceased [six months before the redemption which was exodus]; in Nisan they were redeemed and in Nisan they will be redeemed in the time to come" (Finegan 1998, 79).

It was on the first day of Tishri that Ezra brought the Book of the Law, which was fortuitously found. And on that day, he read it to the people who were rebuilding the Temple after returning from the Babylonian captivity (Neh. 8:2-3). Hence, upon that glorious day, the Law of Moses was remembered again in Israel and read out loud to all the people in commemoration of the building of the Second Temple of God. The same will happen at the end of this age when the Third Temple is built by the Son of David.

The First Ice Age reaches its optimum level when the glaciers reached as far as the 35th or 40th parallel. That was the first maximum glacial extent. The entire planet was gripped by cold. Only a thin belt surrounding the Earth's equator was then habitable. But the climate of the Land of Shinar was temperate and ideal for farming. It must be noted that after the natural creation in the month of Tishri, the world was quickly plunged into the darkness of sin so the very nature of our seasons symbolized the spiritual decline of humanity from the very first. For that reason, this was quite important symbolically to our ancient forefathers.

After the Great Flood, ascendancy into the cold and dark winter following the month of Tishri became even more pronounced due to the destruction of the water vapor canopy and the change in Earth's axis. The winters were more acute, and the time of the autumn now plainly heralds the coming of the cold, dark winter. And so it was with mankind that soon after his creation, sin entered the world, and the curse of death took hold of our planet. Likewise, soon after the Great Flood, the Earth once again plunged into rebellion against God. For this reason, the judgment of the Tower of Babel came shortly after the Great Flood.

The Hebrew Scriptures consider the time from the first of Tishri to the 10th of Tishri as a time of personal introspection and repentance. It is a time when one considers the cost of judgment before the awesome Day of Atonement. It is a time of repentance with respect to the holy judgment of God. Yom Kippur thus symbolizes the atonement of the redeemed who choose to believe and follow the way of God. It is a time of restitution for those who repent of their unfaithfulness and turn to God. But it also indicates a time of retribution that brings the judgment of the unredeemed and wicked who choose not to believe. Their own blood shall be the sacrifice required of God to cleanse the Earth that is profaned by their wickedness. And for that reason it is also known as Yom Hadin, the Day of Judgment.

kk. On the 10th day of Tishri, the atonement for the Earth was completed. It is the Day of Atonement. It is Yom Hadin, the Day of Judgment, when the Earth was declared covered for her previous transgression. It was sanctified and ready for the new beginning. Noah is still within the ark under the protection of God. On the 10th day of Tishri at the end of the Second Earth, Israel shall be under the Eagle's wings, protected by God, and the atonement for the Second Earth shall be completed. In that day, Jesus shall judge the Antichrist and the False Prophet and throw them into the Lake of Fire. It is symbolized by the ritual of Yom Kippur (Rev. 19:19–20). In that day, Lucifer shall be cast into the Abyss until the end of the Third Earth (Rev. 20:1–3). The demons who led the Fourth Insurrection will be punished as the firstfruits of the Lake of Fire, along with the Antichrist and the False Prophet, and the Earth will be cleansed for the new beginning, the Third Earth. But Noah is not yet allowed to come out of the ark.

11 Five days later, Noah is still kept inside the ark during the time of the Feast of Tabernacles from the 15th of Tishri to the 22nd of Tishri. It is the Festival of the general harvest, Succoth, and symbolizes God's protection over Israel during her wandering in the desert for 40 years before entering the Promised Land. During this festival, they are required to build booths of protection, and all God's people were required to live in them for seven days.

This is a prevision of the time of Jacob's Trouble, known in the New Testament as the Great Tribulation, and of the Great Succoth in which Israel is given a place of refuge underneath the Eagle's wings for 1,260 days. There in the wilderness, God will be the manna, the Living Bread, and the Rock who gives forth living water in the desert (Rev. 12:13–14). He who flees to the Eagle's wings shall bask in His light, shining in the midst of a world in darkness.

> *He will dwell on the heights,*
> *His refuge will be the impregnable rock;*

THE DEATH OF THE FIRST EARTH

His bread will be given him.
His water will be sure.

Your eyes will see the King in His beauty;
They will behold the far-distant land.
—Isa. 33:16–17

The Great Eagle, the Living Ark of the Covenant, shall be the ark of protection for those Jews who hearken to the voice of the two olive trees (Elijah and Enoch) and flee into the wilderness. That begins on the day the King of the North invades Jerusalem in the middle of the seven years of Tribulation foreseen by Daniel (Dan. 9:27). The two olive trees are also symbolized by the two witnesses who warned Lot to leave Sodom and Gomorrah and flee into the wilderness. Do not look back, or your fate will be that of Lot's wife. When you see the King of the North enter the Promised Land and profane the Temple of God, declaring himself a god, flee into the Chukka that God has prepared for you in the wilderness. In that day, the two olive trees shall be killed by Abaddon the War demon, but in three and a half days, they shall resurrect before the eyes of the watching world as a symbol of Israel resurrecting in three and a half years to begin the Third Earth.

mm. Noah was finally allowed by God to disembark from the ark on the 27th day of the second month, the month of Heshvan, exactly one year and 10 days after the judgment of the First Earth started (Gen. 8:14). On that day, Noah made a sacrifice unto the Lord. The Second Earth was consecrated. God made the Rainbow Covenant of the Second Earth with Noah.

It was the dawning of the Second Earth (Gen. 8:20–22, 9:1–13). From that day forward, the seasons were much more pronounced. It will one day also be, at the death of the Second Earth, that the Third Earth will dawn when the Root

APPENDIX A

of Jesse shall rule with an iron scepter from Jerusalem. On that day, the Lion of Judah will make an everlasting covenant with Israel.

> *Behold I will take the sons of Israel from among the nations where they have gone, and I will gather them from every side and bring them into their own land; and I will make them one nation in the land, on the mountains of Israel. . . . And they will be My people, and I will be their God.*
>
> *And My servant David will be king over them, and they will all have one shepherd. . . . They will live on the land that I gave to Jacob My servant, in which your fathers lived; and they will live on it, they, and their sons and their sons' sons, forever; and David My servant shall be their prince forever. I will make a covenant of peace with them; it will be an everlasting covenant with them. And I will place them and multiply them, and will set My sanctuary in their midst forever. My dwelling place also will be with them; and I will be their God, and they will be My people. And the nations will know that I am the* Lord *who sanctifies Israel, when My sanctuary is in their midst forever.*
>
> —Ezek. 37:21–28

nn. The violence of man against man that terrorized the First Earth by the Nephilim will now be severely punished. Every man who sheds the blood of another man shall have his life forfeited because human life is sacrosanct. We are all infinitely valuable because we are all created in the image of God (Gen. 9:5–6). On that day, when the Third Earth dawns, the Lion of Judah will reign with an iron scepter over all the nations of the world, and justice will rule with righteousness. The everlasting covenant shall never be broken. Israel shall dwell in peace. No longer will the wealthy oppress the poor. No longer will there be tyrants who oppress the masses. Justice shall rule in righteousness, and swords shall be turned into plowshares. On that day, the Prince of Peace shall sit on His throne in Jerusalem (Isa. 11:1–10).

oo. Farming became necessary in our Second Earth. The fruit of the land could no longer sustain us as it did before the Great Flood. Our planet had degenerated from the robust biosystem God had intended. We are a shadow of the Earth that was (Gen. 9:20). But in that day, in the Third Earth, the Messiah shall turn our broken planet around. The deserts will flower, the salt waters will be made fresh, and predation shall be done away with. The lion shall lie down with the lamb. Nature shall be reconstituted by the real Aquarius. In that day, God shall pour down His Spirit upon Israel, and a fountain of grace shall be opened unto them (Zech. 13).

> *Do not fear, O Jacob My servant;*
> *And you Jeshurun whom I have chosen.*
> *For I will pour out water on the thirsty land*
> *And streams on dry ground;*
> *I will pour out My Spirit on your offspring*
> *And My blessing on your descendants.*
>
> —Isa. 44:2–3

pp. In the following years after the Great Flood, as the dust in the atmosphere cleared, the temperatures began to rise in the equatorial zones. The rotting vegetation of the debris from the Great Flood infused enormous amounts of greenhouse gases that began to heat our atmosphere. That in turn began the process that eventually led to runaway deglaciation as more bodies and vegetation thawed out and decomposed.

qq. The tropical flora and fauna that had inhabited the whole planet in the antediluvian world became restricted to the equatorial zones around the center of the planet. The habitat for wildlife became more hostile because of the extremes in weather. That caused the vast majority of animals that were dependent on large amounts of vegetation to become extinct, along with the predators that ate them.

rr. As the North and South American continents drifted apart from the European and African continents, the Atlantic Ocean increased in size, and subsequently the Pacific Ocean diminished in breadth. Within a short period of time, as the continents ground to a crawl, they came to the relative position found today. They are moving now at a much-reduced rate due to the friction with the basaltic subterranean base they rest on. This growing distance has restricted somewhat the flow of people back and forth between the Old World and the New World. As the distance between the continents increased by the widening and rising of the Atlantic Ocean, it became harder for people to travel back and forth. Initially, the much lower ocean levels provided land bridges and islands to allow some travel among the new continents that are no longer above water due to our much higher sea levels today.

ss. The meteorological conditions changed drastically. The world was now watered by rain. Those areas that do not receive adequate rain became vast expanses of desert. Those areas that receive too much rain are now subject to periodic flooding. Some areas are washed of their topsoil and become rocky outcrops unfit for farming. Man now has to contend with (1) thunderstorms that batter us with lightning bolts; (2) snowstorms that batter us with hail and sleet; (3) hurricanes that batter us with tidal surges and fierce winds; (4) tornadoes that concentrate their destructive power in a much narrower and lethal area; (5) tsunamis that wash over the land, destroying everything in their wake and then dragging it back out to sea; (6) volcanoes that pour forth magma and kill many through their toxic ash, toxic gases, or pyroclastic flows; and (7) earthquakes that bury people alive. So the world might know that judgment came from God, it came in sevens. The single landmass was broken into seven continents. The single ocean was broken into seven oceans. Our Second Earth shall end with a global earthquake on the seventh bowl of the seventh trumpet of the seventh seal that will destroy every city in the world.

tt. The once pristine water of the antediluvian ocean was now contaminated by the turbulence of the Flood, causing enormous amounts of minerals to be dissolved into the water. The salinity of the ocean increased considerably, creating a more hostile environment for marine life. Many of the marine animals were not able to adapt quickly enough and died as a result of the change in salinity. The reduced numbers also caused the larger marine animals to become extinct. As we approach the end of the Second Earth, our oceans shall progressively become polluted until at a certain point during the Great Tribulation, all marine life shall die (Rev. 16: 3). But when our Champion returns, He shall regenerate our planet. The salt water shall become fresh, and marine life will grow abundantly (Ezek. 47:8–9).

uu. The ocean levels again rose steadily in a very short period of time after the Great Flood due to the rapid heating by the greenhouse gases of our atmosphere and subsequent deglaciation. These gases were expulsed into the air by the outgassing of the underground reservoirs that produced the fountains of the deep and the decomposition of the flora and fauna killed by the Great Flood. This is known as the Flandrian Transgression that raised our ocean levels again, this time in a gradual fashion and not in the dramatic cataclysm of the Great Flood.

APPENDIX A

vv. By this time, the survivors of the Great Flood had already rebelled against God, and the judgment of the Tower of Babel caused the disbursement of the people and the confounding of the languages. I suspect that this coincided with the Second Ice Age as the Flandrian Transgression interrupted the thermohaline conveyor belt. God flooded the area of the Middle East called the Valley of Shinar and forced the descendants of Shem, Ham, and Japheth to scatter.

ww. The cause of the Second Ice Age was the disruption of the ocean currents. As the deglaciation process accelerated, the infusion of meltwater with relatively low levels of salinity disrupted the thermohaline system that powers the ocean conveyor belt currents, which in turn kept our global temperatures moderate. The shutdown of the conveyor belt then thrust us into the Second Ice Age within a few hundred years after the Great Flood. At the end of our Second Earth, the same disruption of the ocean currents created by the melting ice caps will bring upon us the Third Ice Age toward the very end of the Great Tribulation period.

xx. The postdiluvian world became an even more hostile environment for life. It is but a shadow of a shadow of the world God had intended for man. Twice now the world has deteriorated, first through the expulsion from the Garden at Eden and then through the destruction of the First Earth by the Great Flood. Unfortunately, the Scriptures tell of a third time to come, but that story will be addressed in *The Coming Prince of Peace*.

REFERENCES

"Acraman Impact Structure, South Australia." Earth Observatory. February 18, 2010. https://earthobservatory.nasa.gov/images/42813/acraman-impact-structure-south-australia.

Allen, Richard Hinckley. *Star Names and Their Meaning.* New York: Dover Publications, 1899.

Athenagoras. *The Sacred Writings of Athenagoras.* Translated by the Rev. B. P. Pratten. Altenmüster, Germany: Jazzybee Verlag Jürgen Beck

Barrow, John D., and Frank J. Tipler. *The Anthropic Cosmological Principle.* New York: Oxford University Press, 1996.

Bierhorst, John. *The Mythology of South America.* Neew York: William and Morrow Company, 1988.

Blavatsky, Madam. *Isis Unveiled.* Wheaton, IL: The Theosophical Publishing House, 1877.

Book of Jubilees, The. Translated by R. H. Charles. Pantianos Classics, 1902.

Britt, Robert Roy. "Giant Crater Found: Tied to Worst Mass Extinction Ever." Space. June 1, 2006. https://www.space.com/2452-giant-crater-tied-worst-mass-extinction.html.

Bond, Alan, and Mark Hempsell. *A Sumerian Observation of the Köfels' Impact Event.* Great Britain: Alcuin Academics, 2008.

Boissoneault, Lorraine. "What Really Turned the Sahara Desert from a Green Oasis into a Wasteland?" *Smithsonian Magazine.* March 24, 2017. https://www.smithsonianmag.com/science-nature/what-really-turned-sahara-desert-green-oasis-wasteland-180962668/#GMLIh6UwSFFyihso.99.

Boule, Marcellin, and Henry V. Vallois. *Fossil Men* (original in French). Memphis, TN: General Books, 1957.

Bradford, Nick. "Increased Hurricane Intensity." National Environmental Education Foundation. Accessed July 27, 2021. https://www.neefusa.org/nature/water/increased-hurricane-intensity.

Brown, Paul. "Melting Ice Cap Triggering Earthquakes." *The Guardian*. September 8, 2007. https://www.theguardian.com/environment/2007/sep/08/climatechange.

Brown, Walt. *In the Beginning: Compelling Evidence for Creation and the Flood, Seventh Edition*. Phoenix, AZ: Center for Scientific Creation, 2001.

Budge, E. A. Wallis. *The Egyptian Book of the Dead*. New York: Dover Publications, 1967.

Cherfu, J. "If Not a Dinosaur, a Mammoth?" *Science* 253, no. 5026 (1991): 1356.

"Chicxulub Impact Event." Lunar and Planetary Institute. Accessed July 22, 2021. https://www.lpi.usra.edu/science/kring/Chicxulub/discovery/.

Church, George M., and Ed Regis. *Regenesis: How Synthetic Biology Will Reinvent Nature and Ourselves*. New York: Basic Books, 2012.

Clerke, Agnes M. *The System of the Stars*. Quoted in Richard Hinkley Allen. *Star Names: Their Lore and Meaning*. New York: Dover Publications, 1963.

Coe, Michael D., and Rex Koontz. *Mexico*. London: Thames and Hudson, 1977.

Coldewey, Devin. "Ancient Tablet Shows Babylonians Used Calculus to Track Planets." News, January 29, 2016. https://www.nbcnews.com/tech/innovation/ancient-tablet-shows-babylonians-used-calculus-track-planets-n507281.

REFERENCES

Davidson, Hilda Ellis. *The Lost Beliefs of Northern Europe*. New York: Barnes and Noble, 1993.

"Death of Gilgamesh, The." The Electronic Text Corpus of Sumerian Literature. Accessed July 27, 2021. https://etcsl.orinst.ox.ac.uk/section1/tr1813.htm.

Dennis, Brady, and Meeri Kim. "Western Wildfires' Size, Intensity and Impact Are Increasing, Experts Say." *The Washington Post*. July 2, 2013. https://www.washingtonpost.com/national/health-science/western-wildfires-size-intensity-and-impact-are-increasing-experts-say/2013/07/02/f13916ea-e32a-11e2-a11e-c2ea876a8f30_story.html.

Egyptian Book of the Dead, The. Translated by Ogden Goelet. Chronicle Books, 2015.

Epic of Gilgamesh, The. Harmondsworth: Penguin Books, 1972. http://www.ancienttexts.org/library/mesopotamian/gilgamesh/tab11.htm.

Eridu Genesis, The. Translated by Poebel. Flood Stories. July 26, 2020. https://floodstories.wordpress.com/2020/07/26/2-1-a-iv-poevel-1914-1969/.

Extant Works (Julius Africanus). In *Ante-Nicene Fathers, Vol. 6*. Edited by Alexander Roberts, James Donaldson, and A. Cleveland Coxe. Buffalo, NY: Christian Literature Publishing, 1886.

Farrar, Stewart, and Janet Farrar. *The Witches' Bible; The Complete Witches' Handbook*. Blaine, WA: Phoenix Publishing, 1981.

Filby, Frederick A. *The Flood Reconsidered*. London: Pickering and Ingus, 1970.

Finegan, Jack. *Handbook of Biblical Chronology*. Peabody, MA: Hendrickson Publishers, 1998.

Fisher, Robert L., and Roger Revelle. "The Trenches of the Pacific." *Scientific American*. Quoted in Walt Brown. *In the Beginning*. Phoenix, AZ: Center for Scientific Creation, 1972.

Flamsteed, Sam. "Grace in Space." *Discover*. March 23, 2007. https://www.discovermagazine.com/planet-earth/grace-in-space.

Gamkrelidze, Thomas V., and V. V. Ivanov. "The Early History of Indo-European Languages." *Scientific American* 262 (March 1990): 110–116.

Gilbert, Adrian G., and Maurice M. Cotterell. *The Mayan Prophecies*. New York: Barnes & Noble Books, 1996.

Gilgamesh: Man's First Story. Accessed May 21, 2022, http://wigowsky.com/school/civilizations/NearEast/gilgameshstory.html.

Gilgamesh Epic, The, and Old Testament Parallels. Chicago: The University of Chicago Press, 1963.Gill, Sam D., and Irene F. Sullivan. *Dictionary of Native American Mythology*. New York: Oxford University Press, 1992.

Gimbutas, Marija. *The Civilization of the Goddess: The World of Old Europe*. San Francisco: Harper, 1991.

Gleiser, Marcelo. *The Prophet and the Astronomer*. New York: W. W. Norton and Company, 2001.

"Global Climate Report – December 2014." National Centers for Environmental Information, National Oceanic and Atmospheric Administration. August 9, 2021. https://www.ncdc.noaa.gov/sotc/global/201412.

"Global Climate Report – November 2015." National Centers for Environmental Information, National Oceanic and Atmospheric Administration. August 9, 2021. https://www.ncdc.noaa.gov/sotc/global/201511.

REFERENCES

"Global Climate Report – November 2017." National Centers for Environmental Information, National Oceanic and Atmospheric Administration. August 9, 2021. https://www.ncdc.noaa.gov/sotc/global/201711.

"Global Climate Report – May 2016." National Centers for Environmental Information, National Oceanic and Atmospheric Administration. August 9, 2021. https://www.ncdc.noaa.gov/sotc/global/201605.

Guirand, Felix (ed.). *New Larousse Encyclopedia of Mythology*. New York: The Hamlyn Publishing Group, 1968.

Hancock, Graham. *Fingerprints of the Gods*. New York: Three Rivers Press, 1995.

Hancock, Graham. *Underworld: The Mysterious Origins of Civilization*. New York: Three Rivers Press, 2002.

Hanor, Jeffrey S. "Precipitation of Beachrock Cements: Mixing of Marine and Meteoric Waters vs. CO_2-Degassing." *Journal of Sedimentary Petrology* 48 (June 1978): 489–501. Quoted in Brown, Walt. *In the Beginning*. Phoenix, AZ: Center for Scientific Creation, 2001.

Harpending, Henry C., Mark A. Batzer, Michael Gurven, Lynn B. Jorde, Alan R. Rogers, and Stephen T. Sherry. "Genetic Traces of Ancient Demography." Presentation at the National Academy of Science of the United States of America, February 17, 1998. https://doi.org/10.1073/pnas.95.4.1961.

Haywood, John. *Chronicles of the Ancient World*. New York: Metro Books, 2012.

Heidel, Alexander. *The Gilgamesh Epic and Old Testament Parallels*. Chicago: The University of Chicago Press, 1963.

Herm, Gerhard. *The Celts: The People Who Came Out of the Darkness*. New York: Barnes and Noble, 1993.

Hesiod. "The Heavens." In *The Legends*. https://www.sacred-texts.com/atl/rag/rag17.htm.

Hoesch, William A., and Steven A. Austin. "Dinosaur National Monument: Jurassic Park or Jurassic Jumble?" Institute of Creation Research. April 1, 2004. https://www.icr.org/article/dinosaur-national-monument-park-or-jurassic-jumble.

Howden, Jana. "Seven of the Biggest Volcanic Explosions to Rock the Earth." *Cosmos*. December 13, 2016. https://cosmosmagazine.com/earth/earth-sciences/seven-of-the-biggest-volcanic-explosions/.

International Standard Bible Encyclopedia, Volume 3, The. Albany, OR: Books for the Ages, 1997. http://media.sabda.org/alkitab-11/V6F-Z/ISBE_V_3.PDF.

"Instructions of Shuruppag, The." The Electronic Text Corpus of Sumerian Literature. Accessed July 27, 2021. https://etcsl.orinst.ox.ac.uk/section5/tr561.htm.

Josephus, Flavius. *Antiquities of the Jews*. In William Whiston, *Josephus Complete Works*. Grand Rapids, MI: Kregel Publications, 1960.

King, Hobert M. "Vredefort Impact Crater." Geology.com. Accessed July 23, 2021. https://geology.com/articles/vredefort-dome.shtml.

Kluger, Jeffrey. "Global Warming: The Culprit?" *Time*. September 26, 2005. http://content.time.com/time/subscriber/article/0,33009,1109337-2,00.html.

La Haye, Tim F., and John Morris. *The Ark on Ararat*. New York: Thomas Nelson Publishers, 1976.

MacCulloch, J. A. *The Religion of the Ancient Celts*. London: Studio Editions, 1992.

McDonald, Marianne. *Mythology of the Zodiac*. New York: Metro Books, 2000.

REFERENCES

Melina, Remy. "What's the Biggest Volcanic Eruption Ever?" LiveScience. November 10, 2010. https://www.livescience.com/11113-biggest-volcanic-eruption.html.

Menard, H. S. "The Deep-Ocean Floor." *Scientific American* 221, no. 3 (1969): 126–145. Accessed July 26, 2021. http://www.jstor.org/stable/26069612.

Mitrovic, George. "The Legends of the Cataclysms." Accessed July 28, 2021. https://sites.google.com/site/georgemitrovicauthor/the-legends-of-the-cataclysms.

National Geographic. "Is Zealandia Relly the 8th Continent?" February 17, 2017. https://web.archive.org/web/20191030221631/http:/www.nationalgeographic.com.au/nature/is-zealandia-really-the-8th-continent.aspx.

Oskin, Becky. "Russia's Popigai Meteor Crash Linked to Mass Extinction." LiveScience, June 13, 2014. https://www.livescience.com/46312-popigai-crater-linked-eocene-mass-extinction.html.

Patiño. Henry. *Codes.* Los Angeles: Areli Media, 2019.

"Poem of Early Rulers, The." The Electronic Text Corpus of Sumerian Literature. Accessed July 27, 2021. https://etcsl.orinst.ox.ac.uk/section5/tr525.htm.

Poetic Edda, The. Translated by Henry Adams Bellows. Sacred Texts, 1936. https://www.sacred-texts.com/neu/poe/index.htm.

Popul Vuh: The Book of the Ancient Maya. Translated by Delia Goetz and Sylvanus Griswold Morley. New York: Dover Publications, 2003.

Rehwinkel, Alfred M. *The Flood.* St. Louis, MO: Concordia Publishing House, 1951.

Schmandt, Brandon, Steven D. Jacobsen, Thorston W. Becker, Zhenxian Liu, and Kenneth G. Duecker. "Dehydration Melting at the Top of the Lower Mantle." *Science* 44, no. 6189 (2014): 1265–1268. https://doi.org/10.1126/science.1253358.

Second Apology of Justin Martyr, The. In *Ante-Nicene Fathers, Vol. 1.* Edited by Alexander Roberts, James Donaldson, and A. Cleveland Coxe. Buffalo, NY: Christian Literature Publishing, 1886.

Sim, David. "Japan Tsunami: 60 Powerful Photos of the Earthquake and Nuclear Disaster That Hit Six Years Ago." *International Business Times.* March 10, 2017. https://www.ibtimes.co.uk/japan-tsunami-60-powerful-photos-earthquake-nuclear-disaster-that-hit-six-years-ago-1610819.

Snelling, Andrew A. *Earth's Catastrophic Past: Geology, Creation & the Flood, Volume 2.* Dallas, TX: Institute for Creation Research, 2009.

South Dakota State University. "Large, High-Intensity Forest Fires Will Increase." *Science News.* April 10, 2017. https://www.sciencedaily.com/releases/2017/04/170410085510.htm.

Streeter, Michael. *Witchcraft: A Secret History.* London: White Lion Publishing, 2020."Sudbury Basin." Wikipedia. https://en.wikipedia.org/wiki/Sudbury_Basin.

Szczepanski, Kallie. "Zheng He's Treasure Ships." ThoughtCo. August 7, 2019. https://www.thoughtco.com/zheng-hes-treasure-ships-195235.

Tarr, W. A. "Is the Chalk a Chemical Deposit?" *Geological Magazine* 62, no. 6 (June 1925): 259.

Taube, Karl. *Aztec and Maya Myths.* Austin, TX: University of Texas Press, 1993.

Tertullian. *On Idolatry.* In *Ante-Nicene Fathers, Vol. 3.* Edited by The Rev. Alexander Roberts and James Donaldson. New York: Charles Scribner's Sons, 1902.

REFERENCES

Testaments of the Twelve Patriarchs, The. Translated by R. H. Charles. London: Adam and Charles Black, 1908.

"Thoughts and Theology."

Vinther, Dann. "Remains of Gigantic Meteorite Crater Found in Greenland." ScienceNordic, July 15, 2012. https://sciencenordic.com/denmark-geology-greenland/remains-of-gigantic-meteorite-crater-found-in-greenland/1374351.

Whitcomb, John C., and Henry Morris. *The Genesis Flood.* Grand Rapids, MI: Baker Book House, 1971.

Williams, Windsey. *The Energy Non-Crisis.* Kasilof, AK: Worth Publishing Company, 1980. Quoted in Walt Brown, *In the Beginning.* Phoenix, AZ: Center for Scientific Creation (2001): 164.

Williamson, Robert W. *Religious and Cosmic Beliefs of Central Polynesia, Volume 1.* Cambridge, UK: Cambridge University Press, 1933.

Willis, Roy (ed.). *World Mythology.* New York: Metro Books, 1993.

Woolley, C. Leonard. *The Sumerians.* New York: Norton & Company, 1965.

World Religions: From Ancient History to the Present. Edited by Geoffrey Parrinder. New York: Facts on File, 1985.

Yeoman, Barry. "Schweitzer's Dangerous Discovery." *Discover.* April 26, 2006. https://www.discovermagazine.com/the-sciences/schweitzers-dangerous-discovery.

INDEX

A

1996 JE1 142
2012 DA14 145
Acraman meteor 155, 157, 170, 178
Adams, Michael 334
Adam's prediction 3, 199
Adapa 454
Aidophedo 109, 481
Aldebaran 169, 206, 210, 211, 212, 213, 222
Allen, Richard Hinckley 192
Ambrose, Stanley 346
ancient cosmic battle 2, 59, 60, 61, 199
andesite line 315
Andes Mountains 343
Andree, Dr. Richard 9
Andromeda 218
Annwn 472
Antarctica 21, 22, 147, 155, 156, 157, 161, 166, 170, 171, 175, 176, 177, 178, 179, 181, 183, 184, 185, 188, 189, 252, 318, 341, 342, 344, 345, 425, 427, 494
Apep 109, 210, 480
Apsu 36, 41, 182, 455, 534
Aquarius 167, 194, 214, 217, 218, 219, 483, 527, 544
Aries 95, 200, 201, 218
Arza 20, 29, 36, 42, 45, 46, 128, 139, 149, 150, 156, 158, 161, 163, 164, 165, 169, 170, 171, 177, 181, 189, 191, 224, 233, 245, 246, 254, 335, 344, 373, 384, 414, 529, 532

Athenaeus 377
Atrahasis 455, 460
Austin, A. 554
Azazel 57, 71, 72, 73, 101, 102, 208, 437

B

Bacchus 92
baoshan 375
Beatlegeuse 211
Belenos 471
Benioff zones 314
Berezovka mammoth 336, 337, 338
Bhola Cyclone 286
black rain 10, 31, 35, 49, 133, 139, 164, 228, 264, 265, 276, 456, 464, 466, 505, 506, 507, 532
Boissoneault, Lorraine 549
Bond, Alan 549
Boshongo 491
Boule, Marcelline 550
Brahma 493

C

calculus 196, 550
Caligula 376, 377
Cashinaua 493
Catal Huyuk 91, 105, 106, 108, 111
Cepheus 219
Cernunnos 88, 89, 90, 92, 94, 95, 472, 473
Cerridwen 88, 92
Chesapeake Bay of Virginia 40
Chicxulub crater 143, 144, 146, 152, 153, 154, 157

coming night 168, 526, 527
continental crust 313, 318
continental drift theory 122
cornucopia 87, 94
cosmic rays 21, 24, 30, 348
Coxcoxtli 510
Cro-Magnon 29, 66, 78, 81
Cromm Cruaich 472
Curuppag 452, 453
Cyclops 66, 500

D

Dagda 471
Dan 481
Daulatpur-Salturia tornado 287
deep-hole drills 256, 257
deep oceanic trenches 307, 311
demonic hierarchy 13, 55, 61, 62, 64, 83, 92, 454, 482, 524
Dilmun 454
Dinosaur National Monument 355, 554
Dionysus 92
Dispater 475, 476, 480
Douglass, Earl 355
drinking of blood 71, 232
Duat 472
Dyaus Pita 469
Dyeus Pater 469, 470, 472, 475, 476

E

earthquake swarms 179, 189
El 266
Elysium 472
Enoch 57, 58, 67, 69, 70, 71, 75, 76, 83, 101, 102, 110, 111, 112, 115, 201, 387, 449, 542
Eobshin 109, 481
Eochaid Ollathair 471

Epic of Gilgamesh 136, 179, 455, 456, 459, 460, 461, 463, 551
Erech Dynasty 8

F

Filby, Frederick A 551
Filby, Frederick A. 9
First Earth ii, 1, 2, 3, 4, 5, 7, 8, 9, 11, 12, 13, 15, 16, 17, 19, 20, 21, 22, 23, 24, 26, 27, 28, 29, 30, 34, 35, 39, 42, 44, 45, 46, 47, 48, 53, 55, 56, 57, 58, 64, 65, 71, 74, 75, 78, 81, 83, 84, 86, 90, 92, 93, 96, 98, 100, 103, 107, 109, 111, 112, 113, 115, 118, 122, 127, 130, 132, 133, 137, 139, 145, 149, 158, 163, 164, 165, 166, 168, 171, 176, 182, 188, 189, 193, 194, 200, 201, 202, 203, 204, 205, 213, 214, 217, 218, 220, 222, 224, 225, 226, 227, 228, 232, 233, 235, 236, 241, 243, 245, 248, 249, 254, 255, 256, 257, 258, 262, 271, 273, 274, 276, 285, 287, 288, 290, 292, 293, 295, 296, 303, 308, 317, 319, 328, 329, 330, 331, 332, 341, 344, 348, 350, 360, 366, 367, 373, 378, 384, 385, 387, 391, 392, 395, 401, 404, 414, 416, 417, 424, 431, 435, 445, 447, 449, 450, 452, 453, 455, 458, 473, 475, 476, 477, 479, 480, 484, 485, 486, 488, 499, 502, 507, 520, 522, 525, 527, 530, 531, 538, 542, 543, 547

INDEX

First Ice Age 53, 54, 175, 182, 229, 290, 293, 294, 295, 302, 303, 325, 331, 343, 396, 400, 404, 405, 406, 409, 410, 413, 414, 415, 431, 435, 450, 495, 507, 508, 539
First Insurrection 5, 88, 395, 435, 524
First Maximum Glacial Extent 412, 413, 414
Flandrian Transgression 407, 414, 546, 547
flash freeze 250
Flavius Josephus 2, 67, 101, 222, 390, 450
Fohi 109, 481
Four Demon Kings 93
Fourth Insurrection 72, 396, 435, 438, 522, 541
frozen forests 345
frozen mammoths 33

G

Gemini 58, 201, 202, 204, 206, 209, 210, 211, 212, 213, 220, 222
Giant tsunamis 160
Gilgamesh 8, 136, 137, 138, 179, 273, 368, 451, 453, 454, 455, 456, 458, 459, 460, 461, 462, 463, 551, 552, 553
gnosis 63, 75, 92
Gondwana 21, 156
GRACE (Gravity Recovery and Climate Experiment) 172, 427
gradual depositions 360
Grand Canyon 40, 362
Great White Throne Judgment 73

greenhouse effect 20, 23, 24, 26, 27, 28, 46, 49, 52, 53, 54, 175, 227, 327, 329, 332, 343, 359, 396, 400, 401, 404, 407, 410, 411, 412, 414, 529, 535, 544, 546
Gudatri-Gakwitl 496

H

Hactun 502
Hammurabi 451
Hananim 472
Harpending, Henry C. 553
Heart of Heaven 31, 138, 139, 472, 476, 477, 504, 505, 506, 509
Heidel, Alexander 553
Hempsell, Mark 549
Hercules 476, 480, 481
Herz, Otto F 336
Hesiod 1, 137, 138, 226, 249, 446, 447, 465, 554
Himalayan Mountains 178, 258, 343
Hoesch, William A. 554
Hook mammoth 335
Howorth, Sir Henry H. 327
human sacrifices 3, 54, 56, 92, 472
Human sacrifices 47
hydroplate theory 35, 36, 38, 39, 43, 128, 129, 137, 184, 185, 307, 311, 314, 315, 316, 320, 339
Hypogeum 98

I

igneous provinces 185, 304
iridium 41, 161, 176
Iridium 161
Isis 88, 192, 216, 549

J

Jacobsen, Steven 39, 555
James Mellart 105
Jared 69, 75
Jarkov mammoth 334
Jorde, Lynn 346, 553
Jupiter 146, 196, 208, 214, 220, 263, 475, 477

K

Kata Tjuta 364, 365
Kauil 477
Krakatau 264, 265
KT boundary 159, 161
Kukulcan 109, 431
Kundalini 109, 110, 481

L

Lago di Nemi 376, 377
Lake of Fire 72, 116, 117, 118, 541
Land of Shinar 33, 53, 54, 73, 389, 397, 400, 415, 525, 539
Larsa 196
Leviathan 213
life force 56, 111

M

Madagascar 155, 156, 183, 468
Madame Blavatsky 67
Magano 472
MAGE (Multiplex automated genome engineering) 85, 86
Magma Traps 185
Mama Oclo 496
Manco Capac 496
Maniitsoq Crater 147
mantle 43, 122, 172, 184, 185, 306, 313, 314, 328, 474
Manu 8, 489
many fossil graveyards 362
Marija Gimbutas 97
Mayan 31, 159, 296, 297, 298, 389, 401, 459, 476, 492, 504, 508, 509, 552
Mazzaroth 199, 201
McCready, George 328
Medusa 480, 481, 482
megafauna 30, 47
mega-hurricane 224, 231, 251
Mellart, James 105
Menard, H. S 555
meteorological homeostasis 21, 276, 294
Mid-Atlantic Ridge 22, 44, 49, 50, 51, 52, 124, 137, 147, 150, 165, 177, 181, 182, 183, 189, 190, 191, 253, 254, 255, 304, 305, 306, 309, 310, 314, 317, 319, 342, 414, 534
Mid-Oceanic Ridge 43, 170, 188, 225, 247, 253, 306, 533
Morrison Foundation 356
Mount Ararat 53, 73, 234, 235, 448, 466, 483, 484, 490, 536, 537
Mount Baal Hermon 5
Mt. Currie Conglomerate 364, 365
Mt. Olga 364
Müller, Frederick Max 469

N

Nagarajan 109, 481
Neanderthals 65, 66, 78, 79, 82, 86, 102, 201, 204, 210, 339, 384, 397, 476, 482, 496, 500
near-Earth asteroids 144

INDEX

Nephilim 3, 5, 47, 64, 65, 66, 74, 78, 80, 81, 83, 84, 88, 90, 91, 92, 97, 100, 102, 103, 107, 108, 109, 110, 111, 113, 116, 119, 139, 201, 204, 208, 210, 211, 212, 213, 222, 296, 450, 451, 455, 478, 496, 500, 502, 504, 543
Nesham 499
New Dawn 295, 296, 297
New Fire ceremonies 193, 217
New World Order 13
nickel/iron core 122, 123
Nimrod 54, 90, 94, 95, 96, 389, 390, 391, 392, 396, 397, 398, 408, 538
Ningizzida 109, 481
Nippur 138, 450, 454

O

occult doctrine of correspondence 61, 110
Ohlmec 472
Old Babylonian Geometry Tablet 196
Ophiuchus 206, 233, 480
Orion 206, 209, 210, 211, 212, 213, 218, 473, 476, 480
Ossendrijver, Mathieu 196
Ourobouros 109, 481
overriding plate 310, 312, 315
ozone layer 1, 24, 26, 348

P

Palomar Asteroid Comet Survey 142
Pan 91, 92
Pangaea 21, 44, 507
Pehuenche 494

Peleg 32, 206, 392
Perseus 218
Pisces 200, 206, 209, 218, 220, 222
Pleiades 58, 107, 191, 192, 193, 194, 202, 206, 213, 214, 215, 216, 217, 233
Plutarch 377
Poetic Edda, The 555
Popigai meteor 151, 157
precession of the equinoxes 19, 201, 204, 212
Prima Nave 377
primordial prophecy 61
prophecy of the Dragon Doom 5, 61, 64, 73, 81, 90, 100, 204, 211, 384, 497
Ptah Atum Ra 471
Ptolemy Philopator 377
pyroclastic flows 264, 274, 546
Pythagorean theorem 196

R

Rahu 109
Rampino, Michael 136, 346
Ratumaibulu 109, 481
Rehwinkel, Alfred 555
Ring of Fire 177, 188, 256, 257, 533
rite of incubation 98
Rodina 21
Ruad-rofhessa 471

S

Sagitta 206
Samhain Festival 193, 217
Samoan 484
Sanderson, Ivan T. 338
Schmandt, Brandon 555
Scholl, David William 316
scientism 6, 18, 510

seamounts 43
Seconda Nave 377
Second Earth 3, 4, 5, 9, 11, 12, 13, 14, 16, 17, 23, 24, 26, 27, 28, 29, 33, 35, 45, 50, 52, 53, 54, 55, 56, 65, 66, 68, 71, 72, 73, 74, 79, 90, 111, 113, 115, 116, 118, 119, 158, 162, 164, 165, 168, 193, 200, 201, 212, 217, 218, 219, 224, 233, 234, 235, 236, 237, 239, 241, 248, 251, 259, 262, 276, 285, 290, 291, 296, 303, 319, 330, 343, 345, 347, 348, 359, 374, 378, 379, 380, 384, 387, 389, 395, 396, 398, 401, 402, 404, 405, 407, 409, 411, 412, 413, 414, 416, 417, 423, 424, 431, 435, 437, 438, 439, 441, 448, 449, 450, 452, 461, 465, 473, 475, 479, 480, 482, 483, 484, 485, 486, 488, 490, 495, 499, 502, 508, 520, 522, 523, 524, 526, 527, 530, 537, 538, 541, 542, 544, 546, 547
Second Ice Age 54, 55, 175, 303, 331, 367, 387, 404, 407, 408, 409, 410, 411, 412, 415, 430, 431, 435, 450, 456, 506, 507, 547
Second Insurrection 5, 58, 64, 68, 69, 72, 73, 101, 102, 110, 112, 115, 116, 292, 387, 392, 395, 435, 436, 437, 478, 483
Second Maximum Glacial Extent 410
seed of Eve 4, 5, 47, 61, 64, 69, 71, 73, 81, 90, 100, 107, 119, 204, 384, 479, 483, 497, 519
seismic tomography 313

Semjaza (Shemihaza) 57, 71
seven seas 164, 166, 373
Shang Ti 471
Sheol 68, 72, 116
Shinarump Conglomerate 363
Siberia 33, 34, 150, 157, 170, 332, 334, 335, 336, 338, 341, 345, 358, 359, 425
Sippar 222, 450
Smertullos 480
Snowball Earth 290, 291
Spaceguard Foundation 144
St. Lawrence Seaway 405, 406
subducting plates 311
Sudbury Crater 152
sudden cataclysmic deposition 360
Sukachev, V. N. 338
Sumerian 45, 53, 54, 73, 109, 138, 191, 195, 197, 200, 202, 203, 205, 206, 207, 209, 210, 213, 214, 218, 220, 221, 246, 389, 396, 399, 401, 415, 448, 449, 450, 451, 452, 453, 454, 456, 461, 483, 549, 551, 554, 555
super-cold air downbursts 250
supercontinent 15, 19, 20, 21, 22, 26, 29, 30, 34, 36, 38, 39, 40, 42, 45, 121, 128, 139, 149, 150, 155, 156, 158, 169, 170, 171, 177, 178, 179, 180, 181, 183, 188, 224, 226, 243, 244, 245, 246, 248, 254, 304, 335, 342, 344, 373, 384, 458, 488, 507, 527, 529, 532
super-tornadoes 287
super-volcano 178, 347

T

Tamil 468
Tamoanchan 28, 29
Taranis 475, 477
Taurus 58, 88, 95, 96, 104, 107, 130, 132, 169, 192, 194, 200, 201, 204, 206, 209, 210, 211, 212, 213, 214, 215, 217, 218, 222, 233, 292, 401, 467
Tcu-unnyikita 499
Teiwaz 470
Teye 369, 492
thermohaline conveyor belt 175, 400, 404, 417, 424, 441, 507, 527, 547
thin water vapor canopy 1, 25, 35, 46, 228, 344, 529
Third Earth 15, 16, 72, 116, 117, 118, 167, 168, 237, 239, 240, 399, 441, 482, 483, 520, 522, 525, 527, 541, 542, 543, 544
Third Ice Age 15, 345, 412, 424, 431, 434, 435, 441, 526, 527, 547
Third Insurrection 392, 395, 397, 435
Thor 208, 470, 475, 477, 480
Tiamat 481
T'ien 472
time of terror 4, 55, 58, 168
Tirawahat 500
Tir na n-Og 472
Tonatiuh 472, 492
Tower of Babel 32, 33, 46, 54, 73, 196, 197, 205, 298, 299, 301, 302, 303, 367, 373, 386, 387, 392, 396, 398, 399, 400, 404, 407, 411, 415, 416, 430, 431, 435, 449, 450, 456, 463, 467, 497, 500, 501, 506, 507, 509, 510, 521, 524, 529, 540, 547

trickster gods 71
Tuatha Dé Danann 471
Type-3 ice 339
Typhon 109, 481
Typhoon Nina 286
Tyr 470
Tzab ("the rattle") 215

U

Ubara-Tutu 452
Uluru arkos inselberg 364
underground saltwater aquifers 21
Underground Saltwater Aquifers 35
Ur language 467
Utnapishtim 8, 456, 460, 462, 463

V

Venetian canopy 28
Vereshchagin, Nikolai 335
violent outgassing 49, 227, 244, 245, 247, 408, 533
Viracocha 477
von Frese, Ralph 172
Von Schrenck's rhinoceros 338
Vredefort crater 148, 154, 156

W

Wagner, Alfred 122
Wallace, Alfred R. 328
war gods 521
Warramunga 109
white magic 71, 208
whiteout blizzards 289
Wicca 88, 92, 208
Wilkes Land meteor 155, 170, 171, 189
Wollunqua 481
Woolley, C. Leonard 557

X

Xisuthros 460
Xochiquetzal 510

Y

Yara-ma-yha-who 481
Year of Jubilee 194, 216, 217
Yormungand (Iormungand) 480
Younger Dryas 405
Yurlunggur 446, 485

Z

Zamna 472, 492
Zealandia 317, 318, 555
Zep Tepi 66, 485, 500
Zeus 466, 469, 470, 477, 481
Zheng He 375, 556

www.ingramcontent.com/pod-product-compliance
Lightning Source LLC
Chambersburg PA
CBHW060511230426
43665CB00013B/1478